BECOMING

BECOMING TONGAN

AN ETHNOGRAPHY OF CHILDHOOD

HELEN MORTON

UNIVERSITY OF HAWAI'I PRESS

HONOLULU

Library of Congress Cataloging-in-Publication Data

Morton, Helen, 1960–

Becoming Tongan : an ethnography of childhood / Helen Morton.

p. cm.

Includes bibliographical references and index.

ISBN 0–8248–1758–3 (cloth : alk. paper).

ISBN 0–8248–1795–8 (paper : alk. paper)

1. Ethnology—Tonga—Holonga (Tongatapu Island)   2. Children—
Tonga—Holonga (Tongatapu Island)   3. Child psychology—Tonga—
Holonga (Tongatapu Island)   4. Child rearing—Tonga—Holonga
(Tongatapu Island)   5. Ethnopsychology—Tonga—Holonga (Tongatapu
Island)   6. Child development—Tonga—Holonga (Tongatapu Island)
7. Socialization—Tonga—Holonga (Tongatapu Island)   8. Holonga
(Tongatapu Island, Tonga)—Social life and customs.   I. Title.

GN671.T5M67   1996

305.23'099612—dc20   95–41374

CIP

University of Hawai'i Press books are printed on acid-free paper and meet the guidelines

for permanence and durability of the Council on Library Resources

Book design by Paula Newcomb

CONTENTS

Photographs follow page 114

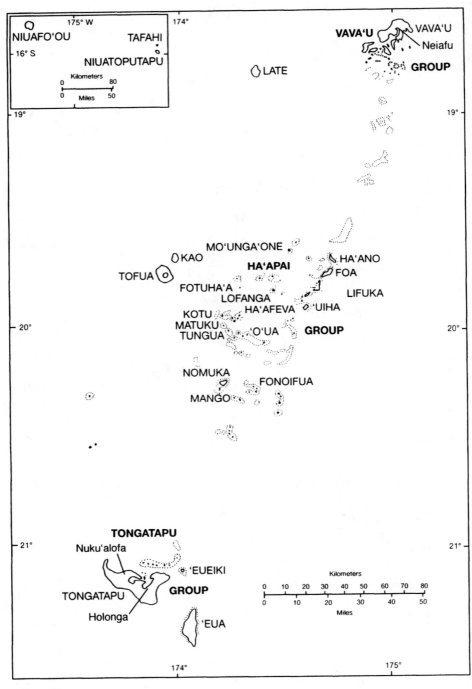

Map 1: Tonga

ACKNOWLEDGMENTS

I first went to Tonga early in 1979 for a one-month visit, which I enjoyed so much that almost immediately I returned to live and work there. Since that first visit, I have spent three years in Tonga overall, including a period of doctoral research from June 1988 to March 1989. I also spent nearly two years living in the households of Tongan migrants in Sydney and Melbourne, Australia (1981–1982). This study is based largely on my doctoral research but also draws on my experiences before I had even heard of anthropology, so there are many, many people to acknowledge as influencing my work, and not all can be included here.

For permission to carry out fieldwork in the Kingdom of Tonga, I thank the government of King Taufa'ahau Tupou IV. I received financial support during my candidature from an Australian Postgraduate Research Award. Further funding for fieldwork was given by the Department of Anthropology, Research School of Pacific Studies, of the Australian National University.

Throughout my doctoral candidature my greatest support came from Dr. Michael Young, my supervisor and a Senior Fellow in the Department of Anthropology, Research School of Pacific Studies. Michael's support and encouragement frequently restored my flagging confidence and spurred me to maintain the pace of my work. Dr. Margaret Jolly first encouraged me in my studies during my undergraduate years at Macquarie University in Sydney. As my adviser during my doctoral research she continued to offer this encouragement, for which I am most grateful. The late Professor Roger Keesing, who was one of my supervisors until his move to McGill University in Canada, also encouraged me in my research.

During my stay in Tonga the people of Holonga (Tongatapu) made me welcome and facilitated my research in many ways. Special thanks to the Kailahi family, particularly Mefa lahi, Semisi, Helenā, Finau, and Tangitangi, and to Vika Lasalo, Latai Tonga, and Manu Ta'eiloa. Thanks also to Lomano and 'Ofa Manukeu for their hospitality while we were in 'Eua. In Nuku'alofa the households of 'Ofa and Vavahe'a Kavapalu and the late Nānisi Helu made my son and me most welcome. We remember with special fondness the little house behind Nānisi's that was our home for some time before my daughter's birth and until we returned to Australia, and in which we—and my field notes—survived a hurricane.

For assistance with transcription and translation in Tonga, thanks to Lātū Manukeu, Palu 'Ilaiu, and Mele Ma'u. Lātū also helped in many other ways during our stay in Holonga. I am grateful to the many government departments, educational institutions, nongovernment organizations, health workers, and others who supported my research and cooperated with interviews.

Throughout this study, except in these acknowledgments, I have used pseudonyms for the Tongans who were involved with my research. I wrestled long and hard with this decision, as I know some people will be disappointed not to be named. However, because many of the people in this book were children at the time of my research I have decided to protect their anonymity, and although it is the children to whom I offer my greatest thanks, I shall not name them even here.

Thanks to the publishers of Oceania and Social Analysis for permission to include some sections of papers published previously in my former married name. To preserve the anonymity of my former husband and his family, I have not referred to these papers in this work.

Discussions with several scholars working on issues in Tongan anthropology and history helped me to develop the arguments in my dissertation (also in my married name and not referenced herein). They include Drs. Aletta Biersack, Wendy Cowling, Kerry James, and 'Okusitino Māhina. Kerry consistently offered support and encouragement while I extensively revised my dissertation for this publication. For assistance with technical details I gratefully acknowledge Margaret Tyrie for her work on the map of Holonga, Beth Robertson for the tables, and the La Trobe University Reprography Unit for managing to develop the photographs from my fungus-ridden negatives. The Multimedia Education Unit at the University of Melbourne also gave valuable assistance.

I would also like to thank the examiners of my dissertation, Professor George Marcus, Professor Geoffrey White, and Dr. Caroline Ralston, as well as an anonymous reader of the dissertation for the University of Hawai'i Press, and especially Professor Alan Howard, who read my manuscript not once but twice before it was accepted for publication. Each of these examiners and readers gave me constructive criticism and valuable suggestions and, most important, helped me to keep believing that I had something interesting to say. I feel immense gratitude to the University of Hawai'i Press, particularly Pamela Kelley, for being willing to consider my dissertation for publication and guiding me through the necessary revisions.

Special thanks go to my mother, Ursula Burt, who first went to Tonga in 1978 with Australian Volunteers Abroad to teach at St. Andrew's High School in Nuku'alofa. It was through visiting her there that my interest in

Tonga was sparked. Our many long discussions about Tonga over the years have been invaluable. My husband, John, has consistently given support and is aware, more than anyone else, of the impact researching and writing this book has had on my life. Finally, I thank my children. Paul has helped me learn that the personal and the intellectual can be a powerful combination. Paul and Rosie shared my fieldwork in very different ways, and they and their little sister Hannah have helped me to keep life's priorities in perspective throughout the long process of writing. Their lives, like mine, have been affected in many ways by my work, and I dedicate this book to them.

BECOMING TONGAN

INTRODUCTION

The first children I knew well in Tonga were the five little girls who became my nieces when I married their father's youngest brother early in 1980. The girls lived in the main house on our *'api* (household compound) with their mother, grandfather, two unmarried aunts, and their formidable great-aunt. My husband and I lived in a tiny room in a ramshackle hut opposite, and every day the girls played in the dusty yard between the two dwellings. Ranging in age from five to twelve, the girls formed a self-contained play group and only occasionally played with neighborhood children. They often sat on the steps outside our door, chatting or playing hand-clapping or juggling games with much laughter and teasing. At other times they played noisy games of marbles in the dust or threw a ball onto our tin roof and caught it as it rolled off. They were a loud, sometimes irritating presence, but they were an ever-cheerful bunch, often breaking into the harmonized singing that is heard so often in Tonga and that always sends little chills down my spine with its beauty. I felt awkward with my nieces at first, as I did with all my new family, but I soon felt very affectionate toward them.

One day not long after my marriage an incident occurred that, in retrospect, was the beginning of my fascination with Tongan childhood. It was Sunday, a day of churchgoing and rest in Tonga. The girls had worn new white dresses to church, and against their mother's orders had kept them on after church while they played in the now muddy yard. To punish the girls for their disobedience their mother lined them up from oldest to youngest and beat each in turn with a piece of wood, on their legs and hands. By the time it was the youngest girl's turn she was sobbing with fear, but her mother, sitting cross-legged on a mat, resolutely administered her punishment.

I watched this scene in horrified amazement. I was a teacher in a girls' college at the time and had heard many stories of the girls being beaten by teachers; I had even seen teachers walking to class with heavy rulers or sticks. Yet I had never actually witnessed a beating, nor had I ever, as I grew up in Australia, seen a child being physically punished in such a manner. In the year I had spent in Tonga before my marriage and in the short time I had been married I had encountered endless cultural differences that variously enchanted, exasperated, amused, and annoyed me, but this incident jolted me into a sense of "culture shock." I was shocked that the children were beaten with a piece of wood, I was amazed that they were expected to stand in line waiting to be beaten, and I was even more amazed that they complied. Their mother's calmness also confounded me: she just sat there and implacably hit her children, one at a time.

My sense of shock was compounded when, very soon afterward, I saw the mother cuddling the youngest daughter. I turned to my husband in bewilderment and asked why, if the mother had been angry enough to beat her children only minutes before, she was now showing affection. I cannot remember his exact words after all these years, but they were something like "She is showing that she loves them. They have to know that she only punishes them because she loves them." I could not even begin to understand his reply. All I felt then was confusion and fear—fear for my as yet unborn children that they, too, would be beaten like that. So strong was this fear that much later it played a part in my decision to end my marriage.

As it turned out, my sister-in-law was a gentle woman who punished her children only infrequently, and her punishments were mild relative to the many incidents I later witnessed. Yet it was that first incident that affected me most profoundly, because it forced me to confront the reality of cultural difference. I had married at nineteen, full of romantic fantasies about living in Tonga and determined to try to *be* Tongan, so keen was I to reject my Australian self.[1] That one Sunday marked the beginning of my realization that my naive dreams could not come true. It also marked the beginning of my interest in child socialization in Tonga, which seemed to me then to be full of contradictions.

The harsh punishments I observed and the infrequency of displays of affection for children, as well as the onerous chores many children were expected to perform and the expectation that they be obedient, respectful, and submissive to all who were of higher status would, I thought, make for a bleak and unhappy childhood. Yet most children, most of the time, appeared to be far from unhappy. The people I knew, of all ages, spent much of their time laughing and joking and seemed to have very close and loving ties with their immediate and extended families. As well, people's attitudes toward children seemed contradictory. "It is paradise (*palataisi*) for one's stay on earth to have children," one woman explained, and another said that without children, marriage—and life itself—would be *ta'eifo* (uninteresting, boring). Children are sometimes referred to as *koloa* (valuables or wealth), and in bearing children a woman is seen to give her husband's extended family (*kāinga*) this special form of *koloa* (Bott n.d., 15; James 1988, 34). A common saying is *"Ko e fānau ko e tofi'a mei he 'Otua"* (Children are an inheritance from God). Yet in their everyday speech to children adults made it clear that they also had very negative views of children, as they constantly told them that they were bad, lazy, silly, tiring, disobedient, and so on and seldom offered words of praise or encouragement.

My fascination with Tongan childhood, and Tongan society more generally, has persisted, and this book is its embodiment. The fascination has remained intensely personal as well as becoming intellectual; always, as my son, Paul, has grown up, I have wondered what his life would have been like if he had grown up in Tonga. What was it that would have made him "Tongan"? I have also wondered, of course, what my own life would have been like if I had remained married to my Tongan husband and enmeshed within the network of his extended kin. My continuing interest in Tongan childhood and family life reflects in part my need to understand the culture that I found so very confusing as a young wife and mother. The interest in language that is evident throughout this book is largely a result of my own continuing struggle to become fluent in Tongan and the insights and immense pleasure I gained by conducting interviews and having conversations in Tongan during my fieldwork.

Paul and I returned to Tonga at the end of 1986, when he was six years old. We stayed in the village of Holonga, on Tongatapu, for two months, with members of a family I first met when I went to Tonga in 1979. We returned in 1988 while I carried out my doctoral research and again stayed in our friends' home in Holonga and later in several other households in Nuku'alofa and 'Eua. Not only did Paul accompany me to the field, I was also in the early weeks of pregnancy when I arrived in Tonga in 1988, and my daughter, Rosie, was born in Tonga in February 1989. My experience supports the observation made by Whitehead and Price that "children often make valuable contributions in observing the attitudes and behavior of their peers in the host community" (1986, 301). I also found, as did many of the authors in Butler and Turner (1987), Cassell (1987), and Whitehead and Conaway (1986), that children and pregnancy both facilitated and hindered fieldwork in numerous ways.

Paul was welcomed as "a real Tongan boy," but he was clearly not Tongan except in his paternally inherited genes and in other people's desire for him to be so. Indeed, so strongly was his sense of self not Tongan when we arrived in 1988 that he initially rejected anything Tongan, including Tongan food, to the point of making himself ill. Even when he had settled in, had learned some language, and spent most of his out-of-school time with a group of Tongan boys, he and I both knew he could only play at being Tongan, just as I had in the early days of my marriage.

To attempt to understand the process of becoming Tongan I initially turned to cross-cultural accounts of socialization. I discovered that the question of how a child becomes a member of a culture has been of concern to anthropologists since the discipline first emerged. However, this question has not been central to the anthropological project because of assumptions that were made about the unproblematic process of socialization, as will be discussed in chapter 1. I have found valuable more recent approaches to socialization from within other disciplines that emphasize its dynamic, interactive nature. In focusing on the question of how children become Tongan I am concerned with questions of identity and of personhood, self, and emotion. My interest is in what Tongans value as "Tongan" as well as how this concept is undergoing constant transformation. To thoroughly explore the ethnography of childhood in Tonga I draw together a number of theoretical strands from recent sociological approaches to socialization, ethnopsychology, language socialization studies, and work on cultural identity and tradition to demonstrate the value of placing children and childhood at the center of anthropological discourse.

My aim is also to redress the lack of any comprehensive study of Tongan childhood. Other Polynesian societies have been the subjects of intensive socialization studies as well as broader ethnographic accounts from a range of theoretical perspectives. Reading these accounts, many of which are mentioned in this book at relevant points, I found much that resonated with my observations of childhood in Tonga and some aspects that seemed to vary significantly. My understanding of Tongan childhood was particularly influenced by my investigation of Bradd Shore's notion of "double socialization" in Western Samoa (1982) in my honors thesis. Shore's complex analysis of Samoan social relations deals only briefly with childhood, but his concept of double socialization raises the issue of children learning apparently contradictory values in the process of socialization, an issue I have explored in the Tongan case.

The absence of a detailed study of Tongan childhood creates a considerable gap in the regional literature. Previously, I have described children as "missing persons" in the history of Tonga (Morton 1990). The earliest accounts of Tonga, by castaways, explorers, and missionaries, seldom gave descriptions of the daily lives of the tu'a (commoner) population, and even less often mentioned tu'a children.[2] These scant early references to children tend to be of three types: very brief generalized portrayals of children as primitive, carefree innocents; detailed descriptions of child sacrifice and finger amputation; and scattered references to particular aspects of childhood, such as children's games. Wherever possible, I have used these early accounts to give some indication of the context of socialization at the time of European contact and the effects of historical processes within the Tongan social system (see Thomas 1989).[3]

On the whole, references to children in accounts of twentieth-century Tonga tend to be as scarce and scattered as those in the historical literature. Accounts dealing with Tonga are notable for their absence in the survey of socialization studies in Polynesia by the Ritchies (1989) and their earlier account of childhood in Polynesia (1979). Gifford's *Tongan Society* (1971b) includes a brief section "Life Crises," with descriptions of birthing practices and "puberty observances" but very little else on children.[4] Like many subsequent ethnographies of Tonga, Gifford's account presents a "noble view" (Decktor Korn 1974) that largely neglects the everyday lives of the *tu'a* population. The Beagleholes' ethnography of Pangai village (1941b) is one early ethnography that does focus on commoners, but as a broad-based village study it does not focus on socialization. The authors admit that "no systematic study was made of the life of children" (82), and their "life-cycle" description contains only two pages on "growing up." Somewhat more useful than these better-known ethnographies is the "Report on a Brief Study of Mother-Child Relationships in Tonga" by Elizabeth Spillius (1958), prepared for the World Health Organization, in which she details practices concerning pregnancy, birth, feeding, and so on. Her report deals mostly with the first year of life, and Spillius states that she "made no special study of older children" (61).

My own study spans the whole of "childhood," from before birth to late adolescence. Throughout my account I indicate which part of this broad span I am discussing, where there is differentiation, by using terms such as "infant," "toddler," "older child," and "adolescent." It should be borne in mind, however, that people in their twenties are often treated as children, as in the demands made on them for obedience and the continued use of physical punishment in many cases. The line between childhood and adulthood is not socially marked and is always blurry. In my account I am concerned to situate children within the wider social context in which they live. I share Toren's (1993, 462) view that to study children as if their social world is somehow separate from that of adults is to provide an inadequate analysis. Thus, one of my central claims is that the power relations, value orientations, and concepts of competent personhood evident in the context of child socialization are also features of relations within the wider social hierarchy.

I begin with a discussion of the theoretical strands that I have woven together to inform my account. The theoretical concerns are then set aside to some extent in the following two chapters, which are primarily descriptive. The second chapter establishes the context of the study, introducing the concept of *anga fakatonga* ("the Tongan way") and briefly describing social structure and organization, household composition, and village life. This chapter also introduces the village of Holonga, the main site of my fieldwork, and a number of the Tongan people who have helped to shape my research. The third chapter focuses on the very beginnings of childhood: attitudes to reproduction, pregnancy, and childbirth. The ways in which infants are cared for are discussed, and the major event of childhood, the first birthday, is described.

Chapter 4 begins the more detailed ethnopsychological analysis with a discussion of Tongan notions of personhood, particularly as related to children, and introduces *poto* (social competence) as the overarching aim of socialization. The cultural values that are associated with the ideals of personhood and the development of *poto* are then discussed: *'ofa* (love, concern), respect, obedience, and independence. The chapter includes an account of gender differences as important components of concepts of self and personhood.

Having established in the previous chapter some of the most salient aspects of cultural knowledge associated with socialization, I move in chapter 5 to examine the contexts in which this knowledge is available to children: in their interactions with kin, in the work they perform for their households, at school, and at play. Chapters 6 and 7 detail the ways in which cultural knowledge is acquired. In chapter 6 several forms of learning are examined: performance, observation and imitation, and language socialization. The following chapter focuses on physical punishment, which I argue is central to Tongan children's socialization. Chapter 7 also considers other forms of violence and their relationship to the processes of socialization.

In chapter 8 a number of threads from the previous chapters are drawn together in an analysis of the socialization of emotion. This chapter considers how Tongan children are encouraged to monitor and manage emotion, particularly negatively valued emotions such as anger. The use of humor as a form of social control is discussed, including the association between anger and humor. Contexts in which intense emotions can be expressed are explored. The chapter concludes with a consideration of relationships between self and other and of the importance of self-control.

The final chapter of this study relates my analysis of childhood in Tonga to recent political developments in Tonga. I argue that at the heart of debates about political reform and the widespread concern about children's "loss of culture" are the issues of cultural identity and tradition. I conclude with some speculations and questions about how future generations will become Tongan.

CHAPTER 1

THE ETHNOGRAPHY OF CHILDHOOD

Socialization has been the subject of research in anthropology, sociology, and psychology: as these disciplines emerged and developed, they confronted the fundamental philosophical problem of the relationship between the individual and society by investigating the process by which individuals become competent adult members of society. The approaches they have taken over time, in examining the processes of socialization, reflect changing views of the individual and society, embodying assumptions about the intrinsic nature of humans and their interactions.[1] Over time, developmental research has also come to recognize that socialization continues throughout life, although the period of life prior to socially recognized adulthood is a period of particularly intensive and influential socialization. It is this period on which I will focus to provide a detailed ethnography of Tongan childhood.

Anthropologists have included descriptions of aspects of childhood, from birth through to the end of adolescence, in their ethnographic studies since the discipline emerged. Yet no comprehensive theoretical approach to the study of child socialization developed within anthropology until the mid-1920s, when the culture-and-personality approach emerged in the United States.[2] Although this approach drew attention to the importance of studying children and childhood, it was deeply flawed by its determinist assumptions that child socialization resulted in adult personality and that culture was personality writ large. This approach was influential for several decades, but by the 1960s wide-ranging critiques had emerged; socialization studies began to draw on other theoretical approaches such as social learning theory and cognitive psychology and became part of the general field of psychological anthropology (see, for example, Hsu 1972; Williams 1975).

Psychological anthropology, like the culture-and-personality approach preceding it, has been subjected to vigorous criticism. The most crucial problem with this work, as has been claimed for much of the empirical research of social scientists, is its "overly Western, middle-class emphasis in techniques, assumptions, and interpretations" (Leiderman, Tulkin, and Rosenfeld 1977, 112; see Strauss 1984). The theories underlying the research were developed using predominantly white, middle-class subjects and often embody assumptions about the nature of persons and society that do not hold in other cultures or even in subgroups of Euro-American societies.

These critiques of psychological anthropology can be seen as elements of a more general "crisis of cultural authority, specifically of the authority vested in Western European culture and its institutions" (Owens 1985, 57). That psychological theories and concepts can no longer be assumed to reflect reality has had a profound effect on psychologically oriented anthropology.[3] One of the specific aims of the ethnopsychological approach used in my own work is to further challenge the Western biases of psychological theorizing (Howard 1985a, 409). The social constructionist approach in social psychology, an important influence on ethnopsychological research, regards psychological theories and concepts as themselves "a form of ethnopsychology, historically and culturally situated, institutionally useful, normatively sustained, and subject to deterioration and decay as social history unfolds" (Gergen 1985, 11; and see Shweder and Miller 1985).

The research into child socialization within the culture-and-personality school and the field of psychological anthropology has not had a major effect upon mainstream anthropology or psychology, particularly outside the United States. In 1970, Mayer observed that British anthropologists had been reluctant "to confront the subject of socialization—to recognize it as a fit subject for analysis in the British anthropological tradition, or even as a major theme of human society at all" (1970, xi). Even the continuing research into developmental psychology did not persuade anthropologists of the importance of children as part of socio-cultural life. In the early 1980s Schwartz commented that "anthropology [has] ignored children in culture while developmental psychologists [have] ignored culture in children" (1981, 4). He claimed:

> Our neglect of the child as a person, participant, and locus of important events in the process of a culture is probably even greater than our neglect until recently of women. . . . [A]t present we know surprisingly little of the cultural competence and content of children as constituent participants in culture. The ethnography of childhood remains a genuine frontier. (Schwartz 1981, 10, 16)

Although many anthropological studies before Schwartz' comments included information about children in descriptions of "growing up" in the "Life Cycle" sections of ethnographies and in the psychologically oriented studies of socialization, the functionalist assumptions informing this work rendered it limited and problematic.[4] The term *socialization* as used until the late 1970s referred to the internalization of culturally appropriate norms and values, with children viewed as basically passive and malleable. As Wentworth points out, creativity, individual preferences, deviance, alienation, misunderstanding, and other factors that did not fit into a given system remained unaccounted for (1980, 71).

By the late 1970s social learning theorists had begun to criticize this unidirectional model of socialization, and developmental psychologists adopted an interactional model of development stressing that social development involves reciprocal influences; according to this approach, "[c]hildren are the architects as well as the victims of their own environments . . . [and] contribute to their own socialisation" (Perry and Bussey 1984, 29–30; and see Goodnow and Cashmore 1982). The notion that the individual in the process of socialization can have some control over that process can be found in some early work, including that of Piaget, some behaviorists such as Skinner, and ego psychologists (for reviews see Bell 1977b; Ochs 1986a), but it remained undeveloped until the 1970s. Bell has shown that the findings of socialization research over many decades can be reinterpreted in terms of the effects of infants and children on their caregivers (1977a).[5] An example of this interactive approach can be found in a U.S. study of the use of physical punishment on children; it discovered "that children contribute to the type and intensity of punishment, not only in their initial behavior . . . but also by their responses to the parents' attempts to discipline" (Mussen et al. 1984, 391; and see Bell 1977b). My own account of physical punishment in Tonga supports these findings and shows that viewing socialization from an interactive perspective reveals it to be a highly complex and sometimes confusing process for the participants.

This interactive view of socialization has also influenced sociological theory, as in Wentworth's socialization-as-interaction approach (1980) and Hurrelmann's contextualistic-interactive model (1988). In examining this "re-visioning of children" Thorne notes of recent studies: "While acknowledging the effects of structural constraints and the importance of children's subordination, they grant children agency and seek to understand the complexity of their experiences" (1987, 101).

Despite the emergence of an interactive model of socialization within developmental psychology and sociology, anthropology has not drawn upon this work and has made little effort to take up Schwartz' challenge to explore the ethnography of childhood. As recently as 1993 Christina Toren commented that "anthropologists tend still to assume that the endpoint of socialization is known. This assumption is at the root of contemporary anthropology's lack of interest in children" (1993, 461). In the present study I propose to use the interactive perspective on socialization to weave together several recent strands of research—ethnopsychology, work on cultural iden-

tity and tradition, and language socialization studies—to demonstrate that
the study of childhood needs to be integral to the fabric of anthropological
analysis. Although my concern is primarily with the interactive process, my
study also focuses on Tongans' own ideas about the end point of socialization. My interest is with the whole of childhood, including the often neglected middle period of childhood between the more frequently studied
periods of infancy and adolescence.

   The critiques of earlier studies of childhood raise the question of whether
socialization remains a useful term. The phrase used by Schwartz, "the ethnography of childhood," describes the broader focus of my own study, which
goes beyond the usual parameters of socialization studies to encompass all
aspects of children's lives. However, I have retained the use of the term *socialization*, as in Wentworth's socialization-as-interaction model, to indicate the
processes by which children are constituted, and constitute themselves, as
actors within a culture. My view of socialization accords with that of Cook-
Gumperz and Corsaro, who view it as "an interpersonal activity of 'becoming' rather than an unfolding of a biologically based plan or an imprinting of
social structure onto the child" (1986, 7). It is in this sense that I am concerned with the process of "becoming Tongan."

ETHNOPSYCHOLOGY

My analysis of this process of becoming Tongan takes the broad focus of an
ethnography, examining the details of children's everyday lives, especially
their interactions with other members of their society. In analyzing so, I draw
on several theoretical perspectives, particularly that of ethnopsychology. In
the discussion that follows I offer an appraisal of this approach, showing how
the work on the interactional nature of socialization, language socialization
research, and accounts of tradition and cultural identity can expand the
scope of the ethnopsychological project. By expanding its scope, we can
address the limitations of the ethnopsychological approach, particularly the
need for a broader conception of context, to include more careful consideration of gender and power relations and the historical processes influencing
ethnopsychological beliefs.

   The emphasis on interaction, agency, and context that is a feature of
recent psychological and sociological approaches to socialization is a feature
of ethnopsychological research in anthropology.[6] These approaches also
share a concern with the contested and negotiable character of meaning and
knowledge. The editors of a volume that explores Pacific ethnopsychologies
have summarized the ethnopsychological approach as seeking "to understand
and describe the cultural significance of social and psychological events as

they are actively interpreted in social context . . . to understand just how, and in what contexts, people do formulate conscious interpretations of social experience" (Kirkpatrick and White 1985, 4). These conscious interpretations "range from the elaborate, overt, and widely shared, to the posthoc, idiosyncratic, and covert" (Lutz 1983, 250n3).

The ethnopsychological approach shares the social constructionist assumption that " 'reality' does not dictate how it is to be categorized or represented" (Shweder and Miller 1985, 60; and see Gergen and Davis 1985). However, it also recognizes the continual interplay between cultural meanings and the world of experience, including bodily and psychological experiences, as well as external events (D'Andrade 1984, 114; and see Morton and Macintyre 1995). Therefore, it does not assume that social experiences are the only determinants of subjectivity. Ethnopsychologists are particularly interested in persons as "points of intersection between the subjective and the social. . . . [P]ersons are cultural bases for formulating and exploring subjective experience. Equally, persons are recognizable as elements of social life, as occupying statuses and participating in social groups and events" (Kirkpatrick and White 1985, 9). A study of socialization can be of value in identifying the dialectical nature of this subjective and social state. In Tonga, the emphasis on molding the subjective self to fit the demands of social life is balanced to some extent by a belief in the relative autonomy of a crucial aspect of that self, the *loto* (heart, mind).

The primary foci of ethnopsychological studies are cultural understandings of person, self, and emotion. This approach is influenced by Hallowell, who, as early as 1955, argued that self-awareness and concepts of the person are universal as well as culturally variable (1955). The concepts of *person* and *self* are used in varying but broadly similar ways throughout the ethnopsychological literature.[7] *Person* is perhaps the most readily understood because it refers to the level of ideals—what someone in a given society "should" be like. How that someone is positioned in terms of the interrelated variables of gender, class, rank, and so on and *who* is determining what she or he should be like complicate the notion of the person, yet there are often widely shared ideas that can be identified, as in the Tongan concept of ideal personhood as chiefly. Lutz has pointed out that many studies have shown that concepts of the person interpenetrate almost every form of cultural knowledge (1988, 33). Yet it is also important to recognize that this cultural knowledge, including knowledge of concepts of the person, is interpreted by experiencing selves in countless ways, and these interpretations, in turn, shape cultural knowledge.

Geoffrey White (1992, 39), who has defined *person* in terms of "collective representations and ideology" and *self* in terms of "reflexive forms of subjectivity," has acknowledged that this distinction reflects the Western dichotomy of society and the self, or individual. This distinction, while problematic, does remain useful for my own study because this is very much how Tongans conceptualize themselves and others: in terms of ideals and subjective experience and of the ways in which these are sometimes congruent and sometimes divergent.

The use of the term *self* is also problematic in the ethnopsychological literature because there is a tendency "to identify the concept of an autonomous, cohesive, bounded self as *the* Western concept of self" (Ewing 1990, 256; emphasis in original), with which *the* concept of self in some other culture can be contrasted. This dichotomy of egocentric, Western selves and sociocentric, Other selves has now been thoroughly contested, as has the more recent deconstructionist tendency to focus on the fragmented Western self (see Morton and Macintyre 1995). The relational nature of personhood and the way in which self is defined and experienced through relationships with others has been a common focus of recent work in Pacific cultures (e.g., Battaglia 1990; Linnekin and Poyer 1990a; Lutz 1988). The interpersonal is, however, inextricably bound up with the personal, and Howard has rightly suggested that "we have exaggerated the extent to which Polynesians are communal in their personal orientations, at the expense of understanding the ways in which they organize experience as individuals" (1985b, 431). He stresses that it is important not to neglect individualized selves by overemphasizing the social nature of persons (415), and I am concerned with both in my account of childhood in Tonga.

Ewing has argued that the culturally shaped "self" that is the focus of anthropological study is better understood as "self-representation" (1990, 255). In all cultures the self is subjectively experienced by each person as whole and continuous, Ewing argues, but people actually construct and project "multiple, inconsistent self-representations that are context-dependent and may shift rapidly" (251). It is therefore important that we examine not only individuals' subjectivity, but also their self-representations—and the dialectic between subjectivity and representation.

A closely related aspect of the self that is frequently not addressed in ethnopsychological studies is the experiencing self and its often problematic relationship with "cultural models."[8] Cultural models are the "taken-for-granted knowledge [that] provides the background against which individuals set their goals, make their plans, try to manipulate their environment, anticipate what others will do and describe their experiences" (Holland and Valsiner 1988, 257). These models can be mundane or central to notions of cultural and personal identity, and the realm of knowledge encompassed by cultural models extensively overlaps with ethnopsychological beliefs. One of the questions I address in this study is how cultural models *become* taken for granted.

As Hollan argues, cultural models and conceptions of the self need to be seen as distinct from the experiential self (1992, 286). What the self experiences may, of course, often be congruent with cultural models. For example, the Tongan model of respect for higher-status persons may, in many contexts, be reflected in genuine experiences of respectful feelings (and see Gerber 1985 on Samoa). An understanding of the processes of socialization can illuminate the ways in which this congruence develops. Hollan states that "one way people actually 'live by' a cultural model of the self [or personhood] is by maintaining childrearing practices which result in deep intuitions about the model's inherent truth and correctness" (1992, 286). Yet what the self experiences may also be in direct conflict with cultural models, as will be seen in my discussion of the physical punishment of children. Such contradictions may go unquestioned or may underlie profound ambivalence toward the models in question. Because cultural models cannot be assumed to be unified and uncontested, the relationship between the self and these models may at times also be self-consciously one of opposition or alignment.

The congruences and contradictions in the relationship between cultural models and the experiencing self can be particularly evident within the realm of emotion.[9] Emotions can be seen as "a primary idiom for defining and negotiating social relations of the self in a moral order" (Lutz and White 1986, 417). Concepts of emotion, Lutz argues, serve "complex communicative, moral, and cultural purposes" (1988, 5). So too do values, the cultural ideals concerning dispositions and behavior that are often discussed as "emotions." Emotions and values do tend to merge: as both abstractions and psychological states they are often impossible to disentangle. That they should not be conflated, however, will be apparent in my discussion of some of the key values deemed appropriate for children in Tonga.[10] Obedience, for example, is a cultural value that cannot be equated with an emotional state. Tongans emphasize the behavior associated with obedience (listening properly, carrying out orders unquestioningly) and do not assume that there is an affective state intrinsic to such behavior. The *ideal* is for obedience to be motivated by both 'ofa (love, concern) and 'apasia (feelings of respect), but people readily admit that other emotions such as fear, anger, resentment, and even sadness can be experienced in their place. However, it would be too simplistic to assume that emotions are a facet of "self" while values are a facet of "personhood." Selves can experience emotion and believe in certain values; concepts of personhood will involve ideals or models of both emotions and values.

Emotion words act as "guideposts to cultural knowledge about social and affective experience" (Kirkpatrick and White 1985, 17). These guideposts are particularly clear during socialization, when theories of emotion are most likely to be articulated. Even when they are not verbalized, these theories are clearly expressed to children, as when a crying child's mouth is covered or when a raised stick silently warns a too-exuberant child to calm down. White has argued that "analysis of patterns of unspoken meaning in emotive discourse may also provide a means of investigating less 'visible' transformations of personal experience" (1990, 64). An example of such an investigation will be found in my discussion of the transformations of anger to sadness and humor in chapter 8.

Recent work focusing on emotion as discursive practice distinguishes between "discourses on emotion (local theories about emotion) and emotional discourses (situated deployments of emotional linguistic forms)" (Abu-Lughod and Lutz 1990, 13). Although this work emphasizes that emotion is tied to sociability and to power relations, the subjective experience of emotion should not be neglected. Strathern argues that in Pacific cultures discourse on emotion centers on the interpersonal, on emotions as aspects of social relations (1987, 158; see Lutz 1988, 81). Yet emotions are both interpersonal *and* personal, and the neglect of the latter may well be a legacy of the tendency to see Others' selves only as sociocentric.

Work on emotion discourse demonstrates that it can be understood as an interactional process (Brenneis 1990, 115). An examination of emotion discourse can therefore be incorporated with the socialization-as-interaction approach, to account for the ways in which children interpret and utilize the messages of emotions and the ways in which they can influence and even manipulate affect and behavior in others. This approach also allows for factors such as ambivalence and creativity, rather than assuming that emotions become neatly integrated within the dominant cultural conceptual framework.

Lutz emphasizes the importance of studying the socialization of emotion:

> As ethnopsychological theories of emotion constitute the model that adults use in understanding the nature, course, and ideal end points of development, they can play a crucial role in the cultural construction of emotional reality for and by the child. . . . [T]he emotions can be seen as both the medium and the message of socialization. . . . [E]motions serve as principles for organizing social life and as vehicles by which children are integrated into adult understandings and activities. (Lutz 1983, 247, 260–261)

Here Lutz appears to be conflating emotion with values to some extent, a conflation that can mask some of the complexities of cultural ideals and practices, as well as subjective experience. However, her point that emotions are crucial to socialization has been ignored for too long in studies of childhood.

Very few ethnopsychological studies have focused on child socialization, although Lutz and several contributors to White and Kirkpatrick (1985) acknowledge the value of such an approach. My claim is that an examination of the cultural construction of the self inevitably leads to a consideration of child socialization, for it is through socialization, especially during childhood, that the constitution of subjectivity takes place. As Howard points out, "The primary means of becoming a person is, of course, to be born and socialized" (1985a, 416). Lutz argues that examining theories of development can point to perceived differences between children and adults and therefore reveal aspects of broader theories that might otherwise have been overlooked (1985, 58–59). Central to my analysis of Tongan theories of development is the concept of *poto* (social competence), which is posited as the opposite state to that of children, who are seen as *vale* (foolish, crazy), and therefore socially incompetent. This dichotomy is in fact a crucial element of the broader notions of personhood which I will explore in detail. As will be shown, beliefs about the process of development can also reveal theories of how and why behavior can change and how "aspects of personhood vary within and across adults" (Lutz 1985, 59).

Whereas socialization reveals important aspects of ethnopsychology, the reverse is also true. Particular beliefs and practices associated with child socialization become comprehensible in the light of the wider ethnopsychological context. Attempts to affect children's development—by instructing, disciplining, and so on—are conceived in terms of broader notions of personhood and culturally appropriate behavior. Lutz argues that "the strong evaluative weight on terms for feeling and acting indicates that the role of ethnopsychology is not simply to describe and explain but also to evaluate behavior vis-à-vis cultural values, and thereby to begin to exercise some control over that behavior" (1988, 102).

An examination of the ways in which children's behavior is evaluated and controlled is both illuminated by and offers insights into power relations in the wider society. Power relations play a central role in the construction of subjectivity, but this dimension is often lacking in the ethnopsychological literature. It is important to consider "the production, control, distribution, and ideological force of cultural knowledge" (Keesing 1987, 388). Thus, although my focus is on the interactive nature of socialization, I am also concerned with the unequal status of the participants. In language socialization, for example, the bidirectionality of influence between adult and child is asymmetrical (Ochs 1990, 302). In Tonga this often means that the child should only speak in certain respectful ways or should remain silent.

An examination of the nature of this kind of asymmetry can reveal much about the power relations between the participants in interactions, an element that cannot be excluded from analyses of the interactional nature of socialization. By acknowledging the power relations inherent in socialization we can incorporate adult/child and child/child relations within our understanding of the term political (Thorne 1987, 100). Given the complex social hierarchies pervading every social context, child socialization in Tonga is very much a political process.

The importance of addressing power relations in child socialization has also been acknowledged in the recent work on emotion discourse and by feminist scholars concerned with "the harsh realities of children's subordination" (Thorne 1987, 98; and see Ennew 1986). Influenced by this concern, a number of recent anthropological studies of "the darker side of parenting" (Scheper-Hughes 1987a, 7) have emerged. I will discuss this literature further in chapter 7, where I examine in detail the most starkly subordinating element of the treatment of children in Tonga, the use of physical punishment.

One aspect of this broader conception of the political that has been largely neglected by ethnopsychological studies is gender relations. The failure of many of these studies to address the intrinsically gendered nature of concepts of person, self, and emotion reflects the essentialist tendencies of this work. The neglect of gender differences may also be a result of the emphasis in the ethnopsychological literature on public attempts to modify "deviant" behavior, which have been seen as the contexts in which ethnopsychological beliefs are most readily discernible (see Watson-Gegeo and White 1990). Women are often excluded from or rendered peripheral to such events, by the male participants or the ethnographers or both, so that gender relations are given little attention. A focus on childhood once again offers a valuable alternative. Caregivers' concerns with socialization are, after all, largely focused on modifying or avoiding deviant behavior. In caregivers' interactions with children, ethnopsychological beliefs are frequently made explicit, and the gendered nature of these beliefs is often readily apparent.

The language in which these beliefs are made explicit is closely examined in ethnopsychological studies. Informing this work is research into language socialization, which examines "the role language plays in the acquisition and transmission of sociocultural knowledge" (Ochs and Schieffelin 1984, 276). Influenced by Wentworth (1980) and Vygotskian socio-historical psychology (Holland and Valsiner 1988; Vygotsky 1978; Wertsch 1985), this research emphasizes the context of discourse and the interactional nature of language acquisition; the ways meaning is negotiated between caregiver and child (Ochs and Schieffelin 1984, 286).[11] Language socialization research thus utilizes the interactive or "dynamic" (Miller and Hoogstra 1992, 89) model of socialization found in developmental psychology and sociology. The influence of language socialization research on my own approach is evident throughout this study, particularly in chapter 6, in which I examine the messages about status relations embedded within the ways children learn and use language.

Broader aspects of language are also important in ethnopsychological studies, especially the language used to talk about the self and social relations. The discursive strategies used in the context of negotiating and asserting meaning, knowledge, and power frequently draw on concepts of person, self, and emotion. It is important not to privilege language, however, and the unsaid, the presuppositions and implications of every act of saying (Tyler 1978), is equally important. One task of an ethnopsychological study is to make explicit the "cultural assumptions that often go unspoken and social practices that often go unrecognized, but that make ordinary speech interpretable, pertinent, and socially forceful" (Kirkpatrick and White 1985, 14). White argues that "inferences about matters of shared importance and personal concern are a connective tissue giving shape and durability to the body of ethnopsychological interpretation" (1985, 358). Again, a study of childhood can be of great value in discovering these inferences, which are often made more obvious as caregivers attempt to influence children's behavior.

One of the obvious dangers of ethnopsychological research is to assume that there is a bounded and cohesive "body of ethnopsychological interpretation." As Howard states,

> To the extent to which we do intervene with propositions of our own and force the strands of our observations into a coherent package, we subvert the intent of ethnopsychological analysis. . . . Instead of logical consistency and systematic coherence, order must be sought in praxis, in the way our subjects *do* psychology. (1985a, 411; emphasis in original)

Psychology is "done" in context, and it is by paying attention to context that both order and inconsistency can be discerned. Examining the context-dependent nature of ethnopsychological knowledge can reveal the extent to which theories are shared, their historical development and change (for individuals throughout the life cycle and for whole societies or subgroups over time), and their degree of salience and daily use (Lutz 1985, 41).[12]

However, in examining the context of ethnopsychological knowledge, some studies have neglected broader historical processes such as conversion to Christianity, colonialism and post- (or neo-) colonialism, and the impact of their associated ideologies.[13] In contemporary societies such as Tonga, ethnopsychological beliefs may at times be self-consciously constructed in accordance with, or as resistance against, these ideologies. Cultural values, as essential components of these beliefs, can become especially significant symbols of cultural identity and tradition in the context of rapid modernization and social change. Here, the recent literature on tradition and cultural identity can usefully inform ethnopsychological work.[14] Sissons points out that the literature on the construction of tradition looks at the politicization of tradition as an aspect of national, subnational, and regional identity politics and at strategic rationalizations of tradition for, or in response to, colonial and state administration (1993, 98). Lacking is an analysis at the level of individuals' experiences of tradition and the ways in which their understanding of tradition is constructed through socialization. This gap in research exploring the construction of tradition is widened by a common tendency for analyses to remain at the level of discourse; as Norton (1993) argues, there is a need to focus on the social relations and cultural practices associated with concepts of tradition. In addressing these gaps, my study provides a better understanding of the concept of tradition in relation to child socialization.

Poyer argues that "cultural identity reflects local ideas of personhood" (1990, 129), and the reverse is also surely true. Rather than delineating a deterministic view of the relation between "culture" and "personality," my concern is to emphasize the dialectical and often contentious relationships between and among cultural identity, notions of personhood, and the experiencing self. Important aspects of this relationship can be discovered through an examination of the processes of socialization, an examination that also reveals how cultural identity is constructed: how *does* a Tongan become a Tongan, and how does being Tongan change over time? In regard to the rapid social change that has become of considerable concern to Tongans as a force detrimental to *anga fakatonga*, other questions can be asked: how does a Tongan remain a Tongan through these changes, and can one possibly cease being Tongan? In the context of increasing globalization juxtaposed with a renaissance of cultural identity within many social groups in the Pacific and elsewhere, such questions have significance beyond the case of Tonga.

Incorporating an interactional approach to socialization with an ethnopsychological study merges a sociologically oriented account of "practice" with a form of psychological anthropology (see Ortner 1984, 151). The approaches that I draw together share a common concern with agency, interaction, and context, and these are the foci of my own study. The two chapters that follow are largely concerned with context, first by establishing the ethnographic context of Tongan childhood by examining broader social structures and describing everyday life in a rural village, and second by exploring the beliefs and practices surrounding reproduction and the care of children.

CHAPTER 2

THE KINGDOM OF TONGA

The world of children should not be seen as separate from that of adults, as their daily activities involve almost constant interaction. Even when playing together children are inevitably connected to adults, who supervise them, chastize them, join their play, or are implicit presences, shaping the very nature of children's play as the children rehearse, reenact, and ridicule adult behavior. This chapter contextualizes my study of childhood in Tonga by describing certain aspects of Tongan society that for both adults and children represent the basis of their daily lives: notions of tradition and identity, social structure and organization, household composition, and village life. In my description of village life I include detailed accounts of children's education, health, and nutrition. These aspects of everyday life are often omitted from ethnographies and relegated to more specialist texts, yet they are vital to children's lives, forming an essential component of the ethnographic context of a study of childhood. Although much of my account of social structure and everyday life is general, I also include a more specific description of Holonga, the village in which I carried out much of my fieldwork, and of some of the households in which I have lived.

TRADITION AND IDENTITY

"The Tongan way" (anga fakatonga) is frequently invoked in everyday life in Tonga as both the defining element of Tongan identity and as the values and behaviors that comprise Tongan culture. Anga fakatonga is also rendered as 'ulungāanga o e fonua or anga fakafonua: the way of the land and the people. Many of the elements that comprise anga fakatonga will be described throughout this book because the concept of anga fakatonga ideally guides the socialization of children and determines proper and appropriate behavior in any given context. Anga fakatonga is used to identify what is seen as a uniquely or specifically Tongan way of being and can be used in any context, from statements of key Tongan values (such as 'ofa) to a description of the Tongan way of peeling vegetables (away from the body, not toward it in the Western way). Tongans speak of anga fakatonga as timeless and essential, yet they are also well aware of its multiple interpretations and historical transformations.[1]

My main concern is with the popular, commoner conception of *anga faka-tonga*, which, although informed by the official church and state definitions, is also very much a grassroots understanding of tradition as it effects everyday life.

Long before Europeans arrived in Tonga there was considerable mutual influence between Tonga and several other Pacific societies, particularly Fiji and Samoa (Gunson 1990; Kaeppler 1978a; Kirch 1984; Māhina 1992). This mutual influence extended to the cultural identities known as *anga faka-tonga*, *vaka viti*, and *fa'asāmoa*, which, while mutually influential, also seem to have been self-consciously opposed. Later, when Tongans were also inter-acting with a diverse group of Europeans, whom they called *papālangi* (now commonly *pālangi*), *anga fakatonga* also began to be contrasted explicitly to *anga fakapālangi*, or "the Western way."

Sustained European contact began in the late 1820s, after a long period of intermittant contact with explorers, whalers, trade s, and the like.[2] Euro-pean missionaries, after a difficult start, had a powerful influence on the social and political transformations of the latter half of the nineteenth century. The self-proclaimed first king of Tonga, Tupou I, or King George, helped to stave off the formal colonization of his country by promulgating European-style codes of law and a constitution. The 1850 Code of Laws prohibited the sale of land to foreigners, protecting Tonga from the influx of settlers experienced in so many other Pacific islands. However, Britain did make Tonga a protectorate, from 1900 to 1970, and the traders, beach-combers, and early tourists were joined by a succession of colonial officials. Under the two subsequent Tupou monarchs, Tupou II and Queen Sālote, Tonga remained relatively isolated and conservative, but a European pres-ence remained.

Marcus has suggested that during this period of the first three Tupou monarchs Tonga developed a "compromise culture," an "early, stable com-plex of institutions, ideas, and practices, which integrated Tongan culture with a version of European culture" (1977, 222). As elsewhere in Polynesia in this period, "older institutions and customs were censored, reorganized, and retraditionalized" (Marcus 1989, 197). It was during this period that much of the current official definition of *anga fakatonga* was established. As James notes, "The designation of what was 'true Tongan custom,' and what was to be abandoned, was the outcome of selective and highly interested negotiations on the part of leading Tongans and Europeans alike, overt or covert, in concert or in opposition with one another" (1992, 99).

When Taufa'ahau Tupou IV, the present monarch, succeeded to Tonga's throne in 1967, he began to open Tonga to the world. The Tongan scholar Epeli Hau'ofa has referred to the subsequent "era of uncertainty and confusion" (1978, 160); certainly it has been a period of rapid change and what Tongans refer to as "progress" (fakalakalaka). This has involved the development of international trade relations; increasing internal and international travel and migration; the introduction of technologies such as television, video players, and a telephone system; and a massive inflow of imported foodstuffs and manufactured goods. There have also been the reliance on aid and remittances, unemployment, land shortages, and other problems associated with a "developing" economy. The influx of tourists has had wide-ranging effects (Bollard 1974; Urbanowicz 1977, 1978, 1979), which will expand with the current push for increased tourism as a source of revenue.

As Marcus has argued for Polynesia more generally, many of the beliefs and practices associated with the compromise culture came to be perceived as "traditions being subjected to rapid change" (1989, 177). Anga fakatonga, regarded as Tongan tradition, is often contrasted today to anga fakapālangi in terms of the old and the new, the indigenous and the foreign. Yet the strands of Tongan and European (and Fijian and Samoan) have been interwoven to such an extent that they cannot be disentangled. Of all the factors contributing to the historical transformation of anga fakatonga, the Tongans' adoption, and adaptation, of Christianity has wrought the deepest and most pervasive changes—so much so that the categories of tradition and Christianity are now inseparable in the minds of many Tongans.[3]

In recent years Tongans have become increasingly self-conscious about their cultural identity, in the context of Tonga's diverse political and economic ties and its participation in regional and international cultural and sporting events. A 1978 study that examined Tongans' identity found that national identity was a component of 37.6 percent of responses ($n = 947$) and Polynesian identity only 9.3 percent (Parr 1981, cited in Helu 1983).[4] If a similar study were carried out today, I surmise it would reveal a far stronger national and regional identity. The renewed concern with asserting the strength and importance of "Tongan culture" has been accompanied and to some extent motivated by growing fears of a weakening or even loss of that culture. Much of this concern is directed at children, and as we will see, the socialization of children has become a critical site for the contestation, construction, and reconstruction of Tongan identity.

SOCIAL HIERARCHY

Tonga is an intrinsically hierarchical society. Kaeppler has referred to hierarchical ranking as "the most pervasive concept in Tongan culture" (1971a, 174). The concept is central to Tongan identity, both in relation to out-

siders, to whom Tongans stress the importance and value of their monarchi-
cal, highly ranked social structure, and to Tongans themselves, for whom
rank and status are fundamental aspects of everyday life and crucial components in the construction of individuals' sense of self. *Anga fakatonga* is
shaped by notions of differential power and prestige and of social ordering.
Tongan hierarchy is complicated as well as pervasive and has been the subject of many previous analyses.[5] Here, I simplify the complexities somewhat
by considering only the basic dimensions of rank, or fixed social category,
and status, or contexual social position.

Rank is fixed at birth, and the most fundamental distinction made in the
ranking system is that between *'eiki* (chief) and *tu'a* (commoner). *Tu'i* (para-
mount chief, monarch) and *matāpule* (chiefs' ceremonial attendants) actually constitute separate categories, but often they are encompassed within
the general category of *hou'eiki* (chiefly people).[6] The ranking system was significantly altered and complicated by the 1875 constitution, which established the *nōpele* (nobles) as the legally entitled, landed aristocracy. This has
meant that legally inherited rank and socially recognized rank do not always
coincide, so that some *nopele* are not *sino'i'eiki* (of chiefly "body" or "blood")
whereas some people legally defined as *tu'a* are *sino'i'eiki* by preconstitution
reckoning.

Overall, the distinction between *'eiki* and *tu'a* has been gradually erod-
ing since the midnineteenth century. Many chiefly customs were diffused
throughout the population, with activities, language forms, and kinship
rules previously used only by or to chiefly persons being widely adopted by
commoners (Lātūkefu 1980, 74). Another important change was the adoption of a new religious ideology in which all people have souls and are equal
in the sight of God. In the twentieth century, the expansion of the media to
include more critical journalism and people's exposure to different social
possibilities through the media, migration, and international travel have
also contributed to this erosion or leveling of the hierarchical order. Today,
there is considerable variation in terms of wealth, power, and prestige across
the whole population. The bourgeoning "middle class" of commoners has
gained a certain amount of wealth and prestige through education and
employment.[7] There is also a small commoner elite who have acquired high
social status and hold important positions within the church and state
bureaucracies and who are sometimes respectfully referred to as *'eiki*
(see Marcus 1993). Some elements of the commoner elite have risen in status as a result of their increasing control of the means of production (Needs
1988, 121).

The *hou'eiki* have lost much of their "personal aura," and as their "hold
over channels of elite formation" has diminished, there has been a "general

lessening of popular forbearance of chiefly power abuse" (Marcus 1989, 199)[8] as church leaders and overseas-educated commoners speak out against economic inequality, the land tenure system, alleged government corruption, and other social issues. Some of the latter group have entered the political arena as elected People's Representatives, and a pro-democracy movement was officially begun in 1992.

Yet despite the changes that have occurred there is still a clear distinction between 'eiki and tu'a, and the ranking system continues to affect people's everyday lives. The hou'eiki have retained a considerable amount of their pule (authority) and their hold over important resources such as land. The government remains dominated by a "noble oligarchy" (James 1994b, 244), with power becoming increasingly centralized in the king.

Cutting across the ranking system is social differentiation based on status. Status is calculated in context and is relative: that is, in any given context, a person's status is relative to that of whoever else is present. Status is primarily determined by seniority (chronological or genealogical), gender, and kinship relations. Another more flexibly determined factor is reputation, which can be enhanced by education, wealth, generosity, and involvement in church-related activities. Unlike ranked relations, status relations can sometimes involve competition and rivalry, particularly in regard to the more readily contested criterion of reputation. Bernstein notes that "there is a continuous struggle for status within households and families. Siblings vie for power and prestige, husbands and wives strive for more status and control, and distant relatives invoke different rules, customs, and circumstances to better their relative position" (1983, 42; and see Marcus 1978).

This cross-cutting system means that in certain contexts, such as funerals or weddings, a titled chief may be of lower status than some of his tu'a relatives. The status system is conceptualized in terms of the distinction between 'eiki and tu'a, so the chief would be "tu'a" in these contexts. Although status distinctions are operative in all social situations, there is considerable variation in the extent to which actors explicitly draw upon them. In some contexts, such as life crises, status relations are highly formalized; in others, such as as interactions between friends, status differences are unlikely to be invoked.

What, then, do 'eiki and tu'a mean as ideological constructs, and what is their significance? In Tonga, ideal personhood is conceived in terms of chiefliness. As Marcus argues for Tonga (and Samoa),

> Chiefliness is an idiom for characterizing virtuous behavior and a formally correct presentation of self. . . . Particularly as it extended to the base of society, chieftainship was not only a position of local leadership and collective

symbolic focus, but also a generally employed idiom for evaluating and controlling common behavior. (1989, 187–189)

Utilizing chiefliness as an idiom entails marking it off from "common" behavior. Indeed, as Linnekin and Poyer have suggested, in highly stratified Oceanic societies such as Tonga, chiefs and commoners are socially distinguished by "mutual stereotyping of behavioral characteristics" (1990b, 10). Historically, for example, commoners were referred to by the *hou'eiki* in derogatory terms, such as *me'avale* (foolish things) and *lauvale* (foolish talk), as well as *kainanga o e fonua*, or *kaifonua*, (eaters of the land [or earth]).[9] This stereotyping extends from ranked to status relationships and involves a set of dichotomies that I will argue can also be seen to characterize the relationship between children and adults. Thus, *'eiki* persons (or adults) are said to exhibit "proper" behavior, to be restrained, and to have authority. Conversely, *tu'a* (or children) exhibit "bad" behavior, have a lack of restraint (i.e., impulsiveness), and must obey and respect those who are *'eiki*.

The term *tu'a* itself has strongly negative connotations in contemporary Tonga. *Tu'a* also means "outside" and "back," and the term acts as a spatial metaphor when applied to social position—as well as being an accurate rendering of the actual spatial location of *tu'a* (in terms of rank or status) during many ceremonial events. For example, those who are *tu'a* will be found at the back of the house, often outdoors, preparing food for a feast, and remaining there to clean up while invited guests eat. The dichotomy between *'eiki* and *tu'a* is also conceptualized as between high and low or above and below.[10] This metaphor of height extends to the notion of "rising" or "falling" in rank or status. Gifford noted that the term *tu'a* was applied to anyone "who is not 'clever in Tongan ways', who does not act according to the prescribed Tongan etiquette, or who is rude or boorish" (1971b, 108). Thus, although they are *tu'a*, commoners strive not to display *anga fakatu'a* ("common" behavior).

The dichotomy between *'eiki* and *tu'a*, central to Tongan notions of identity and personhood, fundamentally shapes child socialization. Children occupy one of the lowest status positions in Tongan society and must learn the values and behaviors appropriate to this status. At the same time, chiefly characteristics are upheld to them as highly valued. A central tension for all Tongans is that in striving for the valued *'eiki* qualities people should not appear to be aiming above their social rank and status. The corollary of this is that respect and obedience are valued *tu'a* qualities, but in excess are debasing and detrimental to status.[11] Tongan children, in the process of becoming *poto*, have to negotiate this tension and learn the complexities of status and power differences.

SOCIAL ORGANIZATION

Status differences based on the *'eiki/tu'a* dichotomy operate even at the level of the family and so are a feature of the social world children first experience. This world expands as children grow and become enmeshed in an increasingly complex net of social relations, all of which are hierarchically ordered. At the center of the kinship network are the household (*'api*) and family (*fāmili*) into which a child is born.

The term *'api* actually refers to the allotments of land that since the Land Act of 1882 have been leased to males over sixteen years old by the Crown or the noble owning the land. "Once a man formally registered his customary allotment with the minister of lands and paid a small fee, the land devolved by male primogeniture ideally forever as long as each successive heir paid his taxes and rates to the government" (James 1994b, 249).[12] The *'api 'uta*, or bush allotment (also called the *'api tukuhau*, tax allotment), is used for agriculture and is ideally 8.25 acres. The *'api kolo*, or village allotment, gives the household its name, as it is on this land (ideally 0.4 acres) that homes are built. *'Api* can refer to the land, the houses, the occupants, or any combination thereof. Household members can be close or distant kin, permanent members, or short- or long-term visitors, but while they reside together they normally eat together and cooperate economically and domestically. Households are rarely economically self-sufficient. Most are part of kin networks that extend beyond Tonga and that circulate food, goods, and money. The links with kin overseas have become a vital aspect of Tongan household economy, with most households reliant on remittances to some extent (see Ahlburg 1991; Campbell 1992b; Gailey 1992; James 1991a).

The most immediate of these networks is the *fāmili*. The term *fāmili* is variously used to indicate anything from the nuclear family unit to virtually the entire *kāinga*, or extended family. *Fāmili tautonu* and *kāinga tautonu* are sometimes used to specifically indicate immediate relatives. Most often, *fāmili* refers to a localized kin group or a kin set maintaining close ties. In the latter sense it includes immediate family members living elsewhere, even overseas, with whom economic and emotional links are maintained. *Fāmili* members give one another economic and other support, and membership can change over time, as when the *fāmili* fissions into smaller units as a result of factors such as conflict, the large size of the original group, or the disparate economic status of sections of the group (see Aoyagi 1966; Decktor Korn 1974, 1977).

Kāinga, used most often nowadays to refer to extended family (including fictive kin), was formerly used to indicate the subjects of a chief. Although the term is still sometimes used to designate the population of a noble's estate or simply the people from a particular place, today *kāinga* does not necessarily imply local boundedness: a person's *kāinga* may be spread throughout Tonga and even overseas. *Kāinga* ties have declined in importance in terms of local organization, as the *fāmili* and *'api* have become more significant. Morton's characterization of social relations beyond the household as "optative, temporary, and ad hoc" (1987, 48–49) is apt for the *kāinga*, as *kāinga* ties are mainly activated for life crises and other ceremonial occasions. People also activate *kāinga* ties that will be advantageous in terms of material or other benefits. Thus, members of the new elite may renew or elaborate distant or forgotten chiefly connections to enhance their positions (Marcus 1981, 1993), or migrants may call on *kāinga* members to assist their settlement overseas.

The home village of most Tongans contains a significant portion of their *fāmili* and *kāinga*, but the village *(kolo)* itself is not structured or organized on the basis of kinship; it is simply an administrative unit. Economic and other activities are usually carried out by the various overlapping groups of kinsfolk and friends within the village, rather than on a villagewide scale (see Decktor Korn 1977). There is some hierarchical structuring of villages, with important figures such as family heads and church ministers who have little formal authority outside the village wielding considerable authority in practice. There are often dominant families, which have accumulated power through their connections to *hou'eiki*, their economic strength, or both. Over two-thirds of the population lives in villages (Central Planning Department 1991, 108), and in addition, parts of Nuku'alofa, particularly the longer-established areas, are socially structured much like the villages.

Village identity is important to Tongans as an aspect of their *fonua* (country and island) identity. Its importance is revealed on occasions in which people from different villages are involved, such as sporting events; on these occasions considerable intervillage rivalry is often evident. However, the village with which a person identifies most closely may not be that in which he or she resides, if migration, marriage, or other factors have led to a change of residence.

These overlapping social units of *'api*, *fāmili*, *kāinga*, and *kolo* constitute most of young children's social world. *Fāmili* and *kāinga* are not geographically bounded, so children become familiar with other villages, other islands in Tonga, and even other countries when they travel to visit or live with kin. In their daily lives children may travel out of their village with their parents or other caregivers for many additional reasons: to go to school, or into town, or to the district health center or central hospital, or even to the beach for a family picnic. However, it is the geographically bounded *'api* and *kolo* in which children spend most of their time and within which they first begin to learn what it is to be Tongan.

HOUSEHOLD COMPOSITION

In recent years there has been a general trend in Tonga for the 'api to comprise nuclear family units, including families in which one partner is absent through death or migration. Interisland migration has slowed this trend to some extent on the main island of Tongatapu, especially in and around the capital, Nuku'alofa. Here, families are extended by in-migrating relatives, or the migrants themselves form often crowded households.[13] In fact, household configuration is widely varied, and membership of individual households may frequently change. In Holonga, the village on Tongatapu in which I conducted much of my fieldwork, there were seventy-seven households in 1988. Families with only parents (or parent) and children comprised thirty-four (44.2 percent) of these households. A similar percentage, 45.5 percent, was found for 235 high school students from Tongatapu and Vava'u (see appendix 1, table 6A; also see Decktor Korn 1975 for an earlier study of household composition).

Holongan households that were not nuclear formed twenty-four different configurations. The most common were nuclear families extended by relatives of the parent or parents and nuclear families extended by children's spouses or offspring or both. In five households children lived with only their grandparents. Eight households were headed solely by women, including two women who were widowed, one who was divorced, one who was unmarried, and four who had husbands working overseas. Household size also varies widely; the Holongan households in 1988 averaged 6.1 residents (6.6 was the average for Tongatapu in 1988: see Statistics Department 1993a, 10, table 13) but ranged between one and twelve.

Households change significantly over time, and to illustrate the kinds of changes that can occur I will describe several of the households in which I have lived, introducing as I do so some of the people who will populate this book (for kinship diagrams of these households see appendix 2).

PITA AND MANU

After living in teachers' accommodations on the grounds of a girls' college in Nuku'alofa in 1979, I moved into a Tongan household after my marriage in January 1980. The 'api in which we lived, in Nuku'alofa, had been my husband Sione's childhood home, where his parents raised their nine children. By 1980 some of these children had moved overseas, and Sione's mother,

Manu, divided her time between Tonga and Australia. The household at that time consisted of Sione's father, Pita, and father's sister, Hina; Sione's sister-in-law Vika and her five children (her husband was working in Australia); Sione's brother, Semisi, Semisi's wife, and their two young children; Sione's two unmarried sisters, Luisa and Palu, and of course Sione, me, and by the end of 1980 our newborn son: a total of seventeen people.

By 1988, when I returned to Tonga for fieldwork and stayed for two weeks in the same 'api, the membership of the household had changed dramatically. Pita, who had spent most of the intervening years in Australia, was present again as the head of the household. Manu and he had returned to Tonga for the birth of Luisa's son, and they, with Luisa, her husband, Ngata, and son, Paula, were the only remaining residents of the household. All the other children of Pita and Manu, and Pita's sister Hina, were now overseas. Vika, the daughter-in-law who had waited many years for her husband to return from Australia, eventually discovered that he had established a new family there. She went to Australia, taking her children, and later remarried.

SEINI AND SIALE

The couple with whom I stayed during part of my fieldwork in 1988, Seini and Siale, were not yet married when I first went to Tonga in 1979. Both lived in Holonga, Siale with his widowed mother, Tonga, and his siblings, and Seini in the household of her maternal great-aunt, Alisi. After their marriage by elopement they lived with Tonga until Siale went to Australia to work, about a year after their twins, Tomasi and Elenoa, were born. When Siale left, Seini moved back to Alisi's home with the twins. When I arrived in 1986 Siale had just returned from Australia (where he had lived with Seini's mother and brother), and they were living with Alisi while building their own home. The twins were three years old; also living in the house were four other children, whom Alisi had adopted: Viliami (eleven) and Finau (four), the children of Alisi's brother's son and his wife, who lived next door to Alisi; Sela (five), the illegitimate daughter of another of Alisi's nephews; and Lopeti (sixteen), the son of a niece who lived overseas.

In 1988 Seini and Siale had moved into their own home in Holonga and lived there with the twins and their year-old daughter, 'Ofa. Seini's mother, Moana, had returned to Tonga from Australia for 'Ofa's birth and remained to care for her while Seini worked. Silia, Seini's nineteen-year-old "sister" (MZD),[14] who was in her final year at a Catholic college in a nearby village, also lived in the household. When Moana returned to Australia in mid-1989 the rest of the household went with her; they have not returned to Tonga. Siale and Seini, having just set up their own home and both earning incomes, were reluctant to go to Australia, but Moana was adamant. Siale suggested sending only the children, but Seini wanted to remain with them; after long discussions they both agreed to abide by Moana's wishes.

THE HOUSEHOLDS COMPARED

The 1988 households of Pita and Manu, Seini and Siale were quite different. The former couple, though conservative and traditional, were also part of the emerging middle class and relatively well off. Because most of their children were overseas they had a ready source of financial assistance and had improved on their large house over the years so that by 1988 it was equipped with a flush toilet, bathroom, and internal kitchen. Both had traveled overseas on many occasions over many years, often living for periods of several years in Australia.

Their daughter Luisa and her husband both had well-paid office jobs, and Ngata had attended university in New Zealand. Their wages enabled them to live very comfortably and to pay a local woman to do their washing and ironing. They did not own a car, but traveled everywhere, even to work, by taxi. Siale and Seini, on the other hand, were struggling financially after spending most of their savings on the construction of their small wooden home. Siale had spent his earnings from his year's work in Australia on the goods and truck he brought back with him. Their house was well-furnished and comfortable; but their daily diet was poor, and they had little disposable income. Seini worked as a clerk and Siale relied on contract trucking work, using his own truck. During my stay he used a bank loan to purchase a second-hand car, which he then used as a taxi. Money remitted from relatives overseas usually went to older family members, not to Siale and Seini.

The households also differed in their contact with neighbors and nearby family, with the Holonga household very much part of village life and the Nuku'alofa household more "suburban." Seini and Siale had a constant stream of visitors, interacted closely with their immediate neighbors, and were involved in village activities such as collective *ngatu* (decorated bark-cloth) production (Seini) and kava drinking (Siale). The household of Pita and Manu was quieter and more isolated from neighbors; there were few informal visitors, and outside involvement centered on church-related activities.

Despite their differences the members of the two households all share one defining characteristic: they are all commoners. My study is one of commoner childhood, and I have chosen not to present "the noble view" (Decktor Korn 1974), that is, the chiefly perspective, which has predominated in much previous research.[15] This earlier research does not include studies of chiefly children, and an investigation of aspects of socialization specific to this group would be a valuable addition to knowledge about the small but powerful chiefly "class" in Tonga. However, such an investigation was not part of my own study. During my fieldwork I deliberately avoided associations with *hou'eiki* because such associations would have made my acceptance into the village of Holonga more difficult. I chose to retain my position as former teacher, former affine, and friend within the social networks of the people I knew; although it was difficult to convince people who knew me in these roles that I was genuinely "doing fieldwork," retaining them precluded any settling-in period and enabled me to begin my fieldwork almost immediately upon arrival in Holonga.

VILLAGE LIFE

My time in Tonga has been spent mainly on Tongatapu, in the residential area close to Nuku'alofa's business district and in the village of Holonga, some twelve miles from town. I have also spent two weeks in Pangai village on 'Eua, living with relatives of my Holongan friends, and two weeks in Vava'u in a small guest house on the outskirts of Neiafu. My experiences support Decktor Korn's claim that there is considerable local-level variability (1977), but I would add that this occurs within a fairly limited range of economic and social activities, house types, religious denominations, and so on.

In many respects Holonga is a fairly typical village (see also Tupouniua 1977), although it also has some unusual characteristics. Holonga is on government land and therefore is not part of a noble's *tofi'a*, or hereditary estate, as are the majority of Tongan villages. Kapukava, the chiefly title associated with Holonga, was not chosen as a *nōpele* title in the political restructuring of the nineteenth century, so that although the present title holder is respected as having *sino'i'eiki* (chiefly blood) and is referred to by villagers as *'eiki*, he has no legal status or *tofi'a*.[16]

Holonga is also atypical because of its high proportion of Catholic residents, attributable to its historical role as one of the earliest sites of Catholicism in Tonga (Lātūkefu 1974, 147). In 1988, some 45.4 percent of Holongans were Catholic, in contrast to the national figure of 16.3 percent.[17] The proportion of Wesleyans (43.3 percent) is similar to the national figure (44.1 percent). Wesleyanism is the predominant religion in Tonga, and Holonga's high proportion despite the large numbers of Catholics reflects the fact that there are only three other denominations represented in the village: the Mormon church (5.8 percent, 12.3 nationally), the Church of Tonga (3.2 percent, 7.5 nationally) and the Ma'ama Fo'ou (2.3 percent, national figures not in census). Not present in Holonga are the Free Church

of Tonga, Seventh Day Adventist, and a number of movements that have
small national congregations (e.g.; Baha'i, New Apostolic Church, Tonga
Muslim League).

As in other villages, Holongans may change religious denomination to
suit the school they attend or the religion of their spouse (usually the wife
changes to the husband's religion) or for "personal re-tooling" (Decktor Korn
1977, 198). Such changes can be the source of family disharmony but are
eventually accepted, and religious differences do not divide communities
today as in the past (see Lātūkefu 1974). Children sometimes attend different churches with different relatives; for example, Seini's children attended
Catholic services with their maternal relations and Wesleyan services with
their paternal kin. Seini herself attended both, despite nominally becoming
a Wesleyan after her marriage, and Siale did not attend at all, although he
had been briefly interested in Mormonism and Islam. Members of different
congregations work together on various projects such as the production of
ngatu, preparation for feasts, and so on. In all Tongan villages and towns,
church activities take up a significant proportion of people's time and money,
with various services, meetings, choir practice, and so on (see Van der Grijp
1993, 205–210). Church activities are also an important context for status
enhancement, as individuals take on roles within the church such as lay
preachers (see Decktor Korn 1978a).

The first settlement of Holonga was along the rocky lagoon shore. As the
population grew the village expanded toward what is now Hahake Road, the
main road along the lagoon coast from Nuku'alofa to Kolonga, at the far
eastern end of the island. Today Holonga sprawls along both sides of Hahake
Road, merging with the village of Malapo to the west and almost reaching
Alaki to the east (see map 2). Houses are being built on bush allotments, and
some town allotments have more than one house crowded onto the land.
Despite this expansion, the actual population has declined, as in many of the
rural villages, as a result of migration to the capital or overseas.[18] The number of households, however, has increased, suggesting a decrease in household size due to the trend toward nuclear family households.

Table 1 indicates the distribution of ages within the Holongan population in 1988, derived from my own household survey. The demographic pattern in Holonga reflects the national pattern (Statistics Department 1991a,
xii), one that shows the effect of migration, particularly from early adulthood. Figures showing the age and sex distribution of persons born in Tonga
and living in New Zealand and Australia for up to nine years before 1986
(Statistics Department 1993b, 48, table F4), clearly show that the largest
numbers for both sexes are between fifteen and thirty-four. The Holongan
figures indicate that there is some difference between males and females in

Table 1: Age Distribution in Holonga, 1988

AGE GROUP	FEMALE (%)	MALE (%)	TOTAL (%)
0–5	37 (14.9)	27 (12.1)	64 (13.6)
6–10	33 (13.3)	40 (18.0)	73 (15.6)
11–15	30 (12.1)	28 (12.6)	58 (12.4)
16–20	34 (13.7)	30 (13.5)	64 (13.6)
21–30	39 (15.8)	26 (11.7)	65 (13.9)
31–40	22 (8.9)	20 (9.0)	42 (8.9)
41–50	11 (4.4)	12 (5.4)	23 (4.9)
51–60	11 (4.4)	10 (4.5)	21 (4.5)
61–70	16 (4.4)	13 (5.8)	29 (6.2)
71–80	13 (5.2)	12 (5.4)	25 (5.3)
81–90	1 (0.4)	4 (1.8)	5 (1.1)
TOTAL	247	222	469 (100)
1986	252	256	508
1976	235	294	529

the twenty-one to thirty group, probably as a result of more young men leaving to work in town or overseas. However, for older groups the distribution is less varied (on migration see Cowling 1990b; Gailey 1992; James 1991a). Table 1 also reflects the relatively high fertility rate common in Tonga. This rate was 5.2 nationally in 1986; in this year 41 percent of the approximately 93,000 Tongans and part-Tongans recorded in the census was under fifteen years of age (Statistics Department 1993b, 1).

Houses in Holonga, as elsewhere in Tonga, vary from traditional constructions with thatched roofs and walls to "pālangi houses" with wooden or concrete walls and steel roofs. The former are now uncommon on Tongatapu, and the latter increasingly popular. Housing styles tend to reflect economic status, and in some wealthier villages and areas around Nuku'alofa quite elaborate structures can be found. Good-quality European housing and expensive consumer goods have become status symbols for the new and aspiring middle-class commoners. European-style furniture such as beds, couches, and cupboards are widely popular, as are household appliances and other imported home goods such as china, glassware, and linen. As well as purchasing goods imported by retailers in Tonga, many returning migrants bring home large quantities of goods. When Siale returned to Holonga in 1986 after working in Australia, he shipped out a large dump truck filled with household appliances, furniture, packaged food, and other goods. Our next-door neighbor in Holonga in 1988 had also returned from overseas, and his relatively poor wooden house was crowded with television and video equipment, a large stereo, electric guitars and

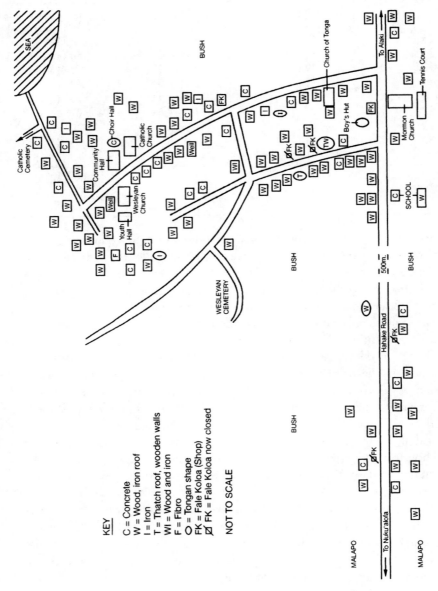

Map 2: Holonga

KEY

C = Concrete
W = Wood, iron roof
I = Iron
T = Thatch roof, wooden walls
WI = Wood and iron
F = Fibro
O = Tongan shape
FK = Fale Koloa (Shop)
Ø FK = Fale Koloa now closed

NOT TO SCALE

drum kit, washing machine, and more, all having arrived crammed into a minivan.

Some houses now have internal kitchens rather than a separate cooking house, though most retain an outdoor kitchen as well, for open-fire cooking. Toilets and showers are usually in separate structures, the majority of toilets being pit style. Access to water is a constant problem in the villages. Most homes on the larger islands, except those in more remote villages, have access to the reticulated water system, with an outside tap and shower and in some cases a flush toilet, but the water supply often fails or is turned off, sometimes for weeks at a time. The piped water can also be contaminated, especially in Nuku'alofa in the low-lying, swampy areas where sewage leaks into the water supply. Rainwater tanks are often inadequate to meet the needs of the household during the dry months, and occasionally water has to be brought in from other villages with larger water stores, such as in-ground concrete tanks. Where electricity is available it is also unreliable; there are frequent blackouts, particularly outside Nuku'alofa. These interruptions to water and power supplies mean that newly acquired household appliances, kitchens, and flush toilets are often rendered temporarily useless. More important, health problems can result from freezers that are repeatedly on and off and flush toilets rendered inoperative.

Most households keep some animals on their 'api kolo, including pigs, goats, chickens, cats, and dogs. Dogs roam free, sometimes in packs, and can be quite aggressive: dog bites are not uncommon injuries. The law requires pigs to be kept fenced in or tied up, but in most villages they can be found roaming free, often causing considerable damage to fences and gardens. The gardens of many homes are well cared for and attractive, and the plants are often used for decorative, medicinal, culinary, and other purposes. As well as homes, villages have at least two or three churches, several small stores (fale koloa) offering a limited range of goods, and sometimes a primary school.

In Holonga, as in many villages, some of the land surrounding the village is cultivated for food crops, but much lies unused, often because leaseholders are living overseas. Village men may have to travel some distance to their bush allotments (or those for which they have gained use rights), and those who work for wages may have younger male relatives work the land for them (see Van der Grijp 1993; Needs 1988). Less than half the men in Holonga (41.3 percent) are solely employed in agriculture, on their own or others' land. Other occupations include, in order of frequency, unskilled labor, office work, teaching, taxi and truck driving, carpentry, shopkeeping, fishing, and employment in the police force or army. Few women (18.2 percent) hold full-time, paid jobs, and those only within a narrow range of occupations (teaching, office work, and nursing).[19] The remainder of women work in the home, as well as producing crafts, contributing to agricultural production, and gathering seafood in the lagoon. Many women in Holonga, and elsewhere in Tonga, are becoming increasingly involved in economic activity and are assuming a greater burden of responsibility for the support of their families (Faletau 1982; Fleming with Tuku'afu 1986). Factors such as migration of males, moves toward more commercial production, and the unreliable nature of many men's incomes contribute to the need for women to be economically active as well as doing work considered to be "female." However, the women of Holonga have not become involved in the recent mobilization of Tongan women into women's groups to obtain funding through international aid agencies for local development projects (Halatuituia, Latu, and Moimoi 1982). Men working the land and women making *ngatu* sometimes work in cooperative groups *(kautaha)* but small, household-based work units are more common.

DAILY LIFE IN HOLONGA

Early mornings in Holonga are busy, as the yards are swept of leaves and rubbish and the household prepares for the day. The smell of smoke as the leaves are burned marks the beginning of a new day. After the morning meal—often bread and butter—the older children go to school. In 1988, the primary school in Holonga had four classes and approximately 120 pupils, some of whom traveled from neighboring villages to attend. Many of the children wear no shoes, and because many have only one school uniform, they wear other clothes on Wednesdays while their uniforms are washed. Once the children have gone to school and the men, and some women, have gone to their jobs or plantations, the village is quiet. The women who are not in wage employment stay mostly at home, and the sound of *tutu*—the beating of bark for tapa—punctuates the stillness.[20] Children not old enough to attend school stay at home, playing with neighboring children or alone, watching the adults remaining at home doing their work, and doing any chores or errands of which they are capable. Occasionally the women organize a *koka'anga*, a gathering to dye huge sheets of tapa, and then there is a flurry of activity as food is prepared for the women and the young children play on the periphery of the women's activities. The older children return home briefly for lunch and then again in the midafternoon when they finish school for the day. They help with household chores and in their spare moments play in noisy groups. As the men begin to return home the sound of kava being pounded replaces the *tutu*. Another sound ringing across the village in the late afternoon is the sound of children being called to *ha'u kaukau* (come and bathe). After the evening meal there may be choir or dance practice to attend or some church-related meeting. If not, most of the men gather to drink kava late into the night, while the women and children, and the men remaining at home, spend the evening watching videos, listening to the radio, or just chatting and perhaps playing cards.

On Saturday the village is busy, with people traveling into Nuku'alofa to shop or thoroughly cleaning the house and yard. Women and teenage girls plough through the mountains of washing accumulated during the week. Sometimes most of the household travel to the family plantation to work and to collect various foods for the Sunday 'umu (underground oven in which heated rocks cook the food). On Sundays it is prohibited to work, play, or trade in Tonga. However, on Sunday mornings households actually work quite hard, with the men and boys preparing the 'umu and the women and girls making the food to be cooked in it. While it cooks people attend church, returning home to feast on the baked food and then rest for the afternoon. Sunday evenings are often spent visiting relatives within the village or having a family religious service at home. Apart from the bustle of the morning's food preparation, Sunday is very much a day of rest in Tongan households.

Daily life in Holonga is, however, far from idyllic. The problems confronted by many Holongans are those faced by the majority of commoners today: insufficient family income and subsequent reliance on remittances; poor diet, sanitation, and water supply and related health problems; inadequate housing; shortage of land; and lack of opportunities for paid employment (see Faletau 1982; Hau'ofa 1977; Sevele 1973). Although many of Holonga's residents experience these problems, they are much more severe in the poorer settlements around Nuku'alofa, populated largely by landless migrants (Lua 1987; Takau and Fungalei 1987).

For Tongan youth, unemployment has been acknowledged as "a major social problem": unemployment for males fifteen to nineteen years old is 27.6 percent, and for females over 50 percent (Statistics Department 1991a, xxxiii).[21] It was partly because of this unemployment problem that few teenagers in Holonga were leaving school early to seek employment. In 1988 only five girls aged eighteen and younger had left school; all were doing home duties. Four males under eighteen had left school, with one working in an office, two as laborers, and one farming. Although few students go on to tertiary education, many remain in high school until they are nineteen or twenty. Some young people are able to move overseas, sponsored by family members who have already migrated. Just as I arrived in Holonga in 1988, Lopeti, who had been in Alisi's household in 1986, was moving to Australia to live with relatives. Silia, in our Holongan household, had made several unsuccessful attempts to find sponsors and eventually moved to Australia with Seini and Siale.

EDUCATION

Unemployment is only one factor encouraging students to complete their high school years. More important, perhaps, is the strong emphasis on formal education in Tonga. The first schools in Tonga were established by the Wesleyan missionaries from 1828, followed by the Roman Catholics in the 1850s. By 1838 adults and children were being taught separately, and for a brief period after 1854 infant schooling was given priority (Cummins 1977, 116, 122). The first secondary school (Wesleyan) was opened in 1866, although it was not until 1870 that girls were admitted to secondary education (Fiefia 1981, 1).[22] In response to a declining interest in schooling after the initial wave of enthusiasm, education was made compulsory in the 1862 code of laws (Lātūkefu 1975, 36).

"Education fever" hit Tonga in the post–World War II period, as people's aspirations for employment and migration grew (Afeaki 1975, 65). Today, all children between six and fourteen living within two miles of a government primary school must attend that or a similar school and complete six years of primary education (Law of Tonga 1967, Act 23, sections 52 and 53), and parents not sending children to school can be fined.[23] The Tongan government now claims a 100 percent literacy rate (Throsby 1987, 9, table 1.4).

There is, as will be shown, a general perception in Tonga of children as vale and unable to learn properly until the end of primary school, and this perception has influenced attitudes toward education. Since "real education" does not begin until secondary school, there has been a "lack of learning intervention activities in the early years" (Tu'inukuafe 1990, 209–210). Perceptions are gradually changing, and a number of kindergartens now operate in Tonga, mainly on Tongatapu. Giving children at least a year of preschool education is becoming an increasingly popular means of improving their chances in the competitive education system and, in the long term, the job market.

The primary education system is predominantly government run and the secondary system mainly church run, with only 19 percent of high school places being at government schools in 1989 (Central Planning Department 1991, 287). There are many more primary schools than high schools, which are in central locations and often have boarding colleges. Most high school students in Holonga travel by bus to the Catholic college at Mu'a or one of the high schools in Nuku'alofa. Since 1944 teachers have been trained in

Tonga at the Teacher's Training College in Nuku'alofa, although some have trained overseas and many remain untrained.

Selection to high schools is competitive, and there is a high rate of repeating students in year six: 20 percent of those who sat the Secondary School Entrance Examination in 1987 (Report of the Ministry of Education for 1987, 11). A serious gap exists between the primary and secondary levels, leading the government to plan an extension of primary schooling into classes seven and eight. The main problem lies in the poor grasp of English many students have on entering high school, where the majority of teaching is in English. High school education has also undergone a restructuring since the late 1980s, toward more Tongan control of subject matter and assessment and away from dependence on the New Zealand curricula on which the system was previously based.

Education is regarded as a means to white-collar employment, creating a conservative attitude toward curriculum planning despite the fact that employment opportunities are limited. Parents and teachers alike are generally conservative in their approach to education, resisting any moves away from an academically oriented curriculum toward an emphasis on practical skills. However, few students who aspire to white-collar work actually attain their goal. Many school leavers go overseas seeking employment or further education; those remaining face high rates of unemployment.

The Tongan education system as a whole suffers from an unequal distribution of facilities and resources between urban and rural areas, adding to internal migration to Tongatapu and particularly to Nuku'alofa, which has the most prestigious schools. Some students are sent to boarding colleges, others to live with relatives near their schools. Sometimes whole families, or at least some members, migrate temporarily or permanently to be near schools. In Vava'u, for example, some families from outer islands set up temporary villages on the main island during school terms.

Overcrowding in classrooms is a problem, and most schools have an acute shortage of educational resources. Despite the high value placed on education, teaching is a fairly low-status profession in Tonga, and the working conditions are poor. Funded from overseas, Mormon and Seventh Day Adventist schools—with their sports facilities, new buildings, modern equipment and textbooks, and extracurricula activities for students—provide a sharp contrast to the other Tongan schools.[24] School fees and other school-related expenses place a great financial strain on many families, and most rely on remittances from overseas relatives to cover these expenses.

There are a number of higher education institutions in Tonga, including business, agricultural, theological, and teaching colleges; a nursing school;

the Tongan extension center of the University of the South Pacific; and the independent 'Atenisi Institute. Many young people nevertheless travel overseas to seek postsecondary education. While there is little difference between males and females in educational attainment at primary and secondary levels, in postsecondary education "males have a clear advantage over females" (Statistics Department 1991a, xx). It is interesting, however, that in my survey of high school students (see appendix 1), six of the female respondents (5.2 percent) claimed they wanted to pursue further education but none of the males gave this response.

HEALTH AND NUTRITION

The education system in Tonga is closely interlinked with the strong primary health care system.[25] Health programs administered through schools include visits by the School Dental Service, Maternal and Child Health personnel, an immunization team, and health education officers, all dependant on the availability of funding (*Report of the Ministry for Health for 1986*, 32). Nearly half of the in-service training given to primary school teachers is in nutrition and health, and the environmental science curriculum for primary schools incorporates health education.

The major health problems for Tongan children are gastroenteritis and respiratory illnesses. Other common health problems for infants and children include parasitic infection, accidental injuries, and skin diseases and infections. Most of the children I encountered had almost continual low-grade infections, with coughs and runny noses. Many children also had sores that were slow to heal; for example, when I arrived in Holonga, Tomasi had an infected cut on his knee and Elenoa had an infected vaccination site on her arm. In both cases the sores took more than two months to heal and were left untreated during that period.

Because some cooking is still done on open fires, kettles, and small gas stoves, and containers of hot food are commonly kept at floor level, burns are also common, particularly for children under three. Soon after her first birthday, 'Ofa was taken to the hospital with a severe burn on her leg after her brother picked up an electric kettle of boiling water and 'Ofa pulled on its cord, causing the water to tip onto her. In another case in Holonga a baby was badly burned when an older child who was carrying her tripped and dropped her into a pot of hot soup sitting on the floor. Burns are often treated at home with Tongan oil (*lolo Tonga*, which is scented coconut oil), coconut cream, or even machine oil.

Many other health problems are not reported to the hospitals or clinics, partly because these conditions, such as diarrhea (unless severe) and various skin infections, are not perceived as sicknesses. Minor problems are left untreated or are treated with herbal medicines prepared by a family member or faito'o (healer).[26] Skin diseases, as well as most respiratory and gastrointestinal illnesses, are generally regarded as Tongan diseases (mahaki fakatonga; see Ikahihifo and Panuve 1983; Parsons 1985) and are therefore usually treated at home. Another category of Tongan disease is the 'āvanga illnesses caused by spirits (Cowling 1990a; Ikahihifo and Panuve 1983, 23; Parsons 1984, 75–77; 1985, 94–96). A further explanation for children's illnesses is family problems, and Parsons shows that in Tongan theories of illness causation, disharmony in relationships between adult kin can adversely affect their children's health. (1984, 81–82).

Medical assistance at a hospital or clinic is usually sought for more serious complaints, although many people fear and distrust hospital treatments and seek help with reluctance. Injections, particularly of penicillin, are regarded as dangerous, and several times I was told stories of people dying after receiving them. Tongan medicine is seen as safer and more rapidly effective than hospital treatments, as well as being the only way to cure Tongan diseases.[27] However, reluctance to take children to the hospital can sometimes have tragic results. The majority of cases of mental retardation in Tonga are caused by complications of meningitis or infections of the central nervous system. A pediatrician from Vaiola Hospital stated that these are "often the result of a sick child taken to a doctor far too late for proper treatment, or in cases where treatment had not been aggressive enough and the infection had gone on to affect areas of the brain resulting in mental retardation, epilepsy, and cerebral palsy" (Matangi Tonga 1989b, 38). Such complications may again be interpreted as spirit caused. Cowling claims that these and other serious illnesses are rarely blamed on the child's caregivers, "unless there is clear evidence of neglect and illtreatment" (1990a, 76n12).

A Tongan medical practitioner now working in Australia blames Tongan children's poor health on physical and emotional neglect caused by a "power struggle" that occurs between parents in the early years of marriage, during which the husband forcibly seeks his wife's submission to his authority. He claims this neglect results in "emotionally disturbed children, poor nutrition, poor hygiene, poor dentition, skin infections and infestation, parasitic infections and delayed development, amongst other things" (Niumeitolu 1993, 76). The dynamics identified here certainly do occur in some families, but this bleak picture cannot be generalized to the entire population. Many other factors need to be considered when examining children's health: for example, the 1986 National Nutrition Survey suggested there may be a relationship between vitamin and mineral deficiencies and the high incidence of skin infections and diarrhea (Maclean and Badcock 1987, 50). These defi-

ciencies result from the lack of fresh fruit and vegetables, other than starchy
root crops, in most Tongans' diets (Englberger 1983).[28] However, severe malnutrition is seldom the cause of illness in Tongan children.

Many children eat only one or two meals a day, usually bread or hardtack
biscuits in the morning and root vegetables with boiled fish or mutton-ribs
(sipi) or "soup" (flour and water with canned fish or meat flavoring) in the
evening. Sometimes a glut of cheap, imported food such as turkey wings adds
variety to this otherwise monotonous diet. A nutritionist attached to Vaiola
Hospital claimed that the eating pattern of the many children who eat little
until the main evening meal can affect their schooling because they are tired
and unable to concentrate during the day (Fonua 1988, 14).

Most families still prepare an 'umu on Sundays, including root vegetables
and various lu (meat or fish with coconut cream, wrapped in taro leaves).
This meal is the most nourishing of the week, with both protein foods and
green vegetables. The feasts that are held at any important event also
provide foods that are not part of the daily diet, particularly protein foods
such as pork, chicken, fish, and eggs. At certain times of the year, such as
Christmas and Uike Lotu (Prayer Week, the first week of the year), people
may attend several feasts in a week, and even at other times they usually
attend a feast every few weeks. However, children attending feasts do not
tend to eat the more nutritious food offered. They prefer the candies, pro-
cessed snack foods, and soft drinks that decorate the pola (trays of food) and
the ice cream that has become a popular dessert at feasts now that many
homes have freezers. Children only benefit from feasts when their family is
given a portion of the leftover food to take home. When their own family
has contributed to the feast they may eat very poorly for several days afterward, as all available money has been spent on the feast food.

Between meals children find or buy various snacks. Boys are more likely
to consume fruit than girls as they are more often in the bush where they can
gather fruit such as lesi (papaya). Children also eat fruit that they knock
down from trees with rocks and sticks, although this is almost always unripe
fruit. Other snacks include edible seeds, bananas that have ripened on
bunches kept for cooking, unripe coconut meat, and imported snack foods
and sweets. A favorite snack food in Holonga in 1988 was uncooked instant
noodles and the contents of their flavor packets (referred to as fifisi, meaning
spicy-hot, and consisting of salt, monosodium glutamate, and spices).

The Tongan government's concern over diet-related health problems has
led to a strong program of public nutrition education in recent years and the
formation in 1982 of a National Food and Nutrition Committee within the
Central Planning Department. The increasing dependence on imported
food, often of low nutritional value, has been associated with increasing

health problems such as cancer, high blood pressure, heart disease, obesity, and diabetes. Apart from the higher prestige of imported foodstuffs, other factors contributing to this consumption pattern include the decline in subsistence production, the lack of availability of some Tongan foods, and the fact that many Tongan foods are now more expensive to buy than imported products.

CHAPTER 3

HAVING CHILDREN:

"PARADISE ON EARTH"

Children are "*me'a mahu'inga taha pe 'i mamani*," Siale's mother, Tonga, said: they are the most important things in this world. Seini's mother, Moana, said, "It is paradise for one's stay on earth to have children." Their words were echoed by most of the women and men with whom I spoke in Tonga, where children are seen as intrinsically valuable social beings who give meaning to life and to social institutions such as marriage. The high value of children is most often talked about in terms of the contribution they can make to their household through their labor and, as they get older, their financial, material, and emotional support of their parents. Both male and female children offer such support, so that in this sense there is no differentiation of value based on sex. Although the greatest emphasis in people's comments to me was on children's role as providers, the continuing emotional attachment between parents and children is also important. This is implicit in the remainder of Moana's comment: "As one gets older (*hoholo hifo*: gradually sink down), one's children are the closest to you; there is no one else who is as close to one's self (*hoto sino*: one's body) in one's old age."[1]

This chapter examines this strongly positive view of children in relation to attitudes to childbearing and childrearing through a discussion of pregnancy and birth, fertility and reproductive control, illegitimacy, and adoption. Throughout childhood the mother has the greatest responsibility for teaching her children "proper" *anga* (behavior, way of being) so that they become *poto* and for caring and protecting her children. Her responsibilities toward them begin even before they are born. During pregnancy the mother's behavior, what she ingests, her relationships with others, and even how she moves her body are all said to influence the physical and mental well-being of the "baby inside" (*pēpē 'i loto*). This influence continues to be particularly strong in the year or so after the birth, in her feeding and general care of the baby. It is in a child's first two years that the high value of children is most clearly reflected in their treatment, with love and affection openly expressed and great importance placed on infants' physical well-being. Also described are the ways in which, from the moment of birth, a child's social identity is acknowledged and how the end of the first year is celebrated.

MARRIAGE

Commoners usually choose their own marriage partners, although ideally the father and the father's sisters of both partners have some influence. Romantic love (manako) and sexual attraction were most commonly cited to me as the reasons for marrying, and these were explained in terms of ideals of masculinity and femininity, trust, and the good nature and good behavior (anga lelei) of the potential spouse. More pragmatic concerns such as socioeconomic status were regarded as secondary considerations. Many marriages are elopements (mali hola): because the couple anticipate objections to the marriage from their families, or because the girl is already pregnant, or even because the couple want to express their freedom to choose (fa'iteliha) or independence (tau'atāina).[2] Seini and Siale eloped after Seini's family attempted to prevent her from seeing him because they thought him ugly and poor. Seini humorously described the elaborate ruses they had taken to evade her relatives on the day of their marriage, which in Tonga requires a trip to the registry office as well as marriage in a church by a minister or priest. My husband and I also eloped, and in our case, as often happens, his family demonstrated their acceptance of the union by attending a church service with us the following Sunday, with both of us wearing formal clothes and thick layers of fine mats (kie hingoa).

Wesleyan missionaries had a profound effect on marriage practices through their influence on the codified laws and through their Christian ideology, which was filtered through their nineteenth-century British ideals (predominantly those of the lower middle class). They encouraged chastity before marriage, fidelity in marriage, and subservience of the wife to her husband. In the latter case, they supported the status relations between spouses that appear to have existed before European contact, in which husbands were 'eiki to their wives. Although different couples vary in the extent to which this status inequality affects their relationships today, it does mean that husbands can exert considerable influence over their wives' reproductive lives. A husband can, for example, reject contraception or insist on adopting out one or more of their children to members of his family. As will be seen below, certain of the husband's relatives are also believed to have some influence on a woman's reproductive capacity.

Most marriages occur when both partners are in their midtwenties.[3] Newlyweds usually live with the parents or other relations of one partner until they have at least one child, mainly out of economic necessity. Tensions often arise between the new spouse and the partner's family, especially when the wife moves in with her husband's family. They will have little privacy, and in many cases will not have a separate bedroom of their own. Also, being low status to all her affines, especially her husband's sisters, a new wife is expected to be hardworking and submissive. Many couples continue to live with other family members after their first child is born, but a large proportion eventually move into their own home and reside as a nuclear family or become heads of a new extended family household.

PREGNANCY: "PREPARING THE CHILD"

Most Tongan women conceive knowing little of the facts of conception, pregnancy, and birth.[4] As girls they are not told the facts of life, and once they are pregnant their female relatives tend to give them only practical advice, instruction about the various *tapu* (restrictions) to be followed, and warnings that the birth will be painful.[5] There is a great deal of reluctance to discuss seriously anything related to sex: "It is a sacred thing," said one young woman. There is a great deal of sexual joking in everyday discourse, mainly through the use of metaphors and double entendre. This banter may give girls some clues about intercourse but is unlikely to be informative about reproduction. Girls are taught from an early age to be modest and embarrassed or ashamed *(mā)* about their bodies.[6]

Pregnant women are given some information about conception and birth from *māʻuli* (traditional midwives) or the antenatal clinics, but the greater part of women's knowledge is gained through experience. According to the doctors and nurses of the Vaiola antenatal clinic, women are slowly beginning to ask questions about pregnancy and birth, particularly younger women. In most cases, however, women's difficulties in talking openly about their bodies, and the power relations between staff and patients, inhibit such discussion.

The term for being pregnant is *feitama* (literally, preparing a child). When people refer to a woman's pregnant state they more often use the term *foʻi kete* (round stomach). This extends even to speaking of the *kete* (stomach), rather than the fetus, becoming weak or strong, or growing larger. There do not seem to have been any Tongan terms specifically for the embryo or fetus, the phrase *tamasiʻi kei ʻi kete* (little child still in the stomach) being used. *Pēpē*, from the English word baby, is also used to refer to the fetus, sometimes as *pēpēʻi loto*.[7]

The process of becoming a Tongan "person" thus begins in the womb. From the time a woman realizes she is pregnant she refers to the growing embryo as a baby, or child, with its own will and *anga*. Her own behavior and consumption during pregnancy are believed to directly influence the baby's development, both physically and psychically. Thus, her concern for her child is demonstrated even before it is born, in the care she takes in her behavior and in the food, drink, and medicines she consumes. The responsibility is considerable, especially as any physical deformities, mental problems, or behavioral abnormalities of her child are likely to blamed on her behavior during her pregnancy.[8] Miscarriages also may be blamed on the mother's behavior, but in the early months until the quickening, known as the *taimi fa'u* (building or forming time), it also may be said that the baby "was not completed" and was "weak." With an early miscarriage the fetus is buried without ceremony. Late miscarriages and stillbirths are given formal burials; but the infant is not usually named, and little ceremony accompanies the interment.

The term *tapu* is used for many of the restrictions on expectant mothers' behavior and consumption. Originally meaning sacred prohibition, or sacredness, *tapu* is frequently used in a very general sense in Tonga today, having virtually lost its sacred quality in most contexts. Many women no longer hold the beliefs about *tapu* in pregnancy, and even those who do may ignore them at times.[9] When a pregnant woman is observed breaking a *tapu* her female relatives may mention it and warn her of the danger, but little disapproval is expressed, and there is no behavior that is supposed to eradicate the ill effects of her actions. Rather, claims that *tapu* have been broken are used as posthoc explanations for a baby's condition.

The *tapu* are based on sympathetic magic, where a direct relationship is assumed between the mother's action and the development of her child. Thus, if the mother ingests cold food and drink or bathes in very cold water, the fetus is thought to become cold and sick. Eating octopus is said to cause the baby to have spotted skin (*kulokula* or *pala*).[10] There are many such *tapu*: some are widely known, and some are the personal beliefs of particular women; some appear to have existed for many generations, and some are new. The clear message of *tapu* is that the mother must obey social rules: *tapu* amount to injunctions against inappropriate expression of emotion, dishonesty, disrespectful behavior, lack of self-control, and so on. In Tonga, it seems, the sins of the mother are visited upon her children. For a Tongan woman, the "observation of pregnancy *tapus* symbolizes the constraints she herself is prepared to accept as a 'good' mother and 'good' member of the household" (Parsons 1984, 78).

Women also assist the correct development of their babies by ensuring that they are properly postioned in utero, avoiding too much heavy work, avoiding bending and twisting their bodies, sleeping on their backs, and taking daily walks. A number of herbal preparations may also be consumed during pregnancy to ensure the infant's proper growth, to treat any pain or problem in pregnancy, and to ease the delivery.[11] Women are also encouraged to eat well, and members of a woman's family may seek out food she craves as an expression of their care and concern for her and the unborn child.

The active role of the mother in ensuring the proper development of the growing fetus is an important factor in the continued reliance of many women on mā'uli.[12] These midwives see women throughout their pregnancies, sometimes daily, and provide advice, support, soothing massage, and herbal preparations. Most women see the mā'uli as an additional source of care to the antenatal clinics run by the Ministry of Health. Attendance rates are generally high at the clinics, but vary according to the accessibility of the clinic, the woman's age, and her parity, so that young urban dwellers expecting their first child are the most likely to attend. Such women are also less likely to visit a mā'uli. The clinics provide basic check-ups and screen for the major problems Tongan women experience in pregnancy: diabetes, high blood pressure, and anemia. Women in Tonga will increasingly rely solely on the clinics, as the number of mā'uli is rapidly declining, and few young women are interested in attaining their skills. In Holonga, for example, the last two mā'uli of the village died in the late 1980s, leaving no successors.[13]

CHILDBIRTH

The development of an extensive health care system in Tonga has seen the majority of women giving birth (fā'ele) in a hospital or with trained medical staff attending them at home.[14] A number of common themes emerged in women's discussion of their experiences of antenatal care and childbirth in the hospital, centering on a general fear, dislike, and distrust of the hospital staff and procedures. Interactions between medical staff and patients follow the pattern of all status relations in Tonga, with the higher-status person (nurse or doctor) issuing orders (and offering little or no explanation) that the lower-status person (patient) obeys unquestioningly.[15] Those who were more positive emphasized the advantages of resting away from other children and the ready availability of equipment to deal with complicated deliveries. In striking contrast to the general view of hospital births, women were unanimously positive in their evaluations of antenatal care and births with mā'uli, with whom they often develop a close and trusting relationship.

The advent of hospital births has seen the decline of certain practices that marked the neonate's identity. Cutting the umbilical cord was formerly an important moment; after it was tied with a strip of tapa it was cut with a bamboo sliver on an implement that symbolized the child's future gender role. A girl's cord was cut on a tapa beater, a boy's on a spade or hoe handle if it was hoped he would be a farmer, an oar handle if a fisherman. The person cutting the cord would call out a wish that the child would do well in its future work and carry out its duties well (Bott n.d., 18).[16] This practice is still referred to when a child follows in its parent's footsteps. Of a boy following his father as a skilled fisherman, for example, people will comment, "His cord must have been cut on his father's oar."[17] Gender identity was also marked by the way in which a birth was greeted: for a boy the *lali* (slit drum) was sounded and exclamations of joy shouted, as the boy would be "a man of the village and the country," but the birth of a girl, destined to stay mainly inside the house, was greeted quietly (Bott n.d., 18). Although there is a lot of speculation about the sex of the baby while the woman is pregnant, based on various indicators (see Morton n.d., 20), there does not appear to be any consistent preference for either sex in first births.

Another way in which the child's identity was marked soon after birth was in the burial of the afterbirth. Although some parents take the afterbirth home from the hospital to bury, this practice is no longer common. Burying the afterbirth near the child's home seems to have metaphorically established a link between the child and its "place" or land. The Ritchies have pointed out that there is an important linguistic association between "land" and "placenta" throughout Polynesia (1979, 16).[18] The Tongan term for both is *fonua*, and a Tongan linguist has suggested that a complex linguistic relationship exists between *fonua* (land, people, placenta), *fanua* (archaic or poetic term for land), and *fānau* (children), in which childrearing is linguistically equated with caring for, and being loyal to, Tonga itself ('Opeti Taliai, personal communication). Certainly, the fact that *fonua* encompasses placenta, people, and land suggests shared identity.

During its first few months the baby is kept within the house as much as possible. Ideally, the mother also stays in the home, resting and eating well for three months. Very few women stay confined to the house for as long as three months these days, but some older women confirmed that they had done so with their first child.[19] Women view this period of seclusion very positively. "It's a good time," said one woman; after a period of rest and plenty of food, "you are beautiful." "To the Tongan eye, this is the time when women are most beautiful—pale, smooth, and plump" (Spillius 1958, 21). The availability of other women to help with household chores is a critical factor in determining the length of a woman's postpartum rest, with some women resuming work within days of the birth, even the day after, if there is no one to help.

Although the seclusion is clearly a time for the mother and baby to "bond," it is also a period of incorporating the child into its network of kin, thereby marking a crucial aspect of the child's social identity. In the hospital a close female relative (usually of the mother) acts as *tauhi* (helper) to the mother, holding the baby while the mother rests and attending to the needs of both. The baby's father and other close relatives also visit the mother in the hospital, bringing food, keeping her company throughout the day and evening, and taking turns holding the baby. When the mother and child leave the hospital, usually after only one or two days, they continue to be attended by relatives and the child's father. This gathering of the *fāmili* to keep the mother company, help care for the baby, and do the household chores is sometimes referred to as a *pō tama*: literally, a meeting for the child. Symbolically, the *pō tama* welcomes the child into the family.

It is common for women who live overseas to return to Tonga when their adult daughters give birth, usually staying at least until the christening and often much longer. This was the case in the households of Pita and Manu, and Siale and Seini, in 1988. Manu had returned to Tonga for the birth of her daughter Luisa's son, and Seini's mother had returned for 'Ofa's birth. Both grandmothers had originally gone to Australia to help after the birth of other grandchildren, and both stayed in Tonga for well over a year, caring for the children while their daughters worked.

On a more formal level, the birth of a child, particularly the firstborn, is an occasion for an exchange of gifts between the parents' families, the child's *kāinga*.[20] *Koloa* (valuables such as mats and *ngatu*) is seldom exchanged after childbirth today, and food is given directly to the mother. These gifts of food usually consist of boiled fish or chicken with boiled root vegetables, rather than feast food (roast pork and food cooked in the *'umu*). Friends and relatives who *vakai fā'ele* (visit the mother after birth) sometimes take baby clothes or bedding as well as food. Some younger women I spoke to did not know of the more traditional gifts such as the *kie hapo tama* ("baby-catching mat": see Spillius 1958, 20), although these are still occasionally presented (I received one from Siale's mother on the birth of my daughter in 1989).

A more important exchange of gifts occurs at the christening, which marks the end of the ideal three-month seclusion. (Catholic christenings are usually held a week after birth.) Again, the christening is especially important for the firstborn; it involves some exchange of *koloa* between the parents' *kāinga*, and a feast, and a gift of *koloa* to the minister who conducts the service. These exchanges of gifts and food at the child's birth and christening act as formal markers of her or his incorporation within the *fāmili* and *kāinga*, the social networks that will have the greatest influence on the child's socialization.

Another practice that reaffirms a child's embeddedness in a network of kinship is the naming (*fakahingoa*). There is little formality about naming today: one of the parents simply asks a relative, or occasionally a nonkin person of high status, to *fakahingoa*. Often the name chosen is that of a relative, living or dead, and there is a strong preference for the father's family to name children, particularly the father's sister or parents.[21]

Many Tongan names are not gender specific (e.g., Tupou), but European names that have been adapted are used as in the West, such as Paula (Paul) for boys and Mele (Mary) for girls. Other names that are not usually gender specific are those that refer to an incident occurring at the time of birth (e.g., Afa, hurricane) or Tongan versions of European words as in Kalasine (kerosene) or Pasifike (Pacific). Children are seldom given their parents' first names, although this is becoming more popular, especially for boys, following the American usage of "Junior." Children so named, or children named after a living relative, often have *si'i* (little) or *leka* (small) appended to their name, and *lahi* (big, senior) may be appended to the relative's name.

The European missionaries introduced the use of surnames, but they were not formally adopted—such as for census purposes—until the 1950s (Neill 1955, 141). The manner in which surnames are used can be confusing. As elsewhere in the South Pacific, children often use their father's first name as their surname, just as many women adopt their husband's first name as their surname. However, children may also use their paternal grandfather's first name or the name he used as his surname. The surname given on a child's birth certificate may thus be different from the name by which he or she is known in the village or at school.

ATTITUDES TO REPRODUCTION

The high social value of children in Tonga is reflected in attitudes toward reproduction. Attitudes to fertility, reproductive control, illegitimacy, and adoption can reveal some of the subtle differences in this value—whether, for example, children are valued differently according to the circumstances of their birth.

FERTILITY

The birth of the first child often comes within the first year or two of marriage, and if not, considerable pressure to have children may be exerted by the couple's families. Fertility is highly valued and is a component of ideal femininity. An inability to conceive may therefore be the cause of some anxiety for the woman, who is assumed to be the infertile partner. Such women may go to the hospital or medical center for advice, but more often will visit a *mā'uli* for treatment with massage and herbal medicine. Anxiety about fertility is moderated, however, by the relative ease of adoption and fosterage in Tonga, discussed below.

Traditionally, it has been thought that certain female relatives of a woman's partner—particularly his sister or his father's sister (his *meheki-tanga*)—can influence her fertility through their power to curse her (*mana'i*). This belief is losing ground: some women now believe that if they are true Christians such curses cannot affect them; others dismiss beliefs in curses as "the old way." The *mehekitanga* also was, and to some extent still is, believed to have the power to make the woman's delivery difficult. Spillius records that if the labor was long and difficult, the father's sister would be asked to come and help massage the mother, overriding the usual *tapu* on her atten-dance at the birth. She would be asked if the parents had done anything to offend her, and if so, to forgive them (1958:18). The *mehekitanga* of the father and the child figure prominently in the exchanges of gifts after a birth—in effect, a show of gratitude for not interfering in the process of con-ception and birth. As will be seen in a later chapter, the *mehekitanga* contin-ues to be an important and powerful figure in the child's life.

REPRODUCTIVE CONTROL

The fertility rate in Tonga has remained at about 5 since 1976 (Central Plan-ning Department 1987, 272), despite the presence of a national family plan-ning program. However, there has been a slight decline.[22] As shown in table 2, Holongan women over fifty-five had an average of 6.8 children in 1988, whereas women between forty and fifty-four averaged only 3.9. Although some women continue to bear children during these years, the rate would not be expected to rise significantly. Fewer women in Holonga, and Tonga generally, are now having the eight or more children that were common in previous generations. The patterns shown in table 2 are consistent with those for Tonga as a whole, according to figures from the 1986 census (Statis-tics Department 1993b, 14–16).

The Ministry of Health's national family planning program offers free contraception through Mother and Child Health clinics and promotes fam-ily planning through public education. Family planning is also promoted through aid-funded organizations, private clinics, the Roman Catholic fam-ily planning center, and a Seventh Day Adventist mobile clinic. It is even advocated through the school curriculum, with lessons on the advantages of small families, complete with songs to learn:

> *Always remember the family:*
> *Father, mother, and little children*

Will be better if there are few—
Enough food, happiness, and ability to go to school;
But many, and they will go short of things—
Hungry, and often sick, and away from school.
If you do not take the responsibility to be moderate
It is a problem for the country.
(Environmental Science Social Studies Lesson Plans, Grade One,
     1985, 3, my translation)

As in this song, the association between fewer children and a higher living standard is a central theme of the family planning programs. Indeed, increasing economic pressure is making this a realistic message for many couples. One of the conflicts couples face in modern Tonga is between the "acquisition of Western-style wealth and provision for many children" (James 1983, 241). The movement of many women into the paid workforce also may have affected average family size.[23] Migrations patterns are also likely to have some effect when couples are separated for often lengthy periods during the woman's childbearing years.

Despite the vigorous promotion of family planning, few practice it, and there are significant factors working against its acceptance (see McMurray and Lucas 1990, 38–39; South Pacific Alliance for Family Health 1991, 10). Both the Roman Catholic and Mormon churches forbid the use of contraceptives, although the former does have a family planning center that teaches natural birth control. Several people working in family planning programs reported a widespread rejection of contraception by males, with some husbands even insisting that their wives have contraceptive devices such as IUDs removed. Women's modesty about such matters, combined with problems involving lack of confidentiality, also contribute to poor acceptance rates. Reluctance to limit family size is also clearly related to the high social value of children, particularly their role as providers for their family.

The high social value of children and the relative ease with which children can be fostered (see below) contribute to the strong disapproval of abortion often encountered in Tonga. Other important factors are Christian ideology and legal sanctions. Abortions are illegal, although cases involving abortion rarely reach the courts and doctors will now perform abortions if the mother's health is endangered. An obstetrician at Vaiola Hospital on Tongatapu told me that women do request abortions, usually because they are unmarried or face economic hardship, but that they cannot be helped under existing laws (Dr. S. Lātū, personal communication).[24]

Table 2: Number of Living Children of Holongan Women, 1988

NUMBER OF CHILDREN				AGE OF WOMEN						TOTAL WOMEN
	15–19	20–24	25–29	30–34	35–39	40–44	45–49	50–54	55+	
0	30	19	8	2	1				1	61
1		2	5	3			1	1	1	13
2			1	1		1	1	2		6
3		2	4	1	4	1	1		2	15
4			2	2	4		1	1	4	14
5				3	2	2			3	10
6					1		2	1	2	6
7							1		6	7
8									4	4
9									4	4
10									4	4
11									1	1
12									2	2
13									1	1
TOTAL WOMEN										148
TOTAL CHILDREN	8	25	31	46	13	29	13		252	417

ILLEGITIMACY

Contraception is mainly used by married women, to control the number of children they bear. Because unmarried women are ideally chaste it is shameful for them to use contraceptives, but combined with the sexual double standard in which young men are implicitly encouraged to be sexually active, illegitimate births are not uncommon.[25] Disapproval is directed most strongly at the mother, and for unmarried men it is still, as Spillius observed in the 1950s, "rather a feather in a man's cap to have had several children by different women" (1958, 13).

It is unclear whether there was a concept of illegitimacy in precontact Tonga. The term commonly used for "illegitimate" today is fā'ele tu'utāmaki (literally, to give birth in adversity or danger), but Churchward gives tama tu'utāmaki (literally, disastrous or dangerous child); tama angahala ("wrong way child") is the abusive term (1959, 451–452). These terms, which were possibly used in earlier times, suggest that children born of "wrong" unions signal trouble between or within families.

The European missionaries were concerned with illegitimacy as an indication of improper sexual activity, and their influence is reflected in the early legal codes, which required fathers to pay maintenance for illegitimate children.[26] Today, the Maintenance of Illegitimate Children Act specifies that the father can be ordered to pay maintenance until the child is sixteen (*Law of Tonga* 1967, Cap. 19, section 2). This act also allows for the father's tax allotment to be given to the mother (or other person applying on her behalf) to support the child. Despite these legal measures most fathers do not pay maintenance, or do so informally in occasional gifts of cash or goods. I often saw fathers giving the children themselves small gifts of money or candy. In any case, illegitimate children cannot inherit their father's land lease or in the case of *hou'eiki*, his chiefly title and estate.

The missionaries' disapproval of improper sexual activity has influenced Tongans' attitudes toward women who bear illegitimate children. Very strong disapproval is expressed when a married woman bears a child to another man, whereas a couple in a de facto relationship who have a child will create less concern.[27] A single woman who falls pregnant is likely to be beaten by her parents, who will attempt to push the father, if unmarried, to marry her. Having an illegitimate child can reduce a woman's marriage prospects, and if she remains unmarried she may, like many others in her situation, leave the child with her parents or other relatives and move away, often overseas. Later, when she is married and settled, she may take the child back. Whether or not she chooses to stay, the child will invariably be accepted into the family, as are all illegitimate children.

Some illegitimate births are viewed positively. A common theme in Tongan mythology is of children being born to chiefly women after brief unions with male gods.[28] The mothers in these myths were of lower status than their godly mates, a pattern replicated in the practice of commoner women bearing children to chiefly men (Bain 1967, 82; Bott n.d., 2,11). A child born of a commoner girl and chiefly male established or strengthened the ties between the chief and her *kāinga* and, in later times, her village (Collocott 1923b, 226; Gifford 1971b, 114). Even today, "women are still willing to become pregnant to nobles and powerful men in Tongan society for reasons of personal advancement, since their offspring are recognized with or without the benefit of wedlock" (James 1983, 240).

Some women I spoke to mentioned the advantages of illegitimacy. One pointed out that if a woman does not marry it is right (*totonu*) for her to have children to help her. "Some think it is bad, but I think it is good," another woman said. "Giving birth to an illegitimate child is a worthwhile, beneficial birth (*fā'ele 'aonga*)." She explained that legitimate children take their father's name, whereas illegitimate children "stay with you" (keep the mother's name).

Illegitimate children do not take their father's surname, which does not even appear on the birth certificate (although legally it *can* be recorded on the certificate).[29] However, it is considered important for the child to know who the father is. This enables the child to know her or his place within the complexities of rights and obligations involved in Tongan kinship. Members of the father's family often want to remain in contact with the child, even when the father is absent or uninvolved with the child. Malia, from Holonga, had two brothers with three children each, all born to different women. Malia said wryly (in English), "So I'm dealing with six women. . . . I don't worry about the mothers, I'm related to the kids, not the mothers." As the children's *mehekitanga* she tried to see the children as often as she could, and she had adopted two of them at their mothers' request. Two of the other mothers had taken the father to court to fight out who had more *pule* (authority) over the father in terms of demanding child support.

ADOPTION AND FOSTERAGE

Despite the existence of laws covering adoption, of both illegitimate and legitimate children, most adoption occurs informally.[30] *Pusiaki*, usually glossed as fosterage, is the most common term used nowadays for both temporary and permanent movements of children between households. Temporary fosterage is sometimes referred to as *ngaohi* or *ngaahi*, terms that also mean bringing up one's own children. When these terms are used the fostered child is said to still "belong" to the natural mother, as when a woman temporarily cares for her grandchildren while their mother is working overseas. *Tauhi* (to care for) includes the care of both natural and adopted children.

The motivations of both the relinquishing parents and the child's new caregiver may be understood in terms of the high value of children, in emotional and pragmatic terms. People may take on the care of others' children because they are childless, or have only boys or only girls, or because their own children are growing older. As well as desiring companionship and household help, they may be especially fond of a particular child. A child also may be relinquished for many reasons. Illegitimacy can be a motive, as can the absence of the mother because of illness, divorce, migration, or death. Such events may precipitate the fostering of children unless their father can either move with his children to another household (often that of his parents) or have female relatives join his own household to care for the children. Migration of the mother or of both parents, one of the primary motives for fosterage, is usually seen as temporary (see Gailey 1992; James 1991a). Sometimes parents living overseas send children to relatives in Tonga, to grow up "in the Tongan way." Economic conditions may also be considered, as when the household is overcrowded or when parents want their children to have educational and economic advantages they cannot provide.

Although the children's best interests may be of some concern in relinquishment, it is in fact the advantages to the adults involved that are stressed in discourse about adoption and fosterage. The care and help the child can provide the adoptive caregiver and the 'ofa of the adults involved for one another are emphasized (see James 1983, 238; Kavaliku 1977, 63). Morton has suggested that Tongan adoptions increase the adoptees' "options for group affiliation and access to resources" (1976, 77), but these advantages tend to be perceived as accruing to the adoptees' natural and adoptive families rather than to the individual child.

For Polynesia more generally, several theories have been put forward about the psychological "message" of adoption (see Brady 1976; Howard and Kirkpatrick 1989, 74–77). These theories variously interpret adoption as encouraging nurturant and dependent behavior (Howard et al. 1970), encouraging interdependence by emphasizing the contingent and replaceable nature of social relationships (Levy 1970), and establishing an identification with a wide group of kin (Borofsky 1987, 153). Each of these theories has some validity, yet in terms of Tongan adoption and fosterage, the great variations in the motives and circumstances surrounding them make me reluctant to speculate about any consistent "message" in these terms. The only clearly generalized message Tongan children receive when they become pusiaki is that it is yet another instance in which their needs and wants are subordinated to those of higher status; adoption is another feature of children's low social status even as it reflects their high social value. In many cases adoption and fosterage also reflect the low status of the parents in relation to certain other kin, particularly the father's mehekitanga.

James has discussed the practice of sending children from migrant communities back to Tonga: "As if they themselves are remittances, children are a bond of love and living confirmations of kinship" (1991a, 16). She also expresses some concern about the psychological effect of such practices, where children are sometimes moved between different households and countries:

> Some relationships appeared to be so highly subject to change and so peripatetic that I came to wonder where the loyalties of these young will ultimately lie, and whether the children will feel called upon to support either set of parents. Thus, while children are sent to ensure social security for themselves, through confirming kinship bonds and also possibly to become effective "second-generation remitters" because of these bonds, I doubt in many

cases that the Tongan notion of 'ofa ("love, generosity") will be successfully instilled into the younger generation born of migrant parents. Instead, they are likely to get more clearly the message of economic individualism, which seemingly dominates the actions of their parents and other relatives, which may mean that they will cut themselves off from wider kinship ties. (James 1991a, 17)

The Tongan pediatrician Dr. Siaosi 'Aho calls babies sent from overseas "brown paper parcel babies" and also expresses concern about the detrimental effect of this practice (Matangi Tonga 1992c, 14).

An increasing problem arising when children are left behind while parents migrate or are sent back to Tonga from overseas is the strain the care of these children places on family members remaining in Tonga. As James points out in relation to this practice, "The ideology of Tongan kinship projects the view that families can cope, and that relatives are happy to take in children. The growing numbers of chidren to be cared for within a rapidly growing population that has a high percentage under the age of 15 years, however, is straining the resources of adults and especially the elderly" (James 1991a, 18).

Not all pusiaki relationships are initiated by the relinquishing parents. Many are initiated by a family member requesting the child, sometimes when the mother is still pregnant. The natural parents may refuse the request, but may be under strong pressure to consent. When a husband wishes to accede to his sister's desire to adopt his child, his wife may not be able to refuse without causing considerable bad feeling between herself and her affines. Even the woman's relatives may place her under pressure to relinquish a child. Gordon tells of a Mormon woman whose father's sister, living overseas, requested her first child. The young woman was distressed about relinquishing her infant but felt unable to refuse, even though Mormon doctrine opposed this practice (1990, 214). Increasingly, however, decisions about matters such as adoption are made jointly by couples. Siale's sister, Tina, was asked by her unmarried sister-in-law for her baby daughter. She and her husband refused, and Tina explained to me, "God may only give us this one child, and if we let someone adopt her who would look after us when we are old?"

Children of all ages can be pusiaki. Babies are not usually taken until they are weaned, between four months and one year, but one adoptive mother I knew acted as midwife at the child's birth and took him home immediately afterward. In many cases the biological parents live nearby and continue to see the child daily. Two of 'Alisi's pusiaki children were the children of her brother's son, who lived next door to her with his wife and other children.

The two households interacted closely, and although Alisi had been their primary caregiver since they were only a few months old, the children were very close to their natural parents. Some children eventually return to their natural parents, and some even go on to live with other adoptive parents.[31] These moves can be distressing and confusing for the children, especially when they involve changing not only household but also village, island, or even country. A child my husband and I fostered for several months, Fonua, had been left as a baby with his maternal grandmother when his unmarried mother migrated to New Zealand. Like many single mothers migrating from Tonga, she left her child behind intending to send for him when she could support him. Fonua's grandmother died when he was twelve; he was sent to Australia, where he lived first with my husband's sister and then with us until his mother moved to Australia and sent for him to live with her, in another city. Fonua expressed some reluctance to go to his mother, as he had formed a strong attachment to us, especially our son, who had become like a little brother to him.

In Holonga in 1988, 48 of the 258 children under sixteen (18.6 percent) were *pusiaki*. Table 3 shows the relationship between each child and the care-giver most directly responsible for that child. The term "caregiver" is used in preference to "parent" because *pusiaki* children may be grandchildren, nieces, nephews, cousins, and so on, and this relationship is acknowledged. Adoptive caregivers take on parenting roles but in many cases are not seen as surrogate mothers or fathers. As with illegitimate children, the circum-stances of the child's birth are discussed openly within the child's hearing.

Table 3: Adopted Children in Holonga, 1988

RELATIONSHIP TO ADOPTIVE CAREGIVER	NUMBER OF CHILDREN
Daughter's son	9
Daughter's daughter	8
Son's daughter	6
Son's son	5
Woman's brother's son	4
Woman's sister's daughter	4
Woman's brother's son's daughter	3
Woman's brother's daughter	3
Woman' sister's son	3
Woman's brother's son's son	1
Woman's brother's daughter's daughter	1
Man's sister's son	1
TOTAL	48

As table 3 shows, in all but one case these children are grandchildren or relatives of the female caregiver, with a tendency for the relationship to be through her brother.[32] Of the forty-eight children, ten were illegitimate and twenty-nine were being cared for while their parents were overseas (eight were in both categories). Twelve households had one *pusiaki* child, four had two, five had three, two had four, and one had five. Those with four and five children were couples caring for grandchildren whose parents were overseas. One aspect of *pusiaki* relationships that the table does not show is that siblings are not always kept together when moved to other households; in fact, they may be sent to different villages or even different countries.

THE CARE OF INFANTS

The great variation in household composition in Tonga means that there is also a good deal of variation in the number of people involved in caring for a child and in their relationship to the child. Children's closest attachments are usually to their parents, even where other members of the household play important caregiving roles. The period of seclusion for mother and baby after the birth is obviously important for the "bonding" between them; but even when little or no seclusion occurs, several factors contribute to the primacy of the mother's role. Breast-feeding (*fakahuhu*) is very important, and even when women work outside the home it is common for them to continue to breast-feed, with other caregivers giving supplementary feeds during the day. Breast-feeding and weaning are discussed in more detail below.

During their first two years, and especially the first few months, infants are given an enormous amount of care and attention. They are lavished with affection, and every part of their development is observed closely and discussed with a mixture of pride and amusement. In many households there are often a number of people at home to interact with babies, so that, as Spillius commented, "they lead an intensely social life" (1958, 51). But in an increasing number of households babies spend long hours during the day with only one or two people caring for them, and it is only at certain times, such as late afternoons, weekends, and school holidays, that these households are busier.

Babies are in physical contact with people much of the time, especially before they can walk, as older people cuddle and hold them or little children lug them awkwardly around, ignoring their loud protests. People holding babies often position them to have eye contact, talking to them and playing games. At other times they face the infants outward so they can watch the activities in the household or play with the older children who gather around to entertain them.

During the first few months babies are usually held lying prone, in some-one's arms or laid across the lap of a person seated cross-legged on the floor.[33] The person holding the baby also may position the child at a distance from her or his body, with one hand supporting the baby's neck and back and the other under the baby's buttocks and legs. In all these positions the baby is *en face*, but the latter position is particularly used when the holder wants to attract the baby's attention. Throughout these early months people smile, laugh, sing, or otherwise vocalize at the baby to elicit a response in the form of a smile or even just eye contact. To further encourage a response the person makes questioning sounds or the facial gesture associated with en-couragement: eyebrows lifted as the chin is dipped. People clearly get a great deal of pleasure and amusement from watching babies who, as they become more responsive and active, continue to hold center stage within the house-hold. Both males and females, of any age or status, give attention to babies, perhaps because babies are in a sense outside the status system, so that play-ing with them and showing affection carry no element of shame or danger of compromising status (see Keeler 1983, 164 for a similar argument for Java-nese men and babies).

When babies are occasionally put down to sleep the *pae* is still sometimes used: layers of soft mats surrounded by a tapa folded to form a wall to keep out drafts and covered by a sheet or mosquito net. At night, babies sleep beside their mothers. In their early months infants are dressed and wrapped up very warmly, often with several layers of clothes, sheets, and blankets. If the baby is taken outside, the blankets are held to shield its face, and extra layers are added. When the baby is asleep the inner layers are wrapped more tightly. It seems likely that early missionaries influenced the practice of wrapping babies, as swaddling was widely practiced in England during the nineteenth century. Before European influence, babies were left naked, covered in sheets of tapa (Bott n.d., 20). There may also be some connection between wrapping the baby and the decline in the practice of seclusion in the early months. Spillius speculated that, like seclusion, wrapping is "an exaggerated form of protecting the baby," with a strong emotional basis (1958, 23). As both Spillius (22–23) and Morton (1976, 70) have pointed out, wrapping the baby signifies to others the mother's competence and concern.[34]

The mothers with whom I spoke claimed that wrapping acted as a protec-tion against colds and coughs, and this belief seemed to be an extension of their fear of the fetus becoming cold in the womb. Similarly, great care is taken to keep babies warm when bathing them. In 1980 I caused great con-sternation when I took my son to a school fair when he was only a few weeks old because he was dressed only in a diaper and cotton shirt and carried upright in a baby harness strapped to my body. In recent years there has been a noticeable trend among younger mothers toward dressing and wrapping babies less warmly. Another rather surprising trend is toward the use of imported (and very expensive) disposable diapers. Again, the influence appears to be current "Western" practices: there is a widespread assumption that all *pālangi* mothers use these diapers. Then, too, because many women still have to wash cloth diapers by hand, the expense of the disposable version may be seen as offset by the labor they save. Shoes for babies are also becoming popular and are often sent as gifts by overseas relatives, as are toys and candy. Clothes are also sent from overseas, including the frilly dresses, tights, tiny suits, and other fancy clothes children wear to church and on special occasions.

The active role of the mother in ensuring her baby's proper development, which began during pregnancy, continues as her infant grows. *Tofo* (or *tofotofo*) is the massage of babies to ensure their limbs and heads are shaped properly and "to make the blood flow properly." It includes massage of the legs, said to prevent knock-knee and to make the legs shapely, and massage of the head to prevent flattening (*'ulu toki*: "axe-shaped head"). The massaging is done with Tongan oil and provides an important source of physical contact for babies, soothing them to sleep and continuing as they sleep.[35] Babies are also turned from side to side occasionally while they sleep to prevent head flattening and to keep the legs and back straight.

The fontanelle is a source of concern because it is believed that the skull bones are not growing together properly. Women explained that babies' heads are "not fully formed inside" and "do not close (*mapuni*)," and the condition is called *mavaeua* ("split in two"). Parsons states that *mahaki mavaeua*, the sickness said to result from an untreated fontanelle, was believed to cause the baby to be restless or sleepy and was said to be fatal if left untreated (1985, 97). Treatment, also called *mavaeua*, is given to ensure the bones knit together as the baby grows. *Mavaeua* is usually done immediately after birth or within the first few months, by a *faito'o* (healer) or *mā'uli*. One method used is to warm the baby's head by holding it or wrapping it in several layers of cloth. Another method, used on Seini's children, is to apply a herbal mixture or Tongan oil to the baby's hands, feet, and head, sometimes placing a little in the child's mouth. *Mavaeua* is still carried out for most babies, although some women said that they did not really believe in it or even know why it was supposed to be important.

Most babies are breast-fed for eight to twelve months, and there are public education programs encouraging women to continue breast-feeding well into the second year.[36] Medical staff now urge women to begin breast-feeding immediately after giving birth, but formerly it was common practice to feed the baby only coconut cream (namoa) for several days. Namoa is prepared by chewing roasted coconut and placing it in tapa or cotton cloth for the baby to suck on or squeezing it into the baby's mouth. Because of its high fat content, this substance acts as a laxative and is used to clear the baby of meconium, which is seen as "bad" or "waste." The namoa thus cleanses the baby internally and nourishes it until the breast milk, described as "thick (fatu) and good," replaces the colostrum. Colostrum is also regarded as "bad," and because of its yellowish color is sometimes called pela (pus). Giving namoa is still common for babies born at home, sometimes for up to three days, although some mothers give boiled or sweetened water instead.[37] Other substances given in these first days can include premasticated banana or root vegetable and infusions of medicinal plants.

Warmth is believed to hasten and increase the supply of breast milk, so the mother drinks warm coconut milk (veifua) and keeps her breasts warmly covered unless feeding the baby.[38] Women who are unable to breast-feed now use bottles, but in the past wet nurses were used, most often from within the mother's family (Bott n.d., 17; Spillius 1958, 21). Some mothers also introduce bottle feeding or solids at an early age for convenience, particularly when they work outside the home. Bottle feeds are mainly used as a supplement: when Seini returned to work only a month after 'Ofa's birth her mother gave the infant bottles during the day, but Seini continued to breast-feed at night and on weekends for more than a year. Formula, diluted condensed or evaporated milk, and even chocolate-malt powder, cocoa, and coffee (often mixed only with water and sugar) are given in bottles.

Breast-feeding is generally approved in Tonga. Women usually are not embarrassed to feed their babies publicly, although they are discreet about it. Breast-feeding is treated calmly; a mother will offer the breast on demand, as well as to soothe or distract the baby, but will also interrupt a feeding if she needs to attend to something else. Food tapu similar to those followed in pregnancy are, to greatly varying extents, followed by lactating women. The mother's diet, rather than the overwrapping of the baby in semitropical weather, is most often blamed for a baby's heat rashes and other skin problems.

The age at which babies are first fed solid foods also varies a good deal, with six months the most common time. The first foods are usually root crops, especially sweet potato and yam, but breadfruit, banana, and other fruits are also frequently given (see Maclean and Badcock 1987, 34). These foods may be chewed first by the mother—a practice known as mama—and contrary to Spillius (1958, 29) I found this still common even in Nuku'alofa. Another favorite food for babies is hardtack biscuits or white bread, softened in warm water, sweetened with condensed milk or sugar, and made into a pulp.

Weaning may be gradual but in some circumstances is very abrupt, as when the mother falls pregnant again, becomes ill, or decides that she is not producing enough milk. If the mother is too thin her milk is said to be "thin and weak," and this may also precipitate weaning (Spillius 1958, 28). Illness is the most common cause of sudden weaning, as it is believed that illnesses are transmitted through breast milk. When Seini was suffering from boils she weaned 'Ofa overnight after discovering that the baby was also developing boils. Seini explained that if she continued feeding, her daughter would not get well. When weaning causes the baby distress, other household members provide distraction and soothing and offer other forms of nourishment; sometimes the baby is taken to another household for several days, away from the mother's breast.

Nutrition surveys over the past thirty years have consistently reported a low incidence of infant malnutrition and undernutrition. The 1986 survey found that "Tongan infants appear to be very healthy and well nourished clinically" (Maclean and Badcock 1987, 47). Nevertheless, there are always rumors in the villages about babies who have died or become seriously ill because they were fed only on chocolate-malt powder and water or some other inadequate diet, such tales serving as constant reminders of the need to protect babies and, as with the wrapping of newborns, to be *seen* to be protecting them.

Mothers are often helped in the day-to-day care of babies by their own mothers, unmarried sisters and female cousins, and other female relatives, as well as by older children, but in nuclear family households the latter are their only helpers. Women without spouses, temporarily or permanently, usually live with relatives who can assist with childcare. If they live alone with young children—as did five women in Holonga in 1988—their situation is regarded as *faka'ofa* (pitiable), and their relatives will offer some material, financial, and emotional support. However, mothers who have no older children and who are living away from their own relatives may have no help because they are often unwilling to ask their affinal relations for assistance.

The father's family, being of higher status than the children and their mother, tends to be proprietary toward his children, a situation that can be daunting for a young mother, as I can attest from my own experience! Fleming and Tuku'afu found "there was a marked reluctance to elicit the support of any in-laws, where a woman has less say than with her own relatives, as she would relinquish some of her control over the children to her husband's family" (1986, 36). The extent to which the mother feels in charge of her baby varies with her own position, so that a young woman with her first child, living with her affines, may feel that much of the responsibility for the baby has been taken from her, whereas an older mother in her own home will assume full responsibility for her infant.

Fathers have much less to do with babies than mothers, as they are often away from home working, drinking kava, and so on. When at home, fathers will hold and play with their babies, increasingly so as the babies become more active and vocal. Although fathers may see little of their babies, they are kept well informed of their development as this is a primary topic of conversation within the household.

With the increasing tendency toward nuclear families, the "multiple parenting" that the Ritchies (1989) distinguish as a major feature of Polynesian socialization is rapidly declining in importance in Tonga. The term is misleading in the Tongan case anyway, given the centrality awarded to the parents' role in both the ideology and practices of child socialization. The child's parents, real or adopted, are clearly perceived as having the primary caregiving role, even when others such as grandparents are the major caregivers during the day when both parents are working. This is not to say that other kin do not have important roles in nurturing, teaching, and disciplining children, but in Tonga today, perhaps as a result of missionary emphasis on the centrality of the nuclear family unit, there is a clear distinction between *parenting* and the role of other kin.

When there are older children in the household they are expected to do the more active work involved in caring for babies and toddlers—fetching things like diapers and bottles, carrying the youngsters around, and running to rescue them from mischief or danger. They quickly learn to keep a close eye on their young charges because they are likely to be blamed if the younger children are hurt, even if there are adults present. What Marcus has called "a supervisory hierarchy among siblings" (1978, 258n9) develops, with the older children delegating responsibility to younger ones and punishing them for inadequate care of babies and toddlers. These child hierarchies, which can include siblings, other children living in the household, and even the children of close neighbors, become much more important once the child is about two years old, as will be seen in the following chapters.

Older children can only help out of school hours, however, and during the day older people such as grandparents are often the major caregivers. This can be onerous for them, particularly when the children are too young to be left to their own devices or to be called upon to do small chores and errands. In our Holonga household Moana cared for 'Ofa during weekdays while the older children were at school and their parents were working. As well as caring for 'Ofa she did various household chores, and for several months she also spent six to eight hours a day beating bark for tapa. Moana was often extremely tired and experienced dizzy spells, and soon after 'Ofa turned one, Moana was admitted to the hospital suffering from exhaustion after collapsing at home.

Older caregivers often restrict children's mobility in order to get on with household work or craft. The child may be kept within one room with the caregiver, with the doorways blocked, or may spend long hours in a stroller or pram (*saliote*: "chariot"). This restriction is also due to the relative immobility associated with higher status: it would be inappropriate for older caregivers to be running around after an active toddler. Playthings are also used to keep babies quiet, and although manufactured toys are becoming more popular, for the most part babies play with whatever is lying around on the floor: sticks, matchboxes, scraps of paper, playing cards, and other odds and ends.

DIFFERENTIAL TREATMENT OF CHILDREN

The ideology of children's intrinsic social value, of their importance in fulfilling one's life, and of the care and concern family members feel for children is clearly reflected in the attention and affection they receive in their first year. Yet in the everyday practices of childcare subtle differences in their treatment become apparent. Obviously, the differential treatment of children is highly dependent upon the personalities of the children and their caregivers and the particular dynamics of their interactions. At a more general level, however, certain patterns can be detected. Adoption and illegitimacy are not in themselves criteria for differential treatment, but the specific circumstances of a child's adoption or illegitimate birth do appear to be influential. A child who is born in circumstances considered shameful is much more likely to be treated harshly, as is an older child who is moved into a relative's household primarily as a household laborer. On the other hand, some adopted children become *pele* (favorites) because their adoptive caregivers have developed a special fondness for them—perhaps because the child is one caregiver's namesake. The children of father's sisters are more likely to become *pele* when adopted than are the children of mother's brothers because the former are of higher status than the caregivers.

In many households one child becomes *pele* and is treated noticeably more favorably than the other children. Such a child may be the oldest, youngest, only girl or boy, or perhaps the most attractive or appealing or a child named after an especially important or beloved relative. Either sex can be *pele*, but girls seem to be chosen more often. This is consistent with the general notion that daughters, who are of higher status, are treated more favorably than sons. *Pele* are typically given less work than their siblings, are punished less often, and are indulged with special food, clothes, and other privileges. Siblings are often ambivalent toward this favored child. One girl said that her only brother was rarely punished or asked to do difficult chores, and she admitted that when no adults were present she and her sisters treated him cruelly—for which they were punished when he reported their actions. A middle-aged woman spoke resentfully of her eldest sister, who she claimed did no work when they were children and "was like a princess."

One of the clearest examples of the differential treatment of children that I encountered was in the household of Alisi, Seini's elderly great-aunt. Two of Alisi's *pusiaki* children were little girls close in age; Sela was five years old and Finau four when I lived in their household for two months in 1986. Sela was the illegitimate child of Alisi's brother's son. Her birth was the cause of great shame to the family because her mother was a married woman whose husband was working overseas. The other child, Finau, was the daughter of the same brother's older son. Her parents and two of her siblings lived next door to Alisi, who had adopted Finau and her older brother as babies because she was very attached to them and wanted their company. The treatment Sela and Finau received, from Alisi and every other member of their families with whom they had contact, was markedly different in virtually every respect. Sela was dressed in old, ragged clothes, made to do numerous household chores, punished frequently and severely, and often sworn at and derided as "ugly." She was one of the few little girls I encountered whose hair was kept very short instead of being allowed to grow long and worn in braids. Finau wore pretty dresses, did fewer chores, and was treated more kindly, with frequent words of praise. She had many more positive interactions, including displays of affection, than Sela. In Alisi's household, Finau was the *pele*, and she was also her natural parents' *pele* because she was their youngest child. They often gave her small gifts of money or goods from their small store in Holonga. Sela was not openly acknowledged by her natural parents and seemed to suffer continually for the shame of her birth.

In our Holonga household Tomasi and Elenoa were treated differently in ways that reinforced their gender identities. As a female, Elenoa was expected to be better behaved, more dignified, and more responsible than Tomasi. She was given more chores to do in the home, particularly minding her baby sister, 'Ofa. Tomasi was not yet old enough to be of much help in the outdoor, "male" tasks, and so had more freedom to play. As a boy he also had more freedom to wander from home, while Elenoa stayed close to home most of the time. These kinds of differential treatment reflected the children's gendered social value and roles, rather than any *pele* status. In our household there was no *pele*, although because she was a baby 'Ofa was given far more attention and affection than the older children.

THE FIRST BIRTHDAY

The end of a child's first year is marked by a birthday celebration (*fai 'aho*) more elaborate than the celebration of the christening and particularly important if the child is firstborn. There does not appear to have been any pre-Christian equivalent of this celebration, but it has become very much a Tongan celebration, with feasting and an exchange of food and *koloa* between the parents' *kāinga*. Spillius noted that there was "a strong element of thanksgiving in the ceremony" in the 1950s (1958, 61) and this is so even today, despite the significant decline in infant mortality. It is also another important marker of the child's inclusion within its *kāinga* and thus of its social identity. Although a few families now celebrate their children's birthdays every year, in most cases the first birthday is one of the very few occasions in a child's life in which he or she is the focus of all the excitement and celebration.

The birthday celebrations are held at the parents' home or sometimes the father's parents' home. While I was living with Siale and Seini they celebrated 'Ofa's first birthday. Preparations began many weeks before the event, as *koloa* was produced for exchange, root crops planted, and pigs fattened for the feast. Several days before the birthday, preparations began in earnest: the house was thoroughly cleaned, curtains and cushion covers replaced, and walls painted. The day before, the root crops were harvested, the pigs were slaughtered, and other food was purchased in town. Various neighbors and relatives came to bring serving plates and dishes and to help prepare the food throughout the night. The next morning the guests began to arrive, and the food and *koloa* they brought were recorded on a notepad so that redistributions could be calculated later; Seini and Siale kept very little. 'Ofa was dressed up in clothes sent by relatives overseas—tights, shiny shoes, and a frilly dress—and taken to church. Afterward the minister came to the feast, sitting 'Ofa on his lap while he said grace and the gathering sang hymns. 'Ofa was then held on the lap of Seini's "sister" (her MBD), who was called the *fa'ēhuki* or, as Seini said, the "cushion" (literally, "the mother who holds in the lap"). So many guests arrived that they had to eat in two shifts, while the children were all seated together on the back porch and given candy and balloons after their meal.

'Ofa's parents did not join in the feasting. Seini stayed outside with the children, and Siale, still in his work overalls, sat in the lean-to kitchen next door with some of the men who had been up all night with him spit-roasting pigs and cooking food in the 'umu. The parents' peripheral role symbolized the importance of the event as an incorporation of 'Ofa into the wider network of kin, as did the replacement of Seini by 'Ofa's classificatory "mother" at the feast. By behaving in a manner appropriate to low-status persons, they also demonstrated their respect for their guests, many of whom were 'Ofa's paternal kin.

The first-birthday celebrations for Luisa's son, Paula, were even more elaborate because he was a firstborn son. The event took place at his father's parents' home and incorporated some "Western" elements. An exchange of *koloa* took place, but unlike 'Ofa, Paula also received gifts of toys, clothes, and sweets and had a huge birthday cake made for him at the town bakery.

Birthdays are sometimes acknowledged by messages of good wishes (*pōpo-aki talomonū*) in the weekly newspaper. They are accompanied by a photograph of the child and often contain greetings from relatives living overseas. One example reads,

> Hoping that you have a happy day on your first birthday, and we sincerely wish that your days will be happy in the future. Being of beautiful appearance is not a trustworthy thing, and being beautiful and well-proportioned is a rare thing, but a boy who respects and obeys Jehovah deserves thankfulness. We have no important gift for you, but we say together Psalm 23. It is a compass for your road to the future and for your journey. Our great love to your dear little face, from [his parents, seven *mehekitanga*, and fourteen "grandparents"]. (*Tonga Chronicle* 1988, my translation)

The following chapters will show that children's "journeys" become increasingly difficult and harsh after the first birthday, as they learn the central importance of respect and obedience, not just for "Jehovah" but for every person of higher status than themselves.

CHAPTER 4

BECOMING *POTO*: WHAT TO LEARN

The process of child socialization is closely tied to cultural ideas about the "nature" of children and the way this must be accommodated, transformed, or replaced in order for them to be regarded as fully adult persons. This chapter begins, therefore, with a discussion of Tongan perceptions of the nature of children, and more generally of personhood. Two key components of personhood—*anga* (nature, behavior) and *loto* (heart, mind)—are introduced and shown to be the main targets of efforts to influence children's development. The overarching aim of socialization, for children to become *poto*, is achieved by the management and molding of children's *anga* and *loto*. Certain aspects of the knowledge that Tongan children need to acquire in this process are then examined: the cultural values of love and concern (*'ofa*), respect (*faka'apa'apa*), and obedience (*talangofua*), as cultural models of proper dispositions and behavior for low-status persons. An apparently contradictory value, that of *tau'atāina* (freedom, independence), is shown to be an aspect of both conformity with and resistance to the hierarchical ordering of social life. Finally, this chapter explores gender difference as an element of this hierarchical ordering and as integral to self and personhood.

CHILDREN AS PERSONS

Once children are walking confidently and beginning to talk, they are referred to as *tamaiki* (children) rather than *pēpē*. *Tamaiki* is properly the dual and plural form of *tamasi'i*, a "child or young person, [especially] boy or youth" (Churchward 1959, 452). However, in common usage *tamasi'i* is used for boys and *ta'ahine* for girls.[1] Ungendered plural terms for children are *kauleka* (literally, short people or dwarfs) and *fānau*. Males aged from about fourteen to their early twenties (unless married) are called *talavou*, a term that can be used for both sexes to mean good-looking. Girls of the same age are *finemui*.[2] Although adolescents can be referred to by these terms, they are still often called *tamaiki* or *tamaiki ako* (school children). As a group youths may be referred to as *to'u tupu*, the "rising generation, young people growing up at the same time" (Churchward 1959, 503). The whole span of childhood and adolescence is regarded as a time for the molding of "natural" qualities and the acquisition of other culturally valued qualities.

Tongan babies are not regarded as "fully formed social beings" (Bernstein 1983, 56) because they have not yet begun to learn the complexities of *anga fakatonga*. However, they are certainly regarded as sociable, willful persons and are treated as such from birth. Babies are thought to be born with distinctive *anga*, which further develops as the child grows. The term *anga* refers to both nature and behavior.[3] Churchward's definition reveals the polysemic nature of this term: "habit, custom, nature, quality, character, characteristic; way, form, style, manner, method; behaviours, conduct, demeanour, way(s) of acting" (1959, 7). Innumerable compounds can be formed with *anga*, such as *anga lelei*, good natured and well behaved.

'Ulungāanga (characteristic behavior or nature) is often used interchangeably with *anga* although it implies a more lasting quality. Both *anga* and *'ulungāanga* can imply a fixed "essence," yet they are more often spoken of as impermanent and changeable. 'Ulungāanga also forms many compounds to describe specific aspects of a person's personality or behavior. The context of speech acts sometimes makes clear whether the speaker is referring to actual behavior or to a person's nature, but nature and behavior are not usually conceptually distinguished. The use of English glosses can therefore be inadequate or misleading, and the Tongan terms are used wherever possible in this text.

The conceptualization of the origin and development of a person's *anga* or *'ulungāanga* is revealed in the following statements by two Tongan women:

> Children already have their *'ulungāanga* from nature (*natula*); it is in the children from nature; they come with good *'ulungāanga* from nature, and there are some children who have bad *'ulungāanga*.
>
> Each child grows up with his or her own *anga*, girls and boys. I don't think the *anga* is the same for one boy and another boy, one girl and another girl . . . and one little boy will grow with *anga lelei* [good *anga*] and the *anga lelei* will grow as he gets bigger. . . . Each one, each person, has his or her own *anga*, and they are that way until they are grown.

To some extent, then, *anga* is an inherited disposition. This is sometimes explicitly associated with certain ancestors or with the child's natal village or island. For example, a child may be said to have inherited a late grandparent's gift for poetry or to have a temperament typical of people from the child's village.

As well as their individual, inherited *anga*, all children are believed to share certain innate characteristics. These are negatively valued characteristics, the most commonly mentioned being that children are *vale* and *pau'u* (naughty, mischievous). Babies were formerly referred to as *valevale*, which Churchward translates as unable to think for themselves (1959, 533). Older children can think, but only foolish thoughts, and the central aim of socialization is for them to become *poto*: clever, socially competent, and capable. Gender and rank are also believed to be "inherited," but as predispositions rather than fixed traits. As with all aspects of children's *anga*, the way in which these predispositions are molded and developed through socialization is important. In Tongan theories of development, the greatest emphasis is on the malleability of the person, not on inherited characteristics.

Koskinen has shown that *vale* is a pan-Polynesian term denoting ignorance, lack of skill, and madness (1968, 37).[4] In Tonga, individuals of any age can be called *vale* or *anga vale* when they have behaved foolishly or been "socially inept." In status rivalry, the participants may be judged to be *vale* or *poto* (Marcus 1978, 266). *Vale* is also used for insane and mentally handicapped persons. Any form of incompetence tends to be treated impatiently or to be regarded as amusing or shameful. For example, a child who trips and falls may be laughed at or slapped for clumsiness. As mentioned previously, the term *me'avale* (foolish thing) is sometimes used to refer to commoners and implies that they lack the proper social graces and knowledge of *anga fakatonga*. Concern with social competence is thus a pervasive theme in Tongan discourse, and it is articulated most clearly in relation to children.

There is no consensus about when children are no longer *vale*. Churchward states that the term *tamasi'i kei vale* (or *tamasi'i vale*), meaning "child who is still foolish," is applied to children of three or four (1959, 452). Ages ranging from four to eleven were suggested to me to be the time when "proper" learning begins, and the end of primary school was frequently cited as a turning point in children's progress in becoming *poto*. It is sometimes said of older adolescents *"kakato hono 'atamai"* (their mind or reason is whole).

Closely related to the concept of *vale* is that of *pau'u*. This is best glossed as mischievous: it implies naughtiness with an element of cheekiness. It is children's *vale* nature that makes them *pau'u*: they know no better. Children's behavior is often interpreted as *pau'u* even from birth, so that an infant who cries, feeds, or needs a diaper change may be called *pau'u*. When my daughter was only a few hours old my friend Seini told her that she was *pau'u* and that "Mummy will have to smack you every day, eh?" Whenever I asked Tongan mothers how their babies were their immediate reply was invariably and emphatically *"Pau'u!"* Although babies are regarded as inherently *vale* and *pau'u*, the latter term also implies agency and intention. This is reflected in active attempts to socialize children, including the use of discipline, within the first year.

The terms Tongans use to describe children in everyday discourse constantly reiterate that children are foolish, naughty, impulsive, and difficult to look after. On one occasion during my fieldwork I jotted down the most frequently used of these terms and quickly had a list of eighteen words. In contrast, my list of positive terms had only three terms: *poto*, *anga lelei*, and *'ulungāanga lelei*. Some of the negative terms are general—describing the child's *anga*, *'ulungāanga*, or *loto* as "bad" (*kovi*), or calling the child disobedient (*leangata'a*, *talangata'a*). More specific terms include *fakahela* (tiring), *fakahoha'a* (troublesome, annoying), *longoa'a* (noisy), *fakapikopiko* (lazy), and *kākā* (cunning). Many terms are combined with *fa'a* (often), as in *fa'a tangi* (often crying), and *fie* (to want, with connotations of pretension), as in *fie poto* (thinking oneself clever, showing off). Still other terms refer to the *vale* nature of children: *fakasesele* (silly), *launoa* (talking nonsense), and *laupisi* (talking rubbish). Like *vale* and *pau'u* these other negative terms used to describe children are sometimes used affectionately, especially with babies and very young children. All of the terms are used for both males and females, although, as will be shown, girls are believed to be "naturally" better behaved.

The negatively valued qualities attributed to children are regarded as normal and natural, and there is a sense in which they are accepted and even seen as an aspect of their Tongan identity, despite the fact that an explicit aim of socialization is to replace or override them with more valued qualities. Whenever I expressed concern that my son was behaving in ways that might annoy other household members, they would laugh and reassure me that "all children are like that." Frequently I was told that he was "a real Tongan boy" because he was so *pau'u*.

Socialization aims to mold "good" people; nevertheless, adults are often characterized as inherently "bad." The bad *anga* with which people are born not only needs molding through socialization but requires social rules and formal and informal social controls to maintain the good *anga* of members of society (see Shore 1982 on Samoa). Again, this is sometimes expressed as a part of Tongan rather than individual nature. One day in Holonga, as I helped search for a missing tool that Siale suspected had been stolen, several people helping in the hunt made passing comments about how bad (*kovi*) Tongans are, how untrustworthy, and so on.

Even when children are not intentionally misbehaving their behavior may be categorized as *pau'u* or *kovi*. Accidental injuiries are often regarded as the child's own fault, particularly if he or she has been hurt while playing.

The child may receive little sympathy and be told he or she has been *pau'u*. When my son cut his leg on some coral while swimming with his friends— an injury that required several stitches—he was taken aback when he showed people his wound, expecting sympathy, only to be told with a laugh how *pau'u* he was.

Children's negatively valued qualities are seen as natural (*fakanatula*) and unsocialized, whereas socially approved qualities such as respect must be learned. Even correct predispositions, such as those to gender or rank, must be developed through socialization. Because the bad qualities are seen as so persistent, emphasis is placed on actively teaching children correct values and behavior. In contrast, the acquisition of physical skills is left to observation and imitation. This process begins long before children are thought to be able to understand properly.

Becoming *poto* entails learning the skills necessary to daily life and acquiring a formal education, but most essentially it entails developing appropriate *anga*. Although some aspects of a person's *anga* are regarded as inherited and fixed at birth, other aspects are acquired through socialization. There are also attempts to alter the natural, inherited *anga* if it is perceived negatively. For example, if a child is said to have inherited a grandparent's bad temper, attempts will nevertheless be made to teach the child to exhibit self-control. One's *anga* should be *totonu* (right, proper), *fe'unga* (befitting, suitable), and *lelei* (good). One reaches this goal by acquiring, or at least manifesting, the values discussed in this chapter. Becoming *poto* also involves learning to match behavior to context. Churchward's definition of *poto* as "to understand what to do and be able to do it" (1959, 416) needs to be expanded to include knowing *when* to do it. Being *poto* means both learning the rules and learning how to manipulate them to one's advantage. Like the English term *clever*, the meaning of *poto* can shade into *cunning*.[5]

The need for children to develop proper *anga* and become *poto* tend to be explained in terms of the importance of other people's opinions. It is important, Seini explained, "because when people come to your home, the children have learned to be *poto* in their *'ulungāanga* to different people." 'Ana's explanation was similar: "When they [children] go to different homes they go and are clever in doing their duty (*fatongia*) in that home. They learn the duties to do at home and they go to different houses and are *poto*." Children are expected to exhibit proper respectfulness and obedience in others' homes and to willingly assist in any chores when asked. Any bad behavior would bring shame (*mā*) to their families.

Protecting and enhancing the reputation of self and family, and avoiding shame, are central motives for proper behavior in Tonga. As Bernstein has pointed out, "an individual's reputation is inexorably tied to his [*sic*] family's reputation" (1983, 126). This reputation is to a great extent dependent on others' judgments of the *anga* of individuals and their families. This protection of reputation is especially important for *'eiki* children, who are often in the public eye at feasts, celebrations, and other events. Though some leeway is given to all children because of their *vale* and *pau'u* nature, people are quick to criticize children and their families for the children's incorrect behavior. Much of this criticism is not intended as a slight on the family's reputation, and information concerning the misdemeanors of children is frequently and freely exchanged between neighboring households. There is a delicate balance, however, between this everyday commentary on children's wrongdoings and more serious criticism or gossip that could be damaging to a family's reputation. Adults therefore tend to be constantly vigilant over the young children in their household, as much to be seen to be monitoring the children's behavior as to appease their own sense of propriety.

People often discussed *anga* in relation to the concept of *mo'ui* (life, existence). Proper *anga* was described to me as part of *mo'ui 'aonga* (a useful, worthwhile life), *mo'ui 'ofa* (a life of concern and love), *mo'ui fai totonu* (a life of doing right), and so on. To live in this way is to adhere to *anga faka-tonga* and to be a good Christian, which to many Tongans are now one and the same. The concept of *anga* is therefore central to Tongan identity, and in rhetoric about national and cultural identity the term *anga fakatonga* is invoked to encompass all positively valued *anga*. In everyday discourse, however, there is also some reference to the negatively valued aspects of *anga* linked to the innately *vale* and *pau'u* nature of children, which are also identified as Tongan.

Another concept crucial to Tongan notions of the person, and thus to ideas about the nature and development of children, is *loto*. *Loto* is best glossed as heart and mind but also means "desire, will, purpose; anger, ire, temper" (Churchward 1959, 302; and see Gerber 1985, 136 on the very similar concept of *loto* in Samoa). As anger or ire it is seldom used nowadays without a qualifying adjective (e.g., *loto 'ita*, angry heart and mind), but it is telling that *loto* has this connotation, particularly because anger has a central place in Tongan theories of emotion, to be described later. *Loto* also means inside, whether of the body (*pēpē 'i loto*: "baby inside") or of objects (*loto fale*: the inside of a house). The term for the physical organ of the heart is *mafu*, a term sometimes used metaphorically for "sweetheart." The term *manava* is similar to *loto* and means "heart, bowels (in Old English), as the seat of affections or courage, etc.," as well as womb or stomach (Churchward 1959, 330; see Smith 1981 on the cognate Maori term, *manawa*). Collocott relates the term *manava* to *mana*, the "living power or force" that was particularly associated with chiefliness, and he suggests that *manava* "perhaps means the place or seat of this power or force" (1921b, 431). *Loto* is now much more commonly used—perhaps, if Collocott was correct, because the concept of *mana* is now seldom invoked.

The *loto* is conceptualized as an entity, which can be hurt (*loto lavea:* "broken hearted"), be big or small (i.e., brave or timid), be cold or hot (i.e., unsympathetic or angry), be "poured out," and so on (see Churchward 1959, 302–305). A person's *loto* can also be "separated" from the body, as described in this statement by a *māʻuli* about the problems of giving birth in hospital: "If you go to the hospital your *loto* stays with your children at home. . . . When you are ready to give birth you are irritable and angry and cry a lot, and if something happens and you die, your *loto* stays at home with your children, husband, and family, and you die unhappy (*mate mamahi*)."

Loto is used in many compound terms to characterize persons' "dispositions" in a temporary or permanent sense. To refer to someone as *loto ʻofa*, for example, may mean either that a particular action was kind or that the person is kind and loving in general. Many of the terms with which *loto* can be coupled indicate emotional states and behavior, so that prefixing them with *loto* associates them with the inner state of a particular person. A woman describing the origin of her angry feelings revealed the association of *loto* with emotion when she said, "I just feel it (*ongoʻi*), feel it in me, it comes from my *loto*. Like feeling sad or happy."

Clearly, *loto* is similar to the terms *anga* and *ʻulungāanga* and, like those terms, does not necessarily imply a fixed or permanent essence. *Anga ʻofa*, kind and loving nature and behavior, could thus be interpreted as almost synonymous with *loto ʻofa*. The difference between these terms is that *loto* refers directly to a person's emotional, subjective state, whereas *anga* is more closely associated with behavior and therefore with social relations. Tongans who distinguished between the two using English glosses defined *anga* as "manner" and "behavior," whereas *loto* was defined as "heart," "inside," and "will." *Anga* was also described as being "more serious." To explain the difference, one woman contrasted the terms *anga kovi* and *loto kovi*. The former could describe an action such as refusing to share a mango, whereas the latter could refer to jealousy. *Loto* is, in an important sense, deeper within the person than *anga*. Mariner captured much of this sense of the term *loto* when he defined it as "disposition, inclination, passion, or sentiment" (Martin 1981, 312).

Mariner also uses *loto* as "mind," translating "*tangata loto lillé*" (*tangata loto lelei*) as "a man with a good mind" (Martin 1941, 318). This definition points to another crucial distinction between *loto* and *anga*: the former is more intentional, more closely bound up with thought and will. Although babies are said to be born with certain *anga*, it is much less common to refer to a newborn baby's *loto*. The term for mind, understanding, and reason, *'ata-mai*, is used less often than *loto*, and when describing a thought or idea, *pehē* or *fakakaukau* (to think) are commonly used. *Loto*, in its dual sense of heart and mind, is used to describe a person's opinion, with a strong connotation of emotion. It could be described as "the emotional mind" (Koskinen 1968, 77).[6] A woman speaking emphatically pressed her fist to her chest and said, "My *loto* as a person is that . . ." (direct transcription). In a less forceful sense, *loto* adds stress to ordinary statements. To say " *'oku ou fie 'alu*" (I want to go) is less forceful than " *'oku ou loto ke 'alu*" (I desire to go).

Mariner claimed that *loto* was also sometimes used for the soul, and he continued, "The soul is rather supposed to exist throughout the whole exten-sion of the body, but particularly in the heart, the pulsation of which is the strength and power of the soul or mind. They have no clear distinction between the life and the soul, but they will tell you that the *fotomanava* (the right auricle of the heart) is the seat of life" (Martin 1981, 312).

Mageo has described socialization in Samoa as "directed toward rooting out the child's willfulness *(loto)*" (1988, 49). Yet in Tonga the *loto* is not only "the source of anti-social behavior" (Mageo 1989a, 182; see Gerber 1975, 1985); it is potentially the source of proper dispositions and behavior. Tongan socialization is directed toward children's *loto*, but in the sense of molding it to conform to Tongan values. Tongan children ideally develop *loto lelei*, a good *loto*. This term is used in the very general sense of "nice" but more specifically means "agreeable, willing, favourably disposed" (Church-ward 1959, 303). The importance of this association between goodness and willingness lies especially in the ideals of obedience and submissiveness for children. Because *loto lelei* precludes animosity and conflict, it is also regarded as essential for maintaining social harmony. To receive others' approval and avoid gossip, women are expected to ensure that their house-hold maintains an atmosphere of cooperation and calmness, so it is impera-tive for them to raise their children to be *loto lelei*.

Although the ideal is to develop *loto lelei* and thus to conform to cultural expectations, a person's *loto* also constitutes "the subjective dimension of the person," as in Samoa (Mageo 1989a, 182). *Loto* allows for individualism, pro-viding a site of "intrapsychic autonomy" (see Ewing 1991). It is often used to express the idea of free will and autonomous choice, combined with desire, as when women claimed they had chosen (or would choose) a spouse accord-ing to their own *loto*. As will be seen below in the discussion of the concepts *tau'atāina* (independence) and *fa'iteliha* (pleasing oneself), this autonomy is highly valued in Tonga as a complement to the strongly hierarchical, inter-dependent nature of social relations, a nature that finds expression in key values such as love and concern, respect, and obedience.

VALUES

The way in which ideal personhood emerges through socialization is described in Tonga in terms of becoming *poto* and acquiring positively valued
anga and *loto*. These in turn are defined in relation to certain salient cultural
values—particularly love, respect, and obedience—that are intrinsically
linked to emotions both as abstractions and as psychological states. In Tongan discourse concerning values and emotions, behavioral aspects rather
than subjective states are emphasized, and it is these aspects that will be
addressed here.

This is not to suggest, however, that subjective states are unimportant.
The relationship between cultural models and subjective experience is often
congruent, with subjective experience reinforcing those models so that
values, emotions, and behavior are mutually consistent. Gerber's analysis of
the Samoan case explains this relationship aptly:

> By defining "right" feelings in a consonant manner, adherence to the values
> of mutual aid and hierarchy is not only made surer; it is rendered less painful.
> A Samoan gives, therefore, not only because he or she has been trained to
> view giving as morally correct but also because his or her training has created
> a disposition to feel such an act as "natural," seeming to arise out of the very
> depths of his or her being. (1985, 153)

While this often appears to be the case, it is important to recognize that
inconsistencies are also frequently present in the relationship among values,
emotions, and behavior. Ambivalence and even outright resistence are commonly expressed, so that behavior that demonstrates appropriate values may
not reflect a person's emotional state or disposition. Children often grumble
about the tasks they are given, for example, and will even resist them to the
point of being physically punished. The following chapters will provide
many examples showing that the process of internalizing cultural values is
often problematic.

In Tongan beliefs about the process of socialization, children not only
need to learn appropriate values and behavior; they must also learn to be
poto he anga: to be able to behave according to context. Learning to match
behavior to context has been described by the Ritchies as "one of the most
important lessons Polynesian children must master" (1989, 103). Context
determines the status of the actors involved and consequently the roles that
they play. Shifting of roles occurs, for example, when in some contexts children behave as high-status persons, usually to younger children, and in other
contexts must demonstrate their low status.

The importance of context has also been identified as an aspect of "the more general Polynesian epistemological bias that things be known in their specific contexts and through their perceptual effects in the world rather than in terms of essential, intrinsic features" (Shore 1989, 138). Consequences of actions are thus more important than motivations, and the clearest determinant of consequences is whether or not actions are appropriate in a given context. Concern is with behavior rather than with internal states or dispositions, although there is no clear distinction between the two in concepts such as *anga* and *'ulungāanga*.

The values to be discussed are those that are particularly salient to child socialization within *tu'a* families and are primarily significant at the level of interpersonal relationships. These values are also appropriate to relationships between chiefs and commoners. Other values were formerly associated only with *hou'eiki*, such as *to'a* (bravery), *hoihoifua* (beauty), *fie 'eiki* (chiefliness), *fie pule* (dominance), *lāngilangi* (honor), and *ngeia* (dignity). Kolo has argued that in precontact Tonga "there were two sets of opposed values and moralities . . . one completely dominating the other, and this continues to the present" (1990, 3). However, it is also the case in contemporary Tonga that "values originating in chiefly culture are shared widely among the population" (Marcus 1980a, 159). Chiefly values have become intrinsic to Tongan notions of ideal personhood, particularly the emphasis on being *poto* and on the high-status characteristics of restraint, relative immobility, proper behavior, and authority. Indeed, chiefliness itself is an ideal to which children are encouraged to aspire.

When 230 teenagers responded to the question "What do you think were the most important things you were taught as a child?" their answers, like those of the adults I spoke with, emphasized the three central values of love,

Table 4: Childhood Learning

	FEMALE (TOTAL RESPONDENTS = 139)	MALE (TOTAL RESPONDENTS = 91)	TOTAL (TOTAL RESPONDENTS = 230)	%
Proper behavior	47	27	74	32.2
Religion	40	34	74	32.2
Obedience	39	30	69	30.0
Respect	17	9	26	11.3
'Ofa	17	5	22	9.6
Household work	12	6	18	7.8
Study	7	7	14	6.1
Tongan customs	9	2	11	4.8
Entertainment	4	4	8	3.5
Other	6	3	9	3.9

respect, and obedience. Table 4 shows their responses (multiple answers were given in some cases).

Most of the answers categorized in table 4 as "proper behavior," such as sharing, helping, *anga lelei*, and kindness, are aspects of love, respect and obedience. Religion also centers on these values, which are seen as traditional values that have been strengthened by Christianity (see Cummins 1979, 180 and Lātūkefu 1980, 75).[7] They are explicitly defined by many Tongans as intrinsic to their cultural identity, and in the context of rapid socio-cultural change they have become especially significant symbols of that identity and are increasingly perceived as under threat.

"Love": 'Ofa

Thus far I have glossed *'ofa* as love, but in fact it has a much wider range of connotations. Kavaliku, in his detailed analysis of this polysemic term, shows that it can mean concern, kindness, hope, sadness, care, help, gifts, sharing, and sexual love. He points out that "no single meaning is a whole unless the other meanings are implicit or explicit." The cluster of meanings that form the concept of *'ofa* is found throughout Polynesia: as *aloha* in Hawaii, *aroha* in New Zealand and the Cook Islands, *alofa* in Samoa and Tokelau, *ka'oha* in the Marquesas, *aropa* in Anuta, and *arofa* in Tikopia and Tahiti.[8] For Tongans, Kavaliku argues that *'ofa* is "the philosophy behind their way of life" (1977, 67). "[T]here seems to be a fervent and constant preoccupation with *'ofa* within Tongan society. . . . [It] seems to represent the supreme justification for their behaviour and activities" (47–48).[9] As Marcus notes, " *'Ofa* is not an exceptional quality in a person but one that should be exhibited and manifested in all social activity" (1978, 247). To be *ta'e'ofa* (without *'ofa*) is to go "against accepted morals and norms" (66), to be unkind, greedy, inconsiderate, and so on.

There is an important distinction to be made between the way the term *'ofa* is used *within* relationships and the way it is used in *talking about* relationships. Within emotionally close relationships, such as between parents and children or between siblings, the term *'ofa* is seldom used in its more emotive sense in everyday conversation. As Ngata commented, "We rarely say 'I love you' in Tonga." Rather, the behavioral manifestations of *'ofa* are emphasized, such as sharing, helping, and serving, as described below. The association of *'ofa* with sympathy and empathy is also stressed, though the derivative term, *faka'ofa* (unfortunate, pitiable) is more readily used in this context.[10] *Faka-'ofa* can be used to express deep sadness and pity, but in ordinary usage it has much less emotional depth, as when a teenage girl commented that it was *faka'ofa* that no basketball was played near my house in town. Another derivative term, *fe'ofo'ofani* (shared emotional closeness, friendliness), is also used within the family context. *'Ofa* tends to be used at emotionally intense times, as during the grief of parting when a family member goes overseas, or on formal occasions, as in speeches at marriage and funeral ceremonies.

'Ofa is used more often by people in less emotionally close relationships, such as distant kin, or in status relations, especially by lower-status to higher-status persons. It is perhaps because there tends to be less emotional involvement in such relationships that *'ofa* must be stressed; ideally, it is a feature of all relationships. This ideal is expressed as *fe'ofa'aki*, to demonstrate *'ofa* to one another. Marcus has pointed out that this grammatical form, in which transitive verbs are made reciprocal (also found in *fe'ofo'ofani*—see above), images "a reversal of the parties involved in an action, regardless of status or categorical distinctions that hold in a particular context." In a hierarchical society such as Tonga, such implied reciprocity "can be quite radical" (1988, 73). However, although the values emphasizing reciprocity ideally cut across status and rank distinctions, in practice they are sometimes expressed in quite different ways. For example, as we will see, high-status persons demonstrate *'ofa* by teaching and guiding, whereas low-status persons do so by being unquestioningly obedient.

'Ofa is used more often and with more emphasis on its emotional aspect when one is talking *about* relationships. Family relationships are ideally characterized by *'ofa māfana* (warm love). The deep love of parents, especially mothers, for their children, is known as *'ofa u'uu'u*, or, in modern usage, *'ofa lahi 'aupito* (very great love). Yet too much love is seen as spoiling a child and is referred to as *'ofa vale'i* (foolish love). *'Ofa* is also used today to refer to sexual and romantic desire; formerly the term *manako* (to be fond of, to desire) was more often used in this sense. Many women I spoke with still used *manako*, not *'ofa*, to describe their feelings for their husbands, or used the English word "love." *Manako* is also used when describing a strong liking for something, as in "I love school."

The tendency of close family members not to use the term *'ofa* to one another in ordinary contexts can be partly attributed to the fact that *'ofa* is expected in such relationships and is therefore not seen as needing constant reaffirmation. However, it can also be regarded as part of a more general tendency to show emotional restraint except in certain contexts (such as those described above). Later, this restraint will be examined further in relation to the context-appropriate expression of emotion, as well as the concern that is shown to evaluate the emotional state of others.

Physical displays of affection, such as kissing, hugging, and other close physical contact, are not a feature of everyday interactions in Tonga, except in people's behavior toward babies and very young children. Another excep-

tion is in same-sex relationships of children and youths, in which hand holding, walking with arms around each other's shoulders, and other forms of
affectionate display are common. In a stylized expression of emotion, Tongan
adults who do not see one another frequently may 'uma ("kiss") on meeting.[11] Touching, leaning, and so on, also frequently mark difficult or stressful
situations, as they provide unspoken reassurance. For example, during more
formal interviews with people who did not know me well it was common for
them to reach for a child to hold or stroke or to lean on another adult.

After their first year, children receive less and less direct physical affection. Young children usually continue to sleep beside an older, same-sex
household member, and this is acknowledged as a sign of emotional closeness. Malia, from Holonga, described how parents show children love, and
explained, "The Tongan way is when you sleep with your children, when
they are young, laying them in your arms and telling them stories, and your
children will feel it [love]." Shumway writes,

> [T]he Tongan concept of mothering is expressed most poignantly in the pro-
> verbial phrase mohe ofi (sleeping close). The image is of a child lying close to
> his or her mother on the bed, head resting on her forearm, listening to her
> wisdom. A supreme compliment to a child (and the parents) is, "Fie lau he
> na'a ke mohe ofi" ("No wonder you excel. You slept close."). (1991, 12)

Children may also be sung to at night, and lullabies are sometimes called
fakapēpē tama (Moyle 1987, 204–206). Moyle translates this as "cradling a
child," but more literally it means treating a child as a baby and implies the
more gentle and openly affectionate treatment of babies. These expressions
of love are infrequent, however, and it is far more common for children to be
left to fall asleep in the living area of the house and carried to a bedroom or
sleeping mat later. In our Holongan household in 1988 baby 'Ofa, who was
frequently lavished with affection and attention by day, slept with her
parents in a separate bedroom. The twins were given very little physical affection at all; the majority of attention directed toward them by older household members took the form of instructions to do chores or run errands, or
scolding and punishment. Elenoa slept with Silia, her teenage "aunt" in
another bedroom, and Tomasi slept on the living room floor with his grandmother, Moana.

Although children of three or four may at times be pulled onto an adult's
lap and cuddled, it is far more common for children to initiate such interactions. When adults are sitting talking, young children often climb onto their
laps (especially their mothers'). They may be ignored, or absentmindedly
held and stroked, but their presence does not activate the same attention as

would babies'. From the age of about four or five, children no longer climb onto adults' laps, but they continue to seek physical contact well into their teens. A child will lean against an adult's back or arm, drape an arm over the adult's shoulders or hug her (or his) arm, usually remaining behind or beside the adult. This physical contact is tolerated, and often the adult will respond by beginning to delouse the child's hair. This entails drawing the child closer to the front of the adult's body, often with the child's head in the adult's lap. Children will be still and quiet for long periods while having their hair searched for lice and often appear to be almost in a trance. Whether being deloused or just leaning comfortably against an adult, children usually remain passive and quiet, never attempting to join in the adults' conversations and seldom daring to interrupt. Another form of physical contact that children seem to like is when they are called on to *faito'o* (heal, in this case by massage) older women of the household who have sore or numb arms or legs after long hours of beating *tutu* or weaving mats.

Children rarely see physical demonstrations of affection between their parents or other adults. The intimacy of parents is expressed subtly, in their teasing banter, their easy cooperation on tasks such as food preparation, their shared delight over their infants' accomplishments, and so on. Siale, for example, was never openly affectionate to Seini in front of other household members, but it was obvious that their relationship was close. On many nights I could hear them talking quietly together into the early hours, and Siale often showed his affection in considerate actions such as driving into town to pick up Seini from work to save her the long, dusty bus trip home. Only when he was drunk did Siale openly express his feelings, and then he would repeatedly proclaim to me, in English, his love for Seini—while she listened, pleased but embarrassed.

Love scenes on videos or *pālangi* couples holding hands or being openly affectionate are viewed with a mixture of amusement and embarrassment. At a beach picnic in 1986 the Holongan women and children I was with were fascinated by a *pālangi* couple in bathing costumes (Tongans swim in their clothes) who were cuddling together on an inflatable raft near the shore. Seini called out in Tongan, "Are you making a baby?" causing gales of laughter among the others. Close physical proximity is not avoided, however, and there are many occasions when adults and children of both sexes are crowded together, as when jammed onto the back of a truck or in an overloaded bus. Any embarrassment that might be felt is concealed by the joking and laughter that characterize such occasions.

The amount of physical affection very young children receive and the age at which it begins to diminish vary considerably. Children who have a lot of contact with grandparents and other older relatives tend to receive

more affection, as do the "baby" of the family and children who are *pele*.[12]
These children also receive more praise and verbal expressions of affection.
As has been shown, there are few words of praise used to children, compared
to critical and disparaging terms. *Poto* and *anga lelei* are the most common
words of praise and are most often used to little children to reward or encourage obedience. Adults are also seldom praised, as praise is thought to encourage people to become *fie poto* or *fie lahi* (thinking themselves clever
or important). Mariner observed that Tongans "avoid the baseness of flat-
tery; and even where a man has performed some achievement really praise-
worthy, they seldom commend him in his presence, lest it should make
him vain" (Martin 1981, 318). In Tonga, as in Pukapuka, where "praise is
simply uncommon," praise, if given at all, tends to be sarcastic (Borofsky
1987, 94).

Open praise is rare, but adults' pride in their children is often apparent.
Parents and other family members are quick to comment that a child is
pau'u, but they almost as readily describe the child's academic or sporting
achievements, amusing behavior, and so on. When children are very little
there is even an element of pride in stories of their naughtiness. Interest and
pride in children's development and achievements continue throughout
childhood. Often when I was playing with children their parents and other
relatives watched closely, anxiously warning them not to break the toys,
grumbling at them for being such nuisances to me, but also smiling with
pride when the children "performed" well. When I taped children singing,
the adults of their household repeatedly asked to hear the tape and listened
attentively each time. At times adults also encourage children more directly,
as when a child spontaneously begins to dance and the adults watching clap,
make a "tch" noise in rhythm for accompaniment, and call out *"Mālie!"*
(bravo).

The many public celebrations during which children are the focus of
attention are also occasions when families' pride in their children is obvious.
When school children march through the streets of Nuku'alofa on the king's
birthday or for the closing of Parliament, when they perform in religious
dramas on Fakamē (White Sunday, or Children's Day, in May) or recite bible
lessons at their confirmation, when they perform traditional dances at school
fund-raising events or take part in singing competitions, whole families are
involved. Tiny Tongan flags are made for the children to wave as they march;
extraordinarily detailed costumes are painstakingly made for the dancers, or
new school uniforms are sewn; some family members march alongside the
children or stand near as they dance to call encouragement; food and drinks
are brought for a picnic after the event, and, increasingly often nowadays,
videos are recorded, to be viewed many times and sent to relatives overseas.

Words of praise and love are rare, but each of these actions is a clear demon-stration of 'ofa.

One of many such events that I witnessed was the schools' march for the king's birthday celebrations in 1988. In Holonga preparations began well before the event, with the local school practicing marching and singing, and family members making new school uniforms and hundreds of paper Tongan flags. Early in the morning on the day of the march, cars and trucks full of people, singing loudly, began to pass through Holonga on their way to town. Our own group packed up the food prepared the previous night and climbed into Siale's huge dump truck, then began the trip to town, picking up passen-gers along the way until the truck was crowded. At the Teufaiva sports ground where the schools were gathering there were thousands of children in brightly colored uniforms, surrounded by proud family members. The chil-dren, many only five years old, marched in school groups from the sports ground on the edge of Nuku'alofa along the main street to the palace. The march took more than an hour in blazing sunshine, and throughout that time the children sang loudly, waved their flags, and shouted "*Tue, tue, tue!*" (a joyous exclamation), urged on by teachers and family and cheered by the crowds who lined the street. I accompanied the Holongan group, and we marched through the palace grounds, waved to the royal family sitting on the palace porch, and gave a final burst of song and cheers. Outside the palace grounds everyone broke ranks and straggled back to the sports ground. Some children clung to their parents or were carried back, some cried, and many limped along in too-tight shoes or missing a shoe that had been lost in the march. At the sports grounds families gathered for picnics before heading home, and in our truck the twins and I were in an exhausted sleep long before we reached home.

'Ofa is also expressed in a concern with others' physical well-being and by generosity *(nima homo)*. To share, as Kavaliku explains, "people must have 'ofa, to share is 'ofa" (1977, 64). In relation to children 'ofa is explicitly associated with the provision of food and other needs and wants. At meal-times family members encourage children to *kai ke 'osi* (eat until it is fin-ished) and offer them special tidbits. Adults are always willing to share special foods with children. Women take candy and other treats home for their children after feasts or other events where they are provided. In our Holonga household the sharing of food was one of the few signs of affection Siale showed to his five-year-old daughter, Elenoa, whom he generally ignored. One night, for example, he came home late and prepared some food for himself. When he saw Elenoa watching him from the doorway as he was about to eat, he immediately offered the food to her, urging her in a kindly tone to share it with him.[13]

As Lutz has noted for the Ifaluk, the sharing of goods in Tonga is "strongly tied to sociability and emotion" (1988, 90). The act of sharing is more important than the goods themselves, so that the sharing of food, rather than its consumption, is associated most closely with the ties between people (95). Children learn to share with their siblings, and this sharing continues throughout life. As Manu explained, her children were taught to share without expectation of return. She said that she gave birth to them "with blood, not silver or gold" so they should honor their bond of blood and help each other.

Sharing within the family is part of a much wider cultural emphasis on giving. All special events are marked by gifts of food and valuables, within and between *tu'a* families and by commoners to chiefs and royalty as either *fatongia* (duty) or spontaneous generosity motivated by *'ofa māfana*. Gifts should be appropriate, however, to a person's (or family's) relative rank or status: giving too much is regarded as *fie lahi*.

Howard, who has noted a similar "association of affection with material giving" for Rotuma, suggests that the generosity of parents establishes a social debt that enables them to control and influence their children's lives (1970, 33). In Tonga this social debt is also recognized in the expectation that adult children will care for their aging parents and make contributions on behalf of their family at feasts and on other occasions. Children accumulate this debt through the food and material goods they receive throughout childhood and adolescence, the education that many parents make sacrifices to finance, and the expectation of some form of inheritance when their parents die. Ngata told me, "The father will get the land, his property, try to get everything in his possession and prepare it for the sons and daughters."

Children begin to be taught to share even during their first year. It can be a hard lesson to learn, as little 'Ofa discovered. Our neighbor Lusi was visiting with her one-year-old son, Saia, who had arrived clutching a packet of cheese-flavored snacks. Lusi took the open packet and put it on the floor so that all the children could share the snacks. The adults present watched as 'Ofa, also one year old, tasted one. They then commented to each other about how 'Ofa and Saia were both trying to grab the packet for themselves. Lusi then let Saia drink from 'Ofa's bottle, and everyone watched 'Ofa closely, saying, "Look at her eyes! . . . Look at her mouth. She's angry!" 'Ofa did get very angry as Saia drank, and when the adults started laughing at her she burst into tears.

Children do learn to share their food and possessions and learn that there is a fine line between requesting something (*kole*) and taking or stealing it. This was clear in another incident in our Holonga home when Tomasi and Elenoa were eating slices of a cake I had bought them. Tomasi finished his quickly then begged Elenoa for some of hers, which she had been eating slowly, savoring every crumb. She willingly offered it to him, and when I intervened and suggested he was being greedy she quickly averred that she was full. However, just as she was speaking to me, he tried to grab the cake, and she became angry and refused to give it to him. At five, Elenoa already had a strong inclination to share, yet was indignant when a reasonable request to share became an attempt at theft.

Anger at having to share does not disappear altogether as children get older, and many adults told me that they had hated having to share everything as children. Children constantly beg things from one another, and little children soon learn to use noisy protests to their advantage, although at considerable risk of punishment for being a nuisance. The begging cry of *mai ia* (give it to me) is frequently heard among groups of children and is one of the earliest expressions learned. If adults are annoyed by the begging cries of children they most often order the child with the desired goods to share, so children are occasionally secretive if they have something they do not want to have to hand over to another child.

Providing and sharing food and other goods is described in terms of *fetokoni'aki* (helping one another, cooperating), *tokoni* (helping), and *tauhi* (looking after, taking care of), and all of these kinds of behavior are demonstrations of *'ofa*. Neighbors take portions of food to one another every Sunday and whenever any special food has been prepared. When people pass by one's house, whether they are strangers or friends, it is polite to call in greeting, "*Ha'u kai!*" (come and eat). Morton has described *fetokoni'aki* as "the spirit and the reality of co-operation. . . . [T]his ideology prevails upon individuals to materially assist kin, neighbors, and friends, particularly those who need assistance" (1987, 62). Failure to share food can be called *kaivale* (foolish eating), and *kaipō* (eating surreptitiously) is particularly frowned upon.

It is in the sense of *tauhi* that *'ofa* is often used in regard to status relations. *Tu'a* are also known as *kakai tauhi 'eiki* (people who look after the chiefs), and as Afeaki points out, this ideology means "it is difficult for them to interpret any of the nobles' actions as exploitation," at least publicly (1983, 71). On the other hand, *tauhi* is also used to describe the obligations of high-status individuals to lower-status persons. This sense of looking after others is distinct from the more specific obligations of ranked relationships (Marcus 1974, 92).

Within the family, *tauhi* as an expression of *'ofa* involves day-to-day attention to children's needs: plaiting girls' hair, rubbing scented oil into children's skin and hair, reminding children to wear warm clothes, and so on. It is providing special clothes for church and feasts and ensuring that children have clean, pressed school uniforms to wear. Seini's mother, Moana, explained: "It ['ofa] is revealed (fakahaa'i) in the way I look after them (tauhi), help them properly (tokoni fe'unga)." Tauhi involves tokanga'i, looking after in the sense of supervising, to make sure children are safe and behaving properly. Caring for children also involves discipline, and the relationship between physical punishment and 'ofa will be examined in chapter 7. Another important form of tauhi is concern for children's health. As I will show later, children are discouraged from complaining about ill health or minor injuries. The initiative for attending to children's health problems comes from adults' concern based on observations and as such expresses their 'ofa.

When I was in Holonga in 1986 Elenoa, then aged three, spent a great deal of her time with her paternal grandmother. On one occasion when she was at home for dinner her father noticed some nasty boils on her arm, which she had not mentioned. He immediately drew Seini's attention to them and told Elenoa she should stay at home more so that they could attend to her health. In 1988, soon after my son and I had arrived in Holonga, Paul was obviously unhappy and unsettled and made himself ill by refusing to eat most of the Tongan food prepared for him. The other members of the household and our immediate neighbors all expressed their concern for him by claiming that he had a throat infection, which was treated several times, by several different people, with poultices of crushed leaves. He was also instructed not to eat sugar and to wear a warm cloth around his throat. Paul kept telling me that his throat felt fine, but the treatment did seem to help, if only to reassure him that these people genuinely cared for him.

Children are discouraged from complaining about minor illnesses or injuries, but when they are more seriously ill or hurt the care they receive is also a sign of 'ofa. When children (or adults) are hospitalized some family members stay with them, with at least one person remaining at night, and other relatives bring food and visit. My neighbor Lupe said of her children, "When they are sick, my life is difficult. I take great care of their illness, take them to the doctor and hospital to get treatment; I really care for them when they are sick."

Getting children the things they want is emphasized, and a common theme of many parents' comments was the difficulty nowadays of satisfying these wants. Several adults described their poor but happy childhoods, during which their needs were few and readily met. Today, they told me, there are many more things available, and even though they have much more money than their own parents had, they cannot afford all that their children want. This dissatisfaction is sometimes identified as a contributing factor in what people see as children's increasing disobedience and the weakening of Tongan tradition.

RESPECT: *FAKA'APA'APA*

The importance placed on the behavioral, over the emotional, aspects of *'ofa* is also a feature of respect in Tonga. The term most often translated as respect, *faka'apa'apa*, actually refers only to the outward expression of "the inward feeling or mental attitude" of reverence and respect denoted by the term *'apasia* (Churchward 1959, 550). *Faka'apa'apa* is used more often in everyday discourse than *'apasia*, and the distinction between the two terms is often blurred. Kavaliku claims that "*faka'apa'apa* is more than just respect. *Faka'apa'apa* encompasses, in Tongan thought, love, humbleness, respect and much more. . . . [W]e could not comprehend or understand *faka'apa'apa* unless we understood *'ofa*" (1977, 50). As this statement indicates, Tongan values are closely interrelated. Children demonstrate their *'ofa* for their family by being respectful and obedient and by generally displaying appropriate *anga*. For parents, *'ofa* entails teaching their children these values and associated behavior. However, it must be added that *pule*, the power and authority of higher-status persons, and fear (*ilifia*) of that authority are other important motives for respect and obedience.

Many of the early European visitors to Tonga commented on the importance Tongans placed on respect. They described the various symbols of respect: wearing a wreath of *ifi* (Tahitian chestnut) leaves, sitting with the head bowed, and wearing mats or *ta'ovala* around the waist. Mariner noted the Tongans' "love and respect for parents and superiors" and stated, "We may readily suppose that the sentiments of veneration and respect are felt in a considerable degree, and, accordingly, every mark of such is shown to the gods, to chiefs, and aged persons" (Martin 1981, 321, 320). As with children's relationships with adults, there was more to the relationship between chiefs and commoners than simply love and respect. Lātūkefu comments that "although *'ofa* existed in . . . traditional social relationships, the coercive elements such as fear of the chiefs' *mana* and absolute power were much stronger" (1980, 75).

One of the first lessons in respectful behavior that children are taught is to respond "*Ko au*" (it's me/I am) whenever someone calls them. 'Ana, with whom I stayed during a visit to 'Eua, told me, "It is right that they [children] grow and have respect for their parents and other people, like when you call 'Tupou!' [her niece] she should say '*Ko au*.' This is the respectful way (*anga faka'apa'apa*) and is helping one another (*fetokoni'aki*)." Children are encouraged to give this response as soon as they begin to vocalize, with older children and adults prompting them as others call their names. What begins as a game becomes more serious as children get older, and children are often punished for failing to say "*Ko au*." One of my neighbors in Nuku'alofa was a grandfather who occasionally gave his three-year-old grandson, Folau, lessons in saying "*Ko au.*" He would call Folau's name repeatedly, in the same even tone, and Folau would respond each time, becoming increasingly frustrated as the lesson wore on. After responding "*Ko au*" some ten or more times he would be angrily sobbing his words, but if he failed to answer, his grandfather's voice immediately became stern and threatening.[14]

Many other lessons in respect are learned through language. In Tongan there are separate lexicons of respect for *hou'eiki* and royalty (see Churchward 1985, 304; Shumway 1971, 602–604; Taliai 1989). Children frequently hear the *fakataputapu*, the respectful prologue to any speech or sermon, and the speeches themselves often use the language of respect. In ordinary discourse there are many terms that are used to indicate respect, humility, and politeness, as in the use of the polite pronouns *te* or *kita* (I or me), rather than the usual *ou* or *au*. There are also respectful versions of kinship terms, such as *fine'eiki* rather than *fa'ē* or *mali* for, respectively, mother and wife. Similarly, *tangata'eiki* is the respectful term for *tamai* (father) or *mali* (husband). These terms are also used as respectful forms of address to older people other than parents.

The use of respectful, polite language is a notable feature of everyday discourse in Tonga. A number of formulaic, polite expressions are used in greetings, to give thanks, and so on, even within the family (see Churchward 1985, 290–297). Children, especially girls, are competent in the use of the more common of these expressions by about five years of age. Children also learn at an early age to use a respectful stance and tone when addressing higher-status persons, and the mixture of deference and fear they exhibit on such occasions contrasts markedly with the aggressive or whining demands they make of their peers and juniors.

Being quiet or silent is another sign of respect, and children learn not to be noisy around adults and not to interrupt adults' conversations. Siale's mother, Tonga, said of her childhood, "If I went where some women older than I were talking I would just stay quiet (*fakalongolongo*) and listen (*fakafanongo*), and if I knew something about what they were talking about I would not say anything." Children who interrupt or offer advice to adults without being asked may be accused of being *fie poto* (thinking themselves clever). For example, one day when 'Ana from 'Eua was visiting our Holonga household, she was preparing to massage Moana with warmed oil when her teenage daughter, Silia, suggested the oil was too hot. 'Ana angrily told Silia not to be *fie poto*.

Another important way in which children show respect is by remaining on the periphery of adult activities. The outside or periphery is generally associated with low status for adults as well. At funerals, for example, people who are of low status in relation to the deceased stay outside and do low-status tasks such as cooking. When people visit someone's home informally they usually remain outside, standing at a little distance from the house or sitting on the porch. When they are asked inside they tend to perch on the doorstep or sit on the floor near a corner. Only close relatives seem to be really comfortable going inside the house for informal visits.

Children follow this pattern and stay mostly outside; if they come in they sit quietly near the door. As long as they remain outside, their presence is tolerated; consequently, groups of children can sometimes be seen standing outside houses, watching through the windows as a video movie plays, a band rehearses, or some other interesting event takes place. At feasts and other social occasions children are expected, as one woman put it, to "stay far away, not crowd around," though some older Tongans told me that this practice is much less strictly observed today than when they were children. Respect is also shown by remaining physically lower than higher-status persons, and children are taught that the correct way to pass in front of someone is to bend low and say *"Tulou"* (excuse me). On formal occasions people sometimes crawl on their hands and knees when passing before or approaching a seated member of Tonga's royal family. Certain kinship relations are marked by the observation of *faka'apa'apa*, particularly the relationship of brothers to sisters and of children to their father's sisters; these relations will be examined in detail in the following chapter. Children therefore are afforded many opportunities to observe adults behaving respectfully, both within and outside their homes. As Marcus has noted, "humility, submission, and deference are normally appproved personal styles" (1978, 255).

OBEDIENCE: *TALANGOFUA*

Like respect, obedience is a sign of children's *'ofa* for their parents and family. As 'Ana explained, "By being obedient (*talangofua*) and doing the work their parents order them to do, the parents are able to know the children love them." Submissiveness, as a sign of both respect and obedience, is a positively valued quality; as 'Ana told me, "Children who are submissive (*faka-ongo*) are pleasing to their parents."

Children's lives should be *mo'ui fakaongoongo* (a life of waiting for instructions), and they should carry out orders unquestioningly. *Talangofua* (obedience) literally means "easy to tell." On one occasion I went for a long and arduous hike into the hills of 'Eua, accompanied by 'Ana and her husband and their six-year-old niece, Tupou. After the day's walk we returned home exhausted, but little Tupou was still given orders to fetch and carry and help with food preparation. Tupou was obedient, but she soon was clearly fed up, and a couple of times when out of earshot she said, "Do it yourself!" then, muttering *"Fakahela!"* (tiring), went to do as she'd been told. On the other hand, when children do tasks they have *not* been told to do they may be accused of being *fie poto*. When five-year-old Elenoa brought in the family washing by herself, her aunt sharply rebuked her for being *fie poto*. When other household members came home later in the day, she told them all what had happened, shaming Elenoa even further.

Obedience, even more than *'ofa* and respect, is regarded as *fatongia* (duty, obligation). *Fatongia* was formerly used to describe the enforced labor of commoners for chiefs (Lātūkefu 1974, 173), but it has a much wider meaning today and is used in many contexts to indicate correct behavior.[15] *Fatongia* specifically refers to the duties involved in social relations, particularly the provision of services and food to higher-status people and *kāinga* members.[16] A related term, *kavenga*, refers to the responsibilities and burdens experienced by the individual or family, such as getting together enough money to pay school fees. Ideally, *fatongia* is seen as reciprocal, so those of higher status also have obligations to those of lower status. This ideology of reciprocal obligation represents "high" and "low" people (such as chiefs and commoners, parents and children) as upholding an ideal of mutual dependency, sacrifice, and service, motivated by warm emotion and loyalty (Biersack 1990a, 1990c, 49–50; Lātūkefu 1974, 32).[17] It is seen as a counterbalance to the unchallengeable authority and unquestioning subservience that otherwise characterize status relations. When Tonga's laws were encoded during the nineteenth century, however, the ideology of reciprocal *fatongia* was not supported by legislation concerning the role of the chiefs. "[W]hile the powers of the highest chiefs were spelled out and made enforceable, their obligations as chiefs could not be enforced" (Powles 1990, 145). Despite the abolition of commoners' *fatongia* in the 1862 Code of Laws (Lātūkefu 1974, 247) and the restraint of chiefly powers and privileges by the constitution, considerable chiefly demands upon commoners continue to the present day.

Children's *fatongia* to their parents (and other family members) continues throughout their lives, and even adult offspring should ideally obey their parents' wishes. The Wesleyan missionaries strongly supported the expectation of obedience to parents. One missionary reported that King Tupou asked them "whether it was the duty of children to consult their parents when they wished to be married; of course we told him it was the duty of children to obey their parents 'in all things in the Lord' " (Rev. P. Turner 1831, 106; cited in Cummins 1972, 98). Obedience to parents is of course only one aspect of the obedience to authority expected both within the Tongan social hierarchy and within the Christian church. Cummins has shown that the early missionaries taught the Tongans that only those who were obedient would receive love, mercy, and forgiveness, while "death and destruction awaited those who were 'disobedient' " (1977, 241–242).

The ideology of obedience and *fatongia* is resisted by children to some extent and sometimes directly challenged by open defiance, which carries a strong threat of punishment. The most common form of resistance is apparent acquiescence—verbally agreeing with but not acting upon parents' wishes. More direct lying is also a means of avoiding parental control. Parents are more often obeyed, however, even when obeying involves life-altering actions such as leaving one's studies to find a job, going overseas, or getting married. Even as heads of their own household, with three children, Siale and Seini obeyed, albeit reluctantly, Seini's mother's request that they move to Australia to be near her. Any anger or resentment that is felt in such circumstances is seldom openly expressed because compliance is simply a matter of *fatongia*.

Responses of teenagers to the question "Are there things you have to do that you don't like?" revealed an ambivalent attitude toward obedience. Of 227 respondents, 61 (26.9 percent) answered "no" and added comments such as "I like the things I must do" and "I learned to be interested in whatever work I'm given." Others averred that they could choose whatever they did (an answer that will be discussed in relation to independence). Of those who answered "yes," 48 gave no further explanation despite instructions to give reasons.[18] Of the rest, only 4 (all female) specifically mentioned obedience, but a further 60 listed various types of household chores. Other activities listed as disliked included doing schoolwork, going to church, staying at home as punishment, sharing, and helping others. The comments that accompanied these listed activities were particularly interesting. Many explained that they did not like whatever they had listed because they were too lazy, too weak, too stupid, and so on. Others added that although they did not enjoy something, they had to be obedient and do what they were told. Having admitted their dislike for various things they had to do, these teenagers were clearly anxious to appear to be "good" in another sense and to accept the blame for their negative feelings.

The ambivalence toward obedience expressed in the students' responses is experienced more generally. Commoners also have an ambivalent attitude toward the obedience expected of them by chiefs, as expressed in the saying *Ngulungulu fei 'umu* (One growls in doing the underground oven but still does it) (Kolo 1990, 3). That is, commoners resent having to provide goods and services to chiefs but nevertheless do so.

Another interesting group of responses to my question about things teenagers did not like doing were twenty-two who misunderstood the question.[19]

These respondents listed things they do that they feel are wrong, such as stealing, smoking, swearing, and being cheeky. Several of these answers indicated concern with others pressuring them to do wrong: "When my boyfriend older than me ask me for drinking beer and smoke but I do not like to do something wrong"; "When someone told me to take something from other homes or other place but I don't like it"; "Yes, I have to do is steal but I don't like it." These answers were given in English and were all from boys, for whom peer pressure is particularly strong within their "gangs." Teenage boys and unmarried men in their early twenties are the most frequently and publicly "badly behaved" of any age group—certainly far more so than their female peers. A number of the young men in Holonga were often in trouble with their families for drinking and fighting, and a few eventually left home and moved into town, seeking greater independence.

Two other questions were asked to discern the ways in which adolescents feel their behavior is restricted and why they often conform with these restrictions. The students were asked, "Are there any things you would like to do but don't do because they are wrong?" and then "Why don't you do them?" Of 232 repondents to the first question, 29 (12.6 percent) answered "no." This does not necessarily indicate that all of these respondents have no desire to do wrong, as many added comments such as, "I just do it" and "I do what I like." Such comments seem to relate again to the value of independence, and of *fa'iteliha*, doing as one chooses, discussed below. Of those who gave affirmative answers, 68 did not elaborate. The other affirmative responses fall into two main categories: first, "modern" forms of recreation such as smoking, drinking, watching videos, and going to dance clubs (a total of 43 responses: 21 female and 22 male). The second category is of activities that are seen as more traditionally restricted: disobedience, rudeness, swearing, dishonesty, going out without permission, and being violent to peers (total of 92 responses: 60 female and 32 male). Table 5 shows the reasons these students gave for not doing the many things they identified as wrong.

The teenagers' responses showed a broader grasp of the sanctions against wrong behavior than younger children would possess—that actions may be dangerous or against the law, for example. The most frequent responses are those that are learned first and clearly continue to provide the most powerful motivations for conformity. Children are taught from a very early age that certain behavior is *kovi* (bad) or *hala* (wrong), and the primary sanction against such behavior is physical punishment. It is only as children get older, at about the time they start school, that they are explicitly taught that it is "against God" or "against *anga fakatonga*."

Obedience is regarded as an expression of *'ofa*, and more generally as a

Table 5: Reasons for Conforming

	FEMALE (TOTAL RESPONDENTS = 152)	MALE (TOTAL RESPONDENTS = 92)	TOTAL (TOTAL RESPONDENTS = 244)	%
Is bad or wrong	54	31	85	34.8
Parents would punish	37	16	53	21.7
Against bible or God	7	12	19	7.8
Obedience to parents	12	5	17	6.9
Is dangerous or harmful	9	8	17	6.9
Not old enough	9	5	14	5.7
Against the law	4	9	13	5.3
For family's sake	7	4	11	4.5
Would cause trouble	4	1	5	2.0
Would make me look bad	4	0	4	1.6
Against Tongan custom	3	1	4	1.6
Would feel ashamed	2	0	2	0.8

crucial element of *anga totonu* (correct nature and behavior). The strong cultural emphasis on the dependence of children on adults, especially parents, for the satisfaction of their needs and for moral guidance has as its corollary a stress on the need for obedience. *Tu'a* children are also provided with clear models of deferential and submissive behavior by their older siblings and adult kin within the context of these relatives' interactions with persons of higher rank or status.

In their discussion of the role of obedience in child socialization, Whiting and Edwards suggest that obedience does not always entail passive compliance, but may involve children becoming "empathic and responsible assistants who can work with their mothers [or others] in a choreography of smooth co-operation" (1988, 268). There are many contexts in which Tongan children's behavior can be interpreted in this way, especially older children's and teenagers', and it would be wrong to imply that Tongan children are passively compliant, whether out of fear or unthinking acceptance of the values and behavior associated with *'ofa.* As Whiting and Edwards point out, however, even obedience that is a form of cooperative behavior does not allow "much opportunity to suggest new strategies or to renegotiate the goal" (149). To do so, or to show initiative by performing tasks unasked, is to risk accusations of being *fie poto*.

FREEDOM/INDEPENDENCE: *TAU'ATĀINA*

Unlike the cluster of values described above—*'ofa*, respect, and obedience, and related values such as *fatongia*—*tau'atāina* is not elaborated to children as a positive value or a model of appropriate behavior. *Tau'atāina* is regarded with ambivalence, and children are most likely to be instructed that it is negatively valued. However, they soon comprehend that there are ways in which it is positively valued as well.

The most common translations of *tau'atāina* are "freedom" and "independence." In the 1862 declaration of emancipation, the Code of Laws stated that "all people are to all intents and purposes set at liberty from serfdom, and all vassalage" (Article 34, section 2; in Lātūkefu 1974, 247). This was followed by the 1875 constitution, which declared "the people of Tonga [shall] be for ever free" (Lātūkefu 1974, 252). The term *tau'atāina*, thought to be a neologism of this period (Biersack 1990b),[20] is used for both liberty and freedom. Hills has pointed out that in Tonga's constitution *tau'atāina* is used variously to mean freedom, liberty, rights, "and perhaps 'independence' in a political sense" (1991b, 11–12).

Biersack has argued that in a political sense *tau'atāina* implied freedom from chiefly control and the introduction of democratic values, as well as freedom from foreign control, or national independence (1990b). She has shown that the 1875 constitution, while espousing these freedoms, in fact reasserted the traditional authority structure and upheld the king's absolute power. Nevertheless, *tau'atāina* continues to be used, in some contexts, as a theme of resistance to chiefly authority and the obligations and duties this implies. In Holonga, which is on a government estate, some people commented that they were more *tau'atāina* than people in neighboring villages, who lived on nobles' estates and were frequently expected to provide them with goods and services. *Tau'atāina* is also used by individuals as an expression of resistance, as when Sālote, who at twenty-one was still dominated and controlled by her adoptive mother (her *mehekitanga*), talked of going overseas to work in order to be *tau'atāina*.

The concept of *tau'atāina* is closely associated with that of *fa'iteliha* (pleasing oneself). Decktor Korn claims that "Tongans perceive their society as one in which there are few prescriptions or prohibitions, where people have alternatives in ordering their lives, and where individuals have considerable autonomy in exercising their options" (1977, 2). Tongans do, indeed, often refer to their personal freedom, and to giving others freedom. The teenagers mentioned previously, who denied disliking anything they had to do, claimed they were free to choose: "I do what I like"; "Everything I want to do I do it."

On the other hand, independence of action and thought is strongly discouraged from an early age, as when five-year-old Elenoa was scolded for bringing the washing in on her own initiative.[21] On another occasion, at a beach picnic near a small resort, some boys from our party wandered off and were eventually found playing billiards in the resort's games room. As one mother scolded her son, she said angrily, "*Tuku ho'o fa'iteliha!*" (stop pleasing yourself). Children are discouraged from acting on their own initiative and from being curious or critical, as well as being taught to be unquestioningly obedient. *Fa'iteliha* and *tau'atāina* are particularly disvalued by many adults when they imply a lack of parental control and the weakening of tradition that many associate with modernization.

Tau'atāina can mean freedom from restrictions and domination, and such autonomy appears to be directly opposed to cultural values such as obedience and obligation. However, some Tongans who discussed this with me did not regard culturally and socially derived restrictions on people's behavior as precluding this form of independence. Siale's older brother, Soane, who had studied overseas, observed that "a lot of people are not aware of the restrictions they have until or unless they face them." Within those restrictions, he claimed, Tongans "can do anything they like." It is in this sense of personal autonomy that *tau'atāina* is especially valued. Yet the emphasis Tongans place on independence, both politically and socially, still appears to contradict the equally strong emphasis placed on social hierarchy and its related values. The high cultural value of independence can seem paradoxical when so many factors operate to encourage the dependence of certain kin on others (especially children on parents) and interdependence between kin.

At the level of society as a whole, the apparent contradictions make some sense if *tau'atāina* is defined as national independence. A young woman's comments in a "People's Opinion" column of a Tongan newspaper exemplify the way in which such independence and the maintenance of the social hierarchy are reconciled by some Tongans. Speaking against the need for political reform in Tonga, she said, "The King is the ruler and has the final word, because he was ordained by God to lead us. He is the only one who loves the people the best, and will do what is right for them. We should be happy with our Monarchy-Government because we are free and have what we need" (*Times of Tonga* 1991, 4). Her argument is that the continuing freedom of Tongans as a nation is dependent upon maintaining the monarchy and the associated hierarchical social order.

At the level of individuals the apparent contradictions of independence and hierarchy are more difficult to resolve. Borofsky has suggested that throughout Polynesia, cultures have dual "ways of knowing": "On the one hand, a hierarchical tendency emphasizes subordination to authority and imitation of it. On the other, a more egalitarian tendency stresses independence and personal experience" (1987, 120). In Pukapuka, he observes, the egalitarian way of knowing dominates. In Tonga, the hierarchical tendency dominates, though both tendencies are clearly present. The Ritchies' analysis of the value of independence in Polynesia also acknowledges these dual tendencies. "Polynesians admire individuals who express a strong sense of independence while acknowledging community consensus. . . . [I]ndependence is a highly valued attribute. It contrasts with, tempers, and balances an emphasis on community goals and processes" (Ritchie and Ritchie 1989, 107, 131). They argue that socialization in Polynesia teaches children "that individuality should always be seen against a collective background, that independence should never be expressed without acknowledging dependence" (1979, 58).

Hierarchical and egalitarian values can thus be seen as complementary, rather than opposed. They may be invoked simultaneously as well as in separate contexts. This was made clear to me during a sermon on tau'atāina that I heard while I was in Tonga, in which the minister explained that tau'atāina can only be achieved through fatongia to God, country, and family (see Williksen-Bakker 1990, 244 on the Fijian notion of freedom through duty). Freedom in this sense is said to come through obedience, which is tau'atāina faka-Kalisitiane (Christian freedom). After quoting a priest who argues that "individual liberty and rights are not incompatible with fatongia towards the community," Van der Grijp claims that the speaker is influenced "by Western ideas of liberty and individuality" and that "two basically incompatible notions of liberty are confused in the speaker's head" (1993, 177 and 177n13). Yet this "confusion" is not found only in those with Western-style educations and, more important, is not perceived as a contradiction by those who uphold the idea that freedom is interrelated with hierarchical values such as obedience and obligation.

In the context of a process of socialization that ideally engenders submissiveness, obedience, and interdependence, the concepts of tau'atāina and fa'iteliha can be seen to foster both "interpersonal autonomy" and "intrapsychic autonomy" (see Ewing 1991). The significant restraints on people's behavior resulting from the complex rank and status hierarchies that permeate their lives may be made less onerous by a belief in independence and the freedom to please oneself. The ideals of independence and freedom seem linked to notions of individualism and autonomy, and maintaining them in the face of interpersonal ties and obligations appears possible. Here, the concept of *loto* as the site of subjectivity and individualism is important. If one's *loto* is believed to be directing one's behavior then that behavior can be seen as chosen rather than imposed, allowing for conformity without a feeling of oppression. Of course, this is an ideal state, often not achieved in practice, hence the resentment, ambivalence, and resistance to authority that frequently occur.

The state of *loto lelei*, in which one is calm and agreeable, is itself seen as a form of *tauʻatāina*. Here the term is used in the sense of freedom from unpleasant or negatively valued emotions, a state in which one is in control and at peace. A teenage boy explained the importance of apologizing to parents after incidents of punishment: "If we feel sorry to our parents we will be free." In the latter sense, freedom may imply a release from (or avoidance of) negative emotion, clearing the mind and heart to restore (or maintain) *loto lelei*.

Many Tongans seem to be able to shift constantly among three clusters of self-representations: those marked by qualities associated with low status, such as humility and obedience; those associated with authoritativeness, punitiveness, and other high-status characteristics; and those involving assertions of autonomy and independence. Each form of self-representation is acquired through the active process of socialization, as are the sets of affective states that individuals experience: the "self" that may or may not be congruent with the "self-representation."

Shore, in his analysis of human ambivalence in relation to moral values, has pointed out that behavior should not be treated "as if it proceeds from a simple activation of cultural values rather than from the problematical and always partial resolution of dilemmas" (1990, 172). He adds: "In normal circumstances, cultural systems *partly* resolve such dilemmas for us by reducing ambiguity, rendering certain choices cognitively more salient and emotionally more acceptable than others" (176; emphasis in original). In Tonga, the importance of context for determining appropriate values and behavior is a crucial means for reducing ambiguity. Context is also the basis for shifts in self-representation, and such shifts are another means of dealing with conflicting values. Ewing's observation that "individuals have a remarkable capacity to maintain an experience of wholeness in the face of radical contradications, by keeping only one frame of reference in mind at any particular moment" (1990, 274) is certainly apt in Tonga. The need to use this capacity is growing as many Tongans negotiate not only apparently contradictory values but also different cultural positions. For example, Gordon has shown that Tongan Mormons can observe Mormon standards of behavior in one context, and Tongan standards in another (1990, 221).

Sometimes contradictions and dilemmas are not so readily resolved and may lead to anxiety and confusion. In the context of cultural change, apparently irreconcilable values identified as "old" and "new" may become a source of internal conflict for individuals and of dissent between different social groups. In Tonga, as the balance between hierarchical and egalitarian values shifts, such conflict and dissent are likely to become increasingly apparent and problematic. One of the cultural arenas within which change may create considerable conflict is that of gender relations.

GENDER DIFFERENCES

Gender was one of the most important distinctions in the precontact Tongan social order. James argues that gender differences were "at the very core of the hierarchical order and the politics that were its stuff of life" (James 1987, 2). A notable feature of the old order was that chiefly women wielded "legitimate secular and spiritual influence and power" and were "not confined by sex-specific, restrictive *tapu*" (Ralston 1990a, 111, 117).

Gender roles, and the ways in which gender, kinship, and status interact, have been transformed, particularly through the influence of the Christian missionaries.[22] James has claimed that gender differences are now important mainly in the domestic and ceremonial spheres (1987, 2). However, gender remains a crucial element in the construction of self for Tongans. A survey of Tongans' "self-views" found that gender was the most frequently cited component of identity, followed by religious identity and occupational identity—which, as will be shown below, is often highly gendered (Helu 1983). Helu comments that these elements of identity are "the *most highly esteemed* departments of our culture. They are also the *most frequently discussed* and *most intensely* advertised (through *indoctrination*). It would be rare, indeed, to find a social situation, private or public, where these values are not openly discussed, promoted, praised, advertised or otherwise activated" (1983, 53; emphasis in original). As in Hawai'i, gender differentiation affects all aspects of life (Linnekin 1990a, 231), and many of the changes in Tonga today are perceived in terms of a dissolution or transformation of gender differences.

When high school students were asked the question "In what ways do you think it is different for boys and for girls growing up in Tonga?" the majority of their responses, summarized in table 6, fell into the categories of work and appearance, with the remainder indicating aspects of behavior and "nature."

Ideas about the sexual division of labor are clearly the most salient to notions of gender difference for these adolescents. As will be shown in the

Table 6: Gender Differences

	FEMALE (TOTAL RESPONDENTS = 131)	MALE (TOTAL RESPONDENTS = 85)	TOTAL (TOTAL RESPONDENTS = 216)	%
Work	56	45	101	46.7
Appearance	30	20	50	23.1
General behavior	21	14	35	16.2
Girls				
Show more respect	19	9	28	12.9
Are better behaved	10	3	13	6.0
Are indulged	4	3	7	3.2
Are "higher"	1	3	4	1.8
Mature more quickly	3	0	3	1.4
Boys				
Sleep separately	6	1	7	3.2
Go (girls stay)	4	2	6	2.8
Are independent	4	0	4	1.8
Go out at night	1	2	3	1.4
Work harder	1	1	2	0.9

following chapter, female tasks are conceptualized as light, easy, clean, and requiring little or no mobility, whereas male tasks are the opposite: heavy, difficult, dirty, and requiring mobility. These distinctions are based on related gender differences, so that women's work is said to be "easy" because they are "weaker," and men's physical strength is matched by the arduous nature of their work.

There is a symbolic association between femaleness and chiefliness in Tonga. The qualities associated with females—especially as sisters—are also those associated with *hou'eiki*: stasis, restraint, sanctity, superiority, dignity, and so on. Similarly, males and *tu'a* are defined by qualities of mobility, lack of restraint, inferiority, and the like. Spatially, the idiom is that females and chiefs are associated with the inside, the center, whereas males and common-ers are associated with the outside, the periphery. Another dimension that can be added to all of these distinctions is the association of adulthood or maturity with the qualities ascribed to femaleness and chiefliness and child-hood with the qualities of maleness and nonchiefliness (this will be discussed further in chapter 9). All of these distinctions are formally expressed in cere-monies such as the *taumafa kava* ceremony (see Bott 1972).

The symbolic association between female and chief is unstable, however, and is therefore open to manipulation by both males and females. One Ton-gan woman, a self-described "radical feminist" living in Australia, argued that this association is a "male construct" that keeps women subservient. As wives, women are *tu'a* and therefore low in status and lacking authority, but they are also expected to exhibit the *'eiki* attributes of stasis and restraint. It is only as sisters that women also have access to the authority associated with chiefliness, and the contexts in which it can be asserted are limited. The patriarchal ideology that has become increasingly predominant in Tonga has served to diminish sisters' rights and powers, although they have remained significant (compare Gailey 1980, 1981, 1987b). Males, who in many respects have *tu'a* characteristics, notably in their outdoor, "dirty" work, are *'eiki* as husbands and fathers and thus wield considerable authority within the familiy. Historically, most titled chiefs have been male, and certain chiefly values said to have originated in the precontact period, such as *to'a* (courage), are strongly associated with masculinity. An important exception to this pattern is Queen Sālote Tupou III, who for Tongans embodied the ideal qualities of chief, adult, and female.

Gender differences are generalized as *anga fakafefine* and *anga fakatangata* (female and male *anga*). To some extent this aspect of a person's *anga* is seen as an innate disposition in the unsocialized child, but much more important to Tongan theories of development is the need for gender-appropriate *anga* to be developed through socialization. In some cases, it is possible for a person's innate gender characteristics to be "wrong" and unalterable despite all attempts to correct them, as in the case of *fakaleitī*, discussed below.

Children's gender socialization begins at birth; even during their first year their sex affects the way they are treated in a number of ways. Boys are often encouraged to be mobile earlier than girls and are also handled and addressed more roughly. These differences are expressed in the following comment by Ngata, father of one-year-old Paula:

> To boys you say, "You stand up and walk, don't fall!" and the girl, you don't. You handle them very delicately. You know, you don't force them to walk . . . when the time comes for them to walk they will walk themselves, but the boys, the mother will . . . you know, be a bit rough with them. . . . You can give a few smacks to the boys, you know, when they cry a lot, you just give a few smacks, to maybe treat them as boys, not to be sissy and cry.

Describing the way in which young boys are addressed Ngata said, "Certain names are called to boys only; you talk a certain language to boys; they don't even understand it, I think, but you talk to them in a masculine language."

Children are dressed differently, even as babies, and it is usually only boys who are allowed to play without clothes. When babies are dressed up to go out, little girls are invariably dressed in frilly dresses, stockings, and ribbons, and little boys in suits or shirts and *tupenu* (a tailored wrap-around garment worn by males). Children are taught Tongan dances from an early age, and the kinds of movements and costumes involved are very different for males and females. Girls learn delicate movements of the hands, arms, and head and make small, almost imperceptible movements with their feet, whereas boys learn to clap, slap their bodies, and stamp their feet.

Throughout childhood, behavior is differentiated by the general notion that "boys go, girls stay." Boys are associated with the outdoors and are seen as *tauʻatāina*; girls' place is indoors and girls' behavior is more restricted. Boys' work involves going to "the bush" (agricultural land) or the sea; girls stay and work at home. A term often used in reference to proper female behavior is *nofo maʻu*. This can mean "sit still" (Churchward 1959, 351) but is also used in its broader sense of staying or remaining fixed in one place.[23] Lupe, our next-door neighbor in Holonga, said, "Men are more independent than women. Women stay put (*nofo maʻu*), and are submissive (*anga nofo*), but men are independent, if they want to go some place at night or during the day, anytime. Women are taught by their parents to stay at home." The relationship between "staying" and proper behavior is expressed in the term *anga nofo*, which means submissive but literally translates as "habitually staying."[24]

Boys are allowed to be freer than girls in several ways. They are given more freedom to wander away from home—at first to play at neighboring homes and by the age of seven or eight to wander much further afield with groups of friends. Older boys also have a considerable amount of freedom within the huts they often use for sleeping and socializing, where they are without adult supervision. Sometimes groups of boys, usually older boys in their mid- to late teens, live with one or more older men (often unmarried). One group, for example, lived with a man in his midtwenties who was teaching them the karate he had learned while living overseas. In such cases the boys still have much more freedom than when living with their parents.

Ngata, who had spent many years in Fiji and Australia, argued that boys' freedom is limited and in any case is lost by later adolescence.

> The boys before they get married, they're not really *tauʻatāina*. They got to build something, they got to prepare the house for the family. If they look for a wife they got to do a few things which they're obliged to do and in fact they're not *tauʻatāina* at all. . . . When they were young they were pressed down, and when they grow up I think that's the time for them to express this freedom.

Ngata claimed that only after marriage, when the husband is able to go out and about while his wife stays at home, does a man feel free. While it is true that adolescent boys' freedom is often restricted by the demanding labor expected of them, most do not make any preparations for marriage in the way Ngata indicates, as most couples live with other family members at first (as did Ngata). Clearly, males have differing perceptions and experiences of their "independence" and "freedom"; perceptions notwithstanding, however, males generally have far more independence than do females.

Boys' association with the outdoors begins very early, as when baby boys are taken outside by older males and shown the animals and vegetation, whereas girls are generally kept indoors. Little boys can move easily between male and female spheres, now sitting inside with the women, then going outside to be with the men or teenage boys. Little girls can do this to some extent but are likely to be called away from the men. One evening in Holonga, Siale came home with a few bottles of beer and sat outside drinking. He encouraged his son, Tomasi (aged five), and my son, Paul (eight), to sit with him and allowed them to share a bottle of beer. They were being silly and acting up for his amusement. Siale's daughter, Elenoa (five), was inside the house and kept going to the doorway to watch. Each time she did, one of the women in the house called her to come and sit down, and finally she was pulled into a bedroom and told to go to sleep.

Boys become increasingly free to wander from home as they get older, but girls are watched all the more carefully. Most Tongan parents keep close tabs on their daughters' whereabouts and insist on a chaperone accompanying them when they go anywhere. This emphasis on girls staying at home is especially important at night. "We Tongan women stay at home at night or lose our honor (lāngilangi)," one teenager remarked. Restriction of girls' movements outside the home, perceived in terms of protecting their virginity and reputation, usually continues until they marry. Thus, when twenty-one-year-old Sālote went swimming with her friends at a public wharf one hot afternoon, her adoptive mother was extremely angry. She accused her daughter of trying to attract men and warned her she had been risking rape. In Holonga, when girls were sent to the store after dark they were never sent alone, even if their "chaperone" was a younger child. Even older, married women rarely walked about alone. The term often used to describe boys' wanderings, 'eve'eva pē (just strolling around), can also mean a boy spending time with a girl. When used in relation to girls' activities it has negative connotations and can even refer to a girl having premarital sex (Churchward 1959, 559). A derogatory term for an illegitimate child is tama 'eve'eva.

Boys' relative freedom also extends to their general behavior, and boys are less strictly raised than girls. When I watched the twins in our Holonga households (first when they were three and then when they were five), it was clear that Tomasi was given far more leeway for naughtiness and silliness than his sister. Although Elenoa was actually more obedient and more timid around adults, she was scolded and punished more frequently. Tomasi was also more likely to be tolerated if he attempted to join in adult activities and generally received more attention and affection from the adults. Daughters are said to be treated more favorably (see below), but because parents expect them to be better behaved and place many restrictions on their behavior, they tend to be punished more often when they are young.

Girls are perceived as "better" than boys: they are easier to control, more obedient, properly behaved (*anga maau*), more dignified (*molumalu*), more polite, and so on. They are also said to grow up more quickly than boys, and in some respects this is verified in their earlier grasp of adult behavior. Even at the age of five, Elenoa was able to give the polite form of thanks when visitors brought food, and she was generally responsible and nurturant with her baby sister. Females' work and bodies are seen as physically clean, and this is associated with their ideally "clean" moral state. Both physical and moral cleanliness are referred to as *ma'a*. Another term sometimes used to describe girls is *melie*, "sweet." Girls are also seen as "higher" (*mā'olunga*) than boys, and as sisters they do outrank their brothers, who should obey and pay attention to them. The restrictions on girls' behavior are said to be balanced by their being treated with special care (*fakalekesi*) and with indulgence and favoritism (*fakapelepele'i*). Though their behavior is closely supervised and they are more likely to be punished for inappropriate behavior than boys, adolescent girls do tend to be more indulged in a material sense. One young woman explained that she saw this as "compensation" for her lack of freedom.

In contrast to the dignity and restraint expected of girls, boys' behavior is in some contexts comparatively unrestrained, particularly during the *talavou* period. Marcus has described this as a liminal period, noting that adolescent boys' behavior "may appear wild and uncontrolled in contrast to the staidness of other aspects of Tongan life" (1978, 257).[25] Boys' cheeky and aggressive behavior is often given covert approval, and boys are handled less gently than girls. Play between young boys and youths or men is usually very physical and rough—wrestling, fighting, and so on.

This rough play between boys and older males often involves an element of sexual joking—grabbing roughly at boys' genitals or making jokes about their uncircumcised state. Other jokes about uncleanliness and scatalogical and sexual jokes are also very common. Boys are given more freedom to go naked as babies and toddlers, and people will touch or make joking reference to their genitals. On one occasion Saia, aged one, was dressed in shorts that

revealed his genitals when he sat down. His mother, Lusi, noticed and
laughed, and called her own mother's attention to this. Mele laughed and
called to him, "*Tuku ho'o anga kovi!*" (stop your bad behavior), then went
over to him and began to tickle his penis, pulling his shorts down and pat-
ting his bottom, laughing all the while, until Lusi put a diaper on him. On
other occasions Lusi also tickled his penis.

Sexual joking does occur with girls, but in a very different manner. Modesty is far more important for girls, even as babies, and sexual joking is
directed at shaming rather than tacit approval. Once when 'Ofa, at eleven
months, was walking along by holding onto a couch, her diaper slipped down
from under her dress. She stepped out of it and kept going, and her mother,
Seini, laughed and said " 'Ofa!" in a mock-reproving tone, then told her to
look at me, to remind her that a visitor was present. Seini gently pushed her
daughter's face around toward me, and several times flipped 'Ofa's dress up,
saying "*Palagu!*" (ugly). Then, continuing to talk to me, Seini lifted 'Ofa up
to sit on the couch beside her. Suddenly she realized that 'Ofa had moved
around and was facing me, with her legs apart, and she exclaimed and pulled
'Ofa's dress down to cover her, saying again "*Palagu!*"

In precontact Tonga children were apparently left unclothed ("in a state
of nature" [Lawry 1850, 111]), but the missionaries encouraged the wearing
of tapa or cloth around the waist except when children were in their own
homes. Spillius claimed in the 1950s that from the time they began to walk
until they went to school many children wore clothes only when there were
visitors in the house or when they went to church (1958, 61). Today, girls are
rarely allowed to go naked, and even little boys are usually dressed in at least
a pair of shorts. Care is taken to keep little girls covered in front of male
household members and anyone from outside the household. Whereas little
boys will sometimes purposely display their genitals as part of their play, girls
are very careful to remain modest. Even when playing energetic games girls
tend to remain aware of the need for modesty, holding their dresses down
with one hand. Much as she tried, Elenoa was never able to master a hand-
stand because she always had one hand holding her dress in place.

Exploration of the genitals is strongly discouraged, especially for girls:

> As the child grows up, she soon realises that her genital area is forbidden—
> must not be exposed nor touched in the presence of others. . . . As soon as a
> child is seen with her hands in this forbidden area, she is soundly smacked
> and threatened with worse punishment if she is caught doing it again. . . .
> [T]he Tongan woman emerges confused, ignorant and very shy about this
> important part of her anatomy, her genital system. (Ikahihifo and Panuve
> 1983, 40)[26]

Adolescent girls are also taught to be modest about their breasts, although older women do sometimes leave their breasts uncovered without embarrassment. In pre-Christian Tonga women did not cover their breasts unless they were pregnant or lactating, but the 1850 Code of Laws made clothing compulsory (Article 41, in Lātūkefu 1974, 237). Knee-length, sleeved dresses, with ankle-length skirts (*vala*) underneath, became the most common dress for women. Standards of modesty are relaxing gradually; at the beginning of the 1980s very few females wore trousers, but today many wear jeans, other long pants, and even shorts.

Earlier observers have commented that Tongan children learn "the facts of life" at an early age, because the one-room houses afforded little privacy (Lovett 1958, 35; Spillius 1958, 62). Whether or not this was so, most modern houses have separate bedrooms, and children are unlikely to observe sexual behavior. Even when household members sleep in one room, or children sleep in the parents' room, great care is taken to preserve modesty in dressing and undressing and in sexual activity. Tongan children rarely see their parents naked, but many now see naked bodies and some sexual behavior on videos. I have on occasion seen such scenes fast-forwarded when children are watching, and once I heard a woman mutter that we should watch a karate movie instead, but there is generally no attempt to prevent children from watching these videos, nor is any explanation given to them about what they are seeing.

FEMININITY

Ideally feminine behavior in Tonga requires the qualities described above: restraint, dignity, politeness, and so on. All these qualities are regarded as *anga lelei*, and they are revealed in a girl's general demeanor and specific aspects of her behavior. For example, girls are taught to sit with their legs to one side (*fāite*), rather than cross-legged (*fakta'ane*) in the male way, for modesty and to protect the skin on their ankle bones from becoming rough. They are also taught not to lean on mats with their elbows, again to keep their skin soft. Older women frequently reminded me how to sit nicely, and I have also heard a Tongan man tell his *pālangi* partner to "sit like a lady."

Physical appearance is a very important aspect of femininity in Tonga, although it is not clear to what extent the ideals of feminine beauty were formerly shared between *'eiki* and *tu'a*. Gifford lists a number of ways in which the beauty of chiefly girls was enhanced, such as rubbing their bodies with masticated *tuitui* (candlenut) to cleanse them, then with scented oil and turmeric; keeping their skin smooth and soft by having them sit on cushions of mats and tapa; and having them wear a corset of tapa to flatten

their stomachs (1971b, 129–130). Both men and women wore a range of
hair styles to enhance their appearance, and there are Tongan aesthetic
ideals of physical beauty for all parts of the face and body (Bott n.d., 30–31;
Bain 1967, 80; Beaglehole and Beaglehole 1941b, 85). Nowadays both male
and female Tongans wear imported clothing, jewelry, cosmetics, and per-
fume, as well as the more traditional beauty aids: Tongan oil and flowers.

Another important element of femininity is virginity. As Bernstein
states, "From a very early age the politics of maintaining a reputation for
chastity is a major focus for Tongan women" (1983, 190). According to
Herda, the emphasis on virginity was partly influenced by Samoan practices
such as tying unmarried girls' legs together when they slept and confirming
the virginity of a bride-to-be (1988, 66). Such practices may have been
adopted only for chiefly girls in Tonga, and one early European observer
claimed that single women slept in groups in large huts and freely received
male visitors for intercourse (Waldegrave 1834, 194).[27] Christianity was also
influential, and today virginity is an important ideal for all unmarried
women. A woman who is believed to be promiscuous has significantly
reduced prospects for marriage. For men the opposite standard applies: as one
man put it, young men "hop from flower to flower . . . it's an addition to their
manhood."

Despite virginity's importance, many adolescent girls are keen to appear
sexually attractive, taking pains with their appearance, wearing fashionable
clothes, and flirting with boys to whom they are attracted. Before a dance
girls spend a lot of time on their makeup, hair style, and clothes, and at the
dances are sometimes what the boys call "sexy" in their movements. I was
surprised at just how uninhibited some girls were when I went with Silia to a
fakasosiale (social night) for several Catholic colleges. After a series of
marches, in which the students marched forward in rows and bowed to the
teachers on the dais, there was a demure waltzing competition. Then there
was a disco competition, and the sudden burst of energy and sexuality was
astonishing. Silia, whom I knew as a quiet and fairly shy member of our
household, did a theatrical dance in which her partner danced away from
her, she followed, tapped him on the shoulder, and beckoned sexily to him,
then he danced toward her and pretended to slap her face. Another couple
did a hip-grinding and body-rubbing dance that was explicitly sexual, as the
nuns and teachers looked on, smiling blandly. The evening ended with a girl
performing a graceful *tau'olunga*, a more traditional means for young women
to display their beauty and attractiveness, and some of the boys responded by
enthusiastically dancing behind her.

When people talk of change in Tonga they often comment that girls are
becoming "like boys": they cut their hair short, wear trousers, drink, smoke,

and go out at night. However, the girls I talked to were not self-consciously attempting to emulate male behavior; they wanted to be "like *pālangi* girls." Some girls are also enjoying more freedom, so that groups of girls can be seen walking around town together even in the evenings, flirting and exchanging banter with groups of boys. Despite these changes, "the dominant images of Tongan women are still beauty, virginity, and fertility" (James 1994, 64). Because females' roles have been able to expand to encompass new roles, they have had much more continuity than have males' roles.

One of the most important aspects of continuity is women's production of *koloa*. As they grow up, young girls are constantly surrounded by this female role and evidence of its significance: the older women of the house doing *tutu*, making dyes, staining and painting the tapa to make *ngatu*, and weaving mats; the exchange of *koloa* at every important event; the yearly village meetings to display women's products, during which huge areas of ground (such as the village sports oval) are covered with *koloa*; and the piles of mats and *ngatu* stored in bedrooms.

MASCULINITY

The fact that early accounts of Tonga focused almost entirely on men means there is ample evidence of masculinity's association with skill in warfare, agriculture, fishing, and ocean voyaging, as well as athletic sports, sexual prowess, and virility. As James has noted, "notions of Tongan manhood" have been profoundly affected by a range of factors such as the cessation of warfare, the devaluation of agricutural skills, and "the abandonment of ancient ceremonies such as the *'inasi* or offering of the 'first fruits' annually to the Tu'i Tonga." She suggests that "the old songs and dances still performed in celebration of these old pursuits may only serve to point up the comparison invidiously with their present routines" (1983, 241).

Tongan songs and dances, myths and legends, may not reflect men's contemporary pursuits, but they do serve to perpetuate to some extent the ideals of masculinity with which they were associated. Masculinity is still defined in terms of strength, invincibility, and courage. One man explained that the old stories of Tongans going to Samoa and Fiji and winning battles give a "psychological lift" to men today. There has also been some transformation of old notions of manhood in modern contexts; for example, the *fautasi* (canoe) racing supported by the king has become very popular, although females also participate in some races. Military clothing is popular for young Tongan males, and heroes of the late 1980s included Rambo, Chuck Norris, and Sitiveni Rabuka of Fiji. Something of a parallel can also be drawn between the boys who formerly followed war parties to train in warfare (Martin 1981, 82; Orange 1840, 176) and the boys who train in karate from older men or who hang around village dance halls watching, and sometimes imitating, the fights between drunken young men. Another aspect of continuity is that manhood is still symbolized by circumcision, and to a lesser extent tattooing, as discussed below.

Since the land reforms of the constitution, the association of masculinity with agricultural skill has been transformed into an association with the land itself. "The land at the very least has served as the ideological basis of male social status and respectability in the new order" (Marcus 1977, 224). However, with increasing land shortages this aspect of masculinity is being seriously eroded for many young Tongans.

Masculinity in Tonga is often defined in terms of not being feminine, and the presence of fakaleitī ("like a lady," i.e., male effeminates, also known as fakafāfine) has been interpreted as providing a model of what not to be as a man (see Cowling 1990c, 195 and Levy 1973, 472–473 for the Tahitian mahu; Schoeffel 1979, 110–112 and Shore 1981, 208–210 for the Samoan fa'afefine). James, however, has rejected this functionalist analysis, arguing that "the phenomenon of the fakaleitī" can be explained in terms of what she calls "the crisis in Tongan men's perceptions of their role and gender identification" (1983, 240). Her argument is similar in some respects to that of Levy for Tahitian males, who he claims have "generalized problems of masculine sexual differentiation . . . a relative lack of differentiation of sex-role orientations and behavior, and special problems for boys in establishing separate masculine identities, and for men in keeping them" (1969c, 42). A main contributing factor to these problems, he suggests, is fathers' lack of input into socialization. In Tonga migration often causes the absence of fathers and other male relatives, which James says "contributes to a growing number of maladjusted and insecure Tongan males." James argues that "in a situation of role contradiction and role confusion for men, more boys are increasingly uncertain of their success within the strongly competitive arena of Tongan masculinity. For the male effeminate, fakaleitī status may provide a viable alternative of identity and survival in the female domain" (1994a, 65).

Morton has claimed that male pele (favorites) are sometimes dressed and groomed as females and otherwise treated as females (1972, 47). As Cowling points out, this is unlikely given that most Tongans only reluctantly accept that a boy is a fakaleitī; she argues that concerted attempts are made to masculinize a boy who is acting "feminine" by assigning him male tasks and teasing and even punishing him (1990c, 188, 190). There appears to be a great deal of variation in the way in which different families react to boys behaving as fakaleitī. James has claimed that some Tongans believe that fakaleitī behavior is learned whereas others believe such boys are "born with certain propensities, which may be encouraged or discouraged" (1994a, 62). In either case, a family may decide to actively discourage a boy or to accept his inclination, and even where the means of discouragement are harsh there is a strong likelihood that the family will eventually accept the boy as a *fakaleitī* if he perseveres in his behavior. In families where boys' *fakaleitī* status is accepted, they are "brought up not quite as girls . . . but in a less harsh way than boys" (54).

Boys are encouraged, from babyhood, to "try to be a man and not a girl, not to be a woman!" as Ngata told me emphatically. *Fakaleitī* is used as a teasing term, as are various English slang terms for homosexuality, particularly when boys appear to be showing weakness. The term *fakaleitī* is increasingly being seen as synonymous with homosexuality and a "camp" lifestyle, a transformation often blamed on Western influences (James 1994a, 63). Ngata, speaking of his boyhood, stated, "It's a disgrace if my mother calls me a sissy, you know, a queer! If my peer group call me a queer I will try to fight it out! To get them back, to [make them] swallow their words." A lot of boys' peer group activity centers on challenging one another to prove their bravery and masculinity. Within the *talavou* gangs status rivalry is particularly evident in regard to courtship and personal skills (Marcus 1978, 256–259). Adolescent boys frequently engage in behavior for which they know they will be punished if caught, such as smoking, drinking, stealing, and petty vandalism, to impress their peers or to prove their loyalty to their "gang." Smoking and drinking alcohol, in particular, have become associated with masculinity.

The adolescent boys of Holonga, who in 1988 called themselves the RBP (Revenge of the Black Power) gang, were constantly vying with each other to prove their masculinity in one form or other, whether it was secret drinking sessions or enduring the pain of tattooing. The adult males with whom they seemed to identify most closely were the unmarried young men who had returned from working overseas, several of whom had been deported. These men, aged in their twenties, were unemployed and spent much of their time drinking alcohol or *kava*. Older villagers considered them a disruptive element.

By adolescence, and sometimes earlier, many boys spend a great deal of their time away from their families in the company of peers. As Cowling argues, this process "encourages the development of strong bonds between male peers and between male siblings, but also helps to confirm the assumption of a masculine heterosexual identity and behaviour" (1990c, 172), despite the common tendency of boys to experiment sexually with one another. Cowling also claims that boys experience "their expulsion from their family's centre" as a loss of family love and that they subsequently

develop a preoccupation with the need for physical affection (185). However, because all children are gradually shifted from their family's center from
the age of about two, in terms of moving to the periphery of adults' activities
and receiving less and less attention, boys' separation is less an "expulsion"
than an expected part of their progression toward manhood. It is true, however, that some boys are left to fend for themselves to the point of being
physically and emotionally neglected (James 1994a, 64). Others remain
closely involved with their families. Once again, there are many variables
that influence each boy's experience. For example, older boys in a female-
headed household, although expected to contribute a great deal of labor to
the household, are also awarded considerable authority within the family.
Such boys seem to take their responsibilities very seriously and are less frequently out and about with their peers.

Many young boys are eager to move into the boys' huts, to be associated
with the older boys, and to experience their comparative freedom. Even boys
who have their own bedrooms in their family home spend most of their time
away from home with their friends. Peer socialization and youth culture thus
have become primary sites for the development of masculine identity. What
is particularly interesting is that this identity is often self-consciously
modeled on youth cultures in Western nations, as perceived through migration experiences, videos, and the media. It contrasts with the Tongan
identity established in the context of the family and village, yet is not incompatible with it. The same youths seen enthusiastically perfoming a traditional dance in costumes of leaves and rattling seedpods, armed with wooden
clubs, might leave the dance ground to don jeans, baseball caps, and sunglasses and saunter back to their boys' huts to watch yet another American
video.

The development of Tongan forms of masculinity occurs through traditional dancing, as well as in everyday activities such as "male" tasks in the
home and plantation. It is also marked by circumcision, carried out when
boys begin to enter puberty. Formerly supercision (slitting of the foreskin)
was performed on groups of boys aged between twelve and sixteeen by a
male, usually a skilled elderly man, who was not brother or cousin to the
boys.[28] After six days the boys were given a feast and *koloa*. Unsupercised
males, according to Gifford, would be "forbidden to eat with the other members of the household, must not touch another's food, and would be spurned
by the girls" (1971b, 187). The Beagleholes, writing of the late 1930s,
claimed that an uncircumcised boy would "suffer shame for the rest of his life
as one abnormal and despised" (1941b, 84). Even today, uncircumcised
males are teased that they are unclean and still young boys.[29]

Today circumcision is carried out by medical officers at health clinics and hospitals, and scalpels have replaced bamboo slivers and shells as cutting implements. Despite an attempt to outlaw the operation in the nineteenth century (Lātūkefu 1974, 225), it retains its importance as a mark of manhood. As Soane explained, "From that they treat you like a man." Less ceremony is attached these days, although for the first son's circumcision a feast may be given. Ngata said, "I think it's getting a bit diluted now, but it used to be the first child of the family, a big feast is put up, a big meal, just for the immediate family, and they come around . . . just to mark the coming of manhood of their eldest son. Some families still put it on." Boys also tend to be circumcised alone nowadays, rather than in groups. Those who have just been circumcised are clearly proud of their new status and associate more and more with the older boys, the *talavou*.

This pride in being circumcised was evident in Viliami, the adopted son of Alisi. While I was staying in Alisi's household in Holonga in 1986, Viliami, then aged eleven, was circumcised at the nearest health clinic, at Muʻa. He was taken to the clinic by an uncle and an older cousin, and when he returned home he stayed in bed for several days recovering. Occasionally he would wrap himself in a sheet and come to sit in the living area, ostentatiously holding the sheet away from his lower body. He was given a lot of attention and special foods, and his behavior changed noticeably as he began to distance himself from the younger children of the household by trying to appear stern and dignified.

Less than three weeks after his circumcision Viliami underwent another, newer form of "initiation" into adolescence when he first attended Holy Communion. In many Catholic families the first communion is followed by a feast at which *kāinga* members give emotional speeches proclaiming the child's new status as a full member of the church and the importance of the first communion as a step toward adulthood. Viliami's natural sister, Losa (aged ten), who lived next door with their parents, had also attended the Holy Communion. The communion was held late at night, and the following day the two households held a large feast. Viliami and Losa, dressed in layers of mats and *ngatu* that had been brought by the guests, sat solemnly at the head of the long row of guests. The importance of this occasion was further emphasized by the keen interest of family members in viewing a video of the event again and again.

For Losa this would be the only formal recognition that she was moving toward adolescence and adulthood. There is evidence that some form of ceremony was formerly held, at least for *ʻeiki* girls, at menarche, and that girls had to observe certain *tapu* (Bott n.d., 27; Gifford 1971b, 180).[30] By the late 1930s, according to the Beagleholes, "there [was] no ceremony connected with a girl's first menstruation," although her mother would tell her it was *tapu* to cook, work, or wash clothes while menstruating and that her relationship of respect for and avoidance of her brother must begin (1941b, 83). In Tonga today, *tu'a* families hold no ceremony at girls' menarche, and the *tapu* mentioned by the Beagleholes are seldom observed. Menarche may be acknowledged within the immediate family. Ngata explained that "when young girls have their first period the family make a good meal and the father will say to the girl: 'Now, you know . . . you make any mistakes now . . . !' It's the time for giving information to the children." This information takes the form of a moral discourse, stressing *faka'apa'apa* and *fatongia*, and is also given to boys at the time of their circumcision.

In precontact Tonga supercision was followed by another symbol of manhood, *tā tatau*, tattooing from the hips to the thighs (Martin 1981, 459). Unlike the attempt to outlaw supercision, the attempt to outlaw tattooing in the nineteenth century (Lātūkefu 1974, 225) was successful, at least in part because the European missionaries were strongly opposed to this "heathen" practice. Some tattooing occurs today, but is most commonly the initials or emblem of the boy's high school. Some girls have tattoos, usually much smaller and often just the initials of their high school.[31] Tattooing had a revival in Holonga during my 1986 visit, when Siale's youngest brother, then sixteen, invented a tattooing gadget using a ball-point pen connected to wires and batteries encased in bamboo. Throughout the school holidays adolescent boys from the village endured the agony of this tattooing (and occasionally the subsequent infections), covering their thighs, chests, and arms with pictures copied from my son's *Masters of the Universe* coloring book.

Clearly, tattooing is no longer associated with any rite of passage. Such rites as do occur—circumcision, Holy Communion, acknowledgment of menarche, and the moral discourse and feasting that may accompany them—do not effect any sudden change in children's daily lives. After the event they go on much as before. They slowly move away from their younger playmates and into the older group, the expectations placed upon them gradually increase, and their acquisition of knowledge that will enable them to become *poto* continues.

Holonga as it fronts onto Hahake Road. From left to right are a boys' hut, an abandoned house, the town officer's house, and a small *fale koloa* (store).

The home of Siale and Seini in Holonga, 1988.

Side view of a typical modern home, with cement water tank, external shower and toilet, and a roofed cooking area.

'Ofa is shown the roasted pigs that will be eaten at the feast celebrating her first birthday. Holding her are her father's sister and Silia, the "aunt" living in 'Ofa's household, with neighborhood children.

'Ofa in her birthday dress before the feast, held by her mother's "sister."

Poor housing in the swampy area on the outskirts of Nuku'alofa, settled by immigrants from the outer islands.

The children of Holonga primary school, with their teachers and parents, march to the king's palace on School's Day. In the front row, second and fourth from the right, are the twins Elenoa and Tomasi.

Young girls in intricately made costumes dance at Kindergarten Day celebrations in Nuku'alofa. Female teachers and relatives clown behind them.

After their dance at Kindergarten Day, the little girls are adorned with money pinned to their hair and tucked into their costumes by onlookers during their performance; this is a common form of fund raising in Tonga.

Elenoa, aged five, dressed up for church.

Local boys play in the rain in the front yard of our Holonga house.

Women clown behind a dancer at a fund-raising event at a Catholic college. To the right of the dancer, a boy has been pulled from the audience by a "clown" who is trying to make him dance with her, and in the bottom right corner a woman clowns with the donations box.

CHAPTER 5

CHILDREN'S EVERYDAY LIVES:

SOCIALIZATION IN CONTEXT

The process of knowledge acquisition Tongans broadly characterize as becoming *poto* occurs in the context of children's everyday lives, in their interactions with kin, their work for the household, their formal education, and their play. This chapter examines these interrelated spheres of children's lives in relation to the knowledge about values and gender discussed in the previous chapter and also explores the wide range of other knowledge associated with these spheres, including the behavior appropriate to different kinship roles and the physical and social skills learned in the home and at the plantation, at school, and at play.

KINSHIP

There is a wealth of literature on Tongan kinship, particularly within ʻeiki lineages and in ritual contexts. However, "the relation of this kinship system to everyday life, patterns of household relations, or recurrent social dramas such as birth, marriage, and inheritance has not been subject to much systematic investigation" (Marcus 1979, 90). There has also been little investigation of the relationship between kinship "rules" and cultural values or of how these rules are learned and how they affect children's lives.

Children's experience of kinship is different in many ways from that of adults. For children, kin relations are largely a matter of behavioral differences—to some people they must be respectful and obedient and with others they can be more familiar. Children are only partial participants in the system of indirect reciprocity in which "goods and services go from ego and his siblings to his patrilateral relatives, while he extracts goods and services from his matrilateral relatives" (Kaeppler 1971a, 179). They are seldom able to engage in the manipulation of rights and obligations that is a feature of adults' relationships, at least until later adolescence when they are approaching adulthood themselves. Because they are not in a position either to demand services or to supply goods, children usually receive goods and give services. One of the earliest lessons children learn is to *kole*, make requests, particularly of their matrilateral relatives. When I first saw youths in town stopping passersby and asking for money I thought they were begging, but I discovered that the people they stopped were always kin (sometimes very distant kin) from whom it was acceptable for the boys to *kole* money, cigarettes, and other items.

The fact that children as a group are low status in relation to adults, by virtue of their age difference, means that the kinship rules they learn may not be applied in many contexts. Children are expected to show respect to *all* adults, and the freedom with which they can treat certain kin is only relative to the restraint characterizing other relationships. That children are nevertheless *'eiki* to some members of their *kāinga* is significant for their understanding of their personal status relative to others and to context.

As has become clear, the most important kin relations in modern Tonga are those within the nuclear family and between extended family members who reside in close proximity to one another. Morton has shown that the "conscious model of kinship reciprocity" does not reflect actual behavior because the model emphasizes the extended family. He shows that most exchanges of goods and children actually occur between parents and children or siblings, even when those nuclear family members have dispersed (1972, 115, 120; see Marcus 1974). The next most significant type of exchanges are therefore those between geographically close *kāinga* members.

The *kāinga* as a whole retains considerable emotional significance for Tongans. As has been shown, nuclear families often form households with *kāinga* members of the husband and/or wife, and adult relatives also visit one another's households for varying periods. In our household in Holonga in 1988–1989, Seini's mother, otherwise resident in Australia, and Seini's "sister" from 'Eua were long-term visitors. Siale's mother, who lived in Holonga, frequently stayed for several days at a time. Another of Seini's "sisters" (MMBDD) from a neighboring village, was also a frequent visitor, often staying for weekends. While I was staying in the house Silia's parents visited from 'Eua for several weeks, as did Siale's sister, also from 'Eua, at another time.

Children's play groups typically contain various relatives of their own generation who live nearby. Many children also form close attachments to one or more households of *kāinga* members in their village. In Holonga in 1986, the twins Tomasi and Elenoa, then aged three, frequently visited their aunt's and their grandmother's homes during the day, and Elenoa sometimes stayed with the grandmother for several days at a time.

This frequent visiting means that children have close contact with many different relatives. Children's notions of who comprises their *fāmili* are, accordingly, highly varied and fluid. During a visit to Holonga primary school I asked the students in each class to draw their *fāmili*, then had each child discuss his or her picture with me, explaining his or her relationship to each person depicted.[1] When I compared these drawings with the data I had gathered in a household survey of Holonga I found that of ninety-five children aged between five and twelve, thirty-one (32.6 percent) drew only members of their household, including resident members of their *kāinga*. Forty-seven (49.5 percent) included nuclear family members who did not reside in the household at that time (e.g., siblings living overseas), and seventeen (17.9 percent) included *kāinga* members not living in the household. Interestingly, eighty-one of the children (85.3 percent) did not include *all* members of their household in their drawings. While some may have simply forgotten certain household members, these figures do indicate that the children were not defining *fāmili* solely on the basis of co-residence.

This drawing exercise also revealed that children have shifting understandings of kin relationships.[2] For example, several children who were being cared for by grandparents while their parents were overseas identified them as "mother" (*fa'ē*) and "father" (*tamai*). The children also tended to call all same-generation relatives siblings when in fact some were cousins or even uncles, aunts, nephews, or nieces—a result of the great age differences that often occur between youngest and oldest siblings. Such terminology is commonly used by adults, too; however, many of the children had not learned the correct use of kin terms for siblings, and *tokoua*, the term for same-sex siblings, tended to be used for opposite-sex siblings as well. If the terms for opposite-sex siblings were given, the term used by sisters for brothers (*tuonga'ane*) was often confused with the term used by brothers for sisters (*tuofefine*).[3] This is not surprising, given that all relatives are addressed by their personal names, not their kin terms, unless respectful terms are being used, such as *fine'eiki* (mother) and *tangata'eiki* (father). Parents do identify relatives to children by kin terms, so that at a feast a parent may say to a child, "That's Sela, she's your father's sister's daughter [*tama 'a mehekitanga*]." Yet, as with so much other knowledge, children are not expected to really understand the complexities of kin terms before the end of primary school.

In Tonga children's personal rank and status are derived from both their mother and their father. In chiefly families, "children derived their social standings, established by the prestige and position of their patrilineal groups in political and economic affairs, from their fathers, while they possessed a personal prestige, in body and blood, transmitted from and by their mothers in procreation" (Marcus 1979, 89).

MOTHERS

Mothers (fa'ē) are of lower status than their children, and there are no tapu between them.[4] A mother is expected to satisfy her children's wants, and their relationship is characterized as familiar and affectionate. Kavaliku comments that "if the child is to be very familiar with anybody, it is the mother, for she gives him his life. A child is pitied most when he has no mother to take care of him" (1977, 49). The close relationship between mother and child is encouraged by the early seclusion of mother and infant and remains particularly intense and affectionate while the child is still breast-fed. Until children are confidently walking and can begin to join the older children's play, they are often very distressed by separation from their mother or main caregiver. Seini returned to work only a month after 'Ofa was born, leaving her in the care of her grandmother. While I was staying with them, when 'Ofa was a year old, she still became distressed each morning when Seini left for work. She would stand crying at the doorway and watch her mother waiting for the bus to town. Seini found this time upsetting too, and she would frequently return home to cuddle 'Ofa and wait until the child was distracted by her grandmother before leaving again.

Mothers are tu'a to their children in kinship terms, but this does not mean that they have no authority over them. Most of the everyday disciplining of children is done by mothers or other primary caregivers, who have higher status by seniority. Mothers also have the major responsibility for teaching their children cultural values and associated behavior, and it is they who will be judged most critically if their children do not demonstrate that they have learned these values. Mothers, in other words, are held responsible for ensuring that children become poto.

MATERNAL KIN

The relationship among children, their mother, and her kin is usually characterized by 'ofa māfana (warm love). This is especially so with the mother's younger sisters and cousins.[5] Unmarried young women often live with older, married sisters or cousins and help with household chores and childcare, as was the case with Silia, Seini's "sister," who had joined the Holonga household from 'Eua to attend the local Catholic college. Silia shared the household chores with Seini and her mother, Moana, and was like a second mother to the children, giving them orders and discipline and forming a very close, affectionate relationship with baby 'Ofa. The older children knew that Silia did not have full parental authority, however, and were more cheeky and naughty with her despite her willingness to punish them.

Mothers' brothers, *tu'asina*, are more commonly referred to as *fa'ē tangata* ("male mothers"). *'Ilamutu*, the children of men's sisters, are *'eiki* to their *fa'ē tangata* and can request goods and services from them and their wives and children.[6] *Fa'ē tangata* are expected to be friendly and generous to their *'ilamutu*, but in the modern cash economy this expectation can cause problems that lead to family tensions. For example, in *anga fakatonga* "uncles should open their stores to their nephews and nieces" (Fifita 1975, 34), yet this obviously causes problems for uncles trying to maintain businesses.

FATHERS

The father and his "side" (his *kāinga*) are *'eiki* to his children, and their relationships are marked by restraint, including a number of *tapu*. The father-child relationship is conceptually associated with the chief-commoner relationship, each being used as a metaphor for the other. Rogers has pointed out that there are sayings in Tonga, "made by women as *mothers* and *wives* about the kind of authority a father and his siblings exert over their children, supporting the principle that the father's side of the family is 'superior' to the mother's side." He gives as an example the saying *"Oku te fānau kae pule tokotaha kehe"* (although you have children somebody else has authority over them). That the father and his side have *pule* over children reflects "an *ideology* of children belonging to a patrilineal unit" (1977, 158, 159; emphases in original). The father and his brothers, all known as *tamai*, have "rights over children, titles, land, houses, and, in the traditional system, political authority" (Bott 1981, 15).

Tapu concerning the father involved a separation of his person from his children: they were not to touch his head, sit in his lap, use his belongings, or eat his leftover food, and if a father was holding a child, the child could not eat at the same time. When the father died, his children could not stay in the house with the corpse during the funeral preparations (Aoyagi 1966, 161; Beaglehole and Beaglehole 1941b, 100; Spillius 1958, 6, 9). These *tapu* are weakening today, and some fathers choose not to adhere to them at all; Siale, for example, made a point of holding his youngest child on his lap and feeding her from his plate. Rogers suggests that the *pule* of fathers has become largely restricted to the economic sphere, with fathers acting as "food production managers" (1977, 159). Although the extent of fathers' authority over their children's lives varies a great deal, certainly while children are young the father's authority is unquestioned. In many families Spillius' comment that "open defiance would be unthinkable" (1958, 6) is still valid, even for adult children. In nuclear family households fathers also have largely taken over the role of 'ulumotu'a, the senior member of the fāmili who gives instructions concerning fāmili participation in ceremonies.[7]

Fathers are ideally "distant and commanding" (Spillius 1958, 6), but many fathers in fact have close and affectionate relationships with their children. There are also notable differences in their relationships with sons (foha) and daughters ('ofafine).[8] Formerly, in chiefly families, sons were potential rivals for the father's position and title, and their relationship was generally one of "distance and reserved respect." A daughter, on the other hand, was a "valued possession, the symbol of the kāinga rank which [was] cherished and given away only as a great prize," and her relationship with her father was one of "warmth and a greater relaxation of tapu" (James 1987, 10). These differences are still apparent in chiefly families.

In tu'a families today there is usually a period of comparative familiarity between a father and his children until they reach puberty. As youths, sons tend to have a strained relationship with their fathers, often characterized by faka'ehi'ehi (avoidance). This is particularly so for the eldest son, who is likely to inherit his father's land and other property. A father will seldom drink kava with his sons, but he will attend faikava (kava-drinking sessions) at which his daughter serves and even join in the men's "crude sex talk" in her presence (Rogers 1977, 159; and see Perminow 1993). When a father is elderly his relationship with his sons becomes more familiar again, but "for warmth and care in old age, men tend to look to their daughters rather than their sons" (James 1983, 240).

Fathers generally have little to do with childcare, especially when the children are very young. Although a father may supervise a young child while his wife is otherwise occupied, he will tend to ask a female relative or affine, or an older child, to take over tasks such as diaper changing, feeding, or bathing. As has been shown, a man whose wife is absent because of death, divorce, migration, or a temporary trip away will usually move in with female relatives or request that they move into his household, rather than attempt to care for the children alone. Where the mother's absence is permanent the children may even be fostered or adopted out. It is unusual to find a man caring for children alone, and I encountered only one such man. Saia lived in Nuku'alofa, and while his wife worked overseas he was caring for his son, aged seven, and daughter, aged three. After some months he sent both children to their mother, claiming that his family had disapproved of the situation, offered little help, and had teased him that his wife had become "the husband," even though he was also working. He complained, "They watched and waited for me to fall on my face."

That fathers have little to do with the daily care of little children does not mean that they are entirely uninvolved. Siale rarely shared the tasks of caring for 'Ofa beyond keeping an eye on her if no one else was available. Yet at mealtimes he often took her onto his lap and fed her or urged her to eat well, and he was always interested in her development. When he returned home from work Seini or other household members often told him what 'Ofa had been doing and encouraged her to show him some cute thing she had done or said that day. This was not the case with the older children, with whom Siale had very little involvement. Tomasi had just begun to help him with chores such as feeding the pigs and preparing the 'umu, so was gradually having more contact with his father. Elenoa, on the other hand, seldom had any form of interaction with Siale beyond his issuing occasional orders to her.

In talking to Tongans about their relationships with their parents, many stated that although their mothers had been the main disciplinarians, their relationships with them were close and "easy" (faingofua). The majority stated that they were afraid of their fathers. Pita commented, "My father didn't say much to us except when he was angry." Some women did say they had felt close to their fathers as young children, and one young woman from Holonga said that when her mother hit her she "always ran and hid in Poppa's arms." However, she added that as she got older and wanted to go out to movies or dances her father had forbidden her to go; he was "very Tongan, so conservative."

FATHER'S SISTERS

Mehekitanga are 'eiki to the father and have considerable authority over his children, especially in the case of his eldest sister.[9] Children are expected to be respectful and obedient to their mehekitanga, who can claim access to their labor and possessions. At the funeral of a mehekitanga, as at their father's, they must liongi: wear mourning clothes, have their hair cut, and do the cooking and other low-status tasks.[10] It is in relation to the mehekitanga that the saying that someone else has authority over one's children is most often used. Several of my informants had heard it from their mothers on occasions when their mehekitanga were given goods or services.

The "dark powers" of mehekitanga that can "affect the health and prosperity" of their brother's children (James 1987, 11) were mentioned in relation to pregnancy and childbirth. Herda notes that "the power to curse, attributed especially to the father's sister, should not be underestimated, for in pre-Christian Tonga, it represented the power of life and death" (1987, 197; and see Rogers 1977; Taumoefolau 1991). This "ritual mystical power," which extended to the children of mehekitanga (Bott 1981, 18) has been undermined by Christianity, and Christian faith is spoken of as a power counterveiling that of *mehekitanga*. Marcus has suggested that "the inherent mystical powers and the efficacy of cursing as the source of the father's sister's influence over her brothers and their offspring have become part of Tongan folklore rather than a natural aspect of routine explanations concerning kinship" (1979, 89). In explications of kinship roles it is most often stressed that the *mehekitanga* have considerable authority over their *fakafotu* and play an important role in teaching them appropriate values and behaviors. In their authoritative role *mehekitanga* can make considerable demands of their *fakafotu*, but they also act as their guides and even protectors (see James 1992, 97).

When a woman adopts her brother's child she has, in a sense, a dual role as mother and *mehekitanga* in relation to that child. Such a child, known as *tama tō he mehekitanga* (a child "fallen" or "born" to an aunt), no longer has to observe *tapu* toward his biological father. He may find, though, that he is treated differently from his cousins (father's sister's children) and is expected to do more work than they. This was the case for Sālote, a young woman who assisted me with some interview transcriptions during my fieldwork. Sālote was sent to live with her *mehekitanga* while in primary school and was still with her in 1989. She said that her aunt treated her harshly and expected her to do most of the household chores. The aunt demanded that Sālote obtain her permission for any outing, and she was very much against Sālote's helping me. When I met her, Sālote was attending 'Atenisi Institute in Nuku'alofa and dreamed of going overseas to work and become "independent." However, not long after I returned to Australia Sālote wrote to tell me that she had left 'Atenisi, married a man her aunt had deemed suitable, and was working as a bank teller. Her *mehekitanga* was able to exert an enormous amount of authority over her, and although Sālote's natural mother had moved to live in the same *'api* some years before, she had not attempted to dispute any of her sister-in-law's actions. Sālote told me that her mother frequently urged her to be a good Christian and to obey her aunt unquestioningly.

GRANDPARENTS

The easiest and most affectionate relationships children have within their families are with their grandparents (*kui*), with whom there are no *tapu*. Even the respect children are expected to show to older people is sometimes allowed to lapse when with their grandparents. Their interactions with them are often more relaxed and physically demonstrative than with any other adults, including their mothers. However, "grandparents' love" (*'ofa'ofa 'a kui*) is recognized as being over-indulgent and yet over-severe at times

(Churchward 1959, 563). Collocott and Havea refer to this phrase as a proverbial saying and explain that "the love of grandparents is very sincere but
their anger is to be dreaded, as in their wrath they may strike the offending
grandchildren how and where they will. [The saying refers to the] love of one
whose affection is undoubted, but whose position of authority is such that he
may punish without let or hindrance" (1922, 120).

Unless they are geographically distant, grandparents usually have a great
deal to do with their grandchildren. In many households grandparents are
present; this was so in twenty-six out of the seventy-seven households in
Holonga in 1988 (33.7 percent), and in a further five households grandparents were the sole caregivers. Grandparents take on much of the childcare, from minding babies and preschoolers while their parents work to
caring for older children—brushing their hair, rubbing their arms and legs
with coconut oil, checking that they are properly dressed, and so on. When
Siale's mother, Tonga, visited the Holonga household, she and Moana,
Seini's mother, were constantly and subtly vying with one another to show
care and concern for the children and to demonstrate their vigilance over
the children's behavior. It was to one or the other of these grandmothers that
the children were most likely to go with tales to tell of other children's mis-
deeds. As we have seen, children learn not to complain about minor illnesses
and injuries, and grandmothers and other elderly female kin seem to be the
only people to whom children readily turn with such problems. These older
women usually respond kindly, rubbing a sore spot with Tongan oil, seeking
some medicinal plants to make an infusion or poultice for the child, or just
letting the child snuggle up to them for comfort. When Elenoa burned her
thigh badly she showed her mother, who did not respond. Later her paternal
grandmother visited and Elenoa showed her. Tonga gently rubbed some oil
on the burn and let Elenoa lie with her head on Tonga's lap for a while, and
when Elenoa was called to do some sweeping, Tonga advised her to take it
easy on her sore leg.

SAME-SEX SIBLINGS

An affectionate relationship also often develops between same-sex siblings
and cousins, although the authority vested in seniority means that their relations are also characterized by a certain amount of restraint.[11] The ideal
for all sibling relationships is that they should have 'ofa for one another.
"Tongan brothers and sisters are very close. Tongans say they live in mo'ui
taha, that is, in one life. There is nothing one would not do for the other:
everything is expected to be shared. Hence, there is a feeling of intense personal oneness" (Kavaliku 1977, 60). As Manu explained, siblings should

help one another and share their possessions because of the bond of their blood, made by God.

Formerly, brothers of the same father but different mothers were seen as rivals, especially sons in chiefly families, and were referred to as *uho tau* (literally, fighting umbilical cords). Brothers with the same mother but different fathers were *uho taha* (one cord) and were expected to be loyal to each other (Bott 1981, 17; Rogers 1977, 171; Wood-Ellem 1987, 211). Today, the main source of sibling rivalry during childhood is vying for the attention of parents and others in the household. This is particularly noticeable in children two or three years old when a new sibling is born, and the "dislike of new babies by the next older child is marked" (Spillius 1958, 61). However, the sibling hierarchy, based on seniority and on the higher rank of sisters (see below) precludes much rivalry, and most sibling groups (including half-siblings, adopted siblings, and cousins) have a well-established pecking order. Sibling relationships are also marked by a lack of cooperation against parents, as shown by their willingness to report each other's misdemeanors to them.

Older siblings play an important role in younger children's socialization (see Weisner and Gallimore 1977). They share the adult family members' responsibility for nurturing, teaching, and punishing, and by doing so, they are able to participate in the adults' world in various ways, so that their caregiving of younger children becomes part of their own socialization. While interacting with an infant sibling, an older child will encourage the infant to be amusing or to acquire new skills or will call adults' attention to some aspect of the infant's behavior. When adults respond positively, by being interested and amused, the older child has succeeded not only in allying herself or himself with the adults, but also in obtaining indirect attention and praise. Later, when the younger child is past infancy, the older one is able to continue this pattern by being protective and nurturant and by being involved in the younger child's discipline—reporting misbehavior, taking the child to an adult for punishment, or even punishing the child.

The role of sibling caregiver therefore enables a child to behave as a higher-status person. However, sibling caregivers are only high status in relation to their young charges. Their low status in relation to adults is frequently highlighted in the context of their responsibilities toward young siblings. One characteristically high-status behavior is to remain relatively immobile while those of lower status do one's bidding. This pattern can be observed in adults' use of children to run errands, chase straying toddlers, carry out the more active childcare, and so on, while the adults remain seated. Also, if older siblings are in any way negligent in their duties as caregivers—if younger ones are hurt, or naughty, or disruptive—the caregivers are likely to be punished by a parent or other higher-status person.

BROTHERS AND SISTERS

Of all the kin relations it is the brother-sister relationship that has received the most attention in the literature on Tongan kinship.[12] This relationship is one of *faka'apa'apa* and is characterized by avoidance and restraint. Marcus has suggested that brother-sister avoidance "has traditionally been associated with the broader cultural feature of combined avoidance and respect for sacred or mystical powers, embodied by persons of chiefly status." Sisters and their children are said to be *'eiki* in relation to their brothers and their brothers' children. Marcus further notes that referring to sisters as *'eiki* suggests that brothers' avoidance of them is "out of respect for the mystical or sacred qualities of the patriline, which females as sisters embody and pass to offspring in sexual reproduction, and which as father's sisters they control and use as advisors in their brothers' families" (1979, 89). Similarly, in her discussion of "the ancient Tongan polity," James has argued that *mana*, "the mysterious power derived from the gods" (1992, 82) and closely associated with chiefliness, was also associated with females as sisters. This *mana*, James asserts, was "derived ultimately from the deity Hikule'o and transmitted only by females. Thus, a man's show of respect to his sister and to his father's sister, and to their descendants can be seen . . . [as] a civil gesture by which he is affirming the basis of the Tongan order" (James 1991b, 304; and see Herda 1987, 197).[13]

In Tongan mythology brother-sister sexual unions are a recurring theme. Many deities, including the god Tangaloa and the goddess Hikule'o, were born of such unions, often from twins, and the origin of intercourse was mythically attributed to a brother-sister pair (Collocott 1921a; Gifford 1971a). James has argued that brother-sister incest is also a pervasive, though implicit, theme "in the creation of the Tu'i Tonga's polity." Pursuing this theme of incest she points out that "symbolically brother and sister are acting the role of mother and father respectively to each other's issue" (1991b:304).

In precontact Tonga *kāinga* were led by a brother and sister pair, who were not necessarily true siblings. This pair joined their "authority and mystical powers in guiding the external and internal relations of the *kāinga* set" (James 1987, 11; see Wood-Ellem's analysis [1987] of the reign of Queen Sālote Tupou and Tungi). Wood-Ellem describes the role of chiefly sisters in precontact Tonga as guardians of knowledge (especially genealogies), who supervised the production of *koloa* and its distribution and ensured that the younger *kāinga* members worked for the advantages of the *kāinga* as a whole; their brothers were responsible for matters requiring physical strength, defense, and strengthening of the *kāinga* and arranging the most advantageous marriages for their daughters and sisters (1987, 211).

It is not clear to what extent these roles were important for *tu'a*, but some *tapu* associated with sisters do appear to have been observed throughout the population. These *tapu* involved a range of behavior and avoidances that spatially separated brother and sister and precluded any familiarity between them. Different accounts of this respect and avoidance relationship as it persisted into the twentieth century vary in their details of the *tapu*, and I will summarize here those *tapu* that are most frequently mentioned (see Aoyagi 1966, 162; Beaglehole and Beaglehole 1941b, 72; Gifford 1971b, 21–22). Sisters and brothers did not sleep under the same roof after they were about ten years old, and when they were in the same house they could not sit near one another or lie down in one another's presence.[14] They could not enter one another's rooms, use each other's belongings (comb, bed, clothes, and so on), or eat each other's leftovers. When they spoke, their conversation was respectful and did not touch on romantic or sexual matters, and they were not supposed to speak ill of one another to other people. They could not dance together, the brother could not drink kava his sister served, and on occasions such as funerals and weddings they could not both attend. These *tapu* were generally relaxed when the brother and sister were older. "After marriage, or after reaching a certain age, however, freedom in every activity is granted in brother-sister relationships, for it is assumed they are old enough to know better" (Kavaliku 1977, 60).[15]

I have used the past tense in the list of *tapu* because in many families brother-sister *tapu* are not always strictly observed today, and even elderly people sometimes claimed that their relationships with opposite-sex siblings during childhood were *faingofua*. The forms of *tapu* that are observed also vary. Some people told me they had been able to talk freely except about romantic matters; others said they could discuss romances but not use swear words in their sibling's presence. Teenagers described similarly varying *tapu*, with teenage girls particularly emphasizing avoiding behavior that could shame their brothers—going to dances when their brothers were there, talking to boys on the street, wearing immodest clothing, or using bad language. It is teenage girls whose behavior is most restricted by these *tapu*, as part of the general expectation that they will stay close to home. Sālote told me about a two-week visit she had made to Holonga, where many of the boys were her classificatory brothers. Her family was very strict about the brother-sister *tapu*, so her social activities were highly restricted, and for much of her visit she stayed inside her aunt's house.

In some Tongan families today much of this avoidance relationship has disappeared. Ngata described his relationship with his sisters during adolescence as close:

> We talk about our love affairs, we share things when it comes to problems, because we are the closest ones to give a hand. If we don't give a hand, who else is going to? . . . [He talked to his sister when she was let down by a boyfriend.] But in the Tongan way you're not supposed to talk about that! . . . But I think as a brother, I think I have more experience, I know how boys treat girls and I help my sisters in that situation. So it's a Christian value, you know if I'm not a "brother," a Christian, she's in trouble, in a problem, in a chaos, and if I'm going to be a Christian I'm the first one to give a hand.

Ngata added that at first his family did not know that he was talking so closely with his sisters, but that when they found out they encouraged him, even urging him to talk with his sisters when they were upset.

Avoidance behavior, when observed, becomes especially important after puberty, but some aspects begin much earlier. Once they are about two or three, boys are not allowed to sleep close to their sisters, and often sons sleep with their father, and daughters with their mother (or other same-sex relatives). Where brothers do not sleep in separate huts once they or their sisters are approaching adolescence, they have separate rooms or partitioned areas and do not go into their sisters' sleeping areas. Such avoidance behavior is found even with classificatory and adopted siblings, so that sixteen-year-old Lopeti, who had been adopted originally by Alisi's brother, moved to Alisi's house because his adoptive sister, Losa, was approaching puberty.

The modesty encouraged in little girls is particularly important when their brothers are present. In the Holonga household Seini would quickly cover 'Ofa's genitals if Tomasi came near when she was changing 'Ofa's diaper. On one occasion Tomasi was playing with 'Ofa and pulled her on top of him as he lay on his back on the floor, so that her body was between his legs. Seini quickly snatched 'Ofa away, angrily telling Tomasi to "ai fakalelei" (do it nicely).

Marcus claimed that "adolescent boys spend most of their time away from home in casual peer groups or gangs . . . as part of sister avoidance" (1979, 85). However, Tongans tend to explain this behavior more in terms of the boys' "freedom" and "independence," thus constructing it as an advantage rather than as the result of behavioral restrictions. Marcus has also suggested that the brother-sister relationship is "an important model in early socialization for the development of generalized personal orientations to relations of rank which structure a broad range of contexts in an individual's later life" (1978, 258n9). The brother-sister relationship is certainly important in this respect, but the relationship of children to their father and his *kāinga* is also very important. In the context of the weakening of restrictions in the brother-sister relationship, it is perhaps more important. In fact, most relationships children have with persons older than themselves "model" relations of rank in Tonga, both in the respect and obedience expected of children and in the power of higher-status persons to punish them.

Many Tongans strongly disapprove of the weakening of the avoidance relationship between brothers and sisters and claim that their *faka'apa'apa* is being *mole* (lost). Seini's mother, Moana, commented,

> When I grew up I saw the respect between brother and sister was dignified, solemn. The brother didn't enter the sister's room, and if the brother entered the house and the sister was lying down, he would go away. Now, I see the sister lies down and the brother can just come in, with some people. The way of respect is not the same as in the past.

One of the most common criticisms of Mormons in Tonga is that they are said to encourage the breakdown of family ties by allowing *tapu* behavior between brothers and sisters, such as dancing together (Gordon 1990, 206).

The initial weakening of the brother-sister *tapu* can be traced back to the early period of contact between Tongans and Europeans. By 1850, "a transformation of the sister's sphere of influence had occurred, due both to the importation of European Christian values and to the changing indigenous attitudes toward the potency of the sacred realm" (Herda 1987, 207). With this transformation and the establishment of Tonga's laws and constitution came a decline in women's power as sisters, though they have not, as Gailey has claimed, "fallen out" of the kinship structure to "remain as wives only" (1980, 317; but see Gailey 1987c). Marcus points out that "the recognition of brothers' lifelong obligations to sisters and their children remain salient and frequently articulated ideals of behavior" (1979, 89). As with other aspects of Tonga's complex system of rights and obligations, the rights of sisters over their brothers and brothers' children are open to manipulation and negotiation, so that some women are disadvantaged because their brothers and brothers' wives refuse them economic and other support. Their position is worsened because the inheritance of titles and landed property (or land leases) based on primogeniture has excluded them from inheriting property. Other women are more like Seini, who did not let her husband's sisters "boss around" her or or her children. Such women benefit by asserting their rights as sisters but not supporting their husbands' sisters' claims. Thus, personal factors such as assertiveness and the degree of closeness in the marital and sibling relationships create considerable variations.[16]

The extent to which any kin-related obligations or rights are activated varies tremendously in modern Tonga. Many find it difficult to achieve a balance between traditional obligations and more individualistic needs and wants, and this is especially so for those in the emerging middle class. Marcus suggests that the extent of people's conformity to traditional kinship norms relates to a "trade-off between personal ambition in the context of modernity and traditional patterns of rights and obligations both as burdens and advantages" (1974, 92; and see Van der Grijp 1993). For example, a man's obligations to his sister and her children must be weighed against investing in his own children's education. Religious affiliation can affect such decisions, and the increasingly popular Mormon and Ma'ama Fo'ou churches strongly support a focus on the nuclear family.

WORK

As soon as children are physically capable, they are expected to wash and dress themselves, brush their own teeth, and so on, although their caregivers may tell them when to do these things. Caregivers or older siblings do more complicated tasks such as braiding girls' hair but do not usually even supervise simpler activities such as bathing—although the dry soap and dirty towels I often observed indicated the younger children do not always manage these tasks well. They may also be reminded to go to bed, but more often children are allowed to fall asleep of their own accord. Toilet training, which usually begins within the second year, is accomplished with a minimum of fuss. The child may be left without diapers for long periods, and any accident is mopped up without comment. When 'Ofa was one her grandmother began taking her regularly to sit on the toilet, but no fuss was made about whether she actually used it. Being physically independent in these ways is valued as part of the process of becoming *poto* and because it relieves caregivers of some of the tiring tasks of childcare.

Once children can walk, they are taught to follow the orders of other household members. At first this is incorporated into the "performances" they are encouraged to give in infancy: actions that are entertaining or amusing for the household members. These are rewarded with praise, affection, and further attention, as discussed in the following chapter. Fetching things and doing other simple errands are the first tasks children learn in this way. As they become more physically competent the range of tasks is increased and the performative aspect declines rapidly, with the tasks becoming an expected part of the children's daily life. The younger household members are expected to be the most active, in accordance with the association of low status with mobility. When young children are within calling distance, adults tell the children to fetch and carry for them while they remain in one place doing tasks such as preparing food or weaving mats. Initially children's errands are within the house; as they get older they are sent to neighboring houses and even further afield. Most Tongan households do not store much food, so that before almost every meal the children are sent on one or more trips to the local store for supplies.

Kavaliku has claimed that Tongan children are not expected to begin working for their household until they are six (1977, 49). I would argue that as soon as children can understand requests made of them they begin to "work," and that before they are six they carry out a range of tasks, including running errands, watching out for younger children, carrying water, sweeping, and collecting and carrying rubbish. Children's work is highly valued by their families, as a contribution to household labor and as an indication of their acquisition of the positively valued qualities of obedience and 'ofa. Children's work, as a form of helping the family, is regarded as a demonstration of their 'ofa for their family, as well as being an aspect of their fatongia. As they get older and take on more adult tasks, their work is also a sign of their increasing maturity. Formerly a female's first mat or ngatu and a male's firstfruits (agricultural produce or fish) were presented to their chief, and a celebration was held (Bott n.d., 22). Even today, young men and women sometimes present their first produce or craft work, or even their first wages, to their noble and/or high-status kin.

The high value placed on children's contributions to household labor underlies some of the resistance toward the issue of family planning. Alisi, who had only one child of her own, a daughter, adopted several children when her daughter left home. She explained why she believed large families were important:

Yes, it's a good thing to have lots of children. The doctor says to be moderate. And it's partly true in that you can see to looking after them. But you see at this time, during this time, the people with lots of children are special (hau). [The children] go to work, and work, and work, and bring you the means to shoulder the great burdens, and the parents can lie down and rest. One or two [children] is just saddening (fakamamahi). The parents aren't able to rest, because there's only a little [help]. The girl does a little work, the boy does a little work . . . the father has to go to farm, not rest at any time. Same with the mother, like me, she will never stop working at home, beating bark-cloth and doing other things. Because to help with the burdens the children must go to work and get some money—it is true that money is important, to be

able to get these things. But she or he is not able to shoulder the general
responsibilities of the family, the land; without doubt it will just be the parents who shoulder them.

The age at which children are expected to do different tasks varies
according to their physical capabilities, the composition of their household,
and a number of personal factors such as individuals' interests, favoritism,
and interhousehold relationships. These factors also influence the amount of
work children are given. Oldest children often begin to do household chores
at an earlier age, and have far more expected of them, than their younger
siblings. They can lighten their load to some extent by delegating tasks to
the younger ones but may be held responsible if chores are not done properly.
A few adults told me that as children they had not had to do any work at all;
they were *pele*, especially indulged by their families. Many more, however,
told me that they had worked very hard and were given little or no time to
play. Several people admitted that they had resented the work and felt
fakapōpula'i (enslaved). Siale's brother, Soane, the eldest of eleven children,
complained that he had had "no fun, no fun at all."

Children, especially boys, often run away (*hola*) when they think they are
going to be told to do some work. This can be effective if there are other
children around who can do the work instead, but it also carries a high risk of
punishment. Seini told me that she had done a lot of work when she was
young because she was the only child in her household. The job she hated
most was collecting the leaves from around the house and from the empty
block next door each morning. She would *hola* to her aunt's house down the
road to try to avoid this work, but another aunt, from her own household,
would come every morning and find her, hit her, and make her do the work.
Boys can avoid work far more successfully than girls, being freer to go away
from the house. As the Beagleholes commented, the amount of work a boy
does is partly dependent on "his ability to disappear with a gang of playmates
whenever he senses his services may be in demand" (1941b, 47).

Children who try to avoid work, or who work badly, may be accused of
being *fakapikopiko* (lazy) and are very likely to be punished. The Wesleyan
missionaries brought with them the sternest of work ethics, and the early
written laws sought to discourage laziness. The 1850 Law Referring to Men
stated that "any man not willing to work, he shall be neither fed nor assisted;
all such persons being useless to the land and its inhabitants; and unprofit-
able to their friends." Similarly, the Law Referring to Women stated, "You
must work, women, and persevere in labouring to clothe your husband and
children; unmarried women shall work to be useful to their relatives and par-

ents. If they do not work, they shall not be fed or assisted; for our assisting the indolent, is supporting that which is an evil" (Lātūkefu 1974, 236).

In Tonga today, the sexual division of labor is a crucial aspect of children's gender identification. In answer to the question "In what ways do you think it is different for boys and for girls growing up in Tonga?" 101 of 216 replies (46.7 percent) either said simply "work" or gave some variation of the formula "girls stay at home and help the mother and boys go with the father and work in the bush," often simply stated as "boys go, girls stay." As we have seen, there are very clear conceptual distinctions between *ngāue fakafefine* (women's work) and *ngāue fakatangata* (men's work), with the former conceptualized as light, easy, clean, and involving staying, the latter as heavy, tough, dirty, and involving going (to "the bush" or the sea). Men's work is also described as "bigger" or "greater" (*lahi ange*) than women's. There is a strong sense of these being natural distinctions, and they underlie the broader gender distinctions in Tonga that already have been described.

It appears that a clear division of labor was a feature of precontact Tongan society. Evidence from about A.D. 1200–1500 indicates that women carried out the daily gardening tasks of weeding and hoeing while men fished and traded by canoe (Spennemann 1986, 1990). Women also combed the reefs for food and produced mats, bark-cloth, and other craft. Spennemann speculates that in the shift to village settlement, during the civil wars of the early nineteenth century, men took over the gardening work, as they were better able to "defend themselves against marauding bands" (1990, 108). The altered division of labor that developed was then supported by the European missionaries, who saw women's proper role as homemaking and men's as agriculture.

Significant changes were also wrought by the emergence of a cash economy (Gailey 1980, 1987a; James 1988). The transformation is continuing today, as more women enter paid employment and move into spheres that have been predominantly male, such as the church, business, and bureaucracy (see Faletau 1982; Fleming with Tuku'afu 1986; James 1983; Moengangongo 1988). However, women's contribution to production has always been significant, and even during the conservative period of Queen Sālote's reign, "women may have spent more hours in productive activities than men" (Bollard 1974, 75).

Women's productive activities today include the "female" tasks of producing bark-cloth, baskets, woven mats, and certain other products such as scented coconut oil and collecting reef foods, as well as "male" tasks in agriculture and animal husbandry. The production of *koloa* and the role of sisters in controlling exchanges of *koloa* and food between kin at events marking

life crises have been important ways in which "women's work" has retained a
high value in Tonga.

Primary school children are taught about the ideal sexual division of
labor as part of the social studies curriculum. In class one children are taught
to sing this song:

> The mother's work is always great—
> Sweeping, and collecting the rubbish,
> Always looking after us,
> Doing the washing and ironing.
> The father is the head of the family,
> Working hard, morning and afternoon
> To meet the needs of the family—
> Food, clothes, happiness, and learning.
> (my translation)

In the following song learned in class two, more traditional work is emphasized:

> The work to do in the family:
> Men do the hoeing and digging,
> Trying to get lots of food,
> Going to the sea to fish,
> To get food for the family.
> The women do the washing and sweeping,
> Tidying the house and cooking the food,
> Weaving mats, mats for the floor,
> Beating tapa, staining many tapa
> To get coverings for the family.
> (my translation)

To a great extent the messages of these songs are confirmed by children's
everyday experiences. Even mothers who are in full-time employment do
numerous "female" tasks in the home. Seini would come home from a full
day's work as a clerk and immediately begin cooking, washing, cleaning the
house and yard, ironing the children's school uniforms and her work clothes
for the following day, and sometimes helping her mother with *tutu*. When I
visited primary school classes and asked them to draw their *fāmili*, without
exception the children drew each person doing some form of work, usually
gender-specific tasks. Examples of some of these drawings can be seen in
figure 1.

Figure 1: Holongan Children's Drawings of Family Members

1A: Girl, aged 10: (*clockwise from top left*) child cooking food, father hoeing, sister sweeping and self collecting rubbish, mother beating tapa, mother bathing baby.

1B: Girl, aged 5: (*clockwise from top left*) father hoeing, mother beating tapa, self getting water, house, washing on line, brother playing.

1C: Girl, aged 11: (*clockwise from top*) mother doing washing, father hoeing, self at school, brother fishing, grandfather getting coconuts, grandmother ironing, self preparing food, sister sweeping (*center*).

1D: Boy, aged 11: (*top row L to R*) father building house, mother weaving, brother hoeing; (*bottom row L to R*) self getting water, brother burning rubbish, sister sweeping.

In early childhood, chores are not strongly gendered, with both sexes sweeping and picking up rubbish, carrying water, and running errands. By the time children are about six or seven years old there is much less overlap between the tasks assigned to males and females. Girls do many household chores such as cooking, sweeping, cleaning, washing dishes, helping with childcare, and so on, and boys help with agricultural work and in collecting and cutting firewood. Girls are generally expected to help with chores earlier and to do more work than boys. Boys are often not expected to do much work until they are old enough and strong enough to do properly "male" tasks. Cooking, formerly a male task, is now divided into male and female tasks, the former being the "hard," dirty, outside work such as killing and roasting pigs and preparing the 'umu and the latter being the "easier" preparation and cooking of food indoors.

There appears to have been considerable transformation in the division of labor within the home, apart from the initial transformation in which women became primarily responsible for domestic chores.[17] Lovett (1958, 34) has argued that the majority of children aged from thirteen to nineteen lived away from home in boarding schools in the 1950s, leaving preadolescents with the bulk of household chores. With the construction of more secondary schools and improved roads and transportation, fewer adolescents are now in boarding schools, and they contribute a significant amount of household and agricultural labor.

Another aspect of this transformation is that women's unmarried or younger sisters often move into their households to assist with chores and childcare. Gailey relates this change to migration, arguing that these young women have functionally replaced the brother's wife where the brother is overseas (1992, 59). This change may also be a result of the greater prevalence today of households comprised of nuclear families with one or more additional members, rather than larger extended family households in which sisters-in-law are co-residents.

The household work carried out by adolescent girls is often very tiring and can leave them little or no time for school homework or recreation. By the time they are in their early teens many girls do the bulk of the household work, with the older women of the household occupied with the production of bark-cloth, mats, and baskets, and/or with agriculture or wage employment. In Holonga Silia began her household work when she returned home from school, starting the cooking and other tasks before Seini came home from work, then working with her or looking after 'Ofa so that Seini could work. Young women like Silia usually remain in the household until they marry, sometimes well into their twenties. They are in an ambiguous position, being given the full work load and responsibilities of adult women yet still often treated as children. Silia was expected to be obedient and submissive toward older household members, who would rebuke her sharply if they thought she had neglected her duties in any way.

The teenage girls I knew frequently complained about their work load: it was too tiring, there were too many people in the house to wash and cook for, it was too hard carrying the heavy water containers, and the clothes they had to wash were always so dirty. Washing is still done by hand in most households, with water carried in buckets from the yard tap. In our Holonga household the washing took up most of every Saturday, with other loads done in the evenings as needed.[18] Teenage girls who are puke (sick), suffering from tiredness, headache, and general malaise, are said to have worked too hard. The fact that this illness is attributed to overwork and the concern and attention shown to girls at these times act as an indirect form of praise for their hard work.

That girls do the bulk of the household work is not always obvious when discussing the division of labor with adults. Fleming and Tuku'afu, in their investigation of women's work in Tonga, found that women said that they did the housework, helped by young girls, "whereas in fact the younger women performed the bulk of these tasks. . . . It seems likely that the person controlling or deciding about an activity regards that work as primarily hers. . . . [I]t is possible that the same mechanism is in operation in attitudes towards women's involvement in agriculture, where they are seen as 'helping' the men" (1986, 50–51).[19]

A study of the Banana Export Scheme on Tongatapu found that "the numerically largest part of the labour force was unpaid women's and children's labour" (Needs 1988, 29). Needs observed that women and children were vital to production but were seldom acknowledged as such either by the male household heads or by the administrators of the scheme. These unpaid laborers also have no control over the product or the profit (91n4). A similar pattern has emerged with Tonga's recent squash "boom." The contribution by women and children to production is likely to increase as more and more young men emigrate and those who remain either resist working as laborers or insist on higher wages (James 1993, 236, 237n6). Nor do census figures reflect the contribution of women and children. Children's involvement in economic production is not acknowledged, and figures on women's economic activity refer only to their *main* activity (Statistics Department 1991a, xxii). Women who are "housewives" yet do some (unpaid) agricultural work, some reef fishing, some production of craft for sale, and so on, are classified as economically inactive.[20]

When females are involved in agriculture, the older women of the household usually work on crop production while girls, young unmarried women, and elderly women work at home. This is partly due to the avoidance between brothers and sisters, as brothers are likely to be working on the same plantation, but is also related to improving girls' marriage prospects. "Mothers like to keep their marriageable daughters as fair-skinned as possible prior to marriage. Keeping your daughters at home, away from the bush (and physical work) also gives prestige which increases the chance of a high status marriage" (Fleming with Tuku'afu, 1986, 30). Fleming and Tuku'afu note that girls are more likely to do agricultural work on Tongatapu, where traditional beliefs are weaker and the need for female labor is greater as a result of the movement of many males into the cash economy. When males and females work together in the bush they usually do different tasks, as when women distribute the seedlings for the men to plant.

The movement of increasing numbers of men into wage employment, in Tonga and overseas, has affected boys' work load also. In many cases it has increased their share of household tasks, such as preparing the 'umu, and of agricultural work, almost always as unpaid laborers. Where households engage in little subsistence production they may work only at intervals, especially when their family's land is some distance from their house. This is particularly common with urban dwellers, some of whom have no access at all to land. Unlike adolescent girls, many boys can avoid being called upon to do too many onerous tasks because their relative "freedom" means they can go to their boys' hut, or into town with friends, or otherwise escape.

A number of cross-cultural studies, surveyed by Whiting and Edwards, revealed that, as in Tonga, "girls are generally more involved in economic and domestic work than are boys of the same age. . . . There is no question that girls are assigned more work than boys during the childhood years; to state the situation in the baldest terms, girls work while boys play" (1988, 72, 125). Generally, Tongan boys have far more leisure time than girls, and although their agricultural work may be physically taxing, it is viewed more positively than is domestic work. Boys do carry out domestic chores such as washing or cleaning on occasion, but when there are enough females around boys are not expected to do "women's work." The contrast between the expectations placed on boys and girls is especially apparent on occasions such as beach picnics, when boys are free to swim and play, while girls are often restricted by demands on them to help with food preparation and childcare and by expectations of decorous behavior.

Boys tend to work in groups, joking and chatting with each other and any older men present. Girls, depending on household composition, may work alone or only with older women, with whom their conversation should be respectful and restrained. If several older women are present the girl may even be excluded from their conversation. There is therefore an element of fun evident in boys' work that is absent from girls' daily chores, and when girls do go to "the bush," they seem to thoroughly enjoy themselves. At harvest time, whole families may travel to their plantation, taking food to cook, and the trip takes on the excitement of a picnic despite the hard work involved.

SCHOOL

Formal education is an important aspect of children's lives today, with the vast majority of students completing high school. "Western" subjects such as mathematics, history, and geography are taught along with Tongan language and Tongan studies. The recent emphasis on teaching Tongan language and culture can be seen in part as a response to the widespread concern that the younger Tongans are "losing" their culture. Cultural workshops have been held for teachers, traditional singing and dancing is taught in schools, and a Tongan studies curriculum has been developed for high schools. The environmental science curriculum for primary schools has a social studies program that strongly emphasizes "traditional culture." To some extent the teaching of Tongan culture in schools is a process similar to that identified by Sissons for *maoritanga* in New Zealand. Thus, there is a process of "fragmentation, objectification and standardisation of form and meaning" by teaching a "correct" version of *anga fakatonga* (1993, 113). However, most children are able to compare what they learn with their lived experiences, and while some may find the difference confusing, others will recognize that in their daily lives things are somewhat more complicated and often contentious.

Schools are also sites for more indirectly teaching and reinforcing a range of social knowledge. Most obviously, because teacher-student relations are modeled on the chief-commoner pattern of all hierarchical relationships, they reinforce children's knowledge of status relations. Teachers wield considerable authority over students, and many exert this authority through physical and other punishments. Several high schools in Tonga are boarding colleges in which discipline is strict. Many schools also have a student hierarchy in which older students, particularly prefects or their equivalent, have authority over younger students.

At the boarding colleges, and to a lesser extent all other schools, children are expected to do chores similar to those they do at home, such as sweeping, collecting rubbish, gardening, and cooking. When I worked in a girls' boarding school in 1979–1980 the girls were also expected to do teachers' laundry and some housework (often as a form of punishment) and were kept to an exhausting regimen of study, chores, and other activities such as choir practice, leaving very little leisure time. Despite the hard work, schools do provide children with many opportunities for socializing with peers (the nature of those activities will be described below).

Acquiring a formal education is highly valued as a means of both helping one's family and attaining a certain independence, as we have seen. Many parents told me that getting an education was one of the most important goals they had for their children and helping them to do so was their *fatongia mamafa* (important duty). They said they wanted their children to *ako ke fa'iteliha* (study in order to please themselves—that is, to be able to make their own choices in life). This is not seen as contradictory to using one's education to help the family, as education can enable their children to afford the things they want—food, clothes, and the like—and to take care of their families when they marry. "That was the goal I had, the reason for them to study and be clever," Manu said.

Becoming *poto* in this sense is a means to an end and is not highly valued in itself. Students who strive hard may be teased and told they are *fie poto* or *fie lahi*. As with status relations in Tonga, there is a marked tension between ambition and humility in people's attitudes to education. There is also considerable tension between becoming *poto* in the sense of acquiring a formal (Western) education and becoming *poto* in *anga fakatonga*.[21] Being *poto* in both senses is of course possible, and certain Tongans are acclaimed for achieving this balance, most notably the present king and the Tongan scholar Futa Helu. Yet there is also a widespread belief that the two forms of knowledge are somehow incompatible and that "new" knowledge will weaken or diminish the "old," a belief that has its roots in the broader distinction between *anga fakatonga* and *anga fakapālangi*.

The process of Western education can entail questioning, critical thinking, and independent expression, all of which conflict with the cultural values of obedience, respect, and conformity. The ambivalent attitude toward education is therefore linked to the broader ambivalence toward *tau'atāina* and *fa'iteliha*. The formality of Western-style education accords well with the Tongan emphasis on formal instruction and advice, and the presence of formal curricula meets the ideal of controlling acquisition of knowledge. Within Tonga many teachers do model their classroom techniques on the formal instruction that occurs in other contexts. Other teachers break away from this model and encourage or at least allow critical and independent thought, and this certainly occurs when Tongans attend schools and universities overseas.

Thus, despite the role of the education system in asserting a standardized form of Tongan culture and reinforcing the hierarchical social structures, it has also played a contrary role. As Hau'ofa has pointed out, historically the advent of compulsory education meant that "the universalization of knowledge and learning broke one of the main strangleholds that aristrocracy had over the people," and as an increasing number of Tongans are receiving higher education, and being educated overseas, they "have acquired a greater awareness of the world and their potential to excel, as well as a growing confidence in their ability and their new place in an evolving society" (1994, 422). However, this process occurs largely at the level of tertiary, and to a limited extent secondary, education. The independent and critical thinking that is encouraged in educational institutions such as 'Atenisi Institute tends to be strongly discouraged in most primary and secondary schools.

Haberkorn has argued that education is perceived as a kind of "investment" (1981, 16). The wages young adults receive from employment, a large portion of which are usually channeled back into the family, are seen as a return on that investment. When people talk about education, however, they draw on the cultural values of *fatongia*, *tokoni*, and *'ofa*, leaving the notion of investment implicit.

In his survey of 450 students throughout Tonga, Haberkorn found that the majority aspired to white-collar work (1981). The results of my own less extensive survey (180 students) revealed the same preference for white-collar jobs and a lack of interest in farming. I asked, "What do you want to do when you finish school?"[22] It is interesting to note that nearly 30 percent stated that they wanted to work to help their parents and family, whereas in Haberkorn's survey only 18 percent gave this answer (1981, 26). Haberkorn claimed that "to help one's family though receives relatively little importance as an occupational motivation across sex, islands, and school systems, in contrast to what students perceive as being a significant factor in their parents' choice" (17). While it probably is the case that parental expectations of help exceed children's intentions, it is important to note that as well as the 18 percent who answered "help family," a further 71 percent in Haberkorn's study answered "help people, village, Tonga" (17).

Haberkorn also suggested that respondents in Vava'u and Ha'apai showed "stronger other-centeredness" than those of Tongatapu (1981, 20), but my own survey showed no difference between responses from Tongatapu and Vava'u. My survey does give some support to his finding that boys were more "self-centered" than girls (17), with 21.5 percent of male respondents compared to 39 percent of female respondents to my survey expressing a desire to help their parents, family, village, or country.

PLAY

In her detailed study of the anthropology of play, Schwartzman (1978) described many of the functions of children's play, including socialization, satirization, projection, communication, and even learning to learn.[23] As she noted, "Children at play learn how to be sensitive to the effects of context and the importance of relationships; they develop the capacity to adopt an 'as if' set towards objects, persons, and situation; and they continually explore the possibilities of interpretation and reinterpretation and with this the creation of new possibilities" (328).

Moyle studied children's games in Tonga and concluded that "most games . . . are played for their own sake and do not crystallize or confirm behavioral norms" (1987, 211). Yet even when the content of a game appears to fit this description—for example, juggling while reciting nonsense verse—the players are acquiring socially valued abilities, such as dexterousness, balance, grace, and so on. The context in which a game is played is also important, and a positive audience response carries messages about a child's competence and ability.

The *way* in which games are played is especially significant, and children's play in Tonga is particularly interesting for the ways in which children explore status behavior, as in their rivalry and competition. Children also frequently incorporate into their play imitations of the various forms of control used by adults toward children. Often these imitations have a strongly satirical quality. For example, children imitate the speech pattern in which statements and directives are made into questions by using the particle ē? "Give me the ball" will become "Give me the ball, ē?" asked with questioning intonation. The question is then repeated, or just the ē? ē? increasingly loudly and with an exaggeratedly angry tone and facial expression. This delights the other children, who readily recognize the parody. Children also copy the threatening gestures adults use and the typical motions of hitting used in punishment. Usually this is done in fun, but it is sometimes in earnest when the older children are exercising their authority over their younger playmates.

As we have seen, play begins almost from birth, as babies' kin seek their attention by singing, talking, teasing, and otherwise interacting with them and encouraging their responsiveness. In the following chapter I will describe in more detail these early interactions and show how children under two become a main source of amusement and entertainment within their household.

Older children play in mixed-age groups of siblings and neighbors (who are often relations). Mixed-sex play groups are not uncommon until children are about nine or ten years old, but even younger children tend to form same-sex groups whenever possible, partly because of the brother-sister avoidance pattern and partly because boys and girls often play different games. When there are large groups of children they also tend to separate into younger and older groups, but at other times children from toddlers to teenagers play together. While older children are at school, younger children play together and are expected to stay within an adult's sight. It is taken for granted that neighbors keep an eye on each other's children, and they either discipline each other's children or report any problems to the children's caregivers. Sometimes neighbors are explicitly asked to *tokanga'i* (watch out for or care for) children, as when a mother leaves them while she goes to town to shop.

The Beagleholes claimed that in Pangai children from about eighteen months old were "free to go where they will or where they can" and that gangs of mixed-age children roamed the bush and the beach (1941b, 82). Similarly, Spillius stated that by four years of age children were "allowed to roam all round the village and out to the plantations," but she did note that children in Nuku'alofa were kept closer to home (1958, 64). Nowhere did I see children under school age allowed to wander away from home, although they were sometimes allowed to go by themselves to another house within their village. Even older children are generally kept close to home—partly so they can be called to do jobs or run errands—and it is only boys, from about seven or eight years of age, who are sometimes allowed to wander further from home. A factor contributing to the closer surveillance of young children nowadays is the danger posed by the greatly increased number of vehicles on Tongan roads. Children therefore socialize most often with other children in their household and the children of neighboring households. They also have frequent opportunities to play with other children from the village at school, and at any event where some or all of the villagers congregate: for koka'anga, preparations for feasts, celebrations, dance practices, and so on.

In most groups of children some are of higher status than others because of their genealogical relationships, and this disparity has some effect on their interactions. Given the great age range of siblings in many families, children's peer groups can contain siblings, cousins, aunts, uncles, nephews, and nieces. As has already been indicated, these relationships are all marked by unequal status, with a father's kin being of higher status and a mother's kin of lower status. Within the same generation, children's tama 'a tu'asina (children of mother's brothers) are of lower status and their tama 'a mehekitanga (children of father's sisters) of higher status. In anga fakatonga, "sister's children may take what they want from brother's children and eat the foods they leave over" (Aoyagi 1966, 163). Children should not hit the children of their mehekitanga or touch their heads or possessions.

However, the extent to which these restrictions are observed depends largely on how closely families adhere to anga fakatonga and who is present when children are interacting. None of the children I observed were expected to comply with any of these restrictions except on formal occasions or when nonresident adult kin were present, such as during preparations for a feast. Even then, the more specific prohibitions such as not touching the heads of tama 'a mehekitanga were not enforced. There is often considerable status rivalry between children, within the peer group itself, yet this is seldom based on criteria such as social rank or kin-related status. For the most part, children have their own criteria for the flexible hierarchies they establish within their play groups, such as physical strength and ability or popularity.[24]

Early accounts of games and sports in Tonga tended to focus on those played by chiefly men (brief accounts can be found in Beaglehole 1967; Collocott 1928; Ferdon 1987; Gifford 1971a; Orange 1840). Children's games that were described include *matamatakupenga* (cat's cradle), walking on stilts of halved coconut shells, and a game called *sikaulutoa* (or *sika*), which was played by chiefly boys, using a reed throwing-stick with a head of *toa* (casuarina or ironwood) wood. *Hiko* (juggling) was accompanied by rhymes, examples of which can be found in Collocott (1928, 100) and Moyle (1987, 216–219). Anderson, an officer with Cook's 1777 expedition, mentioned that boys and girls boxed as adults did; another officer, Samwell, stated that wrestling tournaments began with boys of six or seven and progressed through age groups up to old men and noted that "these Exercises [wrestling and boxing] are held in great esteem among them, the children are brought up in the Practice of them from their Infancy, especially the Sons of Chiefs" (Beaglehole 1967, 901, 1027, 1028). Whitcombe describes a number of games not listed in earlier reports, including games of skill (bow and arrow, slingshot, and the like) played by boys, and a game played by children of both sexes, *fisi*, in which chips of wood were flicked over an upended, rolled mat. He also describes *aamoa*, in which an old woman covered herself with a tapa or *ngatu* and tried to frighten groups of little girls (1930, 7–8).

In 1988 the most popular game for both sexes was marbles *(mapu)*. (In some schools only boys were allowed to play.) *Mapu* was formerly played with round seeds from a *feta‘u* (calophyllum) or *tuitui* (candlenut) tree, but nowadays imported glass marbles are used. Popular girls' games include *moa* (jacks [knucklebones], played with stones), juggling (with *tuitui* or small hard fruits such as limes, often six to eight at a time), and women's basketball (netball). Both boys and girls play cards, as well as more active games such as rounders and cricket. Rugby is very popular among older boys. Other games are made up on the spur of the moment, as when a group of girls invented a game using a tiny piece of straw one of them had found. They sat in a circle with their eyes shut as one girl hid the straw in the grass; then the others had a mad scramble to find it. Moyle describes a number of games that are accompanied by sung or spoken rhymes (1987). Some of these game songs refer to specific individuals or events (historical or contemporary); others contain nonsense words to provide rhythm for accompanying actions. Though both boys and girls sing game songs, they are most frequently sung by girls, to accompany juggling or hand-clapping games played in pairs. Most girls' games are less active than boys', although when they are playing in mixed-sex groups there is little difference between boys' and girls' behavior.

A great deal of children's play is not in the form of organized games or sports. Children climb trees, chase one another, swim, and so on. Often in

Holonga I sat and watched the children play outside, the girls usually seated in a group playing games like hand clapping and juggling, and the boys throwing rocks, running around with machetes, climbing tree stumps, climbing all over any vehicle parked near the house, riding each other around on the handlebars of bicycles while others chased them and tried to knock them off, wrestling each other, and doing any other energetic activity that occurred to them.

Imported toys are now available in some stores, especially in Nuku'alofa and at Christmas time. Others are sent by relatives living overseas. The majority of village children do not have such toys, and any toys they do have are quickly broken and discarded. Toys are usually limited to marbles, perhaps a few balloons (or more often bits of burst balloon), playing cards, and, for boys, slingshots constructed of wood and tire rubber. Some children also have bicycles. The most popular playthings are sticks, small stones (for *moa*), and other objects found lying around. Empty cans are sometimes nailed to sticks to make a long-handled wheel. During the holidays at the end of the year older boys construct *fana pitu* (bamboo cannons), which make a booming sound when their kerosene contents are lit.

Lovett claimed that games of "make-believe" are not a common part of children's play (1958, 21). However, many games clearly involve an element of fantasy, as when boys pretend to be ninja and do *kalate* (karate). One elderly woman told me that she and her friends used to make little houses on the ground, using shells, but I saw no similar games. However, the little girls in our household in 1986 loved to play at being grown up and would carefully put red flower petals on their nails for nail polish, wear adults' shoes and sunglasses, and carry a teapot around pretending to make tea. Play that involves pretend threatening and punishing is clearly a form of fantasy play, and this element of role playing commonly emerges even in organized games such as cricket or rugby.

One spontaneous game of make-believe that I watched in 1986 was a clear example of children's sorting out and commenting on "rules for relationships" (Schwartzman 1978, 274n15). Losa (aged ten) organized the girls of our household—Elenoa, Sela, and Finau, aged three to five—to play at being her children. After they pretended to talk on the telephone, she pretended to give them money to go to buy ice cream. She then ordered them to go to sleep, first raising a shoe in a threatening gesture, then hitting them with it, shouting *"Mohe!"* (sleep). The other children responded with giggles, at which Losa yelled *"Longo!"* (quiet). As the game progressed she became increasingly violent, hitting the children harder and more often, until she inadvertently hit a sore on Sela's leg, which began to bleed. The game ended abruptly as Sela went off crying and Losa went home.

The sequence of events that the children in this game acted out condensed some of the most significant elements of parent-child relationships in
Tonga. Giving the children money for ice cream represents the emphasis on
material giving and satisfaction of wants that characterizes parents' expressions of 'ofa for their children. The sequence of ordering, threatening, and
smacking occurs frequently in most Tongan households, although in this
case the little children responded with giggles rather than compliance or
resistance. When one child was injured and went to seek help the game
ended because the possibility of real punishment precipitated the abrupt
departure of the "mother."

Children are often rough and aggressive in their play, particularly boys.
Children hit, pull hair, snatch things, punch, and are generally very physical
and competitive. My son commented once, "With Tongan kids someone
always gets hurt." Accusations of cheating are common and often cause
heated arguments or physical fights. When adults are nearby children tend
to be more restrained, but they may try to draw the adults' attention to
others' cheating, hitting, and so on. Adults often do not respond, but sometimes they intervene verbally or with physical punishment if the children's
shouting or crying is annoying them. Very occasionally, adults respond by
further encouraging children's fighting, watching it as a kind of amusing
performance.

Adults seldom play with children, saying it would be "a waste of time"
and that they "don't want to get down" (i.e., demean themselves). When
adults play cards together they sometimes let older children and adolescents
join in, but younger children are considered to be nuisances. The games I
took with me to Tonga (board games, dice games, cards, and the like) were
quickly appropriated by adults, who excluded children unless there was no
one else to play with. Then the children were allowed to "play"—for example, to sit and watch as an adult rolled the dice and moved the pieces on the
board for them. Adults and children share a considerable amount of leisure
time but tend to remain in their own spheres, or the children hover on the
periphery of the adults' activities. The evenings in all of the households in
which I lived were spent peacefully unless preparations for a feast were under
way. The whole household would watch a video or the adults would play
cards, gossip, or listen to the radio and absentmindedly hum and sing along,
with the children either playing together or just watching the adults.

On the infrequent occasions when adults play with children and young
adolescents, the games are usually rough and involve a lot of teasing, hitting,
and mock threatening. One evening a group of men and teenage boys were
playing a loud, boisterous game of cards. Tevita kept saying to the watching
children, "Go and get me a knife, I'll kill him!" referring to one of the young

players, Siaosi (aged twelve). A little girl gave him a small knife, and he held it up mock threateningly. When Siaosi won a hand of cards Tevita jumped up and pushed him over, grasping his hair and holding the knife to his throat, while the other players roared with laughter. Later another man pretended to be very angry with Siaosi and whacked him hard around the head several times. Everyone, including Siaosi, laughed, but he looked shaken and was very quiet for some time.

Children playing with adults sometimes end up in tears because they are teased or hit too hard or because they become overexcited and are shouted at or smacked for being too noisy and rough. In the case above, Siaosi was clearly being put in his place by the men, but he accepted and even encouraged their behavior as part of the fun. Other games involve an adult prompting a young child with rude or teasing comments, such as 'ulu pala (having sores on the head), to shout insults at other children. The latter then try to hit the young child, who shelters behind the adult for protection. In all of these games between adults and children there is overt encouragement of physically rough and cheeky behavior. The approval shown in these contexts for bold and assertive behavior is in stark contrast to the usual emphasis on submission and obedience.[25]

By the time Tongan children reach puberty their socializing, like their work, is almost entirely gender-segregated. They are expected to contribute a considerable amount of labor to their household by then and so have less time for recreation. This is especially so for girls, who by their teenage years spend most of their time at school or doing household chores. Basketball is one of their few leisure activities, and the interschool and intervillage competitions are taken very seriously. Before competition matches there is sometimes a formal exchange of koloa between the two sides, and following the match the home side presents the visiting team with food (usually bread, cakes, and biscuits) and soft drinks. Basketball is played very vigorously and sometimes aggressively, though for the most part good-naturedly.

The boys of seven or eight years old who form groups and spend their spare time together often attach themselves to groups of older boys, the talavou (see Marcus 1978, 257–259). These groups of boys wander into the bush to eat fruit, go swimming or fishing together, or go to town to hang around. They often have their own hut in the village, where they eat, sleep, and socialize—play cards, tell stories, and so on. Many of these groups style themselves as "gangs," in their own version of the gangs seen in popular American movies. Some even have their own identifying graffiti and names.

Some teenagers spend their free time in religious groups and youth organizations (potongaue talavou), the latter being mainly involved with agricultural activities. Such groups are an important arena for socializing, and mixed-sex groups also provide opportunities for courting. More popular are the village dances (*hulohula*) and school *fakasosiale*, which have virtually replaced *faikava* as the primary context for courting (on kava and courtship see Perminow 1993). However, for many Tongans, particularly of the older generation, they symbolize a change for the worse in Tonga today. There is widespread disapproval of the fact that teenagers are sometimes very openly sexual in their dancing; of the unregulated nature of the courtship that occurs (in comparison to the *faikava*); and of the smoking, drinking, and fighting that often marks male, and sometimes female, behavior at dances.

An important modern leisure activity in Tonga, for people of all ages, is watching video movies. By late 1989 up to 30 percent of homes had video-cassette recorders (VCRs), and there were thirty-six privately run video libraries (*Matangi Tonga* 1989c, 29).[26] In 1986 the only home with a VCR in Holonga was that of the "chief," Kapukava. Members of our household some-times went to his home in the evenings to watch videos, and there would be up to thirty other people there, including children and teenagers watching from outside through the louvre windows. The most popular videos were ninja movies (Chinese martial arts movies), though many other types were watched. At that time films were still screened on occasion in the village hall, and the difference in people's behavior then was marked. These film screenings were social events, and people chatted to one another or listened to the radio while watching the pictures on the screen. In contrast, when watching a video people tended to sit silently, only occasionally making comments about the movie or laughing.

This behavior was still notable in 1989, when many more homes owned videos, and movies were viewed almost every night (sometimes all night) and throughout weekends. Often, the same movie is watched many times, and any videos newly rented, or sent from relatives overseas, are passed around among any neighbors with VCRs. The households I lived in during fieldwork all had VCRs. Children living in, or visiting these households, were frequently allowed to watch movies with the adults until they fell asleep late at night. Favorite movies included any with Chuck Norris ("Saki Nolisi") or Rambo and the ever-popular martial arts movies. Tomasi, the five-year-old boy in our Holonga household, had learned to say "Fuck you!" and "Oh, shit!" from movies—the only English words he used confidently!—and like other children he loved to play *kalate* and ninja games.

Home movies are very popular, and Tongan residents and their relatives overseas often send videos of important events to each other. This seems to contribute more to sustaining the ties between them than do letters or phone calls, and the emotional impact of the recorded scenes is sometimes intense. The viewers can watch together and in an important sense participate together in the events they witness. Such occasions are also a context for instructing children on kinship, tradition, cultural values, and so on, as the people and events they observe are explained and interpreted for them. In a study of Tongan videographers in Utah, Hammond showed that their videos emphasize their "cultural heritage." She suggests that "Tongan video imagery will surely play a significant role in the self-definition of future generations of Tongans in the U.S." (1988, 397). To a lesser extent, this could also be true for Tongans at home.

CHAPTER 6

LEARNING TO BE *POTO*

Having discussed certain kinds of knowledge that Tongan children acquire and some of the primary contexts in which they do so, I turn in this and the following chapter to look at ways in which they acquire that knowledge. Children learn continuously. Learning does not only occur through didactic teaching, as when children are given advice, although in Tongan notions of child development direct advice and instruction are the preferred means of imparting cultural knowledge. The process of learning in childhood is enormously complex, and a detailed examination of the cognitive development of Tongan children is outside the scope of this study. My aim here is to identify significant forms of learning and explore the ways in which they are part of culturally specific beliefs about child development and the aims of socialization. Hence, I discuss the "performance" that encourages infants' sociability and also sets the stage for the obedience and helpfulness that are highly valued aspects of their later behavior. Observation and imitation are important for teaching particular skills as well as for establishing an awareness of and receptiveness to the demands of higher-status persons. I examine language socialization, particularly in terms of the messages conveyed to children about status-appropriate language and associated behavior. Overall, it will become clear that the ideal upheld to children is for them to remain quietly on the periphery of adults' activities, paying attention in order to acquire social and practical skills and be ready to respond obediently to instructions. Of course, children's behavior in practice frequently does not match this ideal, and when it doesn't they may be verbally rebuked, as in the grumbling and scolding discussed in this chapter, or physically punished, in ways examined in detail in the following chapter.

PERFORMANCE

Ochs has noted that in Western Samoa "children are directed to perform before they can speak" (1988, 167), and the same can be said of Tongan children. As has been shown, babies are at the center of their household's attention for their first year or so. The Ritchies have interpreted this early "indulgence" as a cultural response to potentially high infant mortality in

Polynesia (1979, 50). As I will show, however, early attention and affection also encourage sociability and obedience. Until children are about two years old much of the attention they receive takes the form of amused, concerned, or interested responses to their movements, facial expressions, and vocalizations. From birth babies' actions are treated as performances, as people closely observe them and comment to one another: "See how she's smiling!" "Look at her eyes!" Before children begin to "perform" on their own, adults help them, as when a proud father amused the other passengers on a bus by balancing his infant daughter on his hand, holding only her feet as she pushed her legs straight. Although amusing behavior is often directed by others, children's spontaneous behavior is also treated as performance. Bernstein commented that "infants, being not yet fully formed social beings, are a source of great amusement for adults. It is funny when they evacuate in public, have a rip in the crotch of their pants, or eat messily" (1983, 56). 'Ofa's spontaneous behavior often caused great amusement in our Holonga household. At mealtimes she would sit on an adult's lap, and everyone would laugh as she made a mess with her food or pulled funny faces. Gender distinctions affect people's responses to babies' behavior, however, and amusement at girls' "immodest" behavior often takes the form of teasing disapproval.

Babies are *valevale*, unable to think for themselves (literally, foolish foolish), and can get away with much behavior that is inappropriate (*ta'e fe'unga*) for only slightly older children. Children of four or five often become overexcited as they watch babies and toddlers behave in ways that, to them, must seem excitingly dangerous. This excitement sometimes prompts them to go beyond the limits of acceptable behavior for them—by copying the baby, or becoming aggressive, or just rushing around loudly laughing and shouting. Sometimes, when the older people watching are relaxed and eager for amusement, the older children's actions will also be treated as performance and they may be urged to act even sillier, but more often they will be brought back into line with a sharp word or slap.

Spontaneous performances that are amusing are encouraged while children are still very young, as when a toddler does a funny dance or attempts to vocalize. However, the performances that are given most encouragement are those involving imitation, and as soon as babies begin to mimic others' actions and vocalizations they are constantly coached to produce amusing performances. The frequent face-to-face contact between babies and others often involves this coaching, or "elicited imitation routines" (Ochs 1990, 290). Babies who respond are richly rewarded with laughter and affection. These routines are carried out to amuse the participants and any audience, and they are also an important form of early learning. The behavior children are urged to imitate is often "bad" behavior that would be punished in an older child. I watched one day as Mele, a teenage girl from next door, played with ten-month-old 'Ofa. Holding 'Ofa on her lap, facing her, Mele moved her head from side to side, which 'Ofa copied. Mele then poked 'Ofa in the chest, and 'Ofa poked back, then hit Mele on the face. Mele pretended to cry and 'Ofa hit her again; then Mele hit 'Ofa gently and 'Ofa pretended to cry. Finally Mele began to show 'Ofa how to raise her finger in a rude gesture, laughing as 'Ofa copied her.

Imitation routines sometimes are carried out with older children as a form of amusement for the older people present, as when they are urged to call out teasing or insulting phrases to someone. Spontaneous performances are not generally encouraged in older children except within their own peer group. On the few occasions when I observed children performing to amuse older members of their households they were exhibiting skills they had acquired, such as dance movements or juggling, rather than inventing words or actions by themselves.

Babies and toddlers are frequently urged to do the actions they learn through imitation routines, and they are encouraged to repeat them many times, often until the baby, rather than the audience, loses interest. 'Ofa acquired an extensive repertoire of amusing behaviors during the second half of her first year. It began when she made a funny face and everyone present laughed and made a fuss over her. They called it her *tēvolo* face—the face of a "devil" or mischievous spirit—and encouraged her to do it again and again. She soon learned many more actions that elicited the same response, mainly through imitation routines rather than spontaneous actions. These included wiping her nose with the back of her hand or her clothing, raising the middle finger of her hand in a rude gesture, crossing herself by tapping at her forehead and chest, bobbing up and down as people sang and clapped and called out *"Mālie!"* (bravo), giving someone whatever she had in her hand when they asked for it with an outstretched hand, kissing people (and pictures in magazines), clapping hands, and waving goodbye. Other behavior she learned through imitation was aggressive, such as raising her hand threateningly, hitting her siblings, and making aggressive gestures and scowling angrily, and these actions were equally enthusiastically encouraged. Teaching her these actions and watching her repeatedly perform them was for several months a favorite activity in the household. When the children came home from school, or the adults home from work, 'Ofa would be urged to do one or more of these amusing acts. She would also be called to come and show them off for visitors, and the people in the household frequently commented to one another about what she had learned. In this way, her behavior became a focal point for the household members' interactions with one another.

The same pattern of encouraging learning occurs in the acquisition of motor skills such as crawling and walking. Babies' efforts to master new skills are regarded as entertaining, and they are encouraged by laughter, praise, and by being urged to repeat the performance. Children will throw things along the floor for a crawling baby to fetch or hold a baby upright by the hands and urge the infant to walk, saying "*Ha'u, ha'u*" (come, come). Toward the end of 'Ofa's first year her older siblings, Tomasi and Elenoa, frequently encouraged her to walk. On one occasion they played a game with her in which they were both seated on chairs with a low table between them, getting 'Ofa to take pens from one to the other and back again by walking along holding the table. This game continued until the older children were tired of it, but while it was proceeding several other household members came in to watch proudly.

Children's behavior is often treated as performance for the first two years, the period in which they have the greatest amount of contact with adults. People's responses to their performances encourage the children's sociability. Their performances are rewarded with attention, affection, and verbal praise, such as "*Mālie!*" and "*Poto!*" These rewards gradually diminish throughout the third and fourth years so that by the age of four they are rarely offered. These years are also the period during which children spend an increasing amount of time in children's play groups or on the periphery of adult activities, so that there are fewer opportunities for performances to adults. The kinds of actions that once constituted amusing performances, such as rude gestures, aggressive behavior, or silliness, are actively discouraged from the age of about two, so that once they are three or four, children know they are likely to be punished for behavior that once captured the attention of the other members of their household. Children continue to perform for each other throughout childhood and adolescence, giving one another the attention and encouragement that they formerly received from adults. Learning to shift their largely exhibitionist and aggressive performative behavior to their peer group is one of children's earliest lessons in the importance of context for determining appropriate behavior.

OBSERVATION AND IMITATION

When children begin to learn household chores it is as part of their "performances." For example, one of little 'Ofa's amusing acts was to go to fetch her father's pillow for him when he asked for it, trotting to the bedroom and lugging back a pillow as big as herself. As with other performances these acts of obedience are rewarded with praise, affection, and further attention. As children get older they learn more tasks by observation and imitation, and the performative aspect of their behavior, and others' responses to it, declines. The early period in which children's actions are praised, rewarded, and otherwise gain adults' attention seems to develop a willingness to help with chores and obey directions that persists after the rewards cease. This is reinforced by the increasingly severe sanctions, especially physical punishment, for *not* obeying.

Children begin to practice tasks before they are expected to be capable of doing them. Toddlers try to sweep up leaves, cut the grass with a machete, or peel vegetables and are usually allowed to handle the tools required for such tasks. Spillius remarked that "small children are also allowed to interrupt their parents' work, and they will be shown how to do it even if they are not old enough to do it properly" (1958, 62). This may be the case when the parents or other adults are not busy or feeling irritable, but a far more common response to such interruptions is to tell the child to stop being *faka-hoha‘a* (troublesome), *fakahela* (tiring), or *fie poto*. By the end of the second year, and increasingly in the third and fourth years, these are also common reactions to children's attempts to gain attention by "performing."

Children learn to watch adults work without being intrusive, then either practice by themselves when they get an opportunity or wait until they are asked to help. Whenever a feast is being prepared little boys can be seen on the periphery of the group of older boys and men preparing and roasting the pigs. They will be asked to do small tasks, such as hold a pig's leg straight so it can be cleaned, until eventually they become part of the group. Until that time they are happy to watch or to sit beside the men and roast bits of offal on sticks. Girls watch the women prepare and cook food, assisting with small tasks and helping to keep younger children out of the way.

Household chores are not the only skills learned by observation and imitation. Explicit instruction is seldom given for skills such as bathing, dressing, and using tools or for using other household items such as the telephone, videocassette recorder, and television. The behavior appropriate to interactions with different kin is also learned to a great extent not by instruction, but by children's observing the interactions of those around them, both in their everyday lives and on formal occasions. Children find that different relatives treat them differently and expect certain kinds of behavior of them. At the same time, they also learn that they can treat different relatives with very different degrees of familiarity.

Formal occasions provide important opportunities to watch and listen to adults' interactions. The alliances, rights, and obligations involved in Tongan kinship are seen most clearly at events such as weddings, funerals, and first birthdays, which are organized according to principles of kinship. Children see how food and *koloa* are prepared, presented, and redistributed, and they listen to speeches and witness status disputes. On the occasion marking the opening of a new youth hall in Holonga, for example, two brothers-in-law, both heads of their own families, nearly came to blows over their relative status and the consequent positioning of their *pola* (trays of food). Their heated argument, and the intervention of others to prevent a physical fight, was watched with great interest and excitement by the children present.

Children tend to hover on the periphery of any adult activity, sometimes being called upon to do an errand, but for the most part simply watching. Bernstein observed that children play a role as spreaders of gossip:

> They wander in bands and are so ubiquitous that their presence ceases to be noticed, allowing them to spend a good deal of time looking in windows and standing outside of doors. They are in a superior position to listen to quarrels and conversations, and to observe adult behavior. A parent or relative will at times send children out to see what is happening in another home. If they are caught listening in, family reputations are not damaged, since parents cannot be taken to task for the behavior of naughty and uncontrollable children. In this way children carry information to adults with little risk of reprimand. (1983, 135–136)

I would argue that parents can indeed be blamed for their children's behavior, but the children are rarely "caught listening in." Although children will stand watching through the windows of a house in which a video movie is on, a band is rehearsing, or some other ordinary activity is occurring, they quickly learn to be circumspect in their observation of more private or controversial events. Children also often overhear personal details about themselves or others being openly discussed because even if they are sitting in the same room, adults tend to ignore their presence. The role of children as gossip spreaders is recognized in their frequent use as chaperones for adolescent girls. As Gifford commented, "The child could not be expected to keep a secret" (1971b, 191).

Observation is acknowledged as an important means of acquiring the knowledge required to behave appropriately, and there is an emphasis on children learning to *tokanga* (to notice, to pay attention). It can be said of an older child "*kuo 'atamai fakatokanga 'a e tamasi'i*" (Bott n.d., 21), meaning the child's mind has begun to pay attention to things. *Tokanga* has strong connotations of listening and is often used to refer to the importance of children listening to parents' instructions and orders. Physical punishment is regarded as an effective method of making children *tokanga*. Because *tokanga* involves observing, listening, and obeying, it is thus central to the process of becoming *poto*. The process of acquiring knowledge must be controlled, however; although it is good for children to begin to *tokanga*, they should do so in relation to what they are expected to know, rather than in the sense of developing an inquiring, curious mind.

The word *'ilo* means "to see" and "to know" (or, as a noun, "knowledge"), and its use in childhood reveals this emphasis on controlling the acquisition of knowledge. Children trying to watch something they should not or asking inquisitive questions may be told to stop being *fie 'ilo*: to stop trying to know more than they should. *Fie 'ilo* is often used to mean "busybody," as when 'Ofa would crawl to the front door or climb up to look out of the window and her mother would snatch her away, laughingly telling her she was *fie 'ilo*.

LANGUAGE SOCIALIZATION

"The process of becoming a competent member of society is realized to a large extent through language, by acquiring knowledge of its functions, social distribution, and interpretations in and across socially defined situations" (Schieffelin and Ochs 1986b, 168). Thus children are socialized through language; they are also socialized to use language (Ochs 1990, 287). This process of language socialization is crucial in the development of their social and cultural identities. Recent work on language socialization by researchers such as Ochs and Schieffelin has shown how a culture's "worldviews" are expressed in the content, forms, and functions of discourse so that language is a vital means by which children learn these world views. Ochs states that "the greatest part of sociocultural information is keyed *implicitly*, through language use" (1990, 291; emphasis in original), so that language carries both covert and overt messages. An examination of language socialization is thus one means by which anthropologists can "figure out the rules and conditions that govern talking and access to knowledge in a society" and investigate "discursive procedures that regulate the production, the circulation, and the consumption of knowledge statements" (Lindstrom 1990, xi–xii).

Tongans talk to babies from birth, although at first this often takes the form of comments indirectly aimed at other adults. When people speak to babies their comments are sometimes meant for some other person present. Instead of saying to the mother, "Isn't the baby fat!" a person will say to the baby, "You're too fat!" or "You eat too often (*fa'a kai*)."[1] There is no distinct baby-talk register, but people sometimes adopt either a gentle and affectionate or a mock angry tone with little babies. When babies respond to others' gestures or vocalizations the people observing will draw each other's attention to the response or call others to come and see, exclaiming *"Sio, sio!"* (look, look).

The most frequent form of speech directed at babies is questioning, and even statements are usually ended on a questioning note by adding the *ē?* sound. The most common kinds of questioning statements made to babies include comments on their behavior or characteristics, such as *"Fa'a kai, ē?"* (eat too much, eh?) or *"Fakapikopiko, ē?"* (lazy, eh?), or directives, such as *"Tokoto, ē?"* (lie down, eh?). Questions about the intentions and desires of children, such as *"Te ke kai?"* (will you eat?) or *"Tau ō?"* (shall we go?), are also asked from birth. Often, *"ē?"* is repeated several times, increasingly forcefully, as if the speaker is urging the baby to respond—as indeed babies do as they get older. When babies begin to babble, their sounds are sometimes given intention by the person holding them, especially if these early vocalizations appear to be made in response to questions. Thus, before babies can speak they are treated as responsive, communicating persons.

Speech is encouraged by urging babies to repeat sounds they make that resemble words; often these sounds are interpreted as names. Pet names sometimes arise from this, as when a teenage girl was always referred to as "Tin-da" to her baby cousin, who had once made those sounds in an apparent attempt to say the girl's name, 'Iha. Unlike some of the actions babies learn as performances, there is little direct attempt to teach new words, although such teaching does occur to a limited extent, as when Alisi tried to teach 'Ofa to say *'uma* (kiss) and some names for parts of the face. More often, the baby spontaneously makes a sound, which is interpreted as a word, and then the baby is encouraged to repeat it many times. Apart from names, these first utterances are usually interpreted as *tā* or *pā* (hit), which, as I will show in chapter 7, is part of the general encouragement of aggression in infancy. Verbal interactions with babies and toddlers rarely involve expansion, where the caregiver expands the child's vocalization into a complete phrase or sentence. Only when children are older and speaking confidently do their elders begin to correct their speech on occasion—for example, when a child uses an incorrect pronoun form that excludes instead of includes the person the child is addressing.

Encouraging babies to perform teaches them to show off, to seek audiences and interact with those around them. A number of features of language socialization in the first year also encourage sociability. One of the most common ways to distract unsettled and crying babies, once they are old enough to recognize household members, is to call these people's names when they are not present. Sometimes the words for various animals, such as *pusi* (cat) or *puaka* (pig), are called instead of people's names. The person calling out injects a tone of excitement into her or his voice so that the baby stops fretting and looks about. This tactic may be repeated many times, with different names, and is often enough to keep the baby quiet for some time. The names of the child's parents (or primary caregivers) are frequently called, as are the names of other household members. This "distracting routine" (Watson-Gegeo and Gegeo 1986, 113) thus not only distracts babies; it also constantly reminds them of their connections with others, even in the others' absence. The primary attachment to the baby's parents is encouraged by making the parents the focal point of many verbal interactions with the baby, such as these routines of calling names.

'Ofa often did not see her father, Siale, all day, because he worked long hours. His name was frequently called out to distract her throughout the day, and when he did come home the others in the house would again excitedly call to her "Siale!" or "Poppa!" She soon learned to recognize the sound of his truck, and by the time she was about ten months old she would scream and shout her own attempts at his name whenever she heard the truck approaching. This whole process encouraged the attachment between the father and daughter, as the excitement generated for 'Ofa by her father's arrival meant that she was responsive to him when he came into the house. In turn, Siale was usually attentive and affectionate to 'Ofa when he came home to her exuberant welcome.

Calling the name of absent persons and of animals is increasingly effective as the baby learns to associate them with their names. The calling of names also functions to encourage babies to acquire these words very early in their language development. Learning to associate the names with the person or animal they signify occurs indirectly, as the baby observes interactions between other people. It also occurs directly, as people point to animals and name them or play a game in which they hold the baby and call the names of people present in the house. Because they are speaking for the baby they use a higher-pitched, playful tone. The people called then automatically respond "Ko au" (it's me), the standard response to being called, or they may make some playful comment to the baby, thus establishing a link between the name and the person. Babies seem to quickly learn that by calling a person's name they are guaranteed a response, even if only "Ko au." At other times the calling of names is used to get nearby children to come to distract a baby. Because the children do appear sometimes to play with the baby, the infant soon associates the names with the children, and calling the children's names even when they are not close by becomes all the more effective as a distraction. A baby's own name is also sometimes called out as a distraction. Later, when the child begins to talk, she or he is encouraged to say her or his own name, as well as to reply to a person calling that name by saying "*Ko au.*"

When people visit the house they often call out the baby's name when they arrive, before greeting anyone else, and when they leave they call good-bye to the baby or call his or her name several times as they walk away from the house, calling the name and then saying "*ē?*"[2] Whoever is holding the child at these times answers, giving the correct greeting formula or replying to the calls of farewell by saying " '*Io!*" (yes). During their visit, guests (par-ticularly women) focus their attention initially on the baby, calling the child's name, smiling and speaking to the child, and holding her or him or, with an older baby, encouraging the child to come to them. The guests con-tinue to make occasional comments and observations on the baby's behavior or characteristics throughout their stay.

As they leave, visitors often act out a sequence in which they pretend to encourage the baby to leave with them. They hold out their hands to the baby, saying "*Tau ō?*" with an encouraging facial expression. The baby is not expected to respond, but if the child does, the visitor will exclaim "Look, look, he's coming to me!" and all will laugh. This sequence is acted out even for newborn babies, and as they get older it is gradually extended, from the person's briefly holding the baby to pretending to move away from the house with the baby. Toward the end of the first year the baby may actually be taken for brief periods with the departing guests if they live close by. When this happened to 'Ofa for the first time, she was so accustomed to being held by the teenage girl who was visiting that she was happy to go toward her out-stretched hands. The older girl withdrew her hands at first and exclaimed, "Look, she's coming to me!" Then she picked 'Ofa up and sat with her for a minute, getting her to wave goodbye to the family members sitting nearby, before walking off with her. As she went she spoke quietly to the litle girl: "We'll go now. 'Ofa's coming with me," and so on, and 'Ofa went off happily for a brief visit to the older girl's home next door.

The aspect of language socialization that Tongans themselves emphasize most strongly is direct teaching, in the form of advice, instructions, and orders. Because the characteristics associated with the unsocialized child (foolishness, aggression, and the like) are negatively valued, emphasis is placed on actively teaching children correct values and behavior. This teaching begins long before children are thought to be old enough to under-stand properly. Household tasks are learned by observation and practice, but the value and importance of work itself is taught more formally, through advice and instruction on "appropriate" (*taau*) values and behavior.[3]

Although children's speech and behavior are initially a focus of positive attention within their household, increasing demands for compliance and deference are accompanied by the clear message, through language socialization, that higher-status persons speak and those of lower status listen and obey. In the wider society this is exemplified in the *fono* (public meeting), at which the assembled people are given information and instructions by a high-status person (or that person's representative), with little or no opportunity for them to question or debate the matter at hand.

Children are expected to listen and not to question the words of their superiors. According to Moana, "It is important for children to learn to listen to the things they are told. We all see the children who listen; they finish up well." Listening is explicitly associated with learning, even when speech is not directed at children. Tonga explained that as a child, if she was present when adults were talking, "I was told to just listen, and if I heard some good talk (*talanoa 'oku sai*) I could take it away with me."

When children are present during adult conversations they are expected to remain silent. Even when adults are discussing a child or an event she or he was involved in or knows about in the child's presence, the child should not join in. These restrictions on a child's contribution to conversation index the child's status and mark the child "as someone not fully in possession of her experience" (Miller et al. 1990, 278; cf. Miller and Moore 1989). Restrictions on a child's speech indicate, as does the adult's editing of narratives the child tells, that she or he is not yet "a full-fledged person" (Miller et al. 1990, 299). Another important aspect of personal narrative in Tonga is the content of tales by adults about children, which I have shown is predominantly of children's negatively valued characteristics and behavior.

Children of all ages are strongly discouraged from asking direct questions; adults either ignore them or treat them with impatience or anger. When young children ask questions or make requests, adults often respond by directing an older child to deal with them. This kind of verbal sequence has also been described by Ochs for Western Samoa (1982, 83–85). Not only should higher-status persons hold the role of speaker; they should ideally initiate all interactions with lower-status persons. In this Tonga contrasts with Pukapuka in the Cook Islands, where, as Borofsky notes, "children have little status to lose vis-à-vis adults. Hence, they frequently ask direct questions." He adds that children later learn to ask questions in a deferential manner, and that to avoid appearing ignorant, they avoid asking direct questions (1987, 85–86). A similar pattern is described by Lindstrom for Tanna in Vanuatu, where small children ask questions but learn that as they get older, questioning is considered to reveal their ignorance (1990, 114).[4] In Tonga, too, asking questions can prove embarrassing (*fakamā*), as it may lead to teasing about one's foolishness, poor manners, or inappropriate desire to appear knowledgeable. Questions are also discouraged by the way in which any person instructing a child frequently asks *"Mahino?"* (understand?), to which the child is expected to respond "yes" whether or not she or he truly understands. The answer affirms the child's submission to the speaker's authority rather than comprehension of the immediate issue.

Given the pattern of language use in Tongan status relations, it is not surprising that in regard to language socialization the greatest emphasis is on didactic teaching and on children's learning to *tokanga*. Koskinen comments that in Western Polynesia acquiring information often takes the form of obeying: "the will of the chiefly [or higher-status] person is often confused with knowledge" (1968, 75). A number of Tongan terms describe adults' roles, such as *fakahinohino* (advise, instruct), *akonaki* (teach, instruct, especially regarding morals), *fale'i* (advise), and *tu'utu'uni* (give instructions, directions, or orders). There are also more specific terms, such as *talatalaifale*, a "household warning not intended for outside ears" (Churchward 1959, 448), usually on topics such as the brother-sister *faka'apa'apa* relationship. This emphasis on instruction accords with the discouragement of questioning and the importance of observation and imitation. As on Tanna, "the grounds of external knowledge and the processes of knowing are sensual and passive, rather than reflective or interactive; epistemology, here, thus echoes discursive practice" (Lindstrom 1990, 45).

Advice and instruction are given both formally and informally, the latter especially as it becomes situationally relevant.[5] Informal instruction includes constant reminders, especially to girls, to sit properly, eat politely, and so on. This kind of instruction is often accompanied by threatened or actual punishment, as children are told what they should or should not have been doing. At other times instruction is given during preparations for events such as funerals. In Ngata's words, "The mother will usually tell you, 'This is what you're going to wear. This is what you're going to do. This is where you're going to go.' "[6] Informal instruction such as this begins at an early age, but it is not until children are in high school that they are really expected to understand and carry out such instructions unaided.

More formal instruction is given in many contexts, including regular family meetings such as evening and Sunday religious observances and family gatherings marking special occasions. Church, Sunday school, school, and speeches at feasts, funerals, and other events are all occasions for moral instruction. Formerly, children were told *fananga* (myths) and *talatupu'a* (legends), many of which contained more or less explicit moral statements.[7] Nowadays most children hear these stories only at school or on the radio. However, all children learn song texts and poems, especially those accompanying dances. These texts are full of references to mythical and historical events, messages about moral values and appropriate behavior, and so on (see Kaeppler 1978c, 1985). Christian hymns, which all Tongan children learn, are a similarly indirect form of moral statement.

Much of the moral instruction children receive is framed in Christian terms—for example, the importance of obedience and respect in order to "honor thy parents." Yet the practice of moral instruction existed in pre-Christian Tonga. For example, Mariner witnessed a *matāpule* giving a moral discourse at the wedding of the Tu'i Tonga "on the subject of chastity," advising against adultery and rape (Martin 1981, 98). The *matāpule*, the "hereditary censors of public morals," used *fono* to expound laws and lecture the young chiefs (Thomson 1894, 86; see Lawry 1852, 444). Later, *fono* were used to address the commoners in their villages. At a less formal level, "instruction" occurred within chiefs' households, particularly during evening discussions (Orange 1840, 122).

Although children seem to learn more from informal instruction, which has more immediate relevance to them, formal instruction is emphasized in the discourse of acquisition of knowledge. Formal instruction allows for closer control of this acquisition and allows less leeway for independent interpretation. In practice formal instruction may be ineffective, as children may not understand or even listen. They simply have to appear respectful and submissive and occasionally say "yes" when the speaker queries "*Mahino?*"

An important focus of instruction is kinship, which is taught in both formal and informal contexts. As we have seen in the previous chapter, knowledge concerning kinship includes both actual kin relations and the values and behavior appropriate to them. During a conversation about knowledge acquisition, Ngata commented, "My mother told me [and] you just listen around; when you go to relatives and things like that they say, 'This is your *fahu*. This is your uncle. You speak like this to your uncle. You are not supposed to say that to your aunties,' this kind of thing; it comes, you grow up with it."

Knowledge of this kind is proffered to children at home in informal conversations and through formal moral discourse at prayer meetings and other family gatherings. Much of the instruction is by mothers and grandmothers, who explain genealogical relationships and the behaviors appropriate to them. Some instruction begins even before children can speak; formal teaching begins in primary school and continues throughout adolescence and into adulthood. Children of primary school age are not expected to understand the intricacies of kinship ranking or of status-appropriate behavior, but if they behave very badly, especially on formal occasions, their parents are criticized through gossip and "dropped remarks" (see Bernstein 1983) for not teaching them properly. If children do behave correctly it is said that their mother has taught them well. Ngata remarked, "When you're a child, you don't really care. Oh, you know, 'That's auntie; that's uncle'—who cares! But when you begin to get a little older you get told off. . . . If [children] go their own way, it doesn't matter. But it's a great compliment to the mother, though, if the children behave accordingly." Children also receive some instruction about kinship in church, at Sunday school, and even at school. The environmental science curriculum for primary schools includes lessons on kinship in its social studies component. In class five, for example, children draw up their *kāinga* genealogy, and in class six they are taught about the rights and obligations of some key kinship roles, such as the *mehekitanga*.

Within the family, Tongans emphasize that it is the *fatongia* of the parents, particularly the mother as the primary caregiver, to teach children properly. Providing this education is also a sign of *'ofa*. In practice all family members play a part in this socialization, especially on an informal level. Children even teach each other, down through the hierarchy of children in the household and the neighborhood play group. The ideal way to advise children is said to be to speak gently and persuasively. Parents should not force (*fakapōpula'i*; literally, enslave) their children, a mother of five told me; they should teach them to pay attention to what they are told. Manu stated that "it is right, or maybe it is good, for me to try to persuade them nicely (*fakakolekole lelei*) and advise them nicely (*fakahinohino lelei*) so they will not be afraid of me." This ideal is supported to some extent by the belief that children are *vale* and therefore unable to understand properly any instruction given to them in their early years. However, everyday interactions tend not to conform to the ideal, and fear—particularly of physical punishment—becomes a central motive for good behavior.

The different sources of direct instruction that I have discussed may at times give varying or even inconsistent perspectives on the cluster of values and behaviors associated with the flexible, unbounded, and constantly transforming concept of *anga fakatonga*. In turn, as children move through adolescence and into adulthood, they construct their own understanding of *anga fakatonga* and, through that, their understanding of themselves as "Tongan."

The important role of language in socialization is also revealed in many of the terms that describe children's characteristics and behavior. *Talangata'a*, meaning "disobedient" and "insubmissive" (Churchward 1959, 448) literally means "difficult to tell or command."[8] Obedient is *talangofua* (easy to tell or command). The word *lea* (to speak) is used with the same pair of suffixes to produce the same meanings (*leangata'a*: disobedient; *leangofua*: obedient). Children's speech tends to be dismissed as silly, as in *laupisi* (talking rubbish) and *launoa* (talking nonsense), until they are competent enough speakers to be understood, at about three or four years of age. Subsequently, these terms are used to tease and shame children and adolescents when they speak unclearly or incorrectly or when they talk about things others consider silly. Disrespectful forms of speech such as *talahu'i* (cheekiness), *lea kovi* ("bad talk," e.g., swearing or abuse), and *kape* (swearing), usually earn children swift punishment.

A great deal of speech directed at children of all ages takes the form of orders, threats, scolding, comments, and other unidirectional speech acts requiring no response. As I have stated, there is no baby-talk register. Much talk directed to babies takes the same form as that directed to older children. Bald imperatives (Ochs 1988, 149) are spoken or shouted at children from birth: "Eat!" "Quiet!" "Go!" "Sit!" and so on. Most frequent are the negative imperatives, such as "Don't!" and "Stop it!" alone or with noun or verb phrases, such as "Stop your noise!" Other orders direct older children to run errands or perform some other action, such as "Get the knife," "Watch the baby," and so on. In the late afternoon shouted orders can be heard from most households, telling the children to *ha'u kaukau* (come and bathe). Sometimes, brief explanations are added to orders, often with the phrase *na'a ke* (lest you, in case you), as in *"Tuku'ia, na'a ke tō"* (stop it, lest you fall). For the most part, however, orders are given, sometimes with threats, and children are expected to obey unquestioningly. A number of sounds are also used to get children's attention, especially to indicate disapproval. These include particles such as *ē*, *sa* and *sh* and a disapproving sound called *kahī*, "a rasping noise more or less like the German or Scotch ch" (Churchward 1959, 243).

Other forms of speech frequently directed at children are grumbling and scolding. Grumbling is a feature of ordinary speech to children, in which adults (or older children) make short, negative statements about the child in an annoyed or mock-reproving tone. A mother doing housework while her toddler messes about nearby will grumble "Tiring boy!" "Annoying boy!" and so on. On my long, difficult walk into the hills of 'Eua, described earlier, six-year-old Tupou kept up with the adults and did not once complain or whine, although her aunt grumbled at her almost incessantly, telling her how troublesome and tiring she was. Tupou cheerfully ignored the grumbles, as most children do. Scolding occurs when a child has done something specific that is annoying or "bad" and most often takes the form of short, sharp rebukes sometimes including a negative statement about the child's *anga* or *loto*.[9] For example, a caregiver scolding a child for being noisy and disruptive might shout, "Stop your noise; stop being annoying; you are *anga kovi*." Scolding often accompanies threatened or real punishment and is discussed further in the following chapter.

Many other comments are directed toward children without any expecta-

tion that they will respond verbally, such as encouragements to eat and rhe-
torical questions such as "We had ice cream yesterday, *ē?*" When children are
expected to respond, as when adults directly question them, the verbal
exchange is usually as brief as possible. Children may be asked where someone or something is, for example, or asked to get information about others'
activities.

In Tonga, as Ochs found in Western Samoa, "whether the higher-ranking
party is speaker or hearer, the higher-ranking party controls meaning" (1988,
143). In other words, when the higher-ranking person speaks, the lower-
ranking person must grasp the higher's intention, but the higher-ranking
person can interpret the meaning of the lower-ranking person's speech as the
higher wishes. This pattern is related to the form of "communicative accommodation" Tongan adults use in speaking to children; the patterns are situa-
tion-centered rather than child-centered (Schieffelin and Ochs 1986b,
174).[10] Higher-status persons may also choose not to attempt to interpret
speech they have not understood clearly. When adults do not understand
what a child has said, they do not usually speculate about the child's intention or thought but either terminate the interaction or demand a reformula-
tion of the speech by simply saying *"Ko e hā?"* (what was that). Another
important aspect of language usage in the context of status relations is that
the lower-status person often tries to say to the higher-status person only
what the former thinks the latter wants to hear.

After an initial period in which household members are intensely interested in children's vocalizations, Tongan children gradually learn that their
role as lower-status persons is largely as listeners and as respondents to, rather
than initiators of, speech acts. By the time they are about three years old,
children are often ignored by the adults of their household unless they are
being given an order or are being reprimanded for something. When Seini
returned home from work in the late afternoon, she would greet baby 'Ofa
with physical and verbal demonstrations of affection but ignore the five-
year-old twins until she had an errand for them. Even at mealtimes when, in
most households, the whole family sits together, the adults do not usually
include the children in their conversations. They may speak to them to
encourage them to eat or remind them to sit or eat properly, but they expect
the children older than about two to be quiet while they eat.

When they ask a direct question of an adult, children may be ignored for
some time or be referred to an older child. Children learn a respectful
manner of asking questions of higher-status people, in which they quietly but
insistently repeat the person's name or their request until they gain some
attention. This same pattern is also used by adults to get someone's attention, especially at night, when a caller stands outside the bedroom window

quietly repeating the sleeping person's name until he or she finally awakens. This unobtrusive, respectful means of making requests differs markedly from the loud, often aggressive or whining demands children make of their peers or younger children.

As has been shown, silence is a demonstration of respect in certain circumstances. Children learn that complaining or whining are ignored or even punished so they learn, as do Hawaiian children, to use silence as part of a "set of subtle, passive tactics to signal needs" (Gallimore and Howard 1969b, 14).[11] As we have seen, even when in pain or feeling unwell, children older than about four often do not complain or seek treatment. Frequently the only indication of their suffering is that they are quiet and listless, so that illnesses or injuries may go untreated for some time. When treatment is initiated it may be by older female relatives rather than the child's parents. In Holonga Tomasi had an infected cut on his knee for several weeks before his aunt 'Ana, visiting from 'Eua, treated it with crushed medicinal leaves.

Children also know when it is acceptable for them to join in conversations. This was clear on one occasion when Tomasi wanted to interact with his parents. Seini and Siale were in their bedroom talking, with baby 'Ofa playing on the bed between them. Tomasi stood quietly at the doorway as they discussed a feast they had attended and other things they had been doing. When they turned their attention to 'Ofa, Tomasi immediately entered the room and played with them, laughing and encouraging 'Ofa to kiss Siale and to perform various of her amusing actions. When the parents resumed their conversation Tomasi stopped playing and left the room.

During this incident it was clear Tomasi knew the cues indicating he could join in, just as clearly as he knew when to withdraw. These cues, or "metacommunicative markers" (Ochs 1988, 167), index the context of interactions, enabling children to interpret contexts and adapt their behavior accordingly. The cues can be verbal, as in the prosodic characteristics of speech such as intonation, voice quality, grammatical forms, and affective particles used, or nonverbal, as in body language, facial expressions, setting, and audience (see Miller and Moore 1989; Ochs 1988, 1990; also Howard 1970, 118 for a discussion of such cues in Rotuma). In the incident above, when the interaction shifted from adult-to-adult to adult-to-child and the adults' tone and gestures became playful, Tomasi knew he could participate at last.

Because facial expressions and other nonverbal cues often replace speech, they are crucial keys to meaning in Tonga. The most common cue is the quick lift of the eyebrows, which means "yes" and also indicates interest. I have seen children as young as ten months who intentionally used this gesture. Children learn to make and respond to other expressions and gestures during their first year. The encouragement gesture, made to babies in the first months, has already been described. This is used throughout early childhood when offering children food and when encouraging them to come toward a person; it is also the gesture used by both children and adults when asking someone to hand something over to them, often with an outstretched hand. Babies also quickly learn verbal and nonverbal expressions of disapproval and aggression, as will be described in the following chapter.

Children's role in socializing their younger siblings provides them with an opportunity to use language in a high-status manner: they imitate the behavioral and speech patterns used by adults to children in ordering, threatening, punishing, instructing, and so on. Yet unless their age difference is too great, siblings also interact in contexts, such as play, wherein status differences are not of primary importance. It is within such contexts that children are able to continue the behavior established during infancy: showing off and acting assertively and at times aggressively. It therefore tends to be with older children, rather than with parents or other adults, that children actively experiment with the behavioral limits imposed by their low-status role, by challenging and resisting the older children's authority. The older children also experiment with their role as when they push their authority to its limits, becoming more harsh and severe than their parents. This use of punishment within sibling groups and other groups of children is examined in the following chapter, within a detailed analysis of the role of physical punishment in Tongan child socialization.

CHAPTER 7

SANCTIONED VIOLENCE: PUNISHMENT

AND AGGRESSION IN TONGA

As has become clear, the ideal Tongan child is obedient, respectful, attentive, and in many other ways *anga lelei*. As has also become clear, Tongan children, like children everywhere, do not always conform to the ideal. They are boisterous, cheeky, rebellious, stubborn—the long list of negative terms by which Tongans characterize children indicates the kinds of behavior that children are realistically expected to exhibit in practice. In the previous chapter I examined several ways in which children are encouraged and expected to learn proper behavior, which will ideally transform these negatively valued, "natural" qualities into those that are positively valued. In this chapter I will discuss what Tongan caregivers see as the most direct and immediately efficacious means of ensuring correct behavior: the physical punishment of children. I begin by placing child punishment into its broader historical context, suggesting that current beliefs and practices are strongly influenced by the European missionaries who went to Tonga during the nineteenth century. The early establishment of patterns of punishment during infancy is then described, followed by a detailed account of punishment —how children are punished, why, and by whom; how they respond; and how the issues of intervention and concepts of maltreatment are addressed. Finally, the broader context of violence in modern Tonga is described.

PUNISHMENT IN PRECONTACT TONGA

Early accounts of Tongan society reveal a "paradox" similar to that described by Shore for Samoa. Shore states that the Samoans have been characterized as "reserved, dignified, even courtly in bearing, . . . [yet] also notably aggressive at times" (1982, 150). In Tonga, one of Cook's officers remarked on "the great harmony which subsists amongst all ranks" and "the general sweetness and mildness of their tempers" (King 1777, in Beaglehole 1967, 174). Another officer, Anderson, also stressed the Tongans' "mildness and good nature" and "peaceable disposition" (1777, in Beaglehole 1967, 928). Yet these and other early accounts also described many forms of aggressive and

violent behavior in warfare, punishments, sporting contests, and sexual relations.[1] Mariner described everyday life among the hou'eiki with whom he
lived as frequently violent, and he also gave many detailed descriptions of
battles (Martin 1981; and see Orange 1840). Mariner claimed that "theft,
revenge, rape, and murder, under many circumstances, are not held to be
crimes." Anyone but "a very superior chief or noble" could be killed if they
gave provocation, and any woman but a married and/or high-status woman
could be raped—such incidents, he claimed, being "matters of indifference."
Aggression was also expressed indirectly, in the form of curses that were
believed to cause illness and death (Martin 1981, 242, 299, 318, 356). These
early accounts of violence in Tonga scarcely mention children. An exception is Edgar's observation that at wrestling and boxing matches both adults
and children in the audience were knocked down with a club if they disturbed the order of the ring (1777, in Beaglehole 1967, 108n2).

Early missionary accounts portrayed the Tongans as violent, and the fact
that Tonga was in the midst of civil war obviously influenced their impressions. Violence motivated by religious and political conflicts continued in
the 1880s with the brutal persecution of the Tongan Wesleyans after the
establishment of the Free Church of Tonga and again after the attempted
assassination of Reverend Shirley Baker in 1887 (Lātūkefu 1974; Rutherford
1977).

One of the forms of violence for which there are many detailed accounts
by early European observers is punishment. According to Mariner, Tongans
held the "firm and fixed belief, that all human miseries are the consequent
punishment of crimes"; in the Tongan cosmology, there was "no state of
future punishment—all rewards for virtue, and punishments for vice, being
inflicted on mankind in this world" (Martin 1981, 306, 314; and see Anderson 1777, in Beaglehole 1967, 948). Only hou'eiki and matāpule were
believed to have access to a spiritual afterlife.[2] Their souls ('otua) "had the
power of dispensing good and evil to mankind," as did other supernatural
beings (also 'otua).[3] The punishments the 'otua dispensed included "chiefly
conspiracies, wars, famine, and epidemic diseases, as public calamities; and
sickness and premature death, as punishments for the offences of individuals" (Martin 1981, 298, 331).[4]

Two practices intended to appease angry gods, and mentioned by many of
the early European visitors to Tonga, were child strangulation and finger-
joint amputation. The former (no'osia) was usually carried out when a high
chief was ill, but Mariner also relates an incident when it was a form of
atonement for the desecration of a tapu place (Martin 1981, 76, 140, 211,
348). He interpreted the Tongans' feelings toward no'osia as follows: "All the
bystanders behold the innocent victim with feelings of the greatest pity;

but it is proper, they think, to sacrifice a child who is at present of no use to society, and perhaps may not otherwise live to be, with the hope of recovering a sick chief" (Martin 1981, 348).

Mariner states that those chosen were the children of chiefs by "inferior female attendant[s]" (Martin 1981, 140). The children were therefore not 'eiki, as rank was inherited through the mother. He also indicates that the mothers sometimes resisted the taking of their children, for example by hiding them. One woman he describes as becoming insane "in consequence of excessive grief, partly occasioned by the death of a near relation, but principally by her child having been taken from her to be strangled as an offering to the gods, for the recovery of his sick father" (76). There does not appear to have been any particular age at which children were chosen for strangulation. Mariner mentions a two-year-old (140), and missionaries reported a twelve-year-old victim (*Wesleyan-Methodist Magazine* 1843, 258, cited in Lātūkefu 1974, 8). It appears that both male and female children were strangled. Mary Lawry (wife of the missionary Walter Lawry) wrote in 1823 that she had seen the sacrifice of a young girl, adding that "they really wanted to sacrifice a young man, but he escaped" (in Reeson 1985, 160).[5]

Despite the horror the early observers felt toward child sacrifice, they tended to romanticize it in their descriptions. Mariner claims one child, before its "horrible immolation" was "delighted with the band of *gnatoo* [*ngatu*] that was put round its neck, and, looking up in the face of the man who was about to destroy it, displayed in its beautiful countenance, a smile of ineffable pleasure" (Martin 1981, 140; and see Biersack 1990a, 96; St. Johnson 1883, 130). A similar view is found in some descriptions of the practice of amputating finger joints (*nima kū*), which was also carried out as a sacrifice to effect a cure for illness (Martin 1981, 249, 349).[6] It was done either by the sick person or by a low-status person on behalf of a higher-status relative (Bott with Tavi 1982, 54; Kaeppler 1971b, 209). Mariner reported that he "witnessed a violent contest between two children of five years of age, each claiming the favour of having the ceremony performed on him, so little do they fear the pain of the operation" (Martin 1981, 249).[7]

It is clear from the early literature that punishments from the gods were amply supplemented by the more direct punishments meted out by *hou'eiki*. There are frequent references to chiefs beating and even killing *tu'a* or lesser chiefs for a range of offenses or to end disputes. Any breach of the complicated etiquette of respect was punishable and, indeed, most misdemeanors could be interpreted as disrespect in the context of the Tongans' preoccupation with status.[8] Disrespectful behavior could have been interpreted as an insult or even a challenge to the chiefs' status. Cook described the punishment meted out by a chief when some men disobeyed his order to leave Cook's post:

> He took up a large stick and beat them most unmercifully, one man he struck over the side of the face so that blood gushed out of both mouth and nostrils and he lay for some time motionless and was at last carried off in convulsions; on his being told he had killed the man he only laughed at it and evidently was not sorry for what he had done. We heard afterwards that the man recovered. (1777, in Beaglehole 1967, 100)

Samwell, with Cook in 1777, commented, "We had seen many instances of the cruel Treatm[en]t the Tooa or lower order of People receive from their Chiefs on the most trifling Occasions" (Beaglehole 1967, 1021).[9]

During the civil war that began in 1799 the chiefs began to push their power over the tuʻa population to its limits, and Lātūkefu claims "there was a marked change in the chiefs' treatment of the common people. It had become increasingly harsh, to the point of being intolerably cruel, inhuman and arbitrary. They came to regard the commoners as mere chattels to be used exclusively for their own benefit" (1974, 22). It was during this troubled period that the Wesleyan missionaries established themselves in Tonga, and in their early attempts at introducing Christianity they denounced warfare and emphasized the values of love and peace; after the religious revivals of the mid-1830s, however, they implicitly supported the newly converted Tongans' wars with the remaining "heathens" (Cummins 1979). They also supported the use of physical force against wrongdoers. The Wesleyans were reported as punishing people with "public floggings, broken teeth, branding on the shoulders, and forced labour on mission plantations" (Monfat 1893, 204, cited in Gailey 1987b, 192). They advised King Tupou to recommend hard labor as punishment for lawbreakers, rather than "beating them in the face with the fist," which the missionary Turner noted was the usual method (1842, cited in Cummins 1972, 103). Yet they continued to support public flogging by the Tongan authorities for some offenses (Lātūkefu 1975, 21, 23). Some European visitors to Tonga during this period were highly critical of the severity and frequency of these violent punishments (Cummins 1977, 242–243).

The laws that were encoded in the ensuing years retained the sanctions of corporal and capital punishment. Although in July 1890 the king ordered that women were no longer to be flogged (Cyclopaedia of Tonga 1907, 37), in current law male offenders under the age of fifteen can receive up to twenty "strokes" with a light rod or cane, with older offenders receiving up to twenty-six strokes (*Law of Tonga* 1967 Cap. 15, section 32).[10] Persons under the age of seven cannot be charged with an offense, but a person aged between seven and twelve can be charged if deemed by the court or jury to be mature enough to understand the "nature and consequences of his conduct" (Section 16). For some offenses, notably sexual assault and carnal knowledge, offenders under fifteen may be whipped instead of imprisoned (Section 120), and any male convicted of certain offenses—for example, child abuse, rape, carnal knowledge, attempted carnal knowledge, indecent assault on a girl under twelve, and incest—may be whipped instead of or as well as imprisoned (Section 130). There are strong community reactions to such offenses, if they become known, particularly when the victim is young. "Sexual offences against girls under 12 years evoke very strong violent agitation by members of the victim's family demanding drastic punishment" (*Report of the Minister of Police for 1986*, 80). Between 1967 and 1974 an average of seven juveniles received whippings each year (Statistics Department 1975, 133, table 158).[11] According to one police officer, such whippings are still carried out several times each year. Capital punishment, by hanging, is still possible in Tonga; it requires the assent of the king and the Privy Council (*Law of Tonga* 1967 Cap. 15, section 34), and last occurred in 1982.

By making punishment of citizens a state matter, the legal codes effectively removed the chiefs' power to use violence as punishment, although reducing chiefly power took some time, as the politico-religious violence of the late 1880s attests. It is interesting to compare this transformation with that concerning *fatongia*, the obligatory provision of labor and goods to chiefs. Although this was abolished in the legal codes, it continues to operate to this day as an integral part of the status system.

PUNISHMENT OF CHILDREN HISTORICALLY

Apart from describing child strangulation and finger amputation, the early accounts of Tonga tended to portray children as primitive, carefree innocents, "indulged" by their parents. Mariner commented that "the women are very kind, tender mothers, and the children are taken exceeding good care of. . . . [T]hey are never neglected, either in respect of personal cleanliness or diet" (Martin 1981, 329, 371). The missionary West claimed that children were "nurtured with great care and affection" (1865, 270). Similarly, Mary Lawry wrote that "Tonga is a place where children are cherished and treasured . . . with endless arms to comfort, numberless houses to shelter and many cooking fires to provide food" (Reeson 1985, 159–160). Comments of this kind are not confined to the early literature. Bergeron, a Catholic priest, commented in the 1930s that "the children make an especial appeal to the observation. The brown mites, 'nature's children,' seem to radiate health, and their life in the sunshine is one long round of pleasure. Their parents are indulgent, and the children for the most part thrive well" (Bergeron n.d., 40).

Despite the fact that physical punishment was so widely used on adults and that it was an assertion of status, it cannot be assumed that it was a feature of child socialization. I have not found any early accounts that mention child punishment. The absence of punitive discipline is strongly implied by Sarah Farmer, in *Tonga and the Friendly Islands*, which is based on missionary accounts; she says of the people of Hihifo (Tongatapu) that "the parents were indifferent to their children's training, indulging them to excess" (1976, 352).

There are many indications throughout Polynesia that the physical punishment of children was not traditional.[12] Although the Ritchies have argued that physical punishment *was* a feature of Polynesian child socialization, they admit that the "punitive framework of fundamental Christianity" has had a widespread impact (1989, 129). In Tonga, whatever the precontact methods of child discipline, the European missionaries clearly influenced the ideology and practice of punishment. There are striking similarities between current Tongan beliefs and practices about discipline in socialization and those of eighteenth- and nineteenth-century Europe. The contemporary practices and the beliefs informing them have been incorporated by many Tongans into their concept of *anga fakatonga*.

The early missionaries arrived in Tonga from a cultural milieu in which the corporal punishment of children was deemed necessary and proper. Historical accounts of the treatment of children in the West reveal that from the early seventeenth century until well into the nineteenth century, children were commonly perceived as inherently "bad," and the central aim of socialization was to break their will and make them unquestioningly obedient.[13] Pedagogical tracts urged parents to be vigilant in correcting the willful and unruly nature of children. Control of emotion in the context of punishment was emphasized, for both parent and child. Parents were warned to "pay special heed that in chastising [children] you not allow yourself to be overcome by anger" (Kruger 1752, cited in Miller 1987, 5). They were also advised that children who persisted in crying after punishment should be beaten again until they ceased crying (e.g., Basedow 1773, in Miller 1987, 25). Biblical injuctions to use "the rod" for the child's own sake were frequently invoked as justifications for these views.[14] The following quotation from Farmer's book, intended for child readers in England, exemplifies the prevailing ideology:

Spoiled children are not the most loving children. They detect the weakness that will not allow a parent to deny himself the pleasure of a momentary caress, nor to inflict upon himself the sharp pain of giving pain to the naughty child whom he loves, even though he knows that correction would work out the child's real good. Those who in manhood love their parents most, are those who in childhood feared the rod in a gentle hand. . . . So it is with us and our Heavenly Father. . . they who have most sorely felt the smart of His stripes, have been drawn closest to Him in adoring and grateful love. (Farmer 1976, 373)

Although Tongans may not have used physical punishment with their children in the precontact period, the precedent of punishments inflicted by chiefs may have made them receptive to its introduction. The Wesleyan missionaries emphasized the role of the father as the "chief" of the household and the importance of absolute obedience to parents at the same time that the power of chiefs to punish commoners was being reduced. This power appears to have been transferred to adults in relation to children, in a melding of Tongan beliefs about chief-commoner relations and Christian beliefs about adult-child relations, particularly relations between parents and their children.

"THEY PUNISH ME WITH THEIR LOVE": CONTEMPORARY TONGA

INFANCY: THREATENING AND SMACKING

As we have seen, Tongan children are the focus of their households' attention for at least their first year, and much concern and affection are directed toward them. When infants cry their caregivers check their diapers, offer food, cuddle them, walk them around to soothe them, or try to distract them. Every effort is made to find the cause of their crying and to quiet them. When asked why babies were not left to cry, people said the noise annoyed them. This was clearly an important factor, but I also observed an element of fear that the baby could be ill. This fear is especially present during the first few months, when a baby is still *vaivai* (weak) and thus particularly vulnerable to illness.[15]

As babies approach the end of their first year their crying is increasingly treated as a nuisance, rather than a cause for concern, and they are more likely to be shouted at or punished for crying. There are numerous terms for kinds of crying, differentiated mainly by loudness and associated actions (e.g., *ngā:* to cry loudly [usually said of a small child]; *tāngitūva'e:* to cry and stamp one's foot). Loud, angry crying is especially discouraged. Annoyance at particularly loud or persistent crying is sometimes even expressed to newborn babies. The most common response to babies' annoying crying is to speak sharply, saying "*Longo!*" (quiet), "*Mālōlō!*" (rest), or "*Mohe!*" (sleep). At other times disapproving noises are made: "*Sh!*" or "*Sa!*" Such responses are made by whoever is near the baby—its mother, a nurse in the hospital, a relative. Sometimes the person is clearly only pretending to be cross, and even when the words are spoken angrily their severity is usually softened by a laugh.

One day, traveling on a bus, I watched a mother with her baby (about six months old), who was crying loudly. At first she pretended to smack him, saying "*Longo!*" but he kept crying so she cuddled him, facing her, and stroked his head and murmured comfortingly to him. He continued to cry, and an older woman on an adjacent seat, who did not seem to be traveling with the mother, took the baby and spoke roughly to him: "*Pē tangi, te u taa'i koe!*" (if you cry, I'll hit you). She shouted "*Sa!*" sharply several times, but the baby kept crying. She then passed him back to his mother, who cuddled him again until alighting from the bus shortly after. Throughout this incident the other passengers laughed at the older woman's shouts, but they were obviously bothered by the baby's persistent crying. When I later related the incident to a friend, she commented that that was why she did not take her own baby on the bus: she was afraid he would cry like that and she would feel embarrassed (*mā*).

Another incident in which anger was softened by laughter occurred when Kalolaine was putting her daughter, Luseane (eighteen months), to bed and Luseane was resisting and crying. Kalolaine said angrily, "*Mohe!*" and threatened to smack her. This continued for the next twenty minutes with Kalolaine leaving Luseane in the room and returning occasionally to order her in increasingly angry terms to *tokoto ki lalo* (lie down), then *ki lalo* (get down), and *lalo* (down). She repeatedly threatened to smack Luseane and did smack her, though not hard, several times. When this renewed Luseane's protests Kalolaine shouted "*Tuku e tangi!*" (stop crying) and "*Longo!*" Throughout this sequence Kalolaine alternately spoke angrily and laughed, and the whole episode was treated as a mock serious game. Although she became more obviously angry as the "game" wore on, she did not lose her temper, but continued to laugh at her daughter's protests and struggles to get up. After twenty minutes Luseane gave in and lay down without further protest.

By the end of their first year babies begin to have angry fits of crying during which they scream, throw themselves about, or wriggle violently in the grip of whoever is holding them. These tantrums, sometimes referred to as 'akafute (to kick or jerk about convulsively), usually occur when their wants are frustrated. At this age the tantrums are often efficacious: if threats do not succeed in stopping their noise, babies are almost always given what they want as well as being cuddled to soothe them. Later, tantrums are more likely to be ignored or punished.

Caregivers threaten to hit babies not only for crying, but for any behavior that is annoying, dangerous, or "bad" (kovi). Threats are used with varying degrees of seriousness, from playful teasing to genuine warnings, though the proportion of the latter increases markedly toward the end of the first year. Much of the speech directed toward babies is in the form of threats, often attached to directives, such as "Sit down," "Get down," and, most common of all, "Stop it" (tuku ia).

Bott recorded that three periods of babyhood were formerly recognized, in which babies' responses to threatening gestures were taken as indicative of their development. In the first stage, the baby is 'atamai noa (knows nothing). Someone can fakapoi (threaten to hit) and the baby does not papaka (shy away, act nervous). The baby who begins to papaka when threatened has reached the stage of 'atamia manu (mind of an animal). Finally, when children know their mothers they have 'atamia tangata (human reason or mind) (n.d., 19).[16]

Threats to babies are physical and/or verbal, the former usually a raised hand or object, the latter either a statement or a noise. The ubiquitous threat Te u taa'i koe (I'll hit you), or the abbreviated version taa'i koe (hit you) or just taa'i (hit), are often spoken as questions, with ē? On its own ē is also used as a threatening noise, as are "sh," "sa," and kahī (the throat-clearing noise described previously). The playful threats made to very young babies are often added to comments about the baby's characteristics. For example, a nurse commented to my own daughter when she was breast-feeding only hours after her birth, "Taa'i koe fa'a kai, ē?" ([I'll] hit you, eating all the time, eh?). Playful threats may also be made in reference to other family members or friends, as when another newborn baby was told by a visitor that her daughter would come to see him and hit him. These threats are a way of expressing affection for the baby, though they are sometimes said with a stern expression or even angrily, as when a baby is crying.

A game that is often played with older babies involves alternating threats with affection. The person holding the baby cuddles and kisses the child, making him or her laugh; then suddenly the adult raises a hand threateningly, frowning and scowling. Just as suddenly, the adult smiles again, and affection replaces the threat. Household members and visiting relatives frequently played this game with little 'Ofa. A typical incident occurred when Alisi was visiting during the preparations for a feast. Alisi was trying to settle

'Ofa to sleep, but 'Ofa was struggling to get out of her arms. Alisi shook her roughly, saying *"Mohe!"* and *"Sa!"* and pretended she was going to hit her. Then she leaned forward and kissed 'Ofa, who laughed and kept struggling. The alternating shakes, threats, and kisses continued until, after a particularly rough shake, 'Ofa reached up and hit her great-aunt full in the face. Alisi laughed, pushed 'Ofa upright and pretended to push her from her lap, saying " *'Alu!"* (go).

Babies react in different ways to this game, but the most common reaction I observed was an oscillation between apprehension and laughter. I have also seen this sequence acted out by people with whom the baby is unfamiliar, as at a feast when a visiting woman was alternately urging a baby about a year old to come to her, using the encouraging facial gesture and outstretched hand, then pulling frightening faces at him while raising her hand threateningly. Needless to say, he did not go to her but stayed snuggled close to his mother.

Threats are used by older caregivers to keep a baby out of trouble without having to chase after the child. Remaining seated, they call the baby's name; if the baby does not respond, they shout threats or make threatening noises to get the child's attention. Sometimes a coconut-leaf-midrib broom is slapped loudly onto the floor mat as they shout, for emphasis. Getting up to fetch the child is a last resort and is further avoided if there is anyone younger nearby who can be called to come and help.

Children are also discouraged from wandering out of reach by warning them of animals or *tēvolo*[17] or by calling animals to come and eat them. This is also done as a way of distracting fretful babies, as we have seen, or just as a teasing game. A caregiver will call, "Pig! Elenoa is here, come and eat her!" A baby about to wander into a darkened room, or outside at night, may be warned that the *tēvolo* will come and get him. Babies are also told people will come and hit them, often as part of the routines of name calling. Caregivers will call out, "Sione, come and hit Mefa!" whether or not Sione happens to be within earshot, just to distract and mildly threaten the child. This is sometimes done with strangers, as when the person holding a fretful baby on a bus points to a fellow passenger, saying, "Be quiet, or that man will be angry and hit you." *Pālangi* are popular bogeymen in such situations, and children were often warned that I was going to hit them. Barlow has suggested for the Murik of Papua New Guinea that attributing anger, threats, and punishment to others (people, animals, and supernatural forces) allies the mother with the child "against possible hostility from others" (1985, 214). In the Tongan case, this is offset to a great extent by the frequency of threats and punishments directly from caregivers.

Older children are often involved in threats made to babies, either because they are used as a threat or because they themselves threaten the baby. Even before they can talk children imitate the threat gestures of raised hands and objects (especially sticks and brooms), and children as young as two can be heard telling even younger children *"Taa'i koe, ē?"* Older children are also included in ritualized threats, as when their mother tells them "Bring me the broom," and then uses the broom to threaten a younger child. This can become a game, when someone who is not seriously angry with a baby or toddler calls to an older child to bring the broom, as a teasing threat. Another playful threat is to tell the baby to *'omai nima* (give me your hand), as would be said to an older child whose hand was going to be hit.

In childhood, as in infancy, threats are more common than actual punishment and are sometimes made jokingly and even affectionately. Thus, a mother may laughingly tell a child who is crying because she is going out, *"Te u taa'i koe!"* with no intention of doing so. Threats can become ritualized sequences in which a direct threat is made, another child is told to fetch a broom or stick, or a hand or object is raised threateningly. If the interaction is taking place outside, the person threatening punishment makes a show of hunting on the ground for a stick or breaking a twig from a plant. When children recognize that the threat is not serious, they ignore it or even challenge it by further misbehavior. As Ochs noted of Western Samoa, some threats are "keyed through facial expressions and other ways as *bluffs*, as *mock threats*. . . . Part of a child's linguistic and social competence is to recognize these keys" (1988, 153; emphasis in original). Children must recognize when the threat has become serious and know when to shift their response to compliance if they want to avoid being hit. Threats are also used as a form of teasing, particularly when a child is crying from previous punishment and is laughingly threatened with further violence.

As with threatening, smacking babies can be playful or serious. The game described previously, in which babies are alternately cuddled and threatened, is sometimes extended to include playful smacks. At other times, an elaborate or exaggerated threat gesture is followed by a light tap, with a grunting sound for emphasis. The threat gesture is then repeated. This imitates more serious threaten-and-punish sequences, playfully introducing the baby to a routine that will become both familiar and frightening before long. In playful smacking, the typical response to the baby's crying is to laugh, then to kiss and cuddle the child. The following are some examples I observed of playful smacking as affectionate interactions with babies, all between ten and twelve months old:

> A mother is cutting sticks into lengths, with her baby beside her crying half-heartedly. The mother raises a stick threateningly then taps the baby on the

foot, saying *"Longo!"* and *"Sa!"* This is repeated several times, as the mother laughs, and the baby begins to laugh too, enjoying the attention.

A baby keeps crawling into mischief despite his mother's attempts to keep him still. His mother tries to breast-feed him, then tries to draw his attention to the television, which is showing a video movie, but the baby crawls off again. The mother tells an older sibling to bring the baby to her and sits him down beside her, saying " *'Omai nima."* Taking each of the baby's hands and then feet in turn, she smacks them with exaggerated movements, wearing a stern expression. Each time he is tapped the baby flinches, then claps his hands and laughs, and when she has finished his mother grabs him and cuddles him hard, laughing with him.

A grandmother is trying to strip bark for tapa making, with her baby granddaughter in a pram next to her trying to stand up and lean out. The grandmother tells her repeatedly, "Sit down or you'll fall," but the baby pays no attention, so the grandmother slaps the child lightly with the flat of her knife, then a piece of bark, then holds her hand up in a threatening gesture. Each time she makes a movement toward the baby, the baby pulls a funny face and the grandmother laughs.

More severe smacking of babies, typically preceded by threats and warnings, does not usually begin until they become mobile. Toward the end of the first year babies are smacked frequently, and mothers of toddlers sometimes commented that they had to smack their babies "all the time" because they got into so much mischief. At this age children are often comforted and cuddled if they cry after being hit. An incident that occurred when Siale was looking after 'Ofa exemplifies this sequence. 'Ofa was playing with a glass and an ashtray near her father's foot, as he sat on a lounge chair. At first Siale growled at her and said *"Tuku ia"*; then he smacked her hand, not hard. She continued to play and he smacked her harder, whereupon she cried and he immediately pulled her close and said " *'Uma, 'uma"* and kissed her. 'Ofa stopped crying and sat up, trying to get at the glass again, and Siale raised his hand and growled threateningly. 'Ofa climbed onto his lap and he cuddled her.

Such soothing may be delayed, however, in attempts to make children restrain their own crying by telling them to be quiet and threatening further smacks or by putting a hand over a child's mouth and saying *"Longo ho ngutu"* (literally, quiet your mouth). There is also considerable variation in the extent to which babies and toddlers are playfully smacked, hit, and threatened. Paula, the toddler son of Luisa and Ngata, was rarely hit either in fun or as punishment. In a household full of adults he tended to be treated gently and was discouraged from being aggressive himself.

My observations suggest that more typically, babies, as well as being threatened and punished during infancy, are allowed to threaten and hit, poke, bite, and roughly pull at both children and adults. This behavior, particularly hitting, is not only tolerated but actively encouraged, and it becomes an important aspect of the "performance" so positively valued in babies. Often when a baby hits out or makes an angry face, the people watching laugh and draw others' attention to the child. Explanations of the encouragement of such behavior center on its amusement value, though one man suggested (in English) that it was to encourage babies to develop "a sort of interrelationship" with others. Later, these behaviors are tolerated only in very specific circumstances, and children must learn at an early age to distinguish between appropriate and inappropriate settings for violent behavior.

Making this distinction is often difficult for children until they are about five years old, and when they are included in games encouraging babies to hit they sometimes forget to restrain their own behavior. This occurred one day when Seini was playing with 'Ofa, at ten months old, playfully smacking her and laughing, and Tomasi, five, joined the game. His mother held 'Ofa's hand and made her hit her brother in return, urging her on by saying "*Tā, tā.*" Tomasi became excited by the game and began to hit harder, so his mother slapped him, saying "Stop hitting, she'll cry." He stopped smacking his sister, but now she had the idea of the game and began hitting him without her mother's help.

Older siblings are the most common target of these games and join in by playfully smacking and encouraging their younger siblings to retaliate or by offering parts of their bodies to be hit, poked, or bitten or their hair to be pulled. Games played with babies, such as getting them to imitate actions or sounds, often lead to the baby's hitting out in excitement. People holding babies will, if an older child comes near, urge the baby to hit, pull hair, and so on. This is also done when two babies are together. A frequent visitor to the household in Holonga had a baby boy of the same age as 'Ofa, and whenever he was brought to the house Saia and 'Ofa were encouraged to hit each other, although they were watched closely and never allowed to hurt. 'Ofa was bigger and stronger than Saia and soon became the aggressor in their encounters. For the most part Saia's mother encouraged 'Ofa, but if 'Ofa hit him hard enough to make him cry she would be told with a laugh that she was a *ta'ahine kovi*.

On one occasion Saia's mother brought him in asleep and laid him on a mat while she talked to Seini. When 'Ofa came in to her mother and began to whine, Seini pointed to Saia, calling his name and telling 'Ofa to look at him. 'Ofa made an angry, grunting noise, jerking her head back and hitting her arm through the air in his direction, making the women laugh. This aggression is not always appropriate even for babies, however, and when 'Ofa, at a year old, hit Saia when they were in the midst of a group of relatives and neighbors preparing for a feast, her grandmother told her she was *kovi* and directed her to *kole fakamolemole* (apologize) to Saia.

When 'Ofa jerked her head back, jutting her chin toward Saia, she was making an angry gesture that is often made by adults to children when telling them to go away. 'Ofa learned this gesture at about ten months and made it whenever she saw certain children toward whom she had been encouraged to be particularly aggressive. Sometimes when she saw neighborhood children playing outside she gestured angrily at them and made sounds that were interpreted as *'alu* by her caregivers. They would laugh and, even before she could walk, tell her to go and hit the children or to chase them.

A certain pride is taken in the aggressiveness and naughtiness of babies, and mothers often told me of their little ones' latest exploits with amusement—a child had hit a grandmother's face, pulled an aunt's hair, spat at someone, or bitten a sister and drawn blood. Babies' actions that appeared nonaggressive to me were often interpreted as intentionally aggressive, so that a baby urinating on her grandmother's sleeping mat was said to be doing so in anger, to retaliate for being punished some time earlier, and a toddler who tried to pick up a smaller baby by holding it around the neck was said to be trying to strangle it.

Similarly, babies' first sounds are interpreted as *pā* or *tā*. Given the games played with babies—encouraging them to hit, threatening them, and playfully smacking them—they quickly associate the word with its meaning and use it intentionally. It is interesting to compare this with Ochs' account of Western Samoan children's first sounds being interpreted as *tae* (shit, as an expletive). As Ochs points out, "In giving meaning to the children's first utterances, caregivers and others construct (or create) the social identity of the child" (1988, 159). Tongan children do remain aggressive within their peer group and with younger children, but they learn very quickly that any form of violence directed toward higher-status persons will be swiftly and often severely punished.

CHILDHOOD: PUNISHMENT'S ROLE IN SOCIALIZATION

Throughout childhood and adolescence, physical punishment is the most common form of discipline used in Tonga. Although there is a considerable amount of variation within and between households in the frequency and intensity of punishment directed at children, there is also a remarkable degree of similarity in methods and motives for punishment. The most general terms for punishment are *tautea* (to punish) and *tā*, but there are at least thirty other lexical items referring to forms of hitting (all applicable to children but some also to adults and/or animals). These terms index the object used for hitting (e.g., *leta'i*: hit with a belt), the force of the blow(s) (e.g., *hahapo*: hit roughly), the effect of the blows (e.g., *tenge*: to beat until bruised or lacerated), or the frequency of the blows (e.g., *nafui*: hit repeatedly).

In my survey of adolescents, 214 out of 232 (92.2 percent) said they were punished by being hit (with open hand, fist, stick, belt, broom, rope, coconut spathe, or piece of wood). Sixty-six respondents gave more than one answer, most stating that they were hit as well as punished in another way. Other forms of punishment include being given extra household chores or having activities restricted (not being allowed to play or watch television, being locked in a room), but these are infrequently used sanctions. More common are other forms of physical punishment, such as hard pinching or pulling of hair or ears. Only 14.6 percent of the students specifically mentioned scolding as a form of punishment. However, because various forms of scolding, shouting, and grumbling make up a significant proportion of adults' speech to children, such speech is often not perceived as punishment.

Not all forms of aggression directed at children can be described as punishment. Children are routinely pushed, pulled, shaken, and otherwise handled roughly. To hurry children along adults may grab them by the wrist or forcefully pull them by the arm or hair. When adults and older children have to handle the bodies of children over three or four years old, as in bathing them, doing their hair, helping them to dress, and so on, they tend to be impatient and abrupt, addressing the children with a string of imperatives ("Stand up," "Sit still") or tersely naming the next part of the body they want to wash, dress, or oil. By this age children are expected to be capable of performing such tasks independently, and they receive a clear message that their caregivers find it a nuisance to have to help them. When children are persistently recalcitrant about bathing, dressing, or other tasks, this rough treatment merges into punishment. Indeed, in many interactions between adults and children, and between older and younger children, the distinctions between punishing, aggression, rough treatment, and even play are often blurred.

After the transition from playful smacking to more serious discipline, the frequency of punishment escalates until children are about four or five years old.[18] Between the ages of two and five children may be punished several times a day. At this age they inhabit the margins of the older children's play groups and often receive rough treatment from them. Also during this time, the requirement of absolute obedience is most strongly impressed upon them. By the time they are four or five they are frequently called to do chores and to help mind younger children. During school hours they are the oldest children at home and are kept busy running errands and doing various tasks for much of the day. Any resistance toward these duties is typically met with punishment, as is any cheekiness or other misbehavior. The children aged between three and four whom I observed were prone to tantrums and tended to cry readily and loudly. One little boy in particular, Folau, who lived next door to me in Nuku'alofa, seemed to spend a large part of the day crying and being punished, and I often found it distressing to listen to his plaintive wails and hysterical screams.

At about five, when children commence school, there is usually some decline in the frequency but an increase in the severity of punishment. Incidents involving punishment continue to occur throughout adolescence and sometimes into adulthood. Lesieli, aged nineteen, who helped me occasionally with tape transcription, told me that she was still being beaten about once a week by her father. A twenty-eight-year-old unmarried woman told me that her mother still beat her with a stick at times. When I asked her if her mother would still do this after she married, she replied that it would be up to her husband. For many women, the beatings from their mothers (or fathers, or other relatives) may simply be replaced, after marriage, by beatings from their husbands. As already stated, girls tend to be punished more often than boys when they are young because they are expected to work more and be better behaved. As teenagers boys tend to be punished more often and more severely than girls. However, these gender differences are only slight and are highly variable.

Just as there are routine sequences for threatening, punishment often follows a particular pattern. This pattern can be seen in an incident during which five-year-old Elenoa was punished for lying. The incident occurred on a Sunday, as the household members were settling down for an afternoon rest. Seini hit Elenoa hard on the cheek, and Elenoa began to cry loudly. Seini said "Longo!" several times and repeatedly hit her on the legs and arms with a sandal. Seini did not shout, but spoke softly and insistently, and each time she said "Longo!" she held the sandal up threateningly first, then hit Elenoa when she did not stop crying. Finally Elenoa controlled herself and sobbed quietly, but after a few minutes Seini grew impatient with Elenoa's muffled noises and hit her again, not as hard as before, while telling her son to get a stick to hit her with. Elenoa quieted then and soon fell asleep, sobbing occasionally as she slept.

This pattern of pausing between blows, with hand or object raised threateningly or speaking to the child (to threaten, order to be silent, or say something about the child's misdemeanor), or both, is widely practiced. In none of the incidents of punishment that I observed were more than one or two blows dealt out without this brief interval, even when the person administering them appeared extremely angry.

Within the household anyone older than a child can punish the child, including siblings only a year or two older.[19] It is likely that, as Whiting and Edwards suggest (1988, 191), the "rules" older children have learned are reinforced when they punish younger children. In punishing their juniors, Tongan children mimic not only adult gestures, but also the verbal behavior associated with punishment, often in a highly exaggerated manner. They are expected to punish younger siblings, and adults often direct them to do so. Children are also involved in various ways when adults are punishing other children, such as catching them or fetching a stick or broom. Even young children of three or four are vigilant with younger siblings, frequently threatening them and reporting any slight misbehavior to adults or older children. Ernest Beaglehole speculated in his field journal that the beatings children receive from adults arouse "repressed aggressiveness," which "seems to find an outlet in the equally sadistic beating that goes on in the children's groups. In these there appears to be a well-defined beating order based on seniority such that the older children terrorise the younger and these last, in turn, whip those younger still" (1938–1939, Jan. 12). I often observed that after a young child had been hit, he or she would turn to a younger sibling and report every wrongdoing, as well as threaten and hit the younger child. My neighbor Folau did this with his younger sister, Luseane, and he also directed his attention toward his puppy, scolding and hitting it as if it were his child.

However, there are limits on the beatings children can inflict upon other children, and the status differences of natural and classificatory siblings according to age and sex affects the patterns of punishment among them. Brothers tend to be less punitive with sisters than with younger brothers, particularly when the girls reach puberty and their avoidance relationship begins. Also, boys of about ten and over are frequently absent from the home, reducing their interactions with sisters and very young brothers. When children are too severe with younger ones, when they are perceived as *fakavalevale* (continually bullying), or especially when the crying of the younger child disturbs the adults, the young punisher may also be hit, or at least scolded. Though adults rarely offer comfort after punishing, a child may try to console another child he or she has beaten, motivated to some extent by fear of retribution from an older person.

One afternoon I heard my next-door neighbor, Folau (three) screaming, and I saw that Ma'ata (eight), his visiting cousin, had beaten him very hard with a stick. He was squatting on the ground, naked, and screaming hysterically. Ma'ata stood over him, still holding the stick, but looking uncertain.

As Folau continued to cry, Ma'ata dropped the stick, squatted in front of him, and used the hem of her dress to wipe his face, all the while glancing nervously toward the house where the adults were gathered. She fetched some coconut husk and wiped the blood from his foot, where her beating had split his skin. Folau calmed down, stood up, and after briefly examining the weals on his buttocks and legs moved off with Ma'ata to continue playing.

Mothers and older female adolescents are typically the most frequently punitive within the household, largely because of their major caregiving role. Fathers are usually either uninvolved in physical punishments or deal out infrequent but severe beatings.[20] Even when fathers are not punitive, children are often more afraid of them than of other family members. Alisi told me, "My father didn't hit me, but just talked. I was afraid because he often shouted, but he didn't hit me. My mother hit me in the morning, hit at noon, hit in the afternoon, all the time, but I didn't care about her hitting." Other caregivers sometimes use "Wait 'til your father gets home!" threats, which help to maintain the image of fathers as frightening. So does the belief that men are harsher: as Seini said, "I think men are cruel, eh? But we women don't like to hit [children] hard; it's really like hurting us." Fathers' frequent absences from the home, their authority within the household, and the respect they must be accorded are also factors recognized as contributing to this fear. 'Ofa had already learned to be more afraid of her father by the time she was one. Her mother commented to me one day that 'Ofa would not do the rude, raised-finger gesture in front of Siale because she was afraid he would hit her. Although Siale had not hit her for this, 'Ofa had been told so many times that he would that she now believed it.

Any relatives having temporary care of a child usually treat the child as their own. Some people spoke of being even more severely punished in such cases, especially when the relatives were from the father's side. Grandparents and other elderly relatives are often said to be the least punitive, even if they are the main caregivers. However, as has been mentioned, grandparents are also spoken of as alternately indulgent and severe.

Children are also hit by certain people who are unrelated to them. In Holonga some years ago, Siale's father was regarded as particularly tough and strong, and parents would take their recalcitrant children to him for beatings. His oldest son told me, "A lot of parents felt that he was doing a good job." In the early mission schools, "flogging and earboxing of the poor reluctant learner were everyday occurances" (Tupouniua 1977, 53). Corporal punishment is still common in schools, despite attempts by some principals to forbid it. A survey reported in the Tonga Today magazine found that "corporal punishment prevails as the most common form of punishment used to discipline or change a student's behaviour" (1987a, 35). One male teacher explained to me that the students were "too naughty" and would play truant if they did not fear punishment. Most parents expect teachers to use physical punishment, and many object when schools attempt to abolish it. Children do not usually report punishment received at school to their parents, who would be likely to punish them again for their misbehavior.

In the school in which I taught in 1979 corporal punishment was forbidden. However, some students showed other *pālangi* teachers and me bruises they claimed Tongan teachers had inflicted. Some of the Tongan teachers openly carried lengths of wood to class. In Holonga primary school in 1988 one female teacher carried a piece of garden hose, and an Australian teacher at another school told me that a male teacher had beaten a boy with an electric cord. The issue of corporal punishment in schools was tested in court in late 1992, when a nine-year-old boy was awarded damages (T$250) for a beating inflicted by a male teacher in the Holonga primary school. The teacher "admitted hitting the plaintiff six times on the buttocks with a manioke stick, and when it broke, a further four times on the buttocks with the flat side of a two-foot-long piece of 2x1 timber. Medical evidence showed bruises on the buttocks, while on the thigh was a foot-long bruise. The injury to the thigh developed into an abscess and septic sores." Interestingly, the judge "said he was satisfied that the plaintiff was being chastised for gross disobedience and that his punishment was not unlawful" (*Matangi Tonga* 1992b, 32). It was only the blow to the boy's thigh that was considered a civil wrong, and for which damages were awarded.[21]

Incidents of punishment are seldom dyadic interactions. Apart from the punisher and the victim, others are involved in several ways. An adult may call someone younger to punish a child or may ask a child to fetch a broom, stick, or other object for them to use themselves. Children's misdemeanors are readily reported to those immediately responsible for them, by adults as well as other children. People will even help to catch a child trying to run away from punishment. At times this becomes a source of excitement and amusement, as when our next-door neighbor in Holonga ran away from a beating. Katalina (twelve) was being beaten by her mother, Lupe, for coming home late from school. Lupe shouted for Katalina to come back, and several neighbors came to watch. Lupe then shouted to one of the onlookers, a teenage girl, to get Katalina, who ran behind the houses and into the bush. Several women and children chased Katalina, laughing and shouting. The children who remained in our home excitedly told Siale, arriving home from work, what was happening, laughing about how Katalina would be beaten when she was caught. He dourly commented that those chasing Katalina were *vale*. Katalina ran so far into the bush that she was not caught, and when she returned late at night the incident was not mentioned. Nor was it mentioned again in our household, once the excitement of the chase was over.

Children are punished for a very wide range of behavior, generalized as *talangata'a* (disobedience), *anga kovi* (bad behavior), and *anga ta'e totonu* (wrong behavior). Disobeying direct orders, lying or otherwise being dishonest, speaking rudely, doing chores poorly, getting home late from school or other activities, and, for older children and adolescents, smoking and drinking, are all typically punished. Young children are also frequently punished for noisy or uncontrolled behavior, particularly that which necessitates adult intervention. When adults have to intervene in interactions between children, as when they are noisily arguing and ignoring orders to be quiet, punishment is a very likely outcome. In most cases, no attempt is made to discover the cause of a dispute or to mediate or judge; punishment is dealt out to any child who appears to be involved. Children may also be punished for physically fighting, especially girls, for whom it is regarded as unbecoming (*ta'e taau*). If another child is hurt, punishment is more likely. For example, a boy who injured another boy by throwing a mango at his eye was beaten, told to *va'inga fakalelei* (play nicely), and given chores to do.

As has been mentioned previously, crying is often punished. When children are mildly ill they may be hit if they cry persistently. When 'Ofa, at twelve months, cried inconsolably because she had several painful boils on her forehead, her mother told me she did not know what else to do except "hit her all the time" to make her be quiet. Children who cry when hurt while playing may be smacked, and any other children involved may also be punished. When three children in our Holonga household in 1986 were playing a chasing game and one (aged three) fell over and began to cry, Seini slapped the other two children, briefly cuddled the crying child, then slapped him, too, saying, "Don't cry, it's a game."

Children who cry after being punished are usually hit until they quiet. However, young children quickly learn to use crying to their advantage when they are hit by other children because if they cry very loudly the aggressors may themselves be punished by an adult for causing a disturbance. In the example given previously, Ma'ata was obviously keen to quiet her young cousin, Folau, lest she too received a beating. Older children are often punished when their younger siblings cry—for whatever reason—because they are responsible for supervising them. Soane, who was the oldest of eleven children, complained that "every time one of my brothers or one of my sisters cried I had to face the beating."

A focal message of punishment is clearly control—control of emotional responses to pain, frustration, or unhappiness, as well as control of behavior in order to appear submissive and obedient. Punishment that is initiated because a child has been disobedient also becomes a lesson in emotional control. For example, a child who is hit for ignoring an order to have a bath may become distressed and just stand still and cry. This is interpreted as continued disobedience, and punishment is likely to follow until the child obeys the order to bathe. If the older person has to bathe the child, the bath is likely to be peppered with liberal slaps and rough handling throughout. This was the case with Folau, who at three consistently refused to go and bathe when ordered. In the several months I lived next door to his family there was seldom a day when he was not beaten for refusing to bathe and then roughly bathed by his grandmother or older male cousin as he continued to scream his protests.

As they get older, the extent of children's self-control is often remarkable. On one occasion a five-year-old girl was whimpering softly after a scolding, and her mother sharply ordered her to stop crying. A visitor to the household (an Australian woman with whom she had formed an attachment) went to her and wiped her face and hugged her on her lap. The child snuggled into the woman's lap and sobbed deeply, her whole body shuddering. Her mother came and smiled at the other woman, took the girl from her and set her firmly on the floor, lightly slapped her cheek, and said *"Tuku e tangi!"* (stop crying). The little girl stopped immediately (S. Burt, personal communication).

Lessons in self-control begin early, as seen in the pattern of pausing after hitting a child to see if he or she stops crying, then using a threat gesture to further encourage restraint. Self-control is sometimes demanded even of very young children. Waiting at Vaiola Hospital one day I watched a mother with a child of about eighteen months, who was sitting on the floor at her mother's feet, crying. The mother ignored her for a while, then leaned down and thumped her twice on the back, without speaking. When the child intensified her crying, her mother picked her up by one arm and dumped her on the wooden bench beside her. The child kept sobbing, and the mother slapped her once then raised her hand in front of the child's face in a threat gesture, glaring angrily at her. The child quieted down and the mother threatened again, to completely silence her. Throughout this incident the mother did not speak to the child.

Whether or not actions are punished, and how severely they are punished, depends to a great extent on context. Behavior that is acceptable within the family may be punished if visitors are present or when one is away from home, and even within the family more strictures are placed on behavior on Sundays. On the other hand, children are less likely to be punished when a *pālangi* visitor is present. During my stay in Holonga in 1986 I was surprised one day when Seini beat three-year-old Tomasi, as previously I had only heard her threaten the children. On this occasion we had been to town for the day and the children fell asleep on the long, hot bus ride home. When we alighted at Holonga, Tomasi kept sitting down and crying, refusing to walk home. In her tiredness and frustration Seini took off her shoe and hit him repeatedly, forcing him to walk home, then took him to the bedroom and continued to beat him until he stopped crying. Afterwards, she laughed about the incident and commented that because I was there she had not been hitting the children as she would normally.

As the above example also shows, the mood of the caregiver is another crucial factor in whether or not a child is punished. To give another example, on one occasion Folau, who was usually punished for even the slightest misdemeanor, was kicking a bucket about in anger and ignoring his grandfather's orders to stop. When his grandfather called him to come to him, Folau clearly expected to be hit, but the grandfather, relaxing in the late afternoon sun, just patted his head and said, "Don't be angry, you'll break it." However, it would be wrong to suggest that punishment is motivated solely by the punisher's mood, as did Lovett:

The attitude of Tongan parents towards their children's behaviour often appears both irrational and inconsistent. At any age from birth to late adolescence, children can often get away with anti-social behaviour. Then for no apparent reason at all, a parent will inflict violent corporal punishment on a child for a small offence, or just because a parent is in a bad temper. . . . Punishment often does not seem to have any connection with the upbringing of the child but is more an expression of the parents' frustrations. (1958, 37)

On the contrary, specific incidents of punishment, and punishment in general as an aspect of socialization, are motivated by very clear precepts in Tonga. Explanations are regarded as important, and most parents claimed to give their children reasons for punishing them. The emphasis in such explanations is the child's action (or inaction) and its consequences, rather than the child's motivation. Vainga, a young father, explained (in English):

You just don't beat them up and let them go. You have to take them to private, you have to respect the dignity of your son, if you beat up your son, you know. If you punish your son you respect his dignity, you take him to your room, privately, you talk to him, and [say], "I give you some punishment because this and that and that." I think it needs explanation. You don't just beat up to the floor and then let go and [give] no explanation at all. And then, so that I think you explain to the son, "You know I love you, you know why I want you to stop this, and you know very well why I got to give you punishment. Because if you do something wrong, you are going to be accountable for it."

As Vainga himself admitted, he was describing ideal behavior, behavior that would be regarded as *anga faka'ei'eiki*, chiefly behavior. Vainga added, "Most of the parents they just [say], 'I told you not to do that!' Bang! Down. And after that, he cries, and finish."

Young children are seldom told *why* their behavior is wrong: they are simply told it's bad. Folau's little sister, who was frequently hit for playing with the yard tap, was always told "Don't play with the water, it's bad." If children are punished, the reason may be expressed through a series of questions directed at them as they are being hit. For example, an adult may say, "Stop your noise on Sunday, eh?" to which the child responds " '*Io.*" The question may be repeated or simply "*ē?*" spoken several times, increasingly loudly and insistently, punctuated with blows, as the child continues to respond " '*Io, 'io.*" Apart from these brief utterances, most speaking during punishment is a series of imperatives: "*Longo!*" "*Tuku e tangi!*" "*Tu'u ki 'olunga!*" (stand up), and so on. There is also a distinctive grunting sound that is made as the child is hit, to emphasize the action.[22] Thus, explanations tend to tell children what they are being punished for, but not why it is wrong.

'*Ofa* is an important justification for punishment in Tonga, as is *alofa* in Samoa (Gerber 1985, 131). As one teenage boy commented, there would be no point in complaining to his parents about being punished, as they would tell him they punished him out of love, to teach him the right things. Many teenagers explained their punishment in similar ways: their parents punish "because of their love," or "they punish me with their love." A thirteen-year-old girl wrote (in English) in response to my questionnaire, "My dad tries talking to us and making us understand that what we did was wrong, but he knows it doesn't work because we don't learn, so he uses the belt, but he never does it with anger but with love and caring. He wants us to learn and not do things that would make ourselves unhappy."

Although punishment is explicitly associated with love, it cannot be assumed that punishment is not also experienced by children as a withdrawal of love. Some children claimed that after being punished they felt unloved and unwanted. Lesieli, the nineteen-year-old whose father beat her frequently, told me that she would show her father her bruises and tell him, "If you loved me you wouldn't hit me so hard." The association between punishment and '*ofa* is an important factor in the ambivalence often felt toward punishment. There is no logic, as in Samoa, of a lack of punishment indicating a lack of love (Gerber 1985, 131,134). A few people claimed they had never been hit by their major caregivers (often grandparents) and saw this as a sign of special love. One of the characteristics of *pele* is that they are punished less often than their siblings.

In response to her claim that he did not love her, Lesieli's father would reply that he *had* to hit her hard to teach her. Punishment is explicitly associated with teaching. My neighbor, Lupe, told me, "It is best to punish [children] so they are able to pay attention to things; if not they will be content and won't pay attention to what they are told." The belief that children are *vale* motivates the use of punishment as a teaching tool. Discussing the punishment of young children, the headmistress of a girls' school commented, "There's no use trying to reason with those kids." While, as I have shown, formal instruction and advice giving are regarded as important components of socialization, punishment is seen as the most directly and immediately efficacious method of teaching. Punishment is also said to expedite these other forms of learning because it encourages children to have a submissive, unquestioningly obedient demeanor.

In their responses to my questionnaire some teenagers described physical punishment as "good for our own benefits," stated "I know it is to teach me," and claimed that they deserved it. One boy wrote that when he misbehaved his parents would "beat the hell out of me . . . I was only asking for it," and another asserted that he was "punished according to what the scripture says: 'put the whip to the back of the ignorant.' " An adolescent girl claimed that after punishment she felt "happy because it was my fault." The belief that punishment is deserved is also shown in the proportion of teenagers surveyed who claimed to feel guilty (*halaia*) and repentant (*fakatomala*) after being punished (36.8 percent).

The students were asked "How do you feel when your parents punish you?" After repentance and guilt the two most common responses were anger (23.8 percent) and sadness (22.9 percent). Despite the comments about punishment being a sign of love and well deserved, the overwhelming majority of responses were negative. Teenagers said that they felt lonely, unwanted, and afraid, not wanting to eat or talk; others said they wanted to run away or even to die. Some claimed that they hated their parents, wanted to punish them, and wished they could die. In a poignant comment one teenager wrote that she felt "as if everything is turned inside out."

Children's reactions to punishment are important to consider because they affect the course of incidents of punishment and on a more general level reveal how children interpret its meaning. Earle observed that the favorable responses Maori children gave when she sought to elicit their reactions to punishment tended to be simple and stereotyped, whereas negative responses were more personal (1958, 21). My survey revealed the same tendency, with the majority of favorable responses being simply "I feel sorry/guilty" and, as seen above, a range of more personal, negative responses. Many of my respondents actually gave two answers, one more socially acceptable and thus favorable and the other indicating their negative personal feelings.

Mamahi, a term that was used by nearly a quarter of the respondents, is a complex and ambiguous term. It can indicate both physical and mental pain and also "to be sorry, to feel sorrow or regret; to feel hurt (take offence); to be annoyed or angry, to harbour ill-feeling" (Churchward 1959, 328). When used alone *mamahi* most often refers to physical pain; a more specific term for this is *ongoʻi mamahi*. *Ongoʻi* means "to feel or perceive" and is commonly used for the emotional as well as the physical sense of "feel." Thus, *ongoʻi mamahi* incorporates both senses of pain, as well as the other connotations of *mamahi*. Some respondents mentioned both *ongoʻi mamahi* and *loto mamahi*, the latter being more specifically associated with the emotional aspect of *mamahi*, as it means "inner" *mamahi*. As such, it has connotations of both anger and sadness. Another response, closely associated with *loto mamahi*, was *"ongoʻi ʻoku tautea hoto loto"*: my heart and mind (my "inside") feel punished. In describing the intended effects of punishment, adults often cited *mamahi*, as both physical pain and inner sorrow or regret, as important. Again, the ambivalence toward punishment is indicated in this term, which can indicate the more favorable response of regret (implying guilt) while also encompassing a range of other, more negative, responses including anger.

Any claims of innocence, resistance to punishment, or angry reaction to it are regarded as *loto lahi* ("big" *loto*, i.e., brave, bold, or in this context, acting tough). A child who persists in crying, despite orders to be quiet and threatened or actual punishment, is *loto lahi*. One day Folau's little sister Luseane was crying, and her mother and grandmother shouted at her to stop crying and come to them. Her mother, Kalolaine, got a broom and hit her twice, saying *"Longo!"* but Luseane screamed louder and squatted on the ground. Kalolaine hit her again, then laughed, threw down the broom, and said, *"Loto lahi, ē?"* She picked Luseane up by the arm, roughly, and took her to her grandmother, giving her a smack accompanied with a loud grunt on the way.

Lesieli described the predicament she was in whenever her father punished her. His beatings and the teasing laughter of her neighbors, who watched her being beaten, made her so angry that she would not cry. Her father would tell her she was *loto lahi* and beat her more, but when she did cry, he would shout *"Longo!"* at her. An acceptable response to punishment is to plead and apologize, in a quiet, monotonous tone, such as begging *"Fakamolemole"* (please or sorry) again and again.[23] Some children exclaim

" *'Oiauē!*" in the same way.[24] Children should also submit to punishment, initially by voluntarily going to the person who wants to punish them. If they dawdle they will be ordered to *laka* (march). Adults often remain seated as they punish a child, and staying within reach is a further demonstration of submission. One rainy day in Holonga the children were being kept indoors with Silia, their aunt, who was seated on the floor finishing the decorative edge of a mat. Each time Silia felt that the children were being too noisy or naughty she called them to her and pinched or slapped them, and although this occurred many times the children always went to her obediently and submitted, tearfully, to their punishment.

Trying to avoid punishment by running away can sometimes be a successful strategy for older children, who can run far enough, and stay away long enough, for the adult concerned to "forget" the incident. Teenagers sometimes go to the home of a friend or relative and return at night, so that by morning their misdemeanor has been forgotten. Younger children also try to escape at times, but they are usually caught and beaten. Folau, my three-year-old neighbor, often ran to the end of the garden to try to avoid punishment, but he was invariably caught and beaten all the way back to the house. He also tried in vain to hide under the house. In another means of avoiding punishment, *fakaongo-tuli*, a child pretends not to hear someone calling him or her to be punished. If the person involved is occupied, feels good humored, or is out of sight, or if the child's misdemeanor is slight, this ploy works very well.

Elenoa had already learned the technique of *fakaongotuli* by the age of three. She used it one day when she had entered my room against her mother's orders and her mother called her father, Siale, to come and hit her. Siale, who was resting in the bedroom, called Elenoa repeatedly, but she went and sat on the couch and did not react. Her mother nudged her and told her, in a low voice, to answer, but she remained immobile and impassive. Siale told her brother Tomasi to go and get Elenoa, but when Tomasi went and stood next to Elenoa, shouting her name, she still did not react. Seini nudged her again and told her to go to bed, but got no reaction, so she left Elenoa sitting there and went to the bedroom with Feleti to rest. After they left the room Elenoa got up and began to play. At the time of this incident the adults concerned were relaxed and good-humored, and still rather self-conscious in my presence, and Elenoa read the situation accurately. On occasions when the adults are not as tolerant, children are unlikely to ignore calls to be punished; rather, obedience and a submission to punishment are then the best strategy for reduced punishment.

Some children respond to frequent punishment by becoming wary and nervous. Such children are called *mataila* (literally, awake eyes) because they often flinch from sudden movements as if expecting a blow. Other children readily express a fear of punishment but are often defiant or ignore threats, warnings, and lighter punishments. A primary school teacher commented that she could tell which children were "raised with the stick" because they would not behave unless threatened with being hit. Many of the young children I observed were frequently silly, cheeky, and boisterous despite the fact that such behavior was usually punished. In my field journal I called them "children living on the edge," and I speculated that because children are so seldom given direct positive attention they accept, even invite, negative attention.

Children may even consciously decide to behave in a way that will lead to punishment, particularly boys who choose to be with their friends rather than help with chores. One boy said, "You get a few hidings but from that you get used to being given a belting. . . . I'd rather be with my group than go to Mum, and I don't care that Mum will give me a little hiding tonight." In her story of setting fire to a cooking hut after trying to smoke a cigarette as a little girl, Pulu wrote, "Inoke [her father] showed his anger in the usual Tongan way. And although the fire in the cookhouse was out, we felt like we were sitting on the hot coals. But even a punishment, when shared with fellow conspirators, is part of the game" (Pulu and Pope 1979, 11).

Talking to older Tongans about their childhood revealed their ambivalent yet intense feelings about the punishment they had received. It was not unusual for adults to cry when they talked of their parents and other caregivers, describing both the love and the punishment they had received. As with the teenagers who answered my questionnaire, people of all ages readily associated punishment with feelings of anger, sadness, and hurt, but also claimed to have deserved punishment and to love their caregivers for having taught them properly. A thirteen-year-old girl commented, "When they punish me I honestly feel angry and hateful at first, but after a while I understand them and see what they want from me. This makes me love them more."

On the other hand, some people also admitted to holding long-term grudges toward those who had severely punished them. Siale's older brother, Soane, claimed that people are not aware of holding grudges: "They think [punishment] is part of growing up, it's part of being Tongan, and it's part of being in a family." However, he added, "Underneath . . . you want to pay back when you get older. . . . It explodes in different ways." Many people remember particular incidents especially vividly, and with intense emotions. As a child, Soane had been severly beaten by his uncle for being late home from school, and he said, "Every time I think of that I can still feel the pain in my stomach, from being, you know, pounded in my stomach. . . . I almost died."

Ambivalence toward punishment is linked to that toward hierarchical relations. In simple terms, higher-status persons are protectors and providers as well as punishers and holders of power. In adult-child relations this is symbolized in the game of alternating threats and affection that has been described. Because punishment is positively valued as a form of teaching and an expression of love and concern, the distinction between protecting and providing and punishing is somewhat blurred, and the ambivalence that has been described is deep-seated and complex.

People's statements about punishment indicate that they accept it as inevitable and even necessary, and despite the ambivalence that exists, the popular view of physical punishment is generally approving. People often comment, after punishing a child or when watching a child being punished, "*Sai, ē!*" (good, eh), implying "Serves you right!" Pita said, "It is right to hit and punish [children] so they will be afraid and not go around [go out without permission]." He added that if parents do not *puke* (seize or hold) their children, they will wander anywhere and could get hurt. The importance of fear was also made explicit by my friend Seini when she explained why our neighbor beat her three-year-old daughter, Kalo, so often. Kalo was "*pauʻu ʻaupito*" (very naughty), Seini told me, and had to be hit "all the time." Kalo's mother later went to Australia, leaving Kalo with her elderly grandmother who could not, as Seini explained, "hit her hard enough." Because of this, Kalo was "not afraid," and Seini was worried she might do something dangerous like wander onto the road. Fear in a broader sense is also associated with learning, as in the sign in a classroom: "Fear of God Is the Beginning of All Knowledge."

THE QUESTION OF "ABUSE"

There is no shame associated with hitting children to discipline them because it is believed to be necessary and important. However, some people admitted to feeling ashamed when they punished primarily out of anger. My neighbor, Lupe, admitted, "I feel ashamed as I'm often very quick to punish and do not have much patience; when they work badly I feel angry." Punishment can also be shameful if it is judged to be *tā vale* (hitting foolishly). This is defined to some extent by the nature of the punishment itself: whether it causes bruising or draws blood, whether the head or face is hit, or whether the punishment is too severe.[25] Contextual factors are far more important, however, as I will show. Behavior defined as *tā vale* may also be derided as *anga manu* (animal behavior) or *anga fakatuʻa* (common behavior).

One of the most common reactions of people watching a child being beaten is to laugh. After the incident, too, people often continue to laugh and to tease the child. Tongans are not usually reflective about this behavior, and when I asked people why it occurred most answered simply "Who knows?" (*hei'ilo*) or "It's just funny." The explanations that *were* offered tended to be of two types. The first type is exemplified in a story Ngata told (in English) about his younger brother, who had persisted in coming home late from school despite his father's warnings that he would be hit. One day the father beat the boy, who promised not to be late again.

> The hiding goes on, and we all laugh, because we know Dad told him before. For us, it's a hiding, but it's something very funny. . . . [The next day, the boy is late again, and is beaten again, and once more his family laughs.] It's not the actual hitting, we know that's hard, it's painful, but really we look from the other corner and we laugh. And the other thing is if we don't laugh, things are very, very serious. And if we make it a bit fun, and the person who is doing the beating they will come to an end soon, and the one who is running around will just think it's a big joke. . . . I think it makes it easier for the person being belted up. . . . If everybody stands still, I think it's something wrong, people think "Oh! this is killing, this is slaughtering."

Others denied that laughter has anything to do with helping the person being beaten or easing the tension of the situation. "It all just comes to the fact that our sense of humor, we seem to be laughing at people who suffer," said Soane. The two explanations are actually closely related, as in the second type the emphasis is again on the person's foolish or out-of-control behavior. Both the behavior resulting in punishment and the behavior caused by it are regarded as *vale*, and therefore humorous.

Laughter at punishment does sometimes have the "helpful," cathartic effects indicated in Ngata's explanation. This was clear in an incident involving an eleven-year-old boy who was being punished for going to bed without having a shower. As his father hit him with a piece of wood, Sione whimpered and in a low, babbling voice begged him to stop. When his father had gone inside the house again, Sione's older, female cousin came and laughed at him and imitated his pleading. Sione tried to punch her, but she jumped back into the house. Sione and another boy went to the shower block and began to wash, and the cousin came outside again. She walked to the toilet, and as she passed the shower she taunted, "Sione was crying!" and imitated him again. The boys began to swear about her to each other (e.g., "She is goat shit.") and by the time they were showered they were both laughing and cheerful.

However, laughter and teasing also serve, at times, to increase the shame of the punishment, and can be very cruel. Kalolaine had beaten Folau (three) for not lying down to rest after the Sunday lunch. She had beaten him until he stopped crying and screaming, but as soon as he was quiet she began to tease him as his older cousins laughed. Folau lay unable to reply as he struggled to suppress his sobs, while she repeatedly asked him "Are you asleep?" and "What's your name?"

The person punishing a child may also laugh while, or after, hitting the child, particularly when the child is very young and the transition from play-ful smacking is continuing. Incidents involving punishment are related as amusing anecdotes, even by the person who dealt out the punishment and even if it was severe. One man laughingly told me that he had so badly beaten his younger brother for drinking home brew (hopi) that the boy lost consciousness and was then bedridden for "several weeks." The same man also used this incident as a teasing threat to warn another young brother not to drink.

Yet punishment is not always regarded as amusing. People seldom laugh when the beating is severe, when the child's misdemeanor is particularly seri-ous, and/or when the punisher has lost his or her temper. Other children watch such incidents with fearful, nervous expressions, but adults often behave as though they are ignoring what is happening. The most distressing incident I observed occurred when one of my neighbors, Hina, lost her tem-per with Kalo, her three-year-old daughter, for not responding to her repeated calls to come home and bathe. Hina sent Kalo's older cousin to fetch her, and she went to Kalo, saying, "Go to Hina, she's going to hit you!" Kalo immediately began to cry as the cousin led her by the hand toward her mother, who was approaching and waving a stick. The cousin was clearly nervous and stopped a short distance from the angry woman. Hina stood still, shouting at Kalo to come to her. She ordered another of the older chil-dren who had gathered at a distance to bring Kalo to her and he did so. Hina hit Kalo across the side of her head, knocking her down, then stooped and slapped her hard on the legs several times. Then Hina dragged Kalo to her feet and pulled her home, slapping her and hitting her with the stick. At the low fence surrounding their home Hina hit Kalo very hard then bodily threw her over the fence and kicked her so that her body shot across the ground. Finally she dragged her out of sight into the bathhouse, where Kalo's scream-ing continued for some time. Throughout this incident I felt frozen to the spot, wondering if I should, or could, somehow intervene.[26] The children who were nearby all watched silently, obviously nervous, yet the other adults around did not watch or react in any way. The incident was not mentioned again, except when I spoke to Seini about it and was told, as mentioned above, that Kalo was a "very naughty" child.

Children who have an emotionally close relationship may not laugh at one another's punishments. Lesieli told me that her sisters would go away and cry when she was being beaten. Sometimes other family members show their sympathy to a child who has been beaten by offering food or even cuddling them. Soane told me that his mother, who was also frequently beaten by his father during Soane's childhood, had been too frightened to intervene when Soane was being beaten. Afterwards, she would always buy the boy something nice to eat; as he put it, "I think a making up for what had happened." When older children run away after punishment to friends' or relations' homes, they may be allowed to stay, in an indirect show of sympathy. Soane told me that when he was beaten by his uncle, with whom he was living temporarily, he ran away to his parents' home in another village, and they allowed him to stay with them. Such movement between households tends to be temporary, however, and is not always an option.[27] The Ritchies have claimed for Polynesia generally that children are "not desperately and irrevocably locked into unchangeable, punitive situations" because they can move to other households (1989, 110). In Tonga, the ability to change households in such situations is limited, and the weakening of extended family ties seems to be further reducing the significance of this option.

The people most likely to interfere with each other's actions are married couples and immediate relatives. Seini told me that she stops her husband, Siale, by shouting at him and pulling the children away, although I did not see this happen as Siale rarely hit the children. She added: "Sometimes I am very angry with [the children]. *Tā pē, tā pē, tā pē* (just hit, just hit, just hit), but Siale doesn't speak to me or stop me. But sometimes when I shout at them Siale says, '*Tuku hoʻo kaila pehe*' (stop your shouting)." Attempts at intervention are often unsuccessful, particularly when someone has really lost his or her temper. On one of the many occasions when Folau was being punished for not cooperating while being bathed, his grandmother repeatedly hit him on the face and body, then picked him up bodily and threw him into the bath and began to wash him roughly. Her husband attempted to push her away from Folau but she shoved him away. She hit Folau several more times, shouting angrily at him, then sent him inside to dress. Her husband, who had watched from a distance after being shoved away, followed them both inside, where she was still shouting, and remonstrated briefly with her.

An important factor affecting the likelihood of intervention is the shared evaluation of the child's *ʻulungāanga*. When a child is considered to be particularly willful and naughty, harsh discipline is more likely to be regarded approvingly. It is for this reason that physical punishment tends to peak in frequency between the ages of three and five, when children are said to be especially naughty and foolish, yet old enough to begin to learn proper behavior. Shared evaluations of the seriousness of a child's misdemeanor also influence the probability of intervention.

The "audience" to punishment is also an important contextual factor. Losing one's temper too publicly can shame the family, and other family members are likely to tell the angry person to stop. The relationship of the onlookers to the punisher also determines their own willingness to intervene, and people unrelated to those involved rarely interfere. In one case a woman was beating her little girl and shouting angrily at her for not washing when she was told. Her husband, waiting for a bus outside the house, did not interfere until he saw me approaching the bus stop. He then went inside and talked to his wife, who stopped immediately.

Who is hitting a child also affects the likelihood of intervention. In their discussion of factors preventing child abuse in traditional Polynesian communities, Ritchie and Ritchie argue that "high status people are always there and have a right to intervene—and do" (1981, 192). In Tonga, high-status people certainly do intervene and otherwise monitor the actions of lower-status persons. A child's paternal relatives may express disapproval if they feel the mother is mistreating the child. On one occasion a paternal aunt questioned her niece about a large bruise on her arm. When she was told that the child's mother had hit her with a shoe, the aunt turned to the mother and sarcastically asked if she wanted a knife "to finish the job." However, high-status persons are not always there or always willing to intervene.

Status relations can also work to prevent intervention. Parents would be unlikely to openly dispute the actions of the father's sister, even when she is hitting their own children. In one incident reported to me in which status difference was clearly a crucial factor, a man with an important role in his village as a public official beat his fourteen-year-old son about the head with a piece of wood. Not only did no one intervene, but when the boy was taken to the hospital, the story given by the father (that the boy had fallen from a horse) was supported by relatives accompanying them. Nor did anyone report the incident when, some days later, the boy nearly died and had to be readmitted to the hospital with blood clots on his brain. Parents and other relatives would be most likely to intervene if a child was being hit by an unrelated person with no direct authority over the child, although this would be a rare occurrence.

People are reluctant to intervene if they are themselves afraid of the person beating a child. In the case above the complex interrelationship of respect and fear for high-status persons restrained other villagers from intervening. The father of Siale and Soane, who acted as disciplinarian for the village some years ago, was so feared that people did not interfere when he frequently beat his wife and children. On one occasion, Soane told me, his

father beat him with a belt "until I just lost all my voice." He ran to his
neighbors for help but they were frightened and let his father come and take
him away and continue to beat him.

Such incidents raise the question of "child abuse." The Tongan Criminal
Offences Act defines child abuse as follows:

> If any person over the age of 16 years, who has the custody, charge, or care of
> any child or young person, wilfully assaults, illtreats, neglects, abandons, or
> exposes such child or young person to be assaulted, ill-treated, neglected,
> abandoned or exposed, in a manner likely to cause such child or young per-
> son unnecessary suffering or injury to his health [, that shall constitute child
> abuse]. (*Law of Tonga* 1967, Cap. 15, section 106)[28]

The punishment recommended for such abuse is a fine and/or a prison term
of up to three years (*Law of Tonga* 1967, Cap. 15, section 106). Charges of
child abuse (referred to in law as *fakamamahi'i tamaiki*: cruelty to children)
are seldom laid, however, and from 1985 to 1987 only five cases were reported (*Report of the Minister of Police for 1986 and Report . . . 1987*).[29] Doctors must report suspected cases of child abuse, but the chief medical officer
at Vaiola in 1988 claimed that there is no great problem with abuse because
community pressure has reduced its incidence (Dr. T. Puloka, personal communication). However, injuries caused by beatings may not be reported as
such, as in the case cited previously.

The rare cases that are reported to the police are also defined by the community as *tā vale*. Incidents regarded as serious enough to warrant community intervention but not serious enough to be reported to the police are
dealt with by the family and village concerned. Reprimands from high-status
kin, shaming through gossip, and moving a child temporarily to a relative's
home are the usual actions taken. Such sanctions are infrequently invoked
because even punishment perceived as *tā vale* is seldom regarded as serious
enough to warrant intervention. As has been shown, contextual features
such as the status of the punisher, the setting, the audience, and so on can
also determine the evaluation of and response to beatings. In the case of
the fourteen-year-old described above, some villagers thought the father's
behavior was *tā vale*, but these private assessments did not result in intervention, public shaming, or moves to initiate legal action. Also, not all violent
behavior that could be legally defined as abuse is perceived as *tā vale*. Even
punishment that physically injures a child may be perceived differently. Pulu
tells of being hit on her foot as she tried to jump away from a beating. A
bone in her foot broke, and her family decided that this happened because

she was "weak." Pulu comments: "It never occurred to them that I might have been hit too hard" (Pulu and Pope 1979, 17).

In Western nations the difficulty of clearly distinguishing between acceptable and unacceptable treatment of children has led to a broadening of the definition of "abuse."[30] From legal and medical perspectives, any form of violence to children, including corporal punishment, is increasingly opposed both in principle and in legislation. Despite this the issue of physical punishment, the most widely encountered form of violence toward children, has not been fully confronted. As La Fontaine stated, "The social pattern of battered babies and wives, or of sexually abused children, have drawn our attention to the misuse of this power [of parents and older siblings over children] but its exercise in less dramatic ways is often ignored" (1986, 27).

In their study of child abuse in the United States, Kadushin and Martin found that, as in Tonga, there is a "gray area" between acceptable punishment and unacceptable abuse[31] and that many incidents of abuse result from "extensions of disciplinary actions, which at some point and often inadvertently, crossed the ambiguous line between sanctioned corporal punishment and unsanctioned child abuse" (1981, 264). Because *tā vale* describes such extensions of disciplinary actions, it is similar to the concept of abuse in this sense. Yet *tā vale*, as a definition of maltreatment, is only partially equivalent to the notion of abuse as defined in Tongan law, as well as in Western laws and popular understanding. The most significant difference is in the use of contextual factors as criteria for identifying maltreatment and the necessity of intervention, rather than the nature of the behavior itself and its effect upon the victim.

In "the West" legal definitions of abuse affect the community primarily through social institutions such as social welfare agencies (see Handelman 1983; Scheper-Hughes and Stein 1987). In Tonga there are no such institutions to mediate between the legal definition and the community's understanding or to intervene in citizens' lives except in rare instances of police prosecution for abuse. Common practice has therefore remained largely unaffected by the legal definition. If and when the bureaucratic base of the Tongan government broadens to include social welfare institutions, the issue of state intervention in legally designated abuse cases (or even potential abuse cases, as has occurred in some Western nations) will have to be confronted.

The issue has already become significant in Tongan migrant populations in Western nations (Teu 1978). The problem has also arisen with indigenous and immigrant Polynesians in areas with large populations of Europeans, such as Hawai'i (Baker 1986, 171; Dubanoski 1982; Dubanoski and Snyder 1980; Gautier 1977), American Samoa (Leacock 1987, 183), and New Zealand (Fergusson, Fleming, and O'Neill 1972; Ritchie and Ritchie 1970, 1981). There have been reports of increasingly abusive practices within the migrant and urbanized indigenous communities where village and extended family sanctions are absent and families are suffering economic hardship and social problems such as alcohol abuse (Dubanoski 1982; Fergusson, Fleming, and O'Neill 1972; Ritchie and Ritchie 1979, 1981, 1989).

The problem of defining child abuse also needs to be addressed in anthropological studies of child socialization. Anthropologists have tended to defend, ignore, trivialize, or "exoticize" practices such as harsh physical punishment, painful initiation rituals, and so on (Scheper-Hughes 1987a, 19) and to avoid the whole issue of abuse. Physical punishment, in particular, is often mentioned only in passing, with its occurrence taken for granted as functional and adaptive within a given culture (e.g., Beaglehole and Beaglehole 1941a; Mead 1966; Middleton 1970; and a more recent example, Kirkpatrick 1983, 128, 130).[32] The Beagleholes, in their brief account of Tongan childhood, mention that children are "unmercifully" and "severely" beaten by women and older children, but go no further than to comment that such beatings "appear to be village-practice in enforcing discipline" (1941b, 82). Yet Ernest Beaglehole's field journal clearly reveals that he regarded these beatings as abusive, as he repeatedly refers to the "sadism" involved: "The Tongan mother has not the slightest hesitation in herself picking up a stick or coconut switch and beating her child with a thwarted fury that seems nine parts pure sadism and one-quarter part altruistic-disciplinary. To us, as we watch the scene, these child beatings seem to exceed all that is reasonable and just" (1938–1939, Jan. 12).

Although the matter is not pursued in the Beagleholes' monograph, Beaglehole clearly saw this harsh physical punishment as an important clue to "the Tongan personality." He states in the journal that the child psychology of his day was inadequate to explain the effects of the "sadism" (1938–1939, Dec. 27) and concludes simply that "the bullying and terrorism that are the naked facts in this Tongan child society and which seems to colour so many of the relations between Tongan child and Tongan mother must be important factors in the formation and development of the typical Tongan adult personality" (Jan. 12). In a subsequent article, Beaglehole suggested that the severe punishment of Tongan children and "the necessities of adjusting to the rather strict morality of the average Tongan home" resulted in "psychic stress" (1940, 47).

Recent anthropological studies dealing with "the darker side of parenting" (Scheper-Hughes 1987a, 7)—such as infanticide, incest, selective neglect, and child abuse—have examined the effects of these practices as well as the problem of cross-cultural comparison.[33] This work has been influenced by feminist scholarship, which has recently, albeit belatedly, begun to pay attention to "the often harsh realities of children's subordination" (Thorne 1987, 98).[34] Korbin argues that the factors involved in "reconciling cultural variability with an acceptable definition of child abuse and neglect" include "the socialization goals of the culture, parental intentions and beliefs about their actions, and the way a child perceives his or her treatment" (1981b, 5). Each of these factors has been considered in the previous discussion of punishment in Tonga, and in each case complex and sometimes conflicting goals, beliefs, and perceptions are involved. What is clear is that the factor most salient in distinguishing between socially sanctioned punishment and tā vale is context. Punishment can be seen as a political action, an assertion of power and status. Where this assertion occurs in an inappropriate context it is perceived as maltreatment by Tongans.

The issue of physical punishment of children is gradually becoming a matter of public concern in Tonga. Punishment has a crucial role in Tongan beliefs about child development, and pālangi childrearing (believed to be lacking in discipline) is often unfavorably compared to the Tongan way. Yet attitudes have been slowly changing for some time. When fifty-four Tongan couples were asked to list weaknesses in Tongan child discipline, all indicated that a lack of discipline was a problem in some families, but each couple also stated that the use of beatings as punishment was a weakness (Finau 1979, 60). Some school principals have been trying for years to abolish corporal punishment in schools, and the Tongan media occasionally raises the issue of physical punishment (e.g., Tonga Today 1987a, 35). The Mormon church discourages the use of physical punishment within the families of its adherents and in its schools. Some Tongans are even using the term "abuse," as in Niumeitolu's assertion that in their first five years, "most Tongan children experience some physical abuse as part of their development; that is, either receiving physical punishment themselves or observing the father's physical violence on the mother" (1993, 76). Cases in court of children being assaulted by nonrelatives—such as teachers (Matangi Tonga 1992b) and policemen (Matangi Tonga 1992d)—are also raising the question of just who has the right to discipline children.

As social support networks become more restricted and broader social and economic changes occur, the incidence of child abuse and neglect can increase (Korbin 1991, 72–74). Yet as Korbin notes, "The impact of change on child maltreatment is a complex issue" (74). Tongan parents are responding in varied ways to change and to their related fear that children are becoming badly behaved and "losing" their culture. Some have become increasingly strict and punitive in an attempt to further control their children's behavior, whereas others have relaxed their control to some extent.

WIDER CONTEXTS OF VIOLENCE

Anthropological accounts of twentieth-century Tonga, which have emphasized the unaggressive, dignified side of Tongan behavior, have not upheld the "paradoxical" image portrayed in the historical literature. Today, the extent to which violence is socially acceptable varies considerably; Bernstein argues that the most acceptable expressions of violence are

> private (within families or away from open view), or involving individuals who were traditionally abused and could not easily fight back (e.g., wives, children, mentally retarded, and animals). . . . [T]hey are an example of accepted, even expected, acts in Tonga which can be as validly criticized in their omission as in their commission, for not to control and punish one's wife, child, or animal, leads to criticism that one is not "teaching" them correctly or is too weak to control them. (1983, 154)

As we have seen, the victims of such violence are usually blamed for what happens. Women who have been beaten by their husbands often describe the incident as being their own fault and laugh about it in retrospect.[35] However, wife beating is not as explicitly associated with 'ofa or teaching as is child beating. Husbands are 'eiki to their wives, but women are seldom subservient to their husbands. Many women described their beatings as being caused by quarrels (kē) and clashes (fepaki) in which they were attempting to assert their own opinions or needs. Faiva has argued that in Tonga wife beating is "often seen as a form of disciplining the wives . . . [and] is often seen as the exercise of authority rather than the abuse of that authority" (1989, 41).[36] Violence to wives most often happens during the first years of marriage when, as Niumeitolu states, the husband may use emotional and physical abuse to "achieve the wife's submission" (1993, 76).

Intellectually handicapped and mentally ill people, who are regarded, like children, as vale, are sometimes threatened or treated violently. An elderly man suffering from senility, living in a village near Holonga, was often taunted and threatened by groups of boys. On one occasion when he approached me to beg money one of these boys broke a stick from a bush and threatened to hit him, until he wandered off. Yet on other occasions teenage boys walked along the road with him, holding his hand to stop him from walking out into the traffic.

In Nukuʻalofa, a young woman who appeared to be mentally disturbed was treated with much more open aggression. Individuals or groups of people threatened her with violence and chased her away or threw rocks at her when she approached them to talk. She became verbally abusive herself at times and would then be hit or kicked away. On one occasion she stole some small items from the house next to mine, and when she was caught in the act she was beaten by a woman from the house and several neighbors.

Animals are also treated violently, as has been remarked in several accounts (e.g., Bergeron n.d., 42; Bernstein 1983, 154; Lovett 1958, 33; Thomson 1894, 390). The cats, dogs, pigs, and chickens that roam freely near homes are frequently hit, kicked, and stoned away from doorways, food, and gardens, and other animals such as goats and horses are also beaten at times. Small children act out threatening and hitting sequences with the cats and dogs allowed into or near houses, and when older children chase animals away they often call out the threat they hear so often: "*Te u taaʻi koe*". Adults sometimes laughingly tell children to stop mistreating animals but rarely interfere any further.

On the *ʻapi* on which I lived for a time in Nukuʻalofa a puppy was on one occasion tormented by a boy, aged two, who was being cared for by Meleʻana, one of the women living in the main house. The boy, Vili, squeezed the puppy to make it squeal, sat on it, chased it, and hit it while the women of the household watched and laughed. Meleʻana called to him to stop it and mildly threatened to hit him, as well as telling him it was *fakaʻofa* (pitiable) to hurt the puppy, all the while laughing and not making any attempt to stop him.

In these various contexts violence is directed from higher-status to lower-status persons and animals. Violence that is in a sense outside the status system, yet receives tacit approval, includes defending the honor and reputation of one's family. This sort of violence, as in revenging the rape of a daughter or responding to offensive behavior (e.g., swearing at a man's sister) can also be seen as a form of punishment. Low-status persons rarely direct violence toward those of higher status, although babies and toddlers are frequently encouraged to be violent toward older children and even adults.

Small children sometimes threaten adults as an extension of the encouragement babies are given to behave violently, but even by the age of two they have usually learned that if they actually hit an adult they are likely to be punished. One day when ʻOfa was crying Seini called a neighbor's son, Vea (aged two), to come and hit her. He ran over and threatened ʻOfa with a stick and then a broom as Seini and Vea's older sister, Katalina, laughed. Vea climbed over Katalina's back and lap, and she rapped him on the head and pretended to smack him, then began drumming with some sticks while he danced. Vea picked up a knife and pretended to throw it at me, then laughed heartily when I instinctively ducked. He began to pretend to throw anything he could find and to wave a stick threateningly at his sister as his "audience" laughed. He hit Katalina, breaking his stick, then poked out his tongue. When Seini commented on this to me, he kept doing it, while threatening to throw a brush at me, until an older woman approached and Katalina warned, "Here comes Moana; she'll hit you!" His "performance" ended as the adults began to talk to each other.

As Borofsky has noted of Pukapuka, Tongan punishment teaches children about their "subordinate role in the learning process. The beating constitutes a lesson in social relations" (1987, 97). What Borofsky does not make explicit is that punishment also teaches children how to behave in a dominant (i.e., high-status) manner. Mageo has suggested of Samoa that "because the assertion of status in Samoa is equated with the ability to inflict physical punishment, punishing another may come to be regarded, in later life, as an assertion of status" (1988, 54). Punishment is a direct and forceful assertion of power and control, and in Tonga such assertion is no longer associated with chief-commoner interactions, as formerly, but continues within the family and in other settings such as schools. Children begin, by the age of two or three, to attempt to dominate younger and same-age children by force. In play and other interactions, they sometimes imitate the sequences of gestures and words used by adults and older children when threatening and punishing; at other times they are more directly and competitively violent.

In children's play groups younger children do hit older children, although far less often than they are themselves hit. A great deal of children's play is rough and physical, with a lot of hair pulling, wrestling, kicking, snatching, shouting, and so on. Whiting and Edwards have argued that "rough-and-tumble play is not necessarily aggressive; in our analysis it appears more as competitive and sociable behaviour. This type of play can quickly become hostile and aggressive, however, when one of the actors is hurt" (1988, 276).

In Tonga, this competitive, sociable aspect of rough play is apparent, and in fact much teasing and roughhouse is affectionate, even between high- and low-status persons (e.g., adults and children). However, there are far more contexts in which it becomes aggressive than simply the injury of one player. Accusations of cheating, disputes over turns, and other elements of discord frequently lead to aggression, as does teasing, which is discussed in the following chapter. The status differences of the chidren (kin- or age-based) are never completely obscured by play and often emerge during these moments of dispute or when higher-status children want lower-status children to follow their orders. Children of similar ages tend to vie for dominance (i.e., status), and boys are especially aggressive to one another in this sense. Within boys' peer groups one is often singled out as the weakest and is treated roughly. He is sent to do messages and, as Ngata explained,

> if he makes a mistake, you'll bring him in front of everybody and have a hiding. And that's a fun hiding. Give him a punch, or fall down, give him a kick. And he accepts it . . . and if he's going to cry, that means he's not a man, first thing; second thing, the beating up is too excessive, and then he will be complaining, and the last thing is, if he cries that means the other people will kick him out of the peer group.

Adults often give both covert and overt approval to violent and aggressive behavior between children, particularly between boys. In relaxed and informal situations adults may laugh at and encourage such behavior as a kind of extension of the aggressive performances by babies. Some children tend to be picked on more than others, and adults rarely intervene. One of Alisi's adopted children, Sela, was constantly being teased and hit by the other children, often in front of adults. Seini told me that they hit her because she was "always crying," although my own impression was that she cried *because* she was hit.

Children who have been hit by other children seldom receive any sympathy if they complain to their caregivers. When Sela came crying to Alisi after her older adoptive brother had punched her on the back, Alisi and the women with her shouted at her to stop crying, and one of her aunts threatened to hit her with a shoe. The reaction of adults in this kind of situation varies, and on some occasions the child who has hurt another child may be punished, or both may be punished for causing a disturbance to the adults. The particular children involved affect adults' reactions: a *pele* may be protected from other children's aggression; an unfavored child, such as Sela, may be left to fend for him- or herself.

There is also a great deal of variation in children's tendencies to behave aggressively and violently. Several people commented that children who receive a lot of physical punishment tend to be more aggressive with other children. As a kindergarten principal observed, these children are often "hard cases," not only more aggressive in play but also harder for the teachers to discipline. Although punishment is sometimes explicitly intended to discourage aggression (e.g., when a child is beaten for hitting another child), it also provides a clear model of violent behavior that is enacted in play, in conflict, and as an assertion of status.[37] However, physical punishment is not the only factor contributing to violent and aggressive behavior. Keene (1978) claimed for Samoa that aggressive behavior is influenced by the anger caused by punishment, aggressive models of behavior, the link between pain and love, frustration, and the cultural expectation that anger be repressed. These factors are all clearly important in Tonga, although the contexts in which violent behavior occurs are more restricted than in Samoa. Other social factors that appear to influence the individual child's aggressiveness to other children include his or her place in the sibling hierarchy, treatment received within the household (e.g., if the child is a *pele*) and opportunities to play away from adult observers. Girls, who are kept close to home and occupied with household chores, have few opportunities to behave aggressively except toward the younger children in their care and in any case are expected to be more restrained in their behavior than males.

Violence and aggression within peer groups continues into adulthood, particularly for men. A great deal of fighting between men is precipitated by consumption of alcohol, so dances, hotels, and other sites for drinking are also sites for frequent brawls. As Bernstein noted, there is a tendency for fund-raising events, Christmas, and other celebrations to be marked by an increase in tension and fighting (1983, 155). Jealousy can also precipitate aggression, especially in the case of sexual rivalry, for both males and females. A rather extreme (and terrifying) case I witnessed while I was in Vaiola Hospital in labor with my second child involved two women, one of whom had just given birth and was resting in the room opposite mine. The other woman, who claimed to be pregnant by the father of the newborn baby, attempted to force her way into the room, shouting that she wanted to kill the baby. She turned over trolleys of equipment in the corridor between our rooms, screaming with jealous rage, before being restrained and removed to the next-door psychiatric ward.

Much of the physically rough behavior between persons in Tonga is treated as "fun," although this fun can be violent at times. Bernstein referred to clowning behavior, discussed in the following chapter, as "happy violence" (1983, 156), and this is an apt description of people's behavior in many other contexts. Greetings between people tend to be either formal and polite or loud and physical with much slapping, playful punching, pushing, and joking. Even clearly aggressive and hostile behavior, as in the incident above, is often perceived, at some point and by at least some of the participants and onlookers, as amusing. In the following chapter this association between humor and happiness and violence and aggression is further explored. The importance, in most social contexts, of restraining emotion—particularly anger—is discussed, and some implications of the socialization of emotion for sociality and the construction of subjectivity are considered.

CHAPTER 8

THE SOCIALIZATION OF EMOTION

The effect of culture on the subjective experience and expression of emotion is acknowledged even by those who maintain that certain emotions (or certain aspects of emotions) are universal.[1] For example, differential emotions theorists, such as Izard, have claimed certain emotions to be innate and universal, yet accept that associated cognitive processes are influenced by factors such as age, experience, context, and culture (Izard 1972, 1977, 1982, 1983; Izard and Buechler 1980).[2] The analysis in this chapter is informed by multidisciplinary research into the social bases of emotion.[3] The strongest statements of this perspective can be found in the work of social constructionists (mainly cognitive theorists) who, while not denying that humans have an innate capacity for emotion, focus on the social constitution and rationality of emotions (e.g., Gergen and Davis 1985; Harre 1986; Rorty 1980). This position is expressed in the philosopher Solomon's definition: "An emotion is a system of concepts, beliefs, attitudes, and desires, virtually all of which are context-bound, historically developed, and culture-specific" (1984, 249). Following social constructionist theory, ethnopsychologists have argued that it is possible to study "the negotiation of emotion as culturally defined elements in social life, leaving to the side questions of their biological basis or the pan human reality of affect" (Kirkpatrick and White 1985, 17; and see Lutz 1988).

Research into the socialization of emotion by developmental psychologists has revealed the incredible complexity of this process.[4] This work varies in the extent to which "culture" is granted a leading role, but increasing recognition is being given to the culture-specific nature of both the content and interpretation of emotional experience. Averill has argued that "emotional concepts . . . help to explain behavior by relating it to systems of judgement (e.g., of a moral or aesthetic nature) and to patterns of social relationships. . . . [A]s a child learns to use emotional concepts correctly, he also learns a great deal about the meaning of emotional roles" (1980b, 321). This culture-specific learning begins at birth and continues throughout life. Social competence is closely linked with the development of emotional competence, as has become clear in the discussion thus far of forms of learning in Tonga—observation, moral instruction, punishment, play, and so on. The central features of Tongan systems of judgment and patterns of social relationships have also been discussed, including cultural values, and the roles and relations involved in the interrelated criteria of social differentiation—status, gender, and kinship. Many of these strands will be drawn together in this chapter, in which I show that the central messages children receive about emotion concern its control, particularly the control of the most negatively valued emotion, anger. The restraint of emotion is a valued aspect of personhood, so that the management and control of emotion as discussed in this chapter are crucial to the process of becoming *poto*. Following my account of emotional control I examine the broader issue of self-control, within a discussion of the nature of self-other relationships.

MONITORING EMOTION

The interpersonal nature of emotion is stressed in many Pacific cultures: relationships between persons are culturally emphasized over individuals' inner states. Lutz argues that the Ifaluk assume "people are oriented primarily toward each other rather than toward an inner world of individually constituted goals and thoughts" (1988, 81; see Gerber 1975, 12 for Samoa). According to Lutz, "The Ifaluk emphasize that feelings come from social relations, that their emotional lives *are* their social lives" (1988, 101; emphasis in original). In Tonga, too, a person's emotional life is seen as inextricably bound up with others. There is a cultural emphasis on learning emotional restraint and learning to read contexts in order to act appropriately with others. However, Tongans also value autonomy and recognize the importance of subjectivity. Emotion and thought emerge from one's *loto* (heart and mind) and may be as much a result of one's *'ulungāanga* as of one's social relations.

The term *ongo'i*, introduced previously, is a transitive verb meaning "to feel," physically and emotionally. The noun *ongo* can be translated as "feeling" or "emotion," though the former is more appropriate because *ongo* implies both corporeal and psychological experience. To explicitly denote emotion, as internal experience, the term *ongo'i loto* (inward feeling) is sometimes used. The primary meaning of *ongo* is actually "sound" or, as a verb, "to sound" or "to be heard" (*ongo'i* can also mean "to hear"). This association between hearing and feeling is probably related to the stress placed on listening as a means of acquiring knowledge and understanding.

Individuals' subjective states can often be at variance with cultural concepts or models of appropriate emotion, as both Gerber (1985, 159) and Myers (1986, 106) have observed. In Tonga, where the expression of negatively valued emotion is highly restrained, interpreting individuals' subjective states is particularly difficult. Tongans interpret others' emotions by reading various subtle cues as well as by imputing affective states according to cultural expectations. Tongan discourse reveals an intense concern with monitoring others' emotions. Assessment of people's present emotional states and the sincerity of their emotional expression and speculation about their future emotional states are all facets of this discourse. This concern begins when babies are born, as people interpret infants' closely observed facial expressions as emotional.

Statements are frequently made about the emotional state of a person, with the statements usually directed to others: "Look at Sione, he's smiling, he's happy." The person to whom the emotion is imputed may or may not be within earshot. People also draw attention to others' *mata* (face, eyes), and *mata* is used in compounds in which facial expression and appearance index emotional states or personal characteristics—for example, *matalili* ("boiling face," i.e., boiling with anger) and *mata kākā* (cunning-eyed, suggesting deceitfulness) (Churchward 1959, 336–343). When speaking affectionately, people may direct their *'ofa* to another's *mata*, though this occurs more in formal circumstances of speech making and letter writing than in ordinary interactions. The first-birthday message recorded in chapter 3 includes the phrase "our great love to your dear little face *(mata)*." In some contexts *mata* can even mean "feeling" (Churchward 1959, 336). There is also much speculation about the future emotional states of other persons. So when 'Ana in 'Eua was sending some mulberry branches with me to give to Moana (her half-sister) in Holonga, she repeatedly commented excitedly about how happy Moana would be.

These forms of monitoring others' emotions tend to be employed mainly by adults in relation to other adults or children to other children. People of all ages also pay a great deal of attention to the emotional states of babies and toddlers, with this attention waning once the child is about two years old. There are very few contexts in which comments about present or future emotions are made by adults and older children about each other. These contexts include shared leisure time, when comments about emotional states may be made as a form of teasing or banter, and situations when adults are commenting negatively to children about emotional expression (such as crying after punishment) and teaching the importance of emotional restraint.

Affect labeling is seldom based on admissions of feeling states by the person concerned, and people are rarely directly questioned about their emotions. However, as a visitor I was repeatedly asked about my emotional state, most commonly to reassure people that I was *lata* (content). This was presumably because my cues were obscure and my cultural difference precluded assumptions based on cultural norms. My relative frankness about my

feelings, in response to such queries, was a source of considerable amusement. I was also asked again and again to compare my emotional state in different settings: was I more *lata* in Tonga or Australia, Tongatapu or 'Eua,
Holonga or Nuku'alofa? My hosts emphasized the importance of generous
services (demonstrations of *'ofa*) such as doing my washing or cooking
special foods as their way of ensuring that I was content.

Children do question one another about their emotions and often appear
to be testing their own judgment of facial expressions and other nonverbal
cues. Of great concern to children is the sincerity of emotional expression.
They frequently accuse one another of false emotional displays, claiming, for
example, that others are *tangi loi* (pretending to cry) or *kata loi* (laughing
falsely). Children and others assert their sincerity by saying "*Mo'oni!*" meaning both "true" and "correct." It is also common for people of all ages to
affirm and support other people's statements, as in "*Mo'oni 'a Tupou!*"
(Tupou is honest or right), suggesting that sincerity is a matter of general
concern.

Tongan discourse about emotion stresses the importance of restraint
(*fakama'uma'u*), particularly of negatively valued emotions such as anger
and jealousy. Informal social controls like ridicule and gossip are activated
when a person shows a lack of emotional control. "To be easily upset is to be
marked as a fool or a 'bad' person" (Bernstein 1983, 56). Another term for
restraint is *kukuta*, "to keep a firm grip on oneself (fig.): e.g., when in great
pain (so as not to flinch or cry) . . . or when angry or deeply in love (so as not
to give vent to one's feelings). . . . Of feelings: to be pent up" (Churchward
1959, 274). Emotional restraint is a facet of the restraint that characterizes
ideal personhood, and later in this chapter the issue of self-control will be
addressed at length.

People seldom directly acknowledge their own affective states, and for
intense emotions restraint is ideally exercized even in facial expression and
other nonverbal cues. However, individuals often reveal their emotions
indirectly in speech by using the prefix *faka-*, which denotes causation and
thus enables the speaker to attribute feeling states to others' behavior. Just as
Tongan parents rarely say "I love you," so they do not say "I am angry with
you" or even "You make me angry." Instead, they tell the child he or she is
faka'ita (irritating) *fakahoha'a* (annoying), or *fakahela* (tiring).

Emotion is also expressed indirectly in speech through the use of emotional forms of possessive pronouns.[5] There are emotional articles as well,
which indicate "that the speaker's thought is coloured, as it were, by feelings
of affection, friendship, pity, humility, or respect" (Churchward 1985, 23).
The emotional article *si'i* (indefinite: *si'a*) can also be used as an emotional
adjective in much the same way. *Si'i* can thus be used, according to context,

much as various emotional adjectives are used in English: "the *poor* boy," "the *dear* girl," and so on.

Generally, the direct expression of negatively valued emotion is regarded as *ta'e taau* (unbecoming), *ta'e fe'unga* (inappropriate) and even *fakamā* (shameful). The importance of restraint was noted in some of the earliest European accounts of Tongan society. Mariner observed that jealousy was "seldom strongly expressed" by the wives of unfaithful husbands, adding that "pride generally causes them to conceal this passion" (Martin 1981, 329). Burney, with Cook in 1777, commented that in combat sports "if anything like ill blood appeared between the combatants, the friends of either party interposed and separated them immediately" (Beaglehole 1967, 108n2). Ferdon states that "it was deemed proper etiquette that no fighter exhibit violent emotions by word or expression before, during, or after a fight, even if he or she lost and was badly beaten up" (1987, 185).

Formal kava ceremonies exemplify the importance of restraint, as well as the undercurrent of ambivalence that is its corollary. As Bott states, "The formal, prescribed events of the ceremony emphasize unity and harmony. Rivalry, jealousy and envy are widely and consciously felt, to varying degrees, but their expression is either unofficial or is left to individual initiative" (1972, 226). The subtle expressions of antagonism that can occur in such ceremonies include whispered comments criticizing the conduct of the ceremony, despite the requirement of silence. Children and adolescents annoyed or upset by adults' demands or punishments often mutter deprecatory comments, thus expressing their own ambivalence or outright resentment of the requirements placed upon them.

Although there is considerable concern with monitoring emotion, both by assessing others' emotional states and by controlling one's own emotions, there is less concern with causation. Emotions are said to arise (*tupu hake*) within the *loto*, becoming part of a person's *anga*. Restraint is sometimes described as *fakama'uma'u hifo* (restrain down), and the expression of emotion can be described as *tōtu'a* (fall or drop outside), a term with negative connotations of losing control. Another term used to describe the origin of emotion is *akeloto* (or *akeakeloto*), meaning "to well or spring up within the heart [or inside]" and derived from *ake*, "to swell or rise," referring especially to waves (Churchward 1959, 3). As I have noted, the most common responses to my attempts to ask why particular emotions arose were "*Hei'ilo?*" (who knows) or "*Fakanatula pē*" ([It's] just natural). When pressed for an explanation most people cited a specific social cause—an insult given, a service carried out, and so on.

One explanation I did not hear, but which has been described in other accounts, is interference by spirits (ancestral spirits or supernatural beings, commonly called *tēvolo* today). *'Āvanga,* or spirit-induced illness, ranging from spirit possession to various forms of depression and sickness, has been described by Parsons as an "idiom of distress" (1984; and see Parsons 1983, 1985). Cowling states that *'āvanga* illnesses are "culturally acceptable forms of evincing distress, fears and concerns. . . . [They] can be seen as a plea for attention and the adjustment of whatever life situation is oppressing the victim" (1990a, 87).[6] The life situation that is most commonly a cause for distress is "infractions of the 'moral good' of kin relations, that is, conflict or distress in family relationships," where the sufferer is most commonly "the subordinate (powerless) member of the relationship" (Parsons 1984, 87).[7] Other incidents of *'āvanga* illness are attributed more directly to the actions of the sufferer, particularly disrespect to the dead.

The explanations of emotion causation that I have described all imply that individuals have no control over the actual arising of emotions. Indeed, people will comment that an emotion "just comes in my *loto.*" This does not mean that emotions cannot be managed—through restraint, for example. In the discourse about emotion particular stress is placed on restraining *'ita* (best glossed as "anger").

THE MANAGEMENT OF ANGER

As well as the conceptual metaphor of inner growth and heightening, the metaphor of heat is used to describe emotions. *Māfana* (warm) is used to describe the experience of positively valued feelings such as love, joy, enthusiasm, and exhilaration. Metaphors of heat are also used for *'ita.* There is an extensive lexicon of anger in Tonga, and several terms derive from this metaphor of heat. *Lili* (to boil) is used in compounds such as *matalili* ("boiling face") and *loto lili* ("boiling inside"). Anger is also described as red hot (*kakaha*), flaring up momentarily (*tafue*), or sparking (*mofisi*). Other anger words are also metaphoric, such as *'ita fakamolokau*—angry like a centipede (i.e., restraining anger for a long time then suddenly expressing it). In Tongan emotion discourse, anger is "hypercognated," and as in Tahiti, there is "a developed and shared doctrine of the forms of anger, its effects, and what to do about it" (Levy 1969b, 370).

Anger is seen as the emotion most important to suppress and yet as the most closely associated with the *loto,* the person's individuality and subjectivity. In negatively evaluating anger, people emphasize its behavioral manifestations, just as positive evaluations of *'ofa* stress actions such as sharing, helping, and giving. In Tonga, as in Samoa, "socially virtuous emotions frequently mark the absence of anger" (Gerber 1975, 307). In both cultures, "the domain of emotions seems to emphasize submissiveness and the manipulation of anger" (280).

The violence and uncontrolled behavior that are conceptually associated with anger are feared as dangerous and shameful. The chiefly term for anger is *tuputāmaki* (literally, growing danger). In her study of informal social control in Tonga, Bernstein claimed that

> violence as an informal means of controlling behavior is frightening and of course dangerous. Even openly expressed anger is feared. Subtler forms of social control such as humor and gossip are more acceptable ways to manipulate. Much of the violence and anger in Tonga is channeled through these less disruptive forms. (1983:4)

This view of violence does not fully accord with the early accounts of Tonga discussed in the previous chapter, but it does partially describe the situation in contemporary Tonga. As I have shown, and as Bernstein admits, there are still certain contexts in which violence *is* socially acceptable, notably in the discipline of children, the control of wives, and the treatment of animals. Violence that is (ideally) intended to teach, control, or demonstrate *'ofa* is appropriate, whereas violence motivated by anger is inappropriate and feared. Alisi explained:

> There are people who are often angry in a bullying way (*'ita fakavalevale*), and they often hit. Especially boys, they have problems—they go and drink and that kind of thing . . . and there is a class (*kalasi*), when they are angry they are able to apologize. It is not the same with all people, there are some people with that *anga*. It is the right thing, to think it is best to keep one's feelings in. . . . If someone is angry and it comes out it is harmful; lots of killing when their anger comes out.

The term Alisi used, *'ita fakavalevale*, expresses the association between aggression and foolishness. The opposite of *fakapotopoto* (sensible, wise), *fakavalevale* means "frequently behaving in a bullying manner." It can also mean "babyish" or "childish," children being regarded as naturally both aggressive and foolish. Bullying behavior therefore is seen as impulsive and unsocialized rather than calculating and learned. As I have shown, people who are *vale*, especially children and mentally disabled persons, receive violence but are also characterized as behaving aggressively. Part of the process of becoming *poto* is learning to restrict aggressive behavior to certain limited contexts.

The Western model of emotion has been described as hydraulic, with "emotions as forces and pressures" within the person that can be contained, channeled, dispersed, redirected, and so on (Solomon 1977, 221; see also Lakoff and Kövecses 1987; Kövecses 1990). Tongans share this model to some extent, as seen in the notions of restraint and of emotions "falling out." Anger is described as being redirected, as in slamming doors and breaking or throwing objects, and people will talk of "long-term grudges" that cause anger to "explode." Often, anger thus described is anger that the person has been forced to restrain because of status considerations, such as a child restraining anger toward an adult. However, the ideal model of anger (and other negatively valued emotions) is of restraint leading to dissipation, without any need for expression. Anger that is restrained (*fakama'uma'u*) or held in (*kukuta*) will eventually finish (*'osi*) and leave the person's *loto* peaceful once more. The two models are often contrasted, as in this statement by Moana, Seini's mother:

> When I'm angry I talk and scold, but there is a class who when they are angry can keep their feelings in until they are finished. But me, when I'm angry I talk, scold until my anger is finished. And when my anger is finished there is nothing staying in my *loto*. I will just stay and get angry, and scold until it is all finished. There is a class who when they are angry just stay silent.

Fakalongolongo (staying silent) is the ideal means of dealing with anger. In talking about her own way of managing anger Alisi said,

> When I'm angry I don't like to talk to anyone. I just like to be silent. But if someone comes and talks to me, then I'll be angry with them but I won't speak. They will know that I'm angry because I'm silent. I think it's better for me to be silent, because my anger finishes quickly. If I speak, I will just speak badly, swear, behave inappropriately. It's all right if I'm silent until my anger is finished.

Remaining silent is also, as I have shown, the appropriate way to demonstrate respect in some circumstances. The primary importance of behavior rather than subjective state thus allows for a certain inner autonomy, in which silence may genuinely express respect and obedience or may conceal hostility.

The appropriate response to another's anger is also silence. Siale's mother, Tonga, who had several grandchildren in her sole care, commented,

> When I'm angry I shout. Just shout at [the children] and they know I'm angry, and they are silent so I'll quickly get into a better mood. I tell them

not to talk to me or answer back when I'm angry about something. If they are quickly silent, I will tell them, "Just wait a bit, be patient, because as I get old I get more irritable."

Silence can be an effective strategy for signaling pain, illness, and other needs. By indicating that a person is *loto mamahi*, silence can provoke sympathy in others. Bernstein notes that "while anger is not an acceptable emotion in Tonga, being 'upset' or saddened, when not wholly out of control, is not merely acceptable but elicits pity" (1983, 97). As mentioned previously, both *loto* and *mamahi* have connotations of anger. Sadness and anger are closely linked in Tongan ethnopsychology, and sadness, turned in on oneself, is more culturally appropriate than anger, turned outward.[8] In disputes between parents and adult children in Tonga, "sadness" is often a means of avoiding hostility and maintaining equable relations. When Seini and Siale were being pressured into moving to Australia by Seini's mother, they always spoke of being saddened by the prospect of having to comply, and although they were both clearly agitated about the issue they did not express this— and perhaps did not experience it—as anger.

Many factors, then, encourage Tongan children to restrain their negatively valued emotions in interactions with persons of higher status. The expectation that family members demonstrate *'ofa* for one another; the association of obedience, duty, and respect with *'ofa*; the relationship among teaching, *'ofa*, and punishment; the importance of restraint as a demonstration of respect and, more generally, for proper presentation of self—all of these factors encourage the acceptance of behavioral restrictions and demands for conformity. Such acceptance may in different contexts be willing or reluctant, depending on the extent to which the expectation of conformity is congruent with the individual's *loto*. Restraint is further encouraged by factors such as fear of retaliatory violence and of bringing shame to self and family, as well as by the value placed on peaceful social relations.

Similar factors operate to encourage restraint and nonaggression in adults' interactions. Bernstein has commented that village peace is "often maintained through the suppression of anger" (1983, 51). Although there is an undercurrent of rivalry, jealousy, and tension beneath the peaceful appearance of village life, it seldom rises to the surface in the form of violence or directly expressed emotion. Rather, there is a continual flow of gossip, ridicule, and other forms of informal social control, as Bernstein shows. The ideal of restraint as a means of dissipating anger and the high value placed on reconciliation (discussed below) are especially important factors contributing to the maintenance of harmonious social relations.

Physical appearance is an important index to emotions, although as with silence the subjective state of a person may remain ambiguous. Anger may be so successfully restrained that no trace of it is revealed in the facial expression—but a blank expression can itself indicate restrained emotion. Children become aware of this ambiguity at an early age, partly through the form of threatening described in the previous chapter, in which caregivers warn children that another person, such as a stranger on a bus, might hit them. Barlow, writing of a similar practice amongt the Murik of Papua New Guinea, points out that as the other person usually shows no sign of anger, "this raises the possibility that someone may be angry and not show it" (1985, 215).

At times, anger and sadness are unambiguously expressed through physical cues and speech. Marcus has described how fathers, angry about their daughters' elopements, may show "deeply hurt feelings expressed in a self-consciously sullen and unkempt appearance in public." A father may also "make an elaborate public display of anger, expressed in his intent to disown his daughter" (1979, 86). Common angry gestures in Tonga include jutting the chin forward while sharply tipping the head back or lowering the chin while frowning and pouting. The latter is often accompanied by vigorous scratching of the side or back of the head. It is closely linked with frustration and is most often employed by children when refused something or by adults toward children when feeling angry but refraining from striking them. Actions performed silently also betray suppressed emotion, as I learned one day in 1980. When Sione, who was then my husband, arrived home with a string of fish he had bought, his younger sister approached him and upbraided him for not providing more food for the family. Sione called the family dog over and, without a word, slowly fed it the fish, one by one, as his sister looked on, also in silence. When he had finished, Sione went to our room and went to sleep.

When teenagers described what they would do if they were angry with their parents, their responses included a number of facial expressions, such as looking ugly, going red, scowling (fakafulofula), and pouting (fakapupula), which I have classed together as "look angry" in table 7. The questions asked were "If you were angry with your parents would you show them? If yes, how? If not, what would you do about your anger?" In answer to the first question, of 225 respondents 110 said yes and 115 said no. In table 7 their answers to the second and third questions are combined, to show how the students claimed they would deal with their anger (some gave multiple answers).

The range of responses the students gave indicates that although many consider restraint and reconciliation important, many also claim to express their anger freely. In part this reflects the fact that restraint is learned only

Table 7: Dealing with Anger toward Parents

	FEMALE (TOTAL RESPONDENTS = 137)	MALE (TOTAL RESPONDENTS = 88)	TOTAL (TOTAL RESPONDENTS = 225)	%
Speech				
Tell parents	53	32	85	37.8
Ask forgiveness	31	13	44	19.5
Be silent	21	3	24	10.6
Speak rudely	9	1	10	4.4
Tell relative or friend	3	1	4	1.8
Facial expression				
Look angry	16	9	25	11.1
Look sad or cry	19	5	24	10.6
Behavior				
Not work or work badly	20	10	30	13.3
Hit someone	7	2	9	4.0
Stay with kin	7	2	9	4.0
Hide in room	7	1	8	3.5
Stamp or throw tantrum	6	1	7	3.1
Slam door or break or throw something	4	3	7	3.1
Run away	3	3	6	2.6
Not eat	5	1	6	2.6
Behave badly	5	0	5	2.2
Other[a]	6	2	8	3.5
Feelings				
Remorse	8	7	15	6.6
Forget it	4	6	10	4.4
Smile or be happy	7	3	10	4.4
Be grumpy	4	4	8	3.5
Restrain it	2	3	5	2.2
Loto mamahi	3	1	4	1.8
Other[b]	5	0	5	2.2

[a] Not go to church; turn away from advice; steal money; "want to kill myself"; go and play

[b] tau'atāina (free); fielahi (proud); fie 'eiki (arrogant), loto lahi (tough)

gradually throughout childhood and adolescence. Another factor is the claim many teenagers make to be *fa'iteliha* and *tau'atāina*. Observed behavior suggests that they are much less likely to openly display anger toward their parents or other adults than their responses indicate. Indeed, many who said they would tell their parents that they were angry added comments that showed they would actually express their feelings in terms of repentance. Such comments included "I show them because I want [them] to tell me the right thing to do" and "Tell them what I am angry about and they will tell me the right thing to do." Others stated that they would wait until family prayers or a family meeting before speaking of their anger, or until they were *loto lelei* (i.e., until they were no longer angry).

Some respondents gave multiple answers. Those who indicated that they would not show their parents their anger gave a variety of reasons, including that it is wrong to be angry with one's parents, that they feared punishment, and that parents are always right. Interestingly, they also described both direct and indirect ways in which they would reveal their feelings, as the table shows.

One of the responses, "I would want to kill myself," became especially meaningful for me when a boy I knew (not one of the respondents) committed suicide. The twelve-year-old boy, who had run away from his mother following a disagreement, was found hanging by a shoelace from a beam in a deserted house. The story that circulated in his village was that the boy and his brother had both wanted a pair of shorts sent in a parcel from overseas, but their mother gave them to the brother. The boy became angry and refused to do an errand for his mother, so she began to beat him and he ran away. The simple motive offered for his suicide was, therefore, "He was angry." More complex factors of circumstance and motive were not discussed (at least not in my presence), and in fact people avoided discussing the incident, claiming it would just cause sadness and "bring shame to the family." Instead, conversations centered on the funeral, fond memories of the boy, and how well his mother had cared for him.

This boy's suicide was the fifth for 1988 (*Tonga Chronicle* 1989, 2). Out of twenty-six suicides between 1978 and October 1990, nineteen of the victims were aged between eleven and twenty-four, and seventeen were male; hanging was the most common method, and 90 percent of the suicides occurred on Tongatapu (Ranger 1990, 10). The incidence of suicide in Tonga is low in comparison to some other Pacific societies, such as Western Samoa and parts of Micronesia, but it appears to be increasing. The popular explanation for these suicides in Tonga is that video movies give children the idea of hanging and that when they are angry they imitate what they have seen, with no understanding of the finality of death. In contrast to this explanation,

Tonga's 1986 police report, discussing three successful and seven attempted suicides in that year, suggested that "family disorganisation is the background to all these cases committed by young people who appealed for the love and affection which they are justified in expecting but which they say they lack" (Report of the Minister of Police for 1986, 82). The 1987 report suggested that "personal factors were important motivating forces. The appeal for love, the cry for help, the act of vengeance and abandonment stemmed from emotional pressure over which the social structure, urbanization, religion or economic conditions were contributory factors (*Report of the Minister of Police for 1987*, 81).[9]

In a review of the literature on suicides in Pacific nations, Hezel suggests that "suicide is linked with the transition to modernization, with the highest rates in the middle rather than at the low or high ends of the scale." Hezel's survey supports the explanation offered in Tonga's police reports, particularly with regard to family disorganization. He argues that "suicide is an indication of the importance that the family continues to have in the lives of contemporary young people" (1989, 54), referring to the confusion and distress associated with the significant transformations in family organization and function in the context of modernization.[10]

Tonga is undergoing such transformation, and the explanations given by Hezel and in the police reports are valid; however, it does not seem surprising that the popular explanation for suicides in Tonga is anger, as any event is typically attributed to its immediate precursors. Also, the association between anger and restraint and between anger and violence means that self-violence is interpreted as an act of redirected anger. Yet a recognition of more complex factors may also be implicit in this explanation because anger is conceptually linked with sadness and mental suffering (as in the term *mamahi*).

RECONCILIATION

Nearly 20 percent of the respondents to the questions tabulated in table 7 directly indicated that they would seek reconciliation if they felt angry with their parents. Another question asked the students to describe how they felt after being punished, and 36.8 percent of the 231 respondents stated that they felt guilty (*halaia*) and repentent (*fakatomala*) after punishment. Though it is true that grudges may linger for years in some cases, reconciliation is ideally sought in order to dissipate anger and hurt. One girl explained: "When I've asked for forgiveness, my hurt feelings leave (*mahu'i atu loto mamahi*) and then I'm happy." Parents also seek reconciliation at times. Malia described this as follows (in English):

Sometimes when you are mad with them [children] in the daytime, and after
giving them a bath and then going to sleep, and then you kiss them and say
"I'm sorry." That's the time you show, even though you were angry but . . . Do
this until they go to school. Then they know their parents love them.

Marcus (1977, 1979) has shown that public conflict resolution in Tonga
centers on restraint and the formal reconciliation process. "Unless intoxi-
cated, kinsmen in dispute usually avoid each other indefinitely or else consult some relative to mediate a resolution of the dispute, usually through one
party asking the forgiveness of the other (called *fakamolemole*, literally 'to
make smooth')" (1977, 288n14). He has also shown that after an elopement,
the "elaborate expressions of anger or hurt" displayed by the girl's father
(mentioned previously) may in fact indicate "that a reconciliation is possible, if not expected, by the girl's family" (1979, 86).

Reconcilation is also used as a "therapeutic strategy" when family discord
is believed to have caused a member's illness. In such cases reconciliation
involves confession, discussion, and forgiveness to restore family relationships. Parsons notes that reconciliation "is frequently a time when those of
superior rank are obliged to ask forgiveness of a person of inferior rank,"
especially in cases of *'āvanga* illness where spirits are said to be punishing the
higher-status person for neglecting his or her responsibilities (1984, 82, 83).

Presentations of food and kava, and the kava ceremony itself, are the
most common means of formal reconciliation and are usually accompanied
by emotive speech making. Adults will sometimes go to great lengths to
avoid dealing directly with conflict. The Beagleholes stated that some villagers even changed their religious denomination in response to interpersonal
conflicts with others in their former congregation (1941b, 129). Among relatives, grudges and disputes sometimes result in one or more family members
declaring themselves, or being declared, *motu*—broken away from the family—until a reconciliation can be effected. An example of *motu* that was
described to me was a father's sister who cut herself off from her *fakafotu*
because she was angry with their mother for not giving her *koloa*.

Table 8 looks at how anger is expressed between friends. It shows that less
emphasis is placed on reconciliation and more on direct expressions of anger
in interactions between peers than between parents and children. The question asked of the teenagers was "What happens if you disagree with your
friends?"

Not only were there fewer respondents who indicated that they would
apologize; the most frequent response was that the friendship would permanently or temporarily cease. Terms such as *mavae* (separate), *li'aki* (leave, dis-
card), *movete* (come apart), and *motu* (break away) were used (see "separate"

Table 8: Disagreeing with Friends

	FEMALE (TOTAL RESPONDENTS = 114)	MALE (TOTAL RESPONDENTS = 64)	TOTAL (TOTAL RESPONDENTS = 178)	%
Separate	35	13	48	26.9
Argue	18	11	29	16.3
Ignore them	25	4	29	16.3
Fight or hit	10	13	23	12.9
Be angry	12	9	21	11.8
Not be with them	14	3	17	9.5
Solve problem	9	7	16	8.9
On bad terms	7	5	12	6.7
Sad feelings	6	4	10	5.6
Loto mamahi	9	0	9	5.0
Apologize	3	4	7	3.9
Hate them	4	0	4	2.2
Feel confused	3	0	3	1.7

in the table). Others stated that they would not help their friends, or share, work, or stay with them (see "not be with them"). Both terms used for "be on bad terms," *vākovi* and *vātamaki*, imply a serious rift. While reconciliation does usually occur when friends disagree, it is not emphasized by these respondents. Their answers are concerned with the immediate response to such a disagreement, which is a disruption of the relationship and the direct expression of their anger or other negative feelings.

Anger can be directly expressed in vocal tone and in the content of speech—emphatic terms and abusive, derogatory, or accusative language. This "language of anger" ('Okusitino Māhina, personal communication) or "language of abuse" (Churchward 1959, 2) is often referred to as *lea kovi* (bad speech) and may be peppered with *kape* (swearing). *Kape* (or *kapekape*) is a lexicon of impolite, disrespectful terms, often metaphoric, for body parts, sexual behavior, and excretion (see Feldman 1981). It is used not only in anger, but also in humorous speech. Other terms of abuse, used in anger, are substituted for ordinary verbs (e.g., *puna*, run, for *lele*) and for commands (e.g., *topuna*, go away, instead of *'alu*).[11]

ANGER AND HUMOR

One means of dealing with anger that did not appear in students' responses is humor. Humor is not usually explicitly associated with anger in Tongan discourse, except in the case of teasing. Rather than assuming humor to be a "channel" for redirecting anger, according to the hydraulic model, it seems more appropriate in the Tongan context to regard humor as an alternative to directly expressing anger or as a means of diluting the effects of anger already expressed (but cf. Feinberg 1990, 59). Humor can also be seen as a form of "re-cognition" (Heelas 1986, 259), which transforms individuals' understanding of emotional experiences so that their affective response to a situation that could have caused anger is actually amusement.[12] As will be shown, both anger and fear are commonly transformed through humor.

The forms of angry speech that have been described are often immediately followed by joking and laughter. Sometimes this occurs when the angry speech is intentionally humorous, as when someone jokingly berates another person for laziness. This humorous angry speech is used frequently, so that when I was first in Tonga I often thought people were angry, because they *sounded* so angry, and I was always puzzled that such angry speech was accompanied by so much laughter. Even genuinely angry speech is often followed by laughter, sometimes after the speaker appears momentarily embarrassed. In this case, someone listening will laughingly call out *"Mālie!"* or will whoop, and the tension of the incident dissipates. During long delays at the city bus terminal, with passengers in overcrowded buses waiting in the humid heat, occasionally a particularly irritated passenger will angrily tell the driver to get going, at which the other passengers roar with laughter. Potential conflict between individuals or groups is often averted by this use of humor, in which insults and verbal aggression are combined with, or take the form of, joking and banter.[13]

Presenting the buttocks (clothed or, on rare occasions, naked) is a form of insult that is associated with anger, hostility, or rivalry, but it is performed humorously. The gesture is used by women on occasions involving rivalry between sports or other groups, as a humorous show of derision. When baby 'Ofa, at twelve months, pulled her pants down and walked away when her teenage cousin scolded her, her actions were interpreted as an intentional insult motivated by anger.

Humor, when used as an alternative to an expression of anger, often involves a certain amount of mock aggression, in the form of threatening gestures or playful slaps, pushes, or punches. One incident involving this mock aggression occurred when a crowd of people were shoving one another in their haste to board a bus. A young woman jokingly scolded a boy who was pushing in front of her, claiming that she was pregnant and should be allowed to board first. During the laughter and humorous comments that ensued, several women and teenage girls roughly pulled the woman's hair, and she responded by laughing loudly and slapping the head of the nearest girl before embarking.

Although adults generally express anger directly to children, particularly in the form of physical punishment, this use of humor is also a feature of some adult-child interactions. The incident described previously, in which a boy was slapped and shoved by men during a card game, typifies the rough play that sometimes occurs during such interactions. Humorous comments to children are often made for the benefit of other adults present. For example, one woman who was cross with her children during a gathering of her extended family told them that if she had known how naughty they would be, she would have squashed their heads between her legs at birth—a comment that greatly amused the other adults present and left the children looking embarrassed.

HUMOR AS SOCIAL CONTROL

Bernstein has examined the operation of informal social controls in Tonga, defining them as controls that "depend for their force on diffuse sanctions, rather than a stated system of laws. The diffuse sanctions depend in turn on cultural assumptions of what is morally right and proper behavior." She went on to argue that ambiguity is "an important and pervasive element in informal social control. . . . [H]umor and politeness obscure the actor's intent or feelings; gossip and harassment leave the identity of the perpetrator questionable; dropped remarks obscure the identity of their victim" (1983, 2–3).

The kinds of informal social control discussed by Bernstein rely heavily on shaming (fakamā). To be shamed is to appear vale, and Marcus has pointed out that mā is a concept that "expresses sensitivity of individuals to appearing inadequate or incompetent in public" (1978, 247).[14] The association between mā and vale is particularly salient during childhood because children are regarded as inherently vale. Teasing and other forms of shaming directed toward children constantly highlight aspects of their incompetence and inadequacy and discourage them from thinking themselves too clever (fie poto) or too "high" (fie 'eiki).

Children are frequently teased, usually in a humorous manner, although teasing in the form of mockery and ridicule can also be carried out with undisguised anger.[15] One of the most common forms of teasing is to ask a child rhetorically, often with an affectionate tone, "Oku ke vale?" (are you crazy or stupid). This is asked in many contexts, particularly those in which children's incompetence is obvious. Teasing is used to speed toilet training and weaning, to encourage sharing, and generally to remind the child that conformity is expected. Whenever I have stayed in Tongan households I have found that teasing directed toward me acts as both a sign of affection and acceptance and a gentle reminder of my lack of social competence or conformity. My son also experienced this, as when Siale and Seini thought it strange that Paul had a "bedtime," when I would read him stories in bed to get him to sleep, and they teased him that he was going to bed to *fakahuhu* (breast-feed). He quickly saw that other children did not have bedtimes and insisted on staying up late watching videos with the rest of the household.

Young children are teased, if not punished, if they have a tantrum, and children of all ages are teased about their reactions to physical punishment. Boys are often teased abut their imputed smelliness or lack of cleanliness or, when older, about their sexual abilities. A girl who fancies herself pretty may be teased about her "ugliness." Physical characteristics are a common target of teasing, and children frequently ridicule one another's real or imputed deformities and weaknesses, calling each other names such as "Big Ears," "Black Skin," and so on. One boy in our neighborhood was called "Abo" (short for Aborigine) by other children because he had been conceived when his mother visited his father, who was working in Australia. Many of the terms in the language of abuse are also used for teasing, though in many cases there are separate derogatory terms used in teasing. For example, the derogatory term for eyes is *poko'imata*, the abusive term, *fela*. The derogatory lexicon is extensive and includes terms for most body parts, for aspects of personal status (sex, marital status, age, and the like), and for many nouns and verbs closely associated with the self (food, clothes, house, and so on and talk, sleep, cry, and so on).

Children are not discouraged from teasing unless it becomes disruptive; in fact, teasing is one of the main forms of communication between siblings. Adults themselves frequently tease children and one another. Teasing can be affectionate or cruel, and as I have indicated it is sometimes clearly a form of verbal (and sometimes nonverbal) aggression. Much of the teasing young children receive takes the form of play. The messages it conveys are subtle and often well hidden, unlike the more direct teasing that targets specific behavior. I watched one day as a young child was teased nonverbally and received some confusing messages about sharing and punishment and about emotional control. Two teenage girls were playing with Keleva (aged two) as she sat on her grandmother's lap. They took off her shoes and gave them to another baby, then offered her some candies, withdrawing them as she reached for them. One of the girls then took a balloon Keleva was holding, picked up a stick and threatened to hit her, and hit the side of her head lightly. The other girl wrapped a piece of boiled taro in a candy wrapper and gave it to Keleva, who opened it and cried. The grandmother, who had been talking to other women and so had ignored the previous interactions, was distracted by the child's crying. She hit her leg lightly, saying crossly, "*Ta'ahine fa'a tangi!*" (girl who often cries).

It is important for children to learn to withstand teasing, preferably by retaliatory humor. The use of humor to disguise distress, anger, and shame is expressed in terms such as *katakatatangi* (to laugh or smile when one feels like crying). Angry or tearful responses to teasing provoke further ridicule. Humor is sometimes glossed as *fakakata pē* (just to cause laughter), and to be unable to withstand teasing is to be *vale he fakakata* (foolish in response to humor). Provocation *can* be carried too far, and a child who causes another child to cry or behave aggressively, and thus disturb the adults, may be reprimanded or punished.

Teasing is only one aspect of Tongan humor (*hua fakatonga*); joking, banter, practical jokes, and clowning also occur in many contexts.

> Humor is pervasive in the daily life of the village, where teasing and banter pepper conversations. The raconteur and the wit are highly prized individuals whose humor lightens tedious tasks. Tongan humor is mulitfaceted in that it is used to many ends—to entertain, to instruct, to provoke, to punish, and so on—often simultaneously. (Bernstein 1983, 53)

Amusement is an important criterion of enjoyment and pleasure, and the term *ta'e oli* (literally, not amusing) is used to indicate something is unpleasant or boring. Marriage without children is regarded as *ta'e oli*, for example.

After describing in his journal the violence directed toward children, wives, and animals in Tonga, Ernest Beaglehole commented that "many people here [in Tonga] get genuine amusement from observing many of these displays of aggression"; he gives the example of onlookers laughing at a girl being beaten by her brother, unable to defend herself because she was holding a baby (1938–1939, Jan. 13). I have suggested that when people laugh about physical punishment it is primarily the foolish behavior of the person being punished that is regarded as amusing. Bernstein has similarly interpreted the laughter that is provoked by any form of foolish or out-of-control behavior. "Personal catastrophes are believed to be God's retribution and therefore the victim's own fault. It is all the more humorous when the victim loses control of his emotions and reacts with fear, sorrow, or mirth" (1983, 58).

The cathartic value of this kind of humor also warrants consideration. When children laugh because a puppy has been run over by a bus, as happened in our Nuku'alofa household in 1980, it seems inadequate to attribute their laughter simply to the puppy's foolishness. Nor is the lack-of-control thesis sufficient explanation for the laughter that followed the incident described in the previous chapter, in which a jealous woman wanted to kill her rival's newborn baby—laughter on the part of the nurses and even the baby's mother. Cathartic laughter is a common reaction to events that are frightening, startling, or otherwise arouse sudden, intense emotion. Gory or violent scenes on video movies, sudden shocks (e.g., nearly falling downstairs), or frights (e.g., a sudden fear of ghosts while walking at night) are all events that precipitate laughter from the person experiencing the emotion and from those who have observed their reaction.

When used as a form of informal social control, humor is largely concerned with conformity to socially appropriate values, behavior, and aesthetic standards, and as such plays a vital role in socialization. In the humor directed toward children, the humor they overhear in everyday conversations, and the humor they direct toward others, children are learning about and exploring the boundaries of social competence. Underlying the shame of foolishness, ineptness, and other targets of teasing and ridicule there often seems to be a deeper shame associated with improper relationships and behavior. Sela, who was constantly teased because, as her aunt explained, "she's ugly," was also an illegitimate child born in particularly shameful circumstances. As well as being teased she was treated harshly by the other members of her household who, the aunt claimed, "all hate her."

The ridicule and aggression that are sometimes directed toward physically and mentally handicapped persons also may be based on more than the fact that their "physical, emotional, or social self-control is wanting," making them "inherently laughable" (Bernstein 1983, 56). A physiotherapist working in Nukuʻalofa's ʻOfa Tui ʻAmanaki Center (Love, Faith, and Hope Center), a facility for the handicapped, commented that "some parents are ashamed of their crippled children and look forward to them to die" (*Matangi Tonga* 1989b, 36). The director of the center told me that some parents hide their children at home and refuse to allow them to go to the center for life-skills training. Until recently, even children with clubfoot "faced a lifetime of ridicule, and were often kept hidden away until adulthood" (*Tonga Chronicle* 1986b, 4). This deeply felt shame may be partly attributable to the fact that disabilities are believed to be caused by the behavior of the mother, and sometimes her husband or close relations, during the pregnancy.

Cowling claims that "mental illness and mental disability are not stigmatized because they are usually considered to be caused by factors other than a sufferer's ability to cope with life" (1990a, 90). She adds that Tongans are reluctant to "blame the victim" and often turn to supernatural explanations instead.[16] Nevertheless, excepting victims of spirit possession or other short-term illnesses, such people are frequently ostracized, ridiculed, or treated violently. A certain uneasiness associated with the possible causes of mental problems and an underlying fear that such people may behave aggressively or dangerously appear to be factors contributing to such responses. Even if they are not aggressive, people who are mentally ill often do not conform to social norms and so can be shocking, amusing, or annoying, in different contexts. The young, disturbed woman who wandered Nuku'alofa broke many social conventions with her loud, assertive, and often disrespectful speech, public swearing, and occasional petty theft and violence, and as has been shown, she was often treated cruelly as a consequence.

EXPRESSING STRONG EMOTION

Evaluations of emotional expression are context-dependent, and although there is a general pattern of not directly expressing intense emotional states, there are times when such expression is appropriate. Expressing strong emotion is acceptable during the discussion of past events. Perhaps because these events are distanced by time, the emotions associated with them tend to be discussed openly, although often in a humorous, self-deprecatory manner. Children also learn that crying motivated by 'ofa (as sadness or love) is appropriate in the context of parting, bereavement, religious experience, and formal speech making. The following section of this chapter briefly examines three contexts in which the expression of strong emotion is positively valued: clowning or "making happy," religious experience, and bereavement. It is significant that in each of these three main contexts for emotional expression, children are not central participants but constitute part of the audience. As I have shown, the contexts in which children can freely express strong emotion tend to be limited to interactions with other children.

CLOWNING

Humor in Polynesian cultures has been interpreted by Marcus as "parodic discourse." The parodic, Marcus argues,

> allows a "breathing space" for self-expression. The personal is said by indirection, and parodic reference to the sacred and chiefly allows for individual as well as critical variation in style of communicating the conventional. The humorous inflection of much of the Polynesian parodic as performed is to save the dignity of those who speak humbly in the shadow of higher authority or status. (1988, 75n1)

Throughout Polynesia the epitome of such parody is clowning (see also Hereniko 1992, 1994; Huntsman and Hooper 1975).[17]

In Tonga, when groups of people have gathered to work, practice dancing, or otherwise interact, clowning occurs at times of concentrated joint effort, emotional tension, or the end of formalities. Clowning particularly occurs at special celebrations: "during times of great joy, people, especially women, 'make happy' or celebrate (*fakafiefia*): they smash each other's possessions, fling food around, and assault onlookers" (Bernstein 1983, 155). Clowning is usually performed by middle-aged and older women, who are ordinarily very staid and dignified. Their clowning is a form of parody (largely nonverbal) that temporarily inverts social norms by burlesque, role reversal, and rule breaking.

There are indications that clowning occurred in precontact Tongan society; for example, Vason stated that after mourning for the dead, people "generally terminate their grief with this ceremony of joy [dancing], in which I have seen the women so eager, that they have forgotten all encumbrance of dress for greater freedom and diversion" (Orange 1840, 128). Clowning is formalized at the ceremony of investiture for the Tu'i Kanokupolu. A Fijian of the title Tu'i Soso is always present, and he "prances about, breaking every *tapu* of the *kava* ritual" (Bott with Tavi 1982, 125; see Kaeppler 1985, 101).[18] Although his movements are *tapu*-breaking, they are also highly formalized.

During any dance performed by young women, individually or in small groups (e.g., *tau'olunga*), women and men from their families dance behind them enthusiastically and humorously. Although this clowning is intended to draw attention to the grace and accomplishment of the girls' performance, it sometimes becomes the center of attention when it becomes especially amusing. At other times the clowns are themselves the sole performers. At a School Day celebration at a Catholic college in 1988 I watched as several middle-aged women clowned to the audience of school students and their families and to members of the royal family, who were the honored guests. This clowning occurred after the formal speech making, while the families were eating picnic lunches, as well as later in the day, when a number of dances were performed by students. The women's clowning included sexually suggestive dancing and masculine dance movements, chasing each other and jumping on one another's backs, threatening each other and students with sticks and raised fists, shouting orders to the bandmaster, lying on the ground and turning somersaults, and wearing the donations box as a hat.

Throughout the women's clowning the audience encouraged their antics with whoops and calls of "*Mālie!*" The children were an especially rapt audience, laughing with delight at the women's outrageous behavior, which in its exhibitionist and aggressive aspects closely resembled the behavior encouraged in infants and toddlers. The adults also laughed and watched attentively. Alisi, old enough to clown but remaining as spectator, commented that they were dancing "with happiness." However, she added derisively that they were *fakasesele* (silly, crazy). Another elderly audience member attempted to intervene when one of the clowning women pulled a male school-committee member from the honored guests' area onto the dance floor and began a wild hip-thrusting dance that the other clowns joined, one behind the other in a line. The audience laughed uproariously as the elderly woman berated first the clowns and then the commentator announcing the dances, and the commmittee member returned to his seat, also laughing.

Not all older women clown. Some women tend to clown at most events and others rarely or never do so. In Holonga there was one woman, aged forty-five, who invariably clowned and who also danced in the *kailau* (a male dance) when the Holonga dance group performed. Some of the older women, like Alisi and Moana, never clowned in public but occasionally did a very abbreviated version—a gay swing of the hips and a soft whoop—within their own homes on particularly joyful occasions. At public events several younger women, in their thirties, were beginning to clown briefly, albeit rather self-consciously and with much embarrassed giggling.

In his analysis of clowning in Polynesia, Hereniko suggests that clowning

> was an avenue through which society inspected itself and commented on its rules and regulations, and the ways in which the imposition of structure and hierarchy constrained and stifled creativity and individual expression. Through role-reversal and inversion of societal norms, an alternative world-view was explored within the frame of play. The message "this is play" masked the seriousness of important messages that were disguised in laughter but nonetheless experienced and felt. (1994, 1)

The clowning of older Tongan women clearly inverts the norms of female behavior. Their actions also invert status norms, as when the women at the school function shouted orders at the bandmaster and made the school-committee member the target of their clowning. However, the clowning I observed drew the line at directly targeting chiefs or royalty, who are frequently present when clowning occurs. By reverting to childish—that is, exhibitionist and aggressive—behavior, the clowns also invert the norm of progression from *vale* to *poto*. Clowning does not completely override social norms, as there are clearly behavioral limits, and onlookers always intervene if these limits are reached.

Although Tongan clowning does subvert important values, Hereniko's comment about Rotuman clowning is apt: "Paradoxically, the clown's violation of these values reinforces them at the same time" (1992, 175). And although it is difficult to assess the effect on children of their intermittent observations of clowning episodes, I believe that the clearest message they receive is the contextual nature of behavior and emotional expression. The behavior of the women, although completely different from their everyday behavior, is appropriate in context because it is associated with intense positive emotions. Whatever elements of parody are contained in clowning are balanced by its conceptual association with happiness and 'ofa. These emotions are directed toward God, the monarchy, the hou'eiki, or Tonga itself. As well as inspiring older women to clown, these emotions can also invoke demonstrations of obedience and submission whereby people prostrate themselves before members of the royal family, calling on them to walk or dance on their bodies (see Cowling 1990c, 4, 96, 271). In such contexts people's intense emotion also causes them to be spontaneously generous and offer lavish gifts of money or goods to the royal family, the church, or whoever (or whatever) is the focus of the celebration.

Intense emotions are conceptualized by the metaphors of warmth and growth, as we have seen. Some Tongans described the feelings of māfana (warmth) and vela (burning) as, in English, "feverish," "electric," and "on fire." The term tafunaki (to stoke a fire) is used metaphorically to describe events that arouse or inspire love, zeal, and other intense, positively valued emotions. It is the intensity of the emotion that evokes a metaphor of heat: as has been shown, similar metaphors are used for anger, the most negatively valued emotion. Exaggerated "growth" of positive emotion is also said to occur, so that people tau e langi (reach the sky).[19] The two metaphors can be combined, as in the phrase tupu māfana 'i loto (the warmth grows up inside), and such a state is said to be melie (pleasant). In the extremes of this state, people are said to be out of control, or as one man put it, "not myself." There are several Tongan terms for "letting oneself go" or being "carried away" with excitement and fervor, including sekia, tāngia, and to'oa.[20] When referring to children, these terms have a distinctly negative connotation, as children who are overexcited are considered disruptive and annoying.

Less intense versions of the positively valued emotions expressed in clowning are also expressed in everyday interactions, although the emphasis is on happiness rather than 'ofa. Unlike 'ofa and negatively valued emotions such as anger, happiness (fiefia) is openly demonstrated in loud laughter, shouting, and joking. At times the expression of joy and amusement is exaggeratedly demonstrative. Friends meeting one another and groups of people talking and joking tend to be very physical with one another. A person laughing will double up, slap her or his knees, lean back, move about, even stagger about as if drunk, and grab others and slap, punch, or push them. A joke is repeated and laughed at for some time, and when the laughter finally dies down members of the group give exaggerated sighs of exhaustion and exclaim, " 'Oiauē!"

RELIGIOUS EXPERIENCE

In precontact Tonga emotional experiences associated with religion occurred during "inspiration" by the gods, or spirit possession. Mariner stated that people thus inspired "are generally low spirited and thoughtful, as if some heavy misfortune had befallen them. As the symptom increases, they generally shed a profusion of tears; and sometimes swoon away for a few minutes." Because the incidents were believed to be caused by neglect of religious duties, he attributed this "visitation" to "an inward compunction of conscience." Priests and priestesses (taula) were also inspired by gods, at which times they sometimes had a "paroxysm" of emotion, which Mariner believed to be a "voluntary act" of devotion (Martin 1981, 84–85). Spirit possession may still precipitate the same symptoms, but it is no longer primarily a religious experience; instead, as has been shown, it is treated as an illness.

The early Wesleyan missionaries put "a tremendous stress on emotionalism" (Lātūkefu 1974, 69) with their hellfire-and-brimstone sermons. A major factor in the mass conversion of Tongans was the revival experience, often involving entire congregations and spreading rapidly throughout the islands. In Ha'apai and Vava'u in 1834, mass revivals led to prayer meetings being held day and night, with hundreds of participants weeping, shaking, beating their chests, and fainting (Cummins 1977, 111; 1979; Farmer 1976, 242–243; West 1865, 162–163).[21]

Today, religious experiences continue to provide a legitimate context for emotional outpourings for Tongans, and on a great many occasions prayers are accompanied by weeping and, less often, shaking and fainting. In the Wesleyan church in Holonga it was the practice for the entire congregation to pray aloud, each saying his or her own prayer, and these were times of heightened emotionalism. The term used to describe this "highly emotional (and often noisy) religious fervour" (Churchward 1959, 563) is 'ofa, and the revival experience was known as "dying with love" (Cummins 1977, 111). Children are not excluded from these intensely emotional religious experiences, and I have seen children as young as nine or ten praying and weeping. Yet my observations suggest that often children and adolescents "tune out" much of the proceedings in church and join in only for hymn singing. When family groups perform part of the service, with each member giving a reading or leading the singing, the children are more likely to cry with nervousness than with religious fervor.

Religion also provides the context for another, very different form of emotional expression. Many families have regular meetings, usually on Sunday evenings, at which prayers are said, hymns are sung, and a short bible reading or homily is given by the head of the family. Some families conclude with an airing of grievances, thereby providing a rare opportunity for even the youngest family member to discuss feelings such as anger and frustration without fear of punishment, although the freedom with which they speak varies greatly. The head of the household usually gives directions for resolving the problem and may use it as the basis for further *akonaki* (moral instruction).

BEREAVEMENT

Several detailed accounts of Tongan funerals have been written, and my concern here is only with the expression of emotion at death (see Aoyagi 1966; Beaglehole and Beaglehole 1941b; Gifford 1971b; Kaeppler 1978b; Rogers 1977). For all that has been written about Tongan funerals, surprisingly little attention has been paid to the emotional experiences of the bereaved. Rosaldo has pointed out the problems that can arise from viewing death only from the perspective of ritual. Doing so, he argues, "masks the emotional face of bereavement" or leads to sentiments expressed at the funeral being interpreted as only ritual and obligatory (1984, 186–187).

In precontact Tonga, relatives of the deceased, particularly if he or she was chiefly, expressed their grief primarily through self-directed violence. Mourners burned themselves (*tutu, lafa*); beat or burned their cheeks (*tuki, fepuhi*);[22] beat their heads (*foa ulu*); and cut their cheeks, thighs, and chests with shells, spears, and other objects (Beaglehole 1967, 946; Martin 1981, 349; Orange 1840, 108; West 1865, 268). At times this violent grief could be fatal, as when prostrate mourners had spears thrust into their bodies (*faletau*) (Cummins 1977, 23).[23] Vason claimed that after the death of Tu'i Kanokupolu Mumui, thousands engaged in self-wounding night after night (Orange 1840, 108–109). Such practices were interpreted by Mariner as demonstrations of respect and loyalty, and he described the ragged mats worn at funerals as "emblematical of a spirit broken down, or, as it were, torn to pieces by grief" (Martin 1981, 218). In most accounts the mourners are said to inflict their injuries themselves, but Collocott claimed that hair cutting and burning and cutting the skin were done by others to low-status relatives of the deceased, who were also dunked in the sea (1928, 76).

Today these practices are usually limited to cutting the hair, done by those lower in status than the deceased, and breast beating during the *tangi* (lament). The *tangi*, which Kaeppler (1993, 476) shows is "characterized by texted weeping (crying with words)," begins at the time of death and continues until the body is taken away for burial, and is performed by the women who stay with the corpse. The changes in grieving behavior were largely missionary influenced and were established as early as 1885 (Cummins 1977,

239; Rowe 1976, 69). Tongans today also wear black mourning clothes for periods that vary according to the closeness of their kin ties with the deceased. Accounts of emotional expression at Tongan funerals have tended to have a cynical tone, as in the claim by Spillius that "people can joke about death right after performing the ceremonialised wailing at a funeral. No-one expects you to pretend to a grief that you did not feel, but if you are a good wailer and you stand in the right relationship, you should do your bit" (1958, 62).

Many Tongans, when I asked them to define the term *mamahi*, gave the example of a funeral, describing it as *fakamamahi* (causing pain or sadness). Levy's interpretation of the Tahitians' tendency to have short-lived emotional outbursts at events such as death or the departure of a relative accords well with my own impressions of Tongan expressions of grief and sorrow. Levy argues that "willful dramatization is a way of controlling emotions as well as expressing them"; events such as death "tapped some deep well of loneliness and sadness in people," which was quickly sealed off again by internal and external pressures for restraint (1973, 273, 303). I would extend this argument to include outbursts of joy and religious fervor, as described above. Intense, positively valued emotions, especially joy and sorrow, can legitimately be expressed in certain contexts such as clowning or bereavement, but even these valued emotions are inappropriate (*ta'e fe'unga*) outside such contexts. The emotions may arise in any context but should ideally be restrained in most situations. Mourners who weep and wail while in the presence of a corpse and laugh and joke outside the house cannot be assumed to be grieving only ceremoniously. Each and every one of them would claim to be *mamahi*, and as their subjective states cannot be known, this claim cannot be disputed. Indeed, Spillius' implication could be reversed, given the argument made earlier in this chapter about the role of humor in contexts of intense emotion. The laughter and joking of mourners could be interpreted as the means by which *mamahi* is kept under control, or even dissipated.

As I mentioned previously, on New Year's Eve 1988 a boy from a nearby house hanged himself, and waves of shock and grief flooded our Holongan household. We first heard about it when our next-door neighbor ran into the yard screaming the news. Members of our household, including the children, who had daily played with this boy, immediately ran to the house in which his body lay. I found myself left to mind baby 'Ofa, wondering what was happening. When the others returned the adults were distressed and quiet, but the children were excitedly chattering, telling me the details of how he had been found, what his face looked like in death, how it was originally thought he must have been electrocuted, and how his mother was in deep shock, rocking on her bed and calling out to him as if he were still alive. After the initial shock eased, the adults began to discuss the matter, and as stated earlier they quickly agreed that his actions had been motivated by anger. Their talk then moved on to planning the funeral and to positive recollections of the boy and his mother's love for him; the death itself was no longer discussed. At the funeral adults and children alike expressed their grief through weeping, but in everyday contexts no grief was expressed, and it was difficult to assess individuals' subjective experience of the event. The children appeared to view the death very matter-of-factly and seemed to have readily incorporated it into their understanding of the nature of existence. When I spoke with them about the death they either followed the adults' lead in focusing on positive recollections or repeated their descriptions of the boy's body.

SELF AND OTHER

There is no "Tongan self" that can be described, any more than there is a "Tongan personality." Here I am concerned with the ideals, the common practices, and the widely shared beliefs that influence—rather than determine—the construction of self and the management of self-other relations.

As we have seen, the very earliest period of a child's life in Tonga is one of intense and affectionate interactions with a range of kinfolk. During this period the child is actively encouraged to be highly sociable, affectionate, aggressive, cheeky, and mischievous and learns to expect others' attentiveness and responsiveness. It seems likely that this period establishes a highly positive sense of self. In later childhood the characteristics that were formerly encouraged are vigorously discouraged in the context of interactions with those of higher status. Once they move from their household's center stage, children are frequently punished and verbally denigrated, rarely praised, expected to work hard for their household, and are largely on the periphery of adult life. What does this do to children's sense of self?

Many of the accounts of child socialization in other Polynesian societies have described a rather abrupt transition between an early period of indulgence and later childhood. The Ritchies have claimed this transition is a "major theme in Polynesian socialization" (1979, 57). The early accounts of this transition often referred to parental "rejection" and claimed that the shock of this rejection had reverberations throughout life.[24] Later accounts also discuss this transition. Levy describes the transition period in Tahiti as a time of "disindulgence"; he details a "dramatic and marked diminution of indulgence" as the child is "pushed from the center of the household stage" (1978, 226–227). For Hawai'i, there are similar accounts of an abrupt decrease in indulgence (Jordan et al. 1969, 57) and a "withdrawal of nurturance and rejection of dependency behavior" (Gallimore and Howard 1969b, 14; and see Gallimore, Boggs, and Jordan 1974; Howard 1974).

All these accounts focus on the discontinuities—the contrast between the affectionate and intense interactions between children and caregivers in infancy and the often punitive and distanced interactions that characterize later childhood. In this respect there are many similarities to be found in the Tongan case as I have described it. Certainly, the response of caregivers to an infant is markedly different from their response to an older child or adolescent. Howard has suggested that "the change in parental response is related to an overriding concern for rank and authority within the family." As babies, children are "passively dependent"—and in a sense outside the status system—so they are intensely nurtured, but when they are older they must learn that as low-status persons they have no right to make demands (1974, 42). Howard's point can be seen from an additional angle: children are nurtured and indulged until they are capable of responding to the demands of higher-status people. Here, there is a certain amount of continuity between infancy and later childhood: the performance encouraged in babies clearly prepares them for the demands soon to be made of them.

I have identified a number of other important continuities between infancy and later childhood and shown that the transition is not dramatic and marked nor abrupt and shocking for Tongan children. The primary continuities lie in both ideology and practice. Continuity arises from the belief that children progress only gradually from *vale* to *poto*, as well as from the high social value of children of all ages. The aspects of later childhood that appear to contrast starkly to infancy, such as punishment, are present in moderated forms from birth, as has been shown. Also, rather than a withdrawal of nurturance and affection, there is a gradual change in their forms and expression. Such continuities may in fact characterize other Polynesian societies, where, as the Ritchies point out, "the warmth and attention that surrounds young children is not normally sharply withdrawn" (1989, 111; and see Martini and Kirkpatrick 1981).

The continuities and discontinuities present in childhood constitute a set of influences on children's sense of self, with each child experiencing a unique combination of these influences according the complexly interrelated aspects of her or his life. A child's subjective self also experiences transformations through time; and with *poto* as a highly valued ideal end point of socialization, this transformation is likely to be perceived as a process of achievement and success. Children who achieve a congruence between their *anga* and *loto* and the cluster of values and associated behaviors expected of them—that is, those who successfully internalize the messages of socialization—will be the most likely to retain the positive sense of self established during infancy. The importance of peer socialization is apparent here, as it gives children the opportunity to experience from an early age the authority and prestige of high status despite the many contexts in which they are of decidedly low status. Importantly, it is also within the peer group that children can continue many of the behaviors encouraged during infancy but later discouraged by caregivers, such as aggression, performance, demonstrative affection, cheekiness, and so on.[25] Although there will be considerable variation in children's sense of self, there are also likely to be aspects that are shared. Sela and Finau, the two little girls adopted by Alisi whom I have described as being treated very differently, could develop markedly different self-concepts as a result of their differential treatment. However, they also share other factors, such as being female, being members of the same kāinga on their paternal side, being from a rural village, being tuʻa, and being Tongan, all of which will influence the way they construct their own subjectivity and identity.

Another powerful influence on children's construction of identity and on their relationships with others is the high social value of kinship. The ideal emotional relationship between members of an extended family and indeed between all people is encapsulated in the concept of ʻofa. ʻOfa, as I have argued, is particularly important within the immediate family, where it is expressed in action and concern—sharing, helping, giving, and demonstrating respect and obedience. There is a very strong ideal of family togetherness and fellowship (feohi). Reflecting on her childhood, Alisi said, "I was just happy to see them all [her family]. Happy that we lived together, we grew up together, and we all had fellowship together, with my sisters and brothers."

This closeness is most often discussed in terms of nofo (a way of living or staying). Families ideally nofo fakataha (live together) and nofo fiemālie (live happily). The anglicized version of these concepts is simply nofo fakafāmili (stay or be like a family), and the term that embraces all positive aspects of nofo is nofo fakatonga (live in the Tongan way). These compounds using nofo were the usual answers to my question "What made you feel happy as a child?" The notion of oneness, expressed in fakataha (as one, together) and moʻui taha (one life), was also stressed. When family members or friends are particularly close they sometimes describe themselves as loto taha (of one heart and mind), a term also used less emotively to mean two or more parties are in agreement about something.

Although household members scatter during the day to work, attend school, and so on, they usually spend morning and evening mealtimes together and share a considerable amount of their leisure time. Mealtimes are particularly important, and usually grace will not be said until all available members of the household and any visitors are seated. Anyone who is tardy is repeatedly called to ha'u kai (come and eat). Sundays are important for families, with household members preparing the 'umu in the morning, attending church together, and then eating the cooked food. Sunday afternoons are typically for dozing or otherwise relaxing; the evenings may be spent watching videos or listening to the radio together. The closeness of family members is also expressed in their grief when parting for long periods and their subsequent experience of manatu, remembering or "brooding memory" (Churchward 1959, 330). Parsons found that manatu was regarded as a new form of illness, afflicting overstayers and small children whose parents are overseas (1984, 86; 1985, 99), although much earlier Collocott also mentioned children's "sickness of remembering," when they pined for absent relatives (1923a, 141).

Another ideal quality of relationships, for both family and friends, is vālelei (to be on good terms). Vā is used to describe people's relationships and feelings for one another, but literally means "distance between, distance apart" (528). Vālelei thus characterizes the distance between persons as good or satisfactory (lelei), while its opposites, vākovi and vātamaki, define it as bad and unpleasant. A loving relationship can be characterized as tauhi vā (Finau 1979, 123), literally, "looking after the distance between." Other spatial metaphors applied both to personal orientation and to interpersonal relationships have been described, for gender differences (e.g., inside or outside) and status relations (e.g., high or low). Improper behavior is sometimes referred to as mafuli (upside down, the wrong way around) or maliu (going in the wrong direction).

Despite the ideals of togetherness and warm emotion, many factors operate to discourage inappropriate expressions of intense emotional attachments. These, which have been discussed previously, include an emphasis on restraint, the use of teasing and ridicule, and the "distancing" that occurs between adults and children past infancy. Marcus has noted a tendency for Tongans to "minimize the number of enduring relationships through time and to limit their intensity" (1978, 248). Romantic feelings are seldom expressed directly, and Tongan love songs and poetry rely heavily on imagery and heliaki (indirect, circular expression) to express desire (see Collocott 1928; Kaho 1988). Friends from outside one's kāinga are ideally treated as kāinga members, and at times kinship terms (e.g., brother) are extended to close friends. Yet adult Tongans who spoke of friendship typically claimed not to trust friends and to maintain only superficial relationships with them.

Friendship is nevertheless regarded as important, and friends (kaume'a or kaungāme'a) are different from people who are merely agreeable companions (popoto or potonga) or acquaintances (maheni). In response to the question

"What makes you happy?" 30 percent (sixty-three) of 209 teenagers indicated being with their friends as most important, and a further 17.2 percent (thirty-six) gave various forms of entertainment that involved friends. By comparison, only 9 percent (nineteen) included being with their family in their replies.[26] Same-sex friends are physically affectionate with one another, often holding hands or walking with arms around each other's shoulders. Children's play groups are important sites for many aspects of socialization, providing a source of attention and affection as well as discipline and lessons in aggression. Older boys, as we have seen, spend a great deal of time in groups and may sleep and socialize in huts separate from their homes. Girls, who spend much of their time indoors carrying out household tasks and childcare, have fewer opportunities to be with friends. However, in 1988 "friendship books" were very popular with adolescent girls. These were school exercise books in which they pasted pictures from magazines; drew hearts, flowers, and other decorations; and wrote affectionate messages and poems to friends. These books constantly circulated among groups of friends and seemed to be an important means of continuing friendships beyond the schoolyard given that the girls could not spend much time together.

SELF-CONTROL

Two interrelated concerns emerge in Tongans' discourse about personhood and interpersonal relations. The first centers on the importance of emotional restraint in maintaining harmonious relationships and avoiding shame. The second concern is with displaying appropriate values and emotions through contextually determined behavior. Marcus describes Tongan males' "personal orientations" as "self-controlled, cautious, timid, sensitive to proper presentations of self in the presence of others, and above all . . . oriented to the maintenance of a smooth, trouble-free social world" (1978, 242). Though I would substitute "reserved" for "timid," this characterization is apt for most of the adult Tongans (male and female) I have known. This "personal orientation" is often masked, however, by Tongans' self-representations. The frequent joking, bantering, and physical expressiveness encountered in everyday interactions belie the self-control and acute awareness of context that are so crucial to being *poto*.

It has been argued for Tahitians (Levy 1973) and Samoans (Gerber 1975) that a social emphasis on external controls results in a lack of internal restraints (i.e., "shame" rather than "guilt"). It could be argued, however, that both formal and informal controls rely, to a great extent, on internal restraints or self-controls. Marcus has argued that a lack of 'ofa (ta'e'ofa, which he translates as "without empathy") can be both a public accusation and a private feeling akin to guilt:

> The feeling of shame is keyed primarily to an awareness of external sanctions, but the feeling of empathy, ideally pervasive in all persons and situations, yet sometimes notably absent, involves a higher level, internal sensitivity to context than does shame. . . . [Shame and *ta'e'ofa*] constitute a set of self controls which integrate a person into social relations with a primary orientation to maintaining his balance with the situation, whatever personal goals are being pursued. (1978, 247)

Self-control is a crucial aspect of social competence in Tonga. Bernstein comments that "underlying informal social control is the concept of self-control. In that keeping oneself within proper behavioral limits is of utmost importance to one's standing as a social being, self-control must be practised, and informal social controls encourage it" (1983, 56). The extent of self-control expected varies according to social context, so that "mutually perceived co-equivalence leads to a lessening of self-control" (Marcus 1978, 267). Among peers, as in the boys' groups, less self-control is required than when those same boys are in the presence of adults. Yet even peers seem constantly alert to indications of inadequate self-control and will readily respond with teasing or other forms of shaming. As shown previously, a lack of self-control is itself shameful and can lead to a loss of prestige. Self-control must be seen in its broadest sense here, as it involves not only the restraint of intense emotions but also a range of other restraints that have been discussed. Children learn that emotional restraint and behavioral restraint are expected in the context of status relations, and the behavioral requirements of respect and obedience are very much tied to this expectation.

Lessons in restraint begin in infancy, with the constant comments to babies about eating too much, crying too much, and so on. The distracting routines used with babies also help to develop emotional control: they encourage children to "decenter" and "detach themselves from their own emotions and focus instead on social concerns" (Watson-Gegeo and Gegeo 1986, 113, writing of a similar practice among the Kwara'ae of the Solomon Islands). Later, children learn the important lesson of emotional control in the context of teasing and punishment. They also learn that being unrestrained in their behavior—for example, being loud, cheeky, and exuberant—may carry a high risk of punishment. Children frequently take this risk, but they also become expert at judging which contexts are safer for less-restrained behavior.

Patience is another important demonstration of self-control, and even children of three or four are expected to sit quietly for long periods, for example during church services or speeches. I once sat at the Nukuʻalofa bus terminal for five hours waiting for an arranged lift back to Holonga. With me were Elenoa, aged three, and her cousin Mele, aged twelve, and their grandmother, Tonga. None of them complained or commented on the length of our wait. Mele occasionally commented that it was hot, and a few times she snapped at Elenoa, but these were the only hints that she might be annoyed or bored. Elenoa sat on the ground playing with bits and pieces she found—a bit of popcorn, a burst balloon—or lay quietly across our laps. Children are strongly discouraged from complaining, and both children and adults seldom complain of hunger, thirst, pain, or other discomforts. The term commonly used for patience, *kataki*, also means "to bear pain or discomfort, etc., without complaining or retaliation . . . to endure" (Churchward 1959, 253). As we have seen, even children who are sick or injured may not tell anyone or complain. Sleep is often used as a means of avoiding frustrating, upsetting, or boring situations.[27] In the previous chapter I described a rainy morning in Holonga during which Tomasi and Elenoa were repeatedly punished for being noisy and annoying. Soon after lunch they went to sleep for the rest of the day. I often noticed that after some form of conflict, or when conflict was brewing, people simply went to sleep—as when Sione went to sleep after feeding the dog the fish he had bought for the family.

Another form of self-control involves suppressing curiosity and critical thoughts. Curiosity is discouraged even in babies, and the term used, *fie ʻilo* (wanting to know) has strongly negative connotations, as we have seen. Hauʻofa has claimed that "the authoritarian attitude which permeates the whole structure of relationships" in Tonga prevents "free, public expression" (1978, 164). There has been mixed community reaction to recent political developments in which certain educated commoners have been publicly advocating political reforms, a situation that will be discussed in the following chapter. While some have welcomed their proposals for reform, others have argued that their criticisms are inappropriate and disrespectful. At the level of the family and institutions such as schools, any behavior that could be construed as *fie ʻeiki*, *fie poto*, or disrespectful still tends to be vigorously discouraged.

Self-control is also manifested in humility, the restraint of pride. Humility is *fakatōkilalo* (making oneself lower) and is a central component of Tongans' self-representations. In the Tongan system of rank and status, the only person without others of higher rank to defer to is the king, and even he is expected to be humble before God. Humility must be demonstrated in demeanor and in speech. The use of self-deprecatory language is one of the most common expressions of humility and tends to pervade any form of self-referential speech. People typically describe themselves as lazy, foolish, impatient, and so on as a matter of course. The providers of a lavish spread of food will apologize for the inadequacy of the *"kai tunu"* (snack), and people giving generous gifts bemoan the poverty of their offerings. Within families, the importance of humility is an important factor in the general lack of praise children receive for their accomplishments. Parents also tend not to discuss their children's achievements with others, lest they be accused of *fie 'eiki*.

According to Marcus, humility is a feature of both "grievance disputes" and male status rivalry, in which participants avoid manifesting any mutual hostility: the aggrieved party visibly expresses *mamahi*, eliciting a humble apology and an exchange of mutual respect. Marcus identifies restraint and withdrawal from competition as "a distinctive phase of Tongan status rivalry" (1978, 244). Writing of Polynesia, he notes that status rivalry involves "distinctive themes of humility as honor, the psychocultural restraint on the expression of anger and aggression, and the importance of interdependence" (1989, 205). In relation to Polynesian status rivalry, Marcus uses the phrase "aggressively asserting pride in humility" (206), which is particularly apt for Tonga.

Mageo has argued that "oral restraint" as socialized in Samoa symbolizes the subordination of self to the community (1989b, 416). This argument can be expanded, for Tonga, to include all forms of restraint, or self-control, which also express subordination within the social hierarchy. In their relations with chiefs, commoners' restraint can signify deference, submission, and powerlessness—as is also the case in adult-child relations. Yet restraint is also valued as a chiefly virtue, and restraint exhibited by chiefly persons signifies their dignity and distances them from their inferiors. Like silence, all forms of behavioral and emotional restraint are ambiguous. In the dignified humility of a low-status person's demeanor and behavior, his or her chiefly qualities can become apparent.

In the concluding chapter, notions of ideal personhood—such as restraint—are examined more closely. In drawing together the various threads of this study, I will show that despite the positive emphasis on subordination, the ideals of personhood center on qualities associated with chiefliness, creating a contradiction that must be negotiated during the progression from *vale* to *poto*.

CHAPTER 9

BECOMING TONGAN: THE FUTURE

As has become clear throughout this study, the process of child socialization cannot be separated from broader social processes; indeed they are inextricably linked. In this final chapter I return to consider in more detail the recent political developments in Tonga, mentioned briefly in chapter 2. I draw out the associations between these developments, wider social transformations, and the commonly expressed concern that young people in Tonga are "losing their culture."

POLITICAL CHANGE IN TONGA

Since its official formation in 1992 the pro-democracy movement has caused a great deal of speculation, both within and outside Tonga, about Tonga's political future.[1] This movement, arising out of members' original concerns with corruption and accountability issues, is now thought by some to constitute "a significant challenge to the whole basis of government in Tonga and the system of privilege which it supports" (Lawson 1994, 2). Although explicitly not opposed to the monarchy itself, the movement has begun to take up social justice and social welfare issues in its call for considerable socio-political reforms.

The emergence of this formalized movement was not unexpected; it was preceded by a period of increasing political activism by a fairly small yet vocal group of commoners and the election of some of them as people's representatives in Parliament. This activism itself can be seen as the latest manifestation of the much more general socio-political changes that have occurred over more than a century. A crucial aspect of these changes has been the gradual erosion of the distinctions between 'eiki and tu'a, as discussed in chapter 2.

An important consequence of this process is the increasing autonomy experienced by commoners. The weakening of tapu, and of chiefly power more generally, has diminished the control of chiefs over the bodies and lives of commoners. Their power to demand goods and services has been reduced, and their authority to inflict physical and other punishments has been transferred to the judicial system. Notions of ideal personhood are still based on chiefly qualities, but the chief as person is no longer "the embodiment" of his people (see Bott with Tavi 1982, 71).[2]

The loss of chiefly power has only been partial, however. As James indicates, "A continuation of the belief in the power of 'blood' works in many ways to counteract democratic or 'levelling' tendencies among the population, and to provide an informal basis for personal strategies involving claims among people" (1992, 96). Chiefly control of land and chiefly demands on villagers for contributions of food and services are two areas in which increasing resentment of chiefly privilege is being expressed, yet these are seldom openly challenged or resisted.

Hau'ofa writes that Tonga's "aristocracy"

> are the foci of our culture and our identity as a single people, as well as being the signposts of our historical continuity as a nation. . . . We still expect to see in our aristocracy, as in no other group in our society, the ideal qualities of our collective personality. In our hurly-burly, free-for-all, dog-eat-dog modern society, we look to them for such qualities in social interaction as civility, graciousness, kindness, and that calming aura of a unifying presence in our midst. This may explain why we get very disappointed whenever they behave as mere mortals, exhibiting the follies and foibles that are the lot of humanity in general. (1994, 427)

Hau'ofa's comments capture well many commoners' ambivalence and confusion about ideals that have become intrinsic to their own sense of self and identity. If "chiefliness" is what people aspire to, in the sense of ideals and cultural values, then resistance against the existing order is difficult. A hegemonic ideology that makes the dominant order the most valued resists challenge, until perhaps there is a perceived split between the individuals and the ideals, as when chiefs are accused of exploiting their privileges. Even so, chiefly behavior in practice may be resented or despised without the *ideal* of chiefliness being directly challenged until, as appears to be beginning now, a self-conscious reexamination of that ideal takes place.

IDEAL PERSONHOOD

The ideal of chiefliness, and the hierarchical relations that pervade Tongan social life, fundamentally influence the process of child socialization. As I have shown, child socialization in Tonga is, broadly speaking, a political process in which children acquire the values and skills necessary to function competently in the context of status and power differences.

The low-status values and behavior children are expected to acquire remain part of their lives throughout adulthood. They will continue to be children to their parents and tu'a to their 'eiki relatives, as well as commoners in relation to chiefs, so that in many contexts they will be required to demonstrate obedience and respect, provide goods and services, and otherwise defer to the pule of those who are 'eiki in rank or status or both.

However, developing social competence is not as straightforward as simply learning to behave as should a low-status person. As children learn how to behave toward higher-status persons they also learn how to behave as higher status persons—to demand submission, to extract labor, to punish. This is clearly evident in children's play groups and within the sibling hierarchy. Because ideal personhood is conceived in terms of chiefliness, it is vital for children to learn high-status behavior. Children also learn to compete for status, which they will continue to do, in a variety of contexts, throughout their lives.

Figure 2 illustrates some basic oppositions between the characteristics ascribed to chiefs and commoners in Tonga and their congruence with the distinctions made between adults and children. It is a highly schematic representation, but it remains a useful means of demonstrating the kinds of idealized dichotomies that appear in Tongan theories of personhood.

The oppositions shown in figure 2 reveal that much of the behavior learned by children as proper and good (i.e., deference, submissiveness, obedience, and other behavior appropriate to low-status persons) is inconsistent with the ideal of chiefliness. To become socially competent persons they need to achieve some kind of balance between these two sets of constructs, for despite the ideal of striving for chiefly qualities, it is essential to remain clearly within one's own social rank and status.

This balance is achieved to some extent through the cultural emphasis

Figure 2: Tongan Concepts of Personhood

COMMONER/CHILD	CHIEF/ADULT
vale	poto
low	high
outside	inside
peripheral	central
mobile	immobile
dirty	clean
badly behaved	properly behaved
impulsive	restrained
inferior	superior
subordinate	dominant

on humility in the presentation of self, for both commoner and chief, and by an emphasis on values that ideally cut across status and rank distinctions to emphasize reciprocity and interdependence, such as fe'ofo'ofani (to be friendly with one another) and fe'ofa'aki (to love one another).

Such emphases mask, to some extent, the unequal power relations inherent in the existing system, as does the notion that the loto is the seat of free will and autonomous choice. Yet they also offer possibilities for questioning that system, as when questions are raised about the extent to which values such as humility, duty, and love are genuinely shared. The ideology of resistance that emphasizes the values of independence (tau'atāina) and freedom to do as one pleases (fa'iteliha), drawing on the concept of the loto as autonomous, constitute challenges to the expectation of unquestioning conformity. I have given many examples of the ways in which children resent, resist, and even directly defy the orders and expectations of those with authority over them. The same processes occur more widely and have had their most public expression in recent political activism.

The pro-democracy movement is indicative of a growing tendency for critical thinking among the commoner population. Lawson has commented upon "the revolution in thinking on the part of Tongan commoners which has taken place over the last few years." She cites Futa Helu's 1992 discussion of the widespread and increasingly public criticism directed at those in power, which he says could not have occurred even twenty years ago (1994, 33).

Yet the seeds of that criticism lie in Tonga's long history of forms of resistance and outright challenges to hegemony, including, as we have seen, the continuing salience of the role of the sister and father's sister throughout this century (and see Gailey 1987c). Even twenty years ago public forms of criticism were not unheard of—even from children. De Bres reports the controversy caused by a winning speech in an interschool competition, which was published by the Tonga Chronicle on August 9, 1973. The winning student was a fifteen-year-old girl who titled her essay "Tonga Should Be More Democratic" and called upon her fellow students "to see that today's oligarchy is tomorrow's democracy" (1974, 25–26). This speech led to heated discussion in Parliament and prompted a letter to the Tonga Chronicle from the women's Langa Fonua Association noting that other speeches included "There would be no loss if Tonga's culture died" and "Tongan culture is a thing of the past." The association strongly criticized teachers for allowing students to express such opinions and suggested that the winning speech "could be interpreted as of a seditious nature"; the women's letter concluded with the more traditional view of critical thinking: that it should be directed only at oneself (27).[3]

As has been noted, critical thinking is sometimes encouraged within educational institutions. The 'Atenisi Institute is well known for its stance: as Hau'ofa states, " 'Atenisi has contributed immeasurably to the process of democratization of Tongan society" (1994, 423). Many of Tonga's more outspoken public figures and scholars have graduated from 'Atenisi. To a lesser extent, critical thinking is encouraged at the secondary school level. In his survey of secondary students' perceptions of the effects of migration, Haberkorn found that students from Catholic schools placed greater emphasis than students from other schools on "new ideas," "alleviating social pressure," and "individual freedom." He comments that "if critical thinking as well as self-critical perceptions are alive in Tongan society, this is to a considerable extent due to the extraordinary commitment of the local Catholic Church" (1981, 21). In modern Tonga some churches are contributing to the swell of social criticism, and some individuals within the church hierarchies are important figures in the pro-democracy movement (see James 1994b, 251).

Those who have contributed to the public discourse centering on sociopolitical change have had to tread carefully because of the deeply emotional issues of cultural identity and tradition that are perceived to be at stake. In regard to both political and familial change the concept of cultural identity has been invoked in various ways, and it is an implicit concern in any discussion of social change.

Those who oppose significant political reform often claim it would lead to a loss of Tongan identity, and they represent *anga fakatonga* as essentially unchanged as yet. The editor of a conservative Tongan publication, for example, wrote of "our Kingdom's unwavering attitude regarding preservation of traditional values despite Western influences" (*Tonga Today* 1987b, 2). James has discussed the connection between an essentialist notion of traditional values and a desire to maintain existing social structures in order to preserve these values:

> The resilience of the old hierarchical structures and ideas is in large part due to the fact that many of the practices have become enshrined as Tongan "custom," and have taken on a new proud meaning for Tongans in a world where they seek to maintain their unique identity amongst people from many nations. (1992, 98)

This position of resistance to political change allows for the kinds of social change that realistically acknowledge the inevitability of continuing modernization, yet seek also to retain tradition. This aim is expressed in the Sixth Development Plan, where it is argued in the context of a discussion of "youth problems" that "it is therefore important that a national effort be made to improve the chances of young people to meet the challenges of modern society while preserving traditional values" (Central Planning Department 1991, 305). Just *which* traditional values will be or can be retained in the face of such challenges, and what meaning they will have for young people, are questions that are not addressed.

Some of those who support political reform also do so in the name of *anga fakatonga*. In this case, there is a desire for a return to an idealized former state in which those with rank and power were honest and served the people's best interests. Change is acknowledged but largely rejected as detrimental to Tongan tradition. One man discussing this referred to *havala* (greed) as the *mahaki fo'ou* (new sickness). He observed that *havala* is particularly dangerous when it afflicts those with political power.

Other supporters of reform are more concerned to move away from, or at least radically interrogate and transform, "the Tongan way." The following comments by prominent Tongan scholar Futa Helu exemplify the way in which the traditional political structure is being reevaluated by some Tongans, primarily those who have been educated overseas: "Most commoners today really feel in themselves a passion to be pushed around (and even abused) by a chief or chiefs. . . . This acceptance of submissiveness is really a socialized and time-honored wretchedness which underlies every aspect of the traditional Tongan character" (Helu 1991, 5).

It is perhaps at the broader level of social organization, within the family and village, that criticism and questioning of hierarchical structures could have a more profound impact. Although much scholarly attention has been paid to the internal critiques of Tonga's government, little has been said of the more general social critique that is slowly and sometimes hesitantly emerging. Sometimes such criticism comes from expatriate Tongans, particularly social workers and doctors working with migrant Tongans. A doctor working in Sydney, Australia, reflected on the hierarchical system in Tonga, commenting that "it is the system that makes one feel whole and gives a sense of well-being and belonging. In other words, it makes a Tongan feel like a Tongan, a very unique and definite identity. . . . There is an emotionalism attached to the system which is actively encouraged as this is one of the binding and motivating forces in such a system." However, Niumeitolu continues, "this overpowering sense of duty and sacrifice is more important to a Tongan commoner, often to the risk of ignoring the needs of their children, health and accommodation" (Niumeitolu 1993, 73).

It is at this level, the personal impact of the hierarchical social ordering, that villagers most often express their dissatisfaction with the status quo. Yet it is also at this level that change is most worrying to people because, as

Niumeitolu's comments make clear, their very identity is tied to that ordering. Among the people with whom I spoke there was even greater acceptance of the inevitability of changes to hierarchies based on kinship and
gender than of change to Tonga's government. It was, nevertheless, a reluctant acceptance, and feelings of ambivalence and confusion about such
change were frequently expressed.[4] There is already a widespread conviction
that cultural change will entail, and to some extent has already entailed, cultural identity becoming weak (vaivai) or even lost (mole). Even among
groups that are seen as most readily accepting change, such as returned long-
term migrants and members of religious groups such as the Seventh Day
Adventists and Mormons, there often is an expressed desire to retain anga
fakatonga. Eric Shumway, a Mormon with a long association with Tonga,
wrote in the introduction to his recent collection of Tongan Mormons' life
stories,

> Many Tongan customs are eroding under the abrasion of modern technology
> and modern thought. Many cultural fixtures will inevitably become relics of
> the past . . . with [Mormon faith] we must preserve also the classic Tongan
> virtues which have traditionally characterized the ideal nature every Tongan
> (indeed every person everywhere) should aspire to: anga 'ofa (a loving
> nature), anga faka'apa'apa (a respectful, reverent disposition), mamahi'i me'a
> (zealousness in a good cause to the point of pain), tauhi vaha'a (maintaining
> good relations, being eager to mend fences), and loto tō (to be humbly will-
> ing, deferential, but keenly committed). (1991, 15–16)

The "virtues" that Shumway identifies are those particularly appropriate
in the context of religious faith. They are also the values associated primarily
with low-status behavior, although it is not clear if Shumway is implying a
need to preserve the hierarchical ordering of Tongan society. However, the
moves for socio-political reforms discussed above do raise the question of
how changes to that ordering could affect notions of tradition and identity
in Tonga. Such reforms are likely to affect the cluster of values, associated
with hierarchical relations, that I have identified as central to the concept of
anga fakatonga, as well as upon notions of ideal personhood. Thus, the concept of chiefliness as the focus of ideal personhood may sit increasingly
uncomfortably with growing criticism of the hou'eiki and of the unequal distribution of power and resources in Tonga. Similarly, submissiveness and deference could become devalued as appropriate elements of self-representation
for low-status persons, with significant consequences for existing values such
as respect and unquestioning obedience. These possibilities and their potential impact on childhood are discussed in more detail below, following an

examination of the views of both adults and children on recent changes to Tongan childhood.

CHILDREN AND THE LOSS OF CULTURE

Tongan children from the age of about five begin to be able to articulate clearly the central values of their culture, as well as the attributes of ideal personhood as shown in figure 2. They also at times express resentment, anger, and other negatively valued emotions that belie any passive and unthinking acceptance of cultural norms. There are many indications of both overt and covert resistance to these norms, as in teenage drinking, petty crime, illegitimate births, and even teenage suicides. Yet overall the behavior I observed did largely conform with adults' expectations and demands; and in contexts in which young people were themselves able to take on a high-status role, as with younger siblings, they tended to reproduce these same expectations and demands. Several factors contribute to this tendency toward conformity, including a fear of punishment for nonconformist behavior, children's subordination within the status system as a whole, and the early discouragement of critical thinking. Another crucial factor is the genuine internalization of values, in which the emotions and dispositions of children as social actors become congruent with cultural models. Children's conformity is also modeled on adult behavior: in many contexts adults have to behave obediently and deferentially and carry out sometimes onerous duties.

Many young people also share the widespread concern that *anga faka-tonga* is being weakened or lost. This was evident in their conversations with me, as when twenty-year-old Lose, from Holonga, told me that she was very worried about the bad behavior of her younger siblings. She said they were disobedient, rude to their parents, and hard to control. She blamed Western influences, saying that children "take all the bad things and do not take the good things. . . . I think the movies and dancing are the most influential things in their lives." The concern of young people was also evident in their responses to one of the questions I asked of high school students: "How do you think things are changing for children in Tonga?" Of 161 respondents, 41.9 percent indicated negative changes, with many simply stating "bad behavior" and others listing disobedience, disrespect, stealing, lying, truancy, rudeness, rebelliousness, and violence. A further 6.8 percent specifically indicated that there had been a "loss of culture." A number of respondents did not explicitly evaluate the changes, including those who stated that there had been "changed behavior" and "fast change" (24.8 percent), new forms of entertainment (13.6 percent), changes in appearance (7.4 percent), girls becoming like boys (4.9 percent), children becoming like *pālangi* (3.7 percent), and more religion (4.9 percent; 1.2 percent indicated that there had been a loss of religion). The clearly positive responses mentioned better behavior (4.3 percent) and better lifestyle, including more Western goods and better education (2.4 percent). Only three students (1.8 percent) indicated that there had been no change. The range of responses these students gave is similar to the comments made by adults when I discussed with them the issue of social change. Most identified material benefits such as better houses, better roads and transport, better schools, and so on but emphasized that social relations and cultural values had deteriorated. There was also a similar range between highly conservative responses and those indicating a ready willingness to embrace change.

Males and females responded differently to this question.[5] A much higher proportion of females commented upon the detrimental effects of change (49.5 percent of the girls and only 18.5 percent of the boys). The girls were also more likely to give "changed behavior" and "fast change" as their response (34.5 percent compared to 5.5 percent of boys). On the other hand, the boys tended to comment on new forms of entertainment, better behavior, and a better lifestyle. Overall, the boys seemed to give more positive responses, which accords with my conversations with adolescents, in which girls were much more likely to express negative and conservative views about social change. To some extent this reflects the different life experiences of males and females, with the latter more restricted in their activities, more frequently in the company of adults, and allotted more responsibility for childcare.

Females may also be less willing to embrace change because in an important sense they have more to lose than males. If we allow that there is at least some congruence between gender differences and the dichotomies expressed in figure 2, it is interesting to note that some recent transformations in gender roles are almost inversions of the form of political change being proposed by some commoners. Certain *'eiki* aspects of ideal female behavior, such as restricted mobility, are being challenged in order for women and girls to enjoy the "freedom" already experienced by males. While females thus are slowly becoming more "male," and so in a sense more *tu'a*, some commoners ("males") are demanding more freedom from their chiefs ("females"). As chiefs forego their privileges to give commoners more freedom, and in the process perhaps loosen some of the cultural restrictions placed upon chiefly behavior, females may lose their own privileges—such as the indulgence daughters are said to receive and their rights as sisters—in order to shed the behavioral restrictions imposed upon them.

That many young people of both sexes continue to identify strongly with traditional values and behavior was clear in their responses to another question: "What will be important to you when you have your own children?" The vast majority of responses repeated what adults had described as their own aims as parents: to teach good behavior, such as respect and obedience; to love ('ofa) and look after their children; to teach them to be good Christians; to advise and instruct them; and to make them work and study hard. The eight students who stated that they would let their children "do what they want" may have been expressing the ideal of fa'iteliha as autonomy, although they equally may have been indicating a resistance to the hierarchical structures of parent-child relationships. Only two responses were unambiguously counter to Tongan norms of childrearing: two girls stated that they would not hit their children. Interestingly, there was much less gender difference in the responses to this question than to the question about the effect of social change, perhaps indicating the students' belief that the basic aims of parenting would not alter, despite those changes.

These students' responses to questions about social change and their own goals as caregivers cannot be seen simply as normative statements somehow concealing their real feelings. Their answers to other questions show that they were willing and able to articulate counterhegemonic views when they so wished. These young people, and those with whom I talked at length, all clearly identified with the concepts of anga fakatonga that I have discussed throughout this book; and although they readily admitted that they often felt ambivalence, resentment, and frustration, they seldom expressed outright rejection of their tradition. They often chafed at the restrictions placed on their behavior, especially girls, for whom the restrictions are the most onerous, but none seemed to seriously question the values themselves.

Like the adults with whom I discussed change and the concept of anga fakatonga, older children and adolescents frequently expressed a deeply emotional commitment to their tradition and to their cultural identity as Tongans. The values of 'ofa, respect, and obedience, as well as the kinship and gender roles and relations that constitute an important aspect of the practice of these values, are central to anga fakatonga. Linnekin has discussed the way in which "particular artifacts and customs" are symbols that "draw on the cultural past yet acquire new meaning and become emotionally weighty in the present" (1990b, 159). She does not specifically mention values, but these are also symbols that, especially in the context of rapid social change, are a fundamental aspect of cultural identity. Tongans are today more self-consciously Tongan than ever before. Both in Tonga and in migrant communities in nations such as Australia, New Zealand, and the United States, many Tongans are proudly and emphatically asserting their unique cultural identity. Yet they are also most fearful of that identity's being lost in future generations. The perceived loss of the central values among the young is widely believed to entail a loss of their very "Tongan-ness."

The fear that children are losing their culture is often expressed in the belief that children are becoming increasingly like "overseas children." Many Tongans perceive *pālangi* children as badly behaved and attribute this bad behavior to a lack of discipline. The differences between Tongan and *pālangi* child discipline tend to be described in terms of extremes, so that *pālangi* are said *never* to hit or even scold their children. My neighbor Lupe commented,

> There is a very big difference in the way children grow up in Australia and Tonga. I see the children in Australia—my brother lives there—they do not hit them. Like, if there is a thing that falls and breaks, I have not seen them hit them. It is very different in Tonga. In Tonga when the mother or father is upset (*loto mamahi*) they hit the children. In Tonga they hit them but over-seas I have seen that they do not hit them. And they do not scold or abuse or hit. The children live happily (*nofo fiemālie*) and I have seen that the chil-dren are able to please themselves (*fa'iteliha*).

The many comments I heard about the differences between Tongan and *pālangi* child-rearing methods indicated mixed feelings, but overall, even among younger people, a negative evaluation of the latter. Although *pālangi* children were said to be "happy," to "have fun with their parents," and to be "not *fakapōpula'i* [enslaved]," these were not seen as necessarily positive traits, and their "freedom" was described in terms of their *tau'atāina* and *fa'iteliha*. As has been shown, these are strongly disvalued concepts when they imply freedom from parental control, except within the more sub-merged discourse of resistance to hierarchical controls.[6] Given Tongan beliefs about personhood and development, the unrestricted freedom attrib-uted to *pālangi* children is understood as allowing the inherently negative qualities of persons to grow unchecked. Combined with a lack of discipline, this unchecked growth precludes the children's acquisition of proper *anga* and *loto*. Because corporal punishment is such an integral part of discipline in Tongan socialization, it is not surprising that there is an immediate associ-ation between a lack of physical punishment and a lack of proper develop-ment. *Pālangi* children are therefore perceived as disrespectful and disobe-dient and as not caring for their parents. By comparison, Moana stated, "I think our Tongan life is better. . . . The children of Tonga are still properly behaved and listen to their parents." However, many people fear that this is no longer true.

Despite most children's apparent acceptance of the primary cultural models associated with the concept of *anga fakatonga*, many people claimed that there has been a decline in children's behavior, as the following comments show:

In Tonga now the children have changed their *'ulungāanga*. The children of Tonga now have very bad *'ulungāanga*. The children's *'ulungāanga* has turned the wrong way around. (Pita, aged 72)

When I was growing up, there were ten children, but there were not a lot of problems, and the way our parents cared for me and all the children, we were not often disobedient. . . . Now, in bringing up my children, I see many more problems; they are disobedient. They are very different from when I grew up. They are growing up in a different way, but the method in which I was cared for is the same as the way I care for them, but their *'ulungāanga* are very different indeed. (Lupe, 35)

Let's look at the low behavior (*'ulungāanga ma'ulalo*) growing: I think this arises from the parents not advising them. Teaching them not to go out at night, see movies. . . . There are children who are well behaved but there is a class, their minds go around and around. The changes are lowering Tonga. (Alisi, 70)

The young generation in Tonga now is changing a lot. They have got *'ulungāanga* like going out at night; the young generation in the past did not go out at night, or go from their home to another home, or go on the road, or go to a dance. This generation, the children begin to go out at night and do many bad things; the behavior of this young generation is very different. Naughty. This young generation is very bad. (Mele, 36)

A lot of kids want freedom these days and yet they seem to lose a lot of the values of things, the responsibilities they should have. . . . They don't seem to be dedicated anymore. . . . I can say that they are very uncontrollable, that's what a lot of people say these days. (Soane, 38; spoken in English)

The common element of concern expressed in statements like these is the increasingly bad behavior of children, especially their disobedience and their freedom. Disobedience seems to signify a more general lack of conformity to cultural expectations and is closely associated with the ways in which children are increasingly unrestricted by social and cultural conventions. Thus behavioral restrictions based on kinship and gender relations are seen to be weakening, with, for example, the brother-sister *tapu* being largely ignored in some families, and many girls now behaving in "male" ways.

To some extent such changes are blamed on parents for not fulfilling their roles as teachers and disciplinarians. Sālote, an unmarried twenty-one-year-old, claimed that parents "don't really care that much about how to teach their children, or tell them how to behave properly. Some people love their children but don't put that love into practice." As we have seen, Sālote's association of love with teaching is a common one. Accusing parents of not teaching their children properly is tantamount to accusing them of not loving their children, so that teaching children traditional values and behavior becomes equated with having *'ofa* for them.

The annual *Report of the Minister of Police* for 1986 and for 1987 blames the increase in petty crime among young Tongans mainly on family problems, such as divorce, one or both parents living overseas, illegitimacy, adoption, diminishing parental authority, and strict physical punishment in the home, as well as on truancy and association with other offenders (1987, 15, 85; 1988, 14, 83). In the 1987 report it is also suggested that internal migration has detrimental effects.

> In the more remote islands of the north and rural villages in the main islands, social solidarity is strong, acting as an informal control on deviant behavior. However in the urban centres, particularly Nuku'alofa . . . the community is increasingly characterized by impersonal relationship and anonymity. The internal migration into these centres brings in its wake an initial shock of adaptation, creating anxiety neurosis in young adults and making them susceptible to delinquency. (1988, 36)

Many other factors are also blamed for the perceived decline in children's behavior, most commonly the broad category of "overseas influences." Tonga's Sixth Development Plan acknowledges the rising incidence of "youth problems such as alcoholism, unemployment and delinquency" and suggests that they

> result from a conflict between the present socio-economic system and the traditional system. The competitive educational system and difficulties to find satisfactory wage labor sometimes contribute to personal dissatisfaction and social destabilization. This is somehow compounded by the influence of western values and lifestyle brought about by the media, tourists, and Tongans returning from overseas. (Central Planning Department 1991, 304)

Video movies have come under particularly strong attack by those concerned with children's worsening behavior (Hosea 1987; Matangi Tonga 1989c; Shumway 1987; Tuʻitani 1986). There are no controls on the video industry in Tonga, and censorship is only carried out on movies for public screening. There is special concern over the ready availability of pornographic videos, which have been blamed for an increase in rape cases, including five reported gang-rapes in 1986 (Report of the Minister of Police for 1986, 79).[7] The adolescent boys in Holonga had ready access to pornographic movies, which they watched in their "gang" huts along with the more usual range of martial arts and American teen movies. There is also a fear that the brother-sister avoidance relationship is being further eroded by videos now that brothers and sisters can sit in the same room watching videos containing love scenes and bad language. As has been discussed previously, questions have been raised about the influence of videos on the "recent phenomenon" of child suicides, particularly by hanging (Matangi Tonga 1989c, 29).

Despite the fact that few restrictions are placed on children's watching of videos, many people expressed concern to me about the possible effects of movies. For example, Pita said,

> There are many changes in Tonga that are bad, maybe from watching a lot of videos, the changes that come are very bad. Tonga has been mafuli [literally, upside down, wrong way round] for a few years. The videos are all right but [children] get many bad ways. Sometimes they grow up with ʻulungāanga lelei but then they go in another direction and become very bad.

Lose, from Holonga, echoed his statement that the videos themselves are not bad, adding that the way they are used is wrong. She claimed that her younger brother, who frequently watched movies at a neighbor's house, had become interested in girls at a much earlier age than his older brothers because of the pornographic movies he had seen. On another occasion Moana pointed out that young children sometimes fashion guns from wood, in imitation of the guns they see in movies.

Clearly, there is a high level of concern about the range of factors that may be detrimentally influencing the young people of Tonga, and some action is being taken to further this concern and translate it into positive action. Police announcements on the radio urge parents to keep their children at home at night, rather than allowing them to wander around watching dances and other activities, such as the drinking of home-brewed liquor (hopi). Church leaders, school principals, and other community leaders also make public their concern about the behavior of young Tongans. They call on families to be more vigilant with their children and to make more strenuous efforts to impart traditional values.[8]

Families have responded in various ways to these calls and to the social changes precipitating them. At one end of a continuum of responses are the parents and other caregivers who have reacted to what they see as a decline in their authority by becoming more repressive and strict. At the other end are those who have actively encouraged their children to embrace change, by relaxing behavioral restrictions and self-consciously disregarding *tapu*. In between are the many families who are still finding their way, attempting to raise children in the context of *fakalakalaka* (rapid modernization) while still grounding them in Tongan culture. Some parents living overseas are sending children to live with relatives in Tonga, to learn the language and *anga faka-tonga*, while others are taking or sending their children overseas to acquire a *pālangi* education and what they believe will be a better standard of living.[9]

REMAINING TONGAN: THE FUTURE

There are clear connections between the concern about young people's behavior and the ongoing debates about political change. The common underlying issue in both cases is the relationship between cultural identity and tradition and the hierarchical structuring of Tongan society. Many Tongans are concerned that if the latter is altered the former will also change, and in an essentialist vision of tradition, change is equated with loss. Yet this is not the only possible interpretation. Indeed, the concept of *anga fakatonga* is undergoing constant reconfiguration, as it always has. Today, as in the past, it has plural and contested, though closely overlapping, definitions. It is possible, then, that it could accommodate considerable sociopolitical change while retaining its profound symbolic significance.

The process of such a transformation would not be smooth, yet its beginnings can already be detected. Some of the central values of *anga fakatonga* have been significantly redefined and reformulated in recent years. The meaning of *poto*, one of the central goals of socialization, has expanded to incorporate knowledge acquired through formal education, competence in business, social mobility, and so on. As we have seen, the idea that some values such as *'ofa* cut across status distinctions is already in place, and this allows for the possibility of an emphasis on their egalitarian aspect over their role within the hierarchical structures. There is also considerable scope for people to formulate individual interpretations of values such as *'ofa* and *fatongia*, as well as the ideals of *anga lelei* and *loto lelei*, while retaining an adherence to the overall concept of *anga fakatonga*.

In other respects is it more difficult to imagine how *anga fakatonga* can accommodate change. The starkly hierarchical values and behaviors found in the context of child socialization, such as unquestioning obedience, unequivocal respect, and ready submission to authority, all enforced by physical punishment, are perhaps the clearest examples. Because socialization *fakapālangi* (in the Western way) is already held as a model of the opposite values and practices, it seems unlikely that changes will be seen as anything but an adoption of (or at least movement toward) *pālangi* ways. This is especially so because changes are likely to be precipitated partly by the discourses of children's rights, and more broadly, human rights, which are clearly Western in origin.

It is intriguing to speculate about the ways in which children will construct their identities as Tongans in the context of an increasingly self-conscious assertion of tradition by some members of their society, more open debate about the definition of that tradition, and its explicit rejection, in whole or part, by others. The process of the "objectification and strategic use of culture" that Sissons identified for Maori culture (1993, 97) may increasingly be a feature of Tongan culture. Can *anga fakatonga* continue to accommodate transformations, so that, as Norton (1993, 748) has said of Fiji, popular and elite discourses about identity remain congruent with the social relations and cultural practices of everyday life? Or does there come a point in the process of "objectifying" culture when the discourses about identity no longer have salience for people's ordinary lives but become restricted to certain special contexts? If in some respects socialization practices are perceived as adopted from outside Tongan culture, can parents continue to believe they are raising their children the Tongan way? Such questions return us to the central concern of this study and lead us to wonder how future generations of children born in Tonga, or in emigrant Tongan communities, will construct a Tongan identity: how will *they* become Tongan?

APPENDIXES

APPENDIX 1

Student Questionnaire and Tabulated Personal Data

Part of the research I carried out in 1988 involved administering the following questionnaire to secondary students. In all, the questionnaire was completed by 235 students from seven high schools (nine classes altogether). The students were directed *not* to give their names, so that their responses were anonymous and could be given freely. This strategy proved successful; although students often gave the culturally "correct" answers, they also voiced many of their own opinions and gave some very interesting responses. One reason for devising the questionnaire was that I had found many teenagers to be reticent and shy (or in the case of some boys, flirtatious and facetious) when talking to me, and the questionnaire format overcame this problem. The questions were given in both English and Tongan, and the students were free to answer in either language. The questionnaires were administered during class, and the students had approximately fifty minutes to complete their responses. The teachers did not remain in the classrooms during this time.

Following the reproduction of the questionnaire are six tables that compile the responses to the personal details at the top of the questionnaire and questions one to three. Table 7A notes the language of the responses. The students' responses to the other questions informed aspects of my discussion of Tongan childhood and are at some points in the text reproduced in the form of tables. However, most of the questions were not designed primarily to produce quantitative data. For all of the questions except one and two some students gave multiple answers. The number at the head of the column therefore gives the number of respondents to the question (not all students answered all questions) and not the total number of answers. Similarly, totals are not given in the percentage columns of these tables as they would always be more than one hundred percent.

QUESTIONNAIRE

Male/Female	Age	Religion	Birthplace	Primary school	Place of residence
Tangata/Fefine	*Ta'u*	*Siasi*	*Kolo fā'ele'i*	*Akoteu*	*'Api nofo'anga*

1. Have your ever been overseas? (Where and for how long?)
   Na'a ke 'alu ki muli? ('I fe, mo fuoloa?)

2. How many other children do your parents have?
   Koe e fānau e fiha ho'o mātu'a?

3. Apart from your parents, brothers, and sisters, who else lives in your house?
   Ko hai 'oku nofo 'i ho 'api, tukukehe ho'o mātu'a mo 'ena fānau?

4. What do you think were the most important things you were taught as a child?
   Ko e hā ha me'a mahu'inga na'a ke ako mei ai 'i ho'o kei si'i?

5. What sort of work did you do in your home as a child?
   Ko e hā ho'o fanga ki'i ngāue na'a ke fai 'i homou 'api taimi na'a ke kei si'i?

6. What sort of work do you do at home now?
   Ko e hā 'e ngāue 'oku ke fai taimi ni?

7. In what ways do you think it is different for boys and for girls growing up in Tonga?
   Ko e hā 'e faikehekehe 'e tamasi'i mo e ta'ahine 'i he taimi 'oku nau tupu hake 'i Tonga ni?

8. Are there things that you have to do that you don't like?
   'Oku 'i ai ha me'a kuo pau ke ke fai, ka 'oku 'ikai ke ke sai'ia 'ia?

9. Are there things that you would like to do but don't do because they are wrong?
   'Oku 'i ai ha me'a 'oku ke fie fai, ka 'oku 'ikai ke ke fai 'ia koe'uhi 'oku hala?

10. Why don't you do them?
    Ko e hā 'oku 'ikai ke ke fai ai?

11. What are some of the things that your parents would punish you for?
    Ko e hā ha me'a tautea ai koe ho'o mātu'a?

12. How would they punish you?
    Ko e hā 'e fa'ahinga a 'e tautea?

13. How do you feel when your parents punish you?
    Ko e hā ho ongo'i kapau 'e tautea koe ho'o mātu'a?

14. If you were angry with your parents, would you show them?
    Kapau te ke 'ita mo ho'o mātu'a, te ke fakahā ki ho'o mātu'a?

15. If yes, how?
    Kapau 'io, te ke anga fefe?

16. If not, what would you do about your anger?
    Kapau 'ikai, ko e hā te ke fakahā ai ho 'ita?

17. What things make you feel happy?
    Ko e hā ha me'a 'e lava ke ke ongo'i 'oku ke fiefia?

18. In what ways are your friends important to you?
    Ko e hā ha me'a mahu'inga 'oku manako ai ho kaume'a?

19. What happens if you disagree/fight with your friends?
    Ko e hā ha me'a 'e hoko 'oku 'ikai ke mo lototaha mo ho kaume'a?

20. How do you think things are changing for children in Tonga?
    Ko e hā ho'o fakakaukau ki he ngaahi liliu ki he fanau 'i Tonga ni?

21. What will be important to you when you have your own children?
    Ko e hā ha me'a mahu'inga 'i he taimi e 'i ai ha'o fānau tonu?

22. What would you like to do when you finish school?
    Ko e hā ho'o me'a te ke sai'ia ke fai 'i he taimi 'e 'osi ai ho'o 'ako?

Table 1A: Ages

AGE	FEMALE	MALE	TOTAL
12	2	1	3
13	10	1	11
14	24	17	41
15	33	25	58
16	48	30	78
17	18	16	34
18	3	2	5
19	1	1	2
?	1	2	3
TOTAL	140	95	235

Table 2A: Participating Schools

SCHOOL	RELIGION	GRADE	FEMALE	MALE	TOTAL
Tongatapu					
Havelu Middle School	Mormon	2	13	7	20
Queen Sālote College	Wesleyan	3	25	0	25
Tupou High School	Wesleyan	3	14	10	24
Tonga High School	Government	4	16	9	25
St. Andrews High School	Anglican	4	17	4	21
Vava'u					
Chanel High School	Catholic	3	13	15	28
		4	16	16	32
Mailefihi/	Wesleyan	3	15	19	34
Siu'ilikutapu College		4	11	15	26

Table 3A: Religious Denomination

RELIGION	FEMALE	MALE	TOTAL	%
Wesleyan	72	49	121	51.5
Roman Catholic	13	28	41	17.5
Mormon	14	8	22	9.4
Church of Tonga	17	2	19	8.1
Free Church of Tonga	10	2	12	5.1
Anglican	8	1	9	3.9
Adventist	2	1	3	1.3
Pentecost	1	1	2	0.8
Baha'i	0	1	1	0.4
Tokaikolo	1	0	1	0.4
Constitution Church	1	0	1	0.4
Assembly of God	1	0	1	0.4
No response	0	2	2	0.8
TOTAL	140	95	235	100.0

Table 4A: Number of Children in Family

NUMBER	FEMALE	MALE	TOTAL
1	1	0	1
2	6	2	8
3	7	12	19
4	27	12	39
5	23	18	41
6	19	12	31
7	18	16	34
8	16	3	19
9	12	5	17
10	6	9	15
11	2	2	4
12	2	1	3
13	0	1	1
No response	1	2	3
TOTAL	140	95	235

Table 5A: Overseas Travel Experience

	FEMALE	MALE	TOTAL	%
No	117	75	192	81.7
Yes	20	18	38	16.2
No response	3	2	5	2.1
TOTAL	140	95	235	100.0

Table 6A: Others in Home outside Nuclear Family

	FEMALE (N = 140)	MALE (N = 95)	TOTAL (N = 235)	%
None	60	47	107	45.5
Grandparent(s)	42	27	69	29.3
Cousins	23	2	25	10.6
Aunt(s)*	8	7	15	6.4
Uncle(s)*	8	4	12	5.1
Father's sister	6	3	9	3.8
Father's brother	6	1	7	2.9
Friends	3	4	7	2.9
Mother's brother	4	1	5	2.1
Sister's husband	3	2	5	2.1
Other maternal relation	3	2	5	2.1
Brother's wife	3	1	4	1.7
Mother's sister	3	–	3	1.3
Other paternal relation	–	2	2	0.8
No response	2	2	4	1.7

*No indication given whether maternal or paternal relation

Table 7A: Language of Responses

	FEMALE	MALE	TOTAL	%
English	72	38	110	46.8
Tongan	58	45	103	43.8
Mixed	10	12	22	9.4
TOTAL	140	95	235	100.0

Kin Diagrams of Household Members

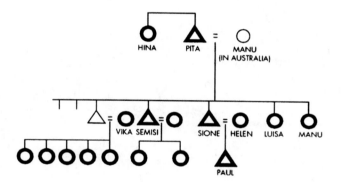

Pita and Manu 1980

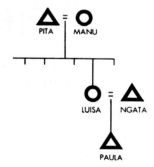

Pita and Manu 1988

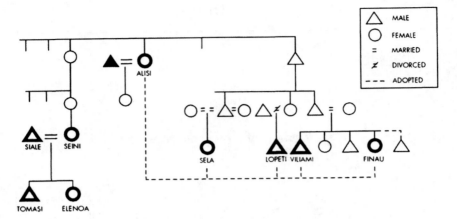

Seini and Siale 1986

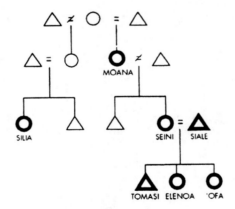

Seini and Siale 1988

NOTES

INTRODUCTION

1. For a fuller reflexive account, see Morton 1995. I am grateful to Don Kulick, one of the editors of the volume in which that paper is published, for pushing me to be more fully reflexive and thus helping me to remember much that I had once needed to forget. Writing that paper has also helped in the revision of my dissertation and enabled me to address the perceptive comment by one of the anonymous readers of the original manuscript, that I was reluctant to convey much of my personal experience of Tonga. However, I am also very much aware that reflexivity, like our "truth," can only ever be partial.

2. That these early visitors to Tonga were almost all male gave their observations an androcentric bias that often excluded women as well as children. Another factor influencing their accounts was the Europeans' appropriation by chiefly persons, limiting their access to the *tuʻa* population. The brevity of the stay of many early observers also limited their view of Tongan life. Captain Cook, one of the most valued sources on Tonga for the late eighteenth century, admitted that he and his men "had but few opportunities of seeing into their domistick [sic] way of living" (July 1777, in Beaglehole 1967, 166).

3. There are some attempts to distill from the historical material comprehensive reconstructions of traditional Tonga, such as Bott with Tavi 1982, Ferdon 1987, and Gailey 1987b; however, these retain the chiefly bias of the early accounts as well as largely neglecting childhood and family life.

4. In any case, this account must be used with caution; as Thomas notes, "Gifford's work was a competent but quite ahistorical distillation of cultural reconstruction, subsequent reinterpretation, and folklore, which like other Bishop Museum Bulletins abstracted particular facts from practices in creating a generalized representation of native culture" (1990, 198).

CHAPTER 1: THE ETHNOGRAPHY OF CHILDHOOD

1. For historical surveys of socialization research see Hurrelmann 1988; Jahoda and Lewis 1988; Schwartzman 1978; and Wentworth 1980.

2. Well-known studies incorporating this approach include *Childhood in Contemporary Cultures* (Mead and Wolfenstein 1955), *Patterns of Child Rearing* (Sears, Maccoby, and Levin 1957), and the work of the Six Cultures project (Minturn and Lambert 1964; Whiting 1963; Whiting and Whiting 1975). Mead's *Coming of Age in Samoa* (1966, original 1928) helped to make the culture and personality approach

popular, and numerous works on other Pacific societies also used this approach; for a survey of this work see Gladwin 1961 and Levy 1969a. For discussions of the culture and personality approach see Barnouw 1963; Draguns 1979; Hsu 1961, 1972; Jahoda 1982; LeVine 1973, 1974; Shweder 1979a, 1979b, 1980; Wallace 1970.

3. The wider implications of the crisis of representation for anthropology have received considerable attention in recent years, with two seminal texts being Clifford and Marcus 1986 and Marcus and Fischer 1986.

4. For useful surveys of anthropological studies of socialization see Harkness 1992, La Fontaine 1986, LeVine 1980.

5. See also Bugental 1985, Mussen et al. 1984, Goodnow and Cashmore 1982, Lewis and Rosenblum 1974, Uzgiris 1979.

6. Ethnopsychology is not a new term, but recent work is significantly different from previous research referred to as such. Ernest Beaglehole and James Ritchie called themselves ethnopsychologists in 1958, in their Rakau Maori studies, but their culture and personality approach is incompatible with recent ethnopsychological work. Another early example of an ethnopsychological study, Valentine's 1963 study of the Lakalai of Papua New Guinea, focuses initially on indigenous concepts and categories but proceeds to translate these into English-language terms and concludes by recommending research methods such as "objective tests, quantifiable measurements, and controlled experimental situations" (1963, 470). Ethnopsychology closely overlaps with cultural psychology (see Stigler, Shweder, and Herdt 1990; Shweder 1991) and indigenous psychology (see Heelas and Lock 1981).

7. See Harris 1989 and Ito 1987 for assessments of the concepts of self, person, and individual; Fogelson 1982 on self, person, and identity; and Morton and Macintyre 1995 on "persons, bodies, selves, and emotions."

8. On cultural models, or "folk theory," see Holland and Quinn 1987; and see Keesing 1987 for a critique of this work.

9. The 1980s saw a burgeoning of research into emotions. Some particularly relevant works include Averill 1982; Harre 1986; Lewis and Saarni 1985a; Levy 1983; Lutz 1988; Plutchik and Kellerman 1980, 1983; Saarni and Harris 1989; White and Kirkpatrick 1985.

10. "Values" is a particularly appropriate term to use in the Tongan case because the metaphor of koloa (valuables, wealth) is used for culturally valued qualities.

11. For language socialization studies see Cook-Gumperz, Corsaro, and Streek 1986; Kulick 1990; Miller and Hoogstra 1992; Ochs 1986b, 1988; Ochs and Schieffelin 1983, 1984; Schieffelin 1990; Schieffelin and Ochs 1986a, 1986b. Although few anthropological studies take account of language socialization, it is a process undertaken by most ethnographers in their initial role as a "child" or "novice" within the culture they are studying.

12. Clearly, an enormous range of elements can comprise context. Tulkin has listed aspects of context that can be considered in studies of infancy and early childhood under the categories of medical-biological, behavioral-situational, and ideological contexts (1977). An examination of his extensive list reveals that no one study

could attempt to account for every aspect of context, so any research involves decisions about which aspects are most salient.

13. In relation to the impact of contact, colonization, and social change there are relevant studies of family life and child socialization that do not have an ethnopsychological approach, such as Gallimore, Boggs, and Jordan 1974 and Gallimore and Howard 1969a (for Hawai'i), and more recently Baker, Hanna, and Baker 1986 (for Samoa) and Jolly and Macintyre 1989a (the Pacific generally). White has argued that the impact of colonialism and nationalism on "culturally constituted selves" has not been addressed "because the 'psychological' issues have been framed as if they pertained solely to individuals rather than persons-embedded-in-collectivities or politics" (1992, 38). This contrasts with analyses of "traditional" concepts of person and self, which do emphasize this collectivity; the assumption may be that effects of modernization are felt mainly at the level of the individual, a position that harks back to the common assumption in the culture and personality literature on the Pacific that change brought "psychic stress" and personality disorders.

14. The question of "tradition" and *kastam* has been widely examined in the Pacific: see Babadzan 1988, Borofsky 1987, Hanson 1989, Jolly and Thomas 1992, Keesing 1989; Keesing and Tonkinson 1982, Lawson 1993, Linnekin 1983, Sissons 1993; and specifically on cultural identity see Linnekin and Poyer 1990a. I find it hard to write the word "tradition" without quotation marks: it is such a slippery term that it seems to need this containment. However, to avoid awkwardness I henceforth let it stand unmarked, reminding the reader that I use this term to indicate a nebulous body of ideas and behaviors that is both widely shared and individ-ually defined by its users.

CHAPTER 2: THE KINGDOM OF TONGA

1. Anthropologists have begun to acknowledge the problems of essentialist accounts that purport to describe such entities as "Tongan culture" or even "the Tongans." Although I have tried to avoid imposing my own essentialist claims, it is important to recognize that Tongans themselves readily use such essentializing notions, even if at times they do so in apparently contradictory ways.

2. Main sources on Tonga's history include Bott with Tavi 1982, Campbell 1992c, Ferdon 1987, Gailey 1987b, Lātūkefu 1974, Rutherford 1977.

3. See Toren (1988) for an interesting analysis of a similar process in Fiji.

4. The study was intended "to determine the nature of modern Tongans' self-view, the conception of their own 'identity'," and was applied to students and teachers in thirteen educational institutions (Helu 1983, 51). The three categories with the highest rate of responses were sexual identity (gender), religious identity, and occupational identity.

5. Some of the main sources on Tongan social structure include Bott 1981; Coult 1959; Decktor Korn 1978b; Gifford 1971b; James 1992; Kaeppler 1971a; Marcus 1975a, 1975b, 1980a. See also the references in note 2.

6. The plural of *tu'a* is properly *kau tu'a* or *kakai tu'a*, but *tu'a* is also acceptable.

7. In her classic study of Tongan social stratification, Bott (1981) was reluctant to use the term "classes" for Tongan social groups, but in recent years it has become increasingly common to see this term used, particularly for the emergent middle class: see, for example, Benguigui 1989.

8. Marcus is discussing Polynesian cultures more generally, but his remarks are particularly apt for Tonga.

9. The derogatory terms for the children of *tu'a* refer to the nonhuman world: *pikilau* (small, secondary tubers growing on the roots of vegetables like yams) and *'uhiki*, the young of birds and animals.

10. See Toren 1990 for a detailed analysis of the Fijian cultural construct of above/below as a model of hierarchical social relations in relation to children's cognitive development.

11. This tension is experienced somewhat differently by *hou'eiki*, who need to demonstrate their chiefly qualities yet retain some common ground with *tu'a*. An *'eiki* person must try to avoid both appearing too pretentious and "lowering" himself or herself by behaving like a commoner (see Marcus 1980b).

12. For details of the land tenure system see James 1993; Maude 1971, 1973; Morgan 1985; Nayacakalou 1959; and Van der Grijp 1993. Problems with access to land are partly fueling the current political unrest. James claims that "by the early 1990s, 75 percent of those who were eligible for land had none" (1993, 221).

13. In 1986, 76.3 percent of the total population of 94,535 dwelt on Tongatapu, and 30.6 percent lived in Nuku'alofa (Statistics Department 1987, 2, table 2). Migration is adding more than 0.7 percent annually to the Greater Nuku'alofa population (Statistics Department 1991b, 4).

14. I have used standard kinship notation throughout this text: F=father, M=mother, S=son, D=daughter, B=brother, and Z=sister.

15. The chiefly bias of historical studies of Tonga is partly due to the Tongans' own view of history. As Herda notes, "The traditional Tongan construction of the past was concerned with only those things which were connected with the *hou'eiki* (aristocracy). . . . [T]he non-chiefly view is sparsely recorded indeed" (1988, 13). Another important factor was that early visitors to Tonga, including castaways, explorers, missionaries, and even ethnographers (e.g., Gifford) associated primarily with chiefly people and presented the chiefly view in their written accounts. Later, the Tongan Traditions Committee vetted research proposals and steered researchers toward chiefly topics. This tendency to present "the noble view" continues to influence much historical and anthropological research even today (e.g., many papers in Herda, Terrrell, and Gunson 1990).

16. For details of Holonga's establishment and Kapukava's position see Bott with Tavi (1982, 120–124).

17. National figures are from the 1986 census (Statistics Department 1991a, xvii, table 8).

18. Between 1976 and 1986 there was an annual average growth rate in Holonga and nearby villages of minus 0.54 percent (Statistics Department 1987, 4, table 3).

The 1986 census (Statistics Department 1991a, 1) gives the population of Holonga in 1986 as 508, and my own survey in 1989 shows a drop to 469. There were 69 households in 1976, 85 in 1986, and 77 in 1989.

19. This percentage for Holongan women had increased from 6.6 percent as recorded in the 1976 census (Census of Population and Housing 1976, 1:146, table 25).

20. See Teilhet-Fisk 1991 on the continuing importance of tapa and ngatu making.

21. For adults, the official unemployment rates are 6.4 percent for males and 18.7 percent for females (Statistics Department 1991a, xxxii).

22. See Cummins 1977, 1980; Paongo 1990; and Roberts 1924 for the history of formal education in Tonga.

23. In the 1903 code of law students over twelve were punished for nonattendance with a fine or in default a fourteen-day prison term, with double this for nonattendance at an examination (Powles 1990, 163n89).

24. In 1979–1980 government expenditure on primary students was T$47 per child whereas in the Mormon schools it was T$386 per child and in the Seventh Day Adventist schools T$478 (Central Planning Department 1981, 312). For 1989–1990 the government amount had increased to T$139; figures for the Mormon and Adventist schools are not available (Central Planning Department 1991, 295).

25. In 1989 Tonga had one main hospital, three district hospitals, fourteen health centers, and thirty-three small clinics. Most doctors work in the hospitals; other centers are staffed by health officers with two years' training and nurses. For an account of some of the problems within the health care system, particularly at Vaiola Hospital, see Fonua 1992a.

26. See Weiner 1971 and Whitcombe 1930, 10–13 for details of herbal treatments used for children's illnesses. The type of treatment different faito'o use varies considerably. Also, each remedy may be used for several kinds of problems, and more than one faito'o may be consulted. Knowledge of medicinal plants is not confined to faito'o: many Tongans know and use a variety of remedies for common complaints.

27. Parsons notes that because of the distinction between Tongan and European illnesses, Western medicine "is unlikely to readily displace the traditional Tongan healing practices" (1985, 105).

28. The 1986 National Nutrition Survey did not examine the diets of males aged between four and twenty or females between four and fifteen, so there are no recent statistics on children's diets.

CHAPTER 3: HAVING CHILDREN

1. Most of the conversations and interviews from which I have derived quotations were conducted in Tongan. In many quotes I include Tongan terms that are difficult to translate and give the closest English translation.

2. There have been many descriptions of Tongan weddings. On traditional weddings see Aoyagi 1966, 167–171; Beaglehole and Beaglehole 1941b, 92; Collocott 1923b; Gifford 1971b, 191–196; Martin 1981, 96–98; Orange 1840, 149–151. On

elopements see Marcus 1979. Since the late nineteenth century, Christian ideology and codified laws have wrought significant changes in the wedding ceremony, the choice of marriage partners, and divorce and remarriage practices.

3. Pulea cites Department of Justice figures for 1980 showing that 70.4 percent of females and 51.6 percent of males married between fifteen and twenty-four (1986, 127). The 1986 census showed that the mean age at first marriage was 27.1 for men and 24.8 for women (Statistics Department 1991a, xiv). Spouses may come from the same village but more often are found elsewhere: of 254 Holongan couples (some of whom lived elsewhere at the time of my research) only 57, or 22.4 percent, had married within Holonga. The number of males and females with non-Holongan spouses was similar: 100 females and 97 males.

4. Ideas and practices concerning conception, pregnancy, and birth historically and in contemporary Tonga are examined in detail in Morton n.d.

5. The plural of tapu is ngaahi tapu, but the use of tapu for both singular and plural is common.

6. It is interesting to note that one of the side effects of the recent public education program for AIDS awareness in Tonga may be a more thorough awareness about sex and sexual practices. As Dr. Puloka, an instigator of the program, commented, "Nothing is hidden . . . there are no tapus at all" (Matangi Tonga 1989a, 4). Some of the educational films on AIDS shown at antenatal clinics, high schools, and other venues are explicit.

7. The Tongan term for baby, valevale, meaning "not yet able to think for itself" (Churchward 1959, 533), has been almost entirely replaced by pēpē, although I did hear valevale used occasionally by older women. To indicate sex, pēpē tangata (male baby) or pēpē fefine (female baby) can be used, or more commonly, tamasiʻi (boy) or taʻahine (girl). Pēpē tends to be used until the child is walking.

8. Less often such problems are blamed on people with whom the mother interacts closely, particularly her husband. Cowling states that some problems also may be blamed on spirits that may interfere "at point of conception, birth or post-natally, with [the] child's mind" (1990a, 76); no women I spoke with, however, offered this explanation.

9. Some women, when asked about pregnancy tapu, replied that too much fat, salt, or sugar is dangerous for the baby. These are the three "don'ts" given in the public health education program of the Ministry of Health, which now have been incorporated into the category of tapu. They are the only tapu many younger women will learn in pregnancy.

10. For descriptions of pala and kulokula see Shineberg 1978, 287 and Spillius 1958, 30–31. It is interesting that even skin problems in older children may be attributed to their mother's diet during pregnancy and lactation. Examples of pregnancy and lactation tapu can be found in Beaglehole and Beaglehole 1941b, 78–79; Bott n.d., 14; Collocott 1921b, 418; and Spillius 1958, 15–16.

11. For details of these medicines see Weiner 1971. For an extensive discussion of medicines and other treatments in pregnancy and birth and in antenatal, postnatal, and neonatal care, see Ikahihifo and Panuve 1983.

12. The role of *māʻuli* has been given little attention in the literature on Tonga. As Rogers has noted, "Another unexplored domain [of women's power] is that of midwives, senior women who hold the power of life and death over babies and parturient mothers" (1977, 180). In Morton (n.d.) I discuss in detail the contemporary role of *māʻuli*.

13. The remaining *māʻuli* in Tonga are being offered training courses in basic midwifery by the Ministry of Health. They are also being used as "motivators" to promote family planning and to advise women to attend antenatal clinics and have hospital births.

14. Figures on rates of hospital births vary. In its report for 1987 (1988, 32) the Ministry of Health claimed that 80.1 percent of women gave birth in a hospital and a further 16.9 percent had a medically assisted home birth (not with a *māʻuli*). For 1988 it was claimed that 93 percent of births were attended by health personnel, and of those births 73 percent were in a hospital (Central Planning Department 1991, 274). This gives a rate of only 69 percent for hospital births. Home births are becoming increasingly popular, although not at the rate these figures would suggest. Of the home births in 1988 it was claimed that 67 percent were delivered by *māʻuli* (274).

15. Practices surrounding hospital births also fit well with the Western model, in which childbirth is treated as a medical condition and the women as passive objects, expected to follow the orders of medical staff: see Davis-Floyd 1988, McBride 1982. However, there is generally less technological intervention in Tonga because of lack of resources.

16. Bott also recorded that the person cutting the cord would "squeeze it between the baby and the afterbirth . . . drawing whatever liquid is there towards the baby as it was thought that the baby's life comes from the afterbirth" (n.d., 16).

17. Collocott and Havea give the saying "*Kuo tā ki hono uho*: it was stuck to his navel cord," used "when anyone is peculiarly apt at some particular task or seems to have been born to meet some special circumstances that have arisen" (1922, 81).

18. The Maori term for land and placenta is *whenua*. See Kinloch 1985, 209 on the Samoan *fanua*; Kirkpatrick 1983, 127 on the Marquesan *pu henua*; and Williksen-Bakker 1990 on the Fijian *vanua*.

19. The term *olopoʻou* is used for the first child, as well as for the primipara during pregnancy and after the birth. The second child is *oloua*.

20. It is not clear whether such exchanges were made on the birth of children, either chiefly or commoner, before European contact. Certainly by early this century such exchanges occurred, especially within chiefly families. Spillius refers to this exchange, in the case of the *olopoʻou*, as "in essence the completion of the wedding ceremony" (1958, 21). Recently, however, this practice has become less common. For accounts of such exchanges see Beaglehole and Beaglehole 1941b, 81; Biersack 1982, 192; Spillius 1958, 19–21; Rogers 1977, 165.

21. For accounts of naming practices see Aoyagi 1966, 165–167; Beaglehole and Beaglehole 1941b, 81; Rogers 1977, 164. When my son was born in Tonga in 1980 I was not aware of naming practices, so was very surprised when soon after the birth one of my husband's paternal relatives, whom I had never met, arrived at the hospital

and proclaimed the baby's name to be Tangatalakepa. We chose not to give him that name and opted for my *pālangi* custom of parents selecting their own children's names.

22. See Bakker 1979 and McArthur 1967 for analyses of earlier population trends.

23. An analysis of the 1986 census claims that "women who are not economically active bear, on an average, 2.3 children more than women who are economically active" (Statistics Department 1993b, 43). The census recorded women as economically active on the basis of their main activity only, thus grossly underrepresenting the economic activities of women (Statistics Department 1991a, xxii). However, it may be cautiously inferred that women who are in full-time employment, and thus categorized as economically active, are on average having fewer children.

24. Abortion was made illegal in Tonga's first written legal code, the 1839 Code of Vava'u (Lātūkefu 1974, 222). By 1862 the punishment for procuring an abortion was to work as a convict for life (243). Traditional methods involved herbal abortifacients and vigorous massage.

25. In 1991, some 14 percent of babies were born to unwed mothers, over half of whom were between the ages of fourteen and twenty-four (*Matangi Tonga* 1992a, 46).

26. The 1862 Code of Laws stipulated maintenance payments of two shillings per week until the child was thirteen (Lātūkefu 1974, 243). An earlier law, in the 1850 Code of Laws, stated that "it shall not be just for a relative to take forcibly a bastard child from its mother, but by her consent only" (231), which suggests that formerly the father's family may have had a right to "illegitimate" children.

27. A "wrong" relationship between the parents seems a more important source of shame than giving birth out of wedlock. Infanticide is rare in Tonga, but one well-publicized case in 1986 involved a woman who had given birth to a child by her husband's brother (*Report of the Minister of Police for 1987*, 30; *Tonga Chronicle* 1986a). Public speculation focused on the shame she must have felt to be driven to killing the baby and attempting to conceal the birth. She was sentenced to life imprisonment for murder.

28. In these myths the illegitimate child journeys to find the father and undergoes some ordeal as a result of meeting him. See Collocott 1928 and Gifford 1971a for collections of myths and Biersack 1990a, Bott 1972, James 1991b, and Valeri 1989 for some interesting interpretations.

29. The mother's consent is needed for the child to be adopted by the father, and if legally adopted the child will bear the father's surname (*Law of Tonga* 1967, Cap. 19, section 18).

30. Several previous accounts have described the forms and procedures of adoption in Tonga: Beaglehole and Beaglehole 1941b, 70–71; Morton 1976; Urbanowicz 1973. For Polynesia more generally see Brady 1976 and Carroll 1970.

31. The term *tonotama* means "to take somebody else's adopted child and keep it as one's own" (Churchward 1959, 494).

32. Comparative figures can be found in Morton 1976. Of eighty-one adoptions he found that 68 percent were related to the adoptive "mother" (68).

33. MacKay (n.d., 2) claims that babies were formerly carried in slings of tapa on their mothers' backs, but I have not been able to find any other evidence of this practice.

34. Mothers' concern to protect babies may be related to the high infant mortality rates in earlier generations, when introduced diseases caused many deaths. Epidemics caused considerable fluctuation in infant mortality rates: in 1925 the rate was 295.61 per thousand; in 1927 it was 33.67. These were the highest and lowest rates in the period between 1925 and 1957 (Spillius 1958, appendix 1; see also Bakker 1979, 121). More recent figures also seem to vary (apparently because of different methods of record keeping): the Fifth Development Plan gives a rate of 9.7 per thousand in 1983 (Central Planning Department 1987, 337), the Sixth Development Plan, a rate of 6.8 per thousand in 1986 (Central Planning Department 1991, 272). The Statistics Department, however, basing its rate on census figures, gives a rate of 25.9 per thousand for 1984 (1993b, 1, 19–21). Certainly the rate has declined significantly, partly as a result of an extensive immunization program.

35. Other practices to shape the baby—such as the use of tapa binders on the arms, legs, and waist when the child is sleeping or placing heavy tapa on top of the baby's head when the baby is asleep to keep the head from elongating—are rare today (Bott n.d., 29–30). These practices may have been carried out only with babies of chiefly parentage.

36. The 1986 National Nutrition survey (Maclean and Badcock 1987) found that 100 percent of babies were breast-fed for the first three months, with 10.8 percent weaned at three to five months and a further 19.1 percent by six to eight months (sample size not given).

37. The 1986 National Nutrition Survey (Maclean and Badcock 1987) reports that 26.2 percent of mothers began breast-feeding immediately after giving birth and 41.1 percent some time during the first day. Another 14.4 percent did not breast-feed until the second day and 15.2 percent until after that. Some other form of nourishment was given to 73.7 percent of babies in the first two days. The sample size is not given, nor is it indicated whether both hospital and home births are included.

38. Formerly, the mother and baby were rubbed with a mixture of turmeric (enga) after the birth and daily for several weeks, as this was believed to help keep them warm and promote the mother's milk (Gifford 1971b, 185; Spillius 1958, 18).

CHAPTER 4: BECOMING POTO

1. Gender distinctions can be further emphasized by the terms tamasi'i tangata (male boy) and ta'ahine fefine (female girl).

2. Gifford states that finemui was the term for tu'a girls who were still virgins; chiefly girls were taahine (ta'ahine) or taupoou (tāupo'ou) (1971b, 191). When no longer virgins chiefly women were still called ta'ahine (girls) but commoner women were called finemotu'a, a term that today can mean elderly women or married women or can be a derogatory term for any female.

3. There is a linguistic relationship between the Tongan anga and other Polyne-

sian cognates, such as the Maori *tika* or *tikanga* and Samoan *aga*. Shore describes these concepts as "a kind of Platonic form appropriate to each thing or activity" (1989, 149; and see Mageo 1989a for an analysis of the Samoan *aga*). An important difference appears to be that these other terms imply *appropriate* conduct, form, and so on, whereas *anga* is a nonevaluative term requiring specifying suffixes.

4. Mariner tells of a man about to strangle a child as a sacrifice referring to the child as "*chi vale*" (*si'i vale*), which Mariner aptly translated as "poor little innocent" (Martin 1981, 140). The perception of children as crazy, foolish, and so on is widely encountered. Kirkpatrick states that for Marquesan children "mature thought" is believed to appear after their first communion and to begin properly with puberty (1983, 88). On Ifaluk in Micronesia children are said to be "crazy" until five or six and therefore not responsible for their actions (Lutz 1988, 106). Many other cross-cultural examples could be cited, such as Briggs' report of the Utku Eskimo belief that children have no *ihuma* (mind, thought, reason, or understanding) (1970, 111).

5. *Kākā* means "deceit" or "trickery," but a combination of the two, *potokākā*, means "cunning and subtlety."

6. Koskinen suggests that this "emotional mind" is believed, throughout Polynesia, to be situated near the center of the body: toward the lower body in eastern Polynesia and higher in the west (1968, 77–78, 55). In Tonga, as in Samoa (Gerber 1985, 136), the location of the *loto* seems ambiguous and can range from the heart to the lower abdomen. It is best understood simply as "inside."

7. Although there are many different denominations in Tonga, "Christianity," rather than particular denominational ideologies, is invoked in discourse concerning appropriate values and behavior.

8. Related concepts also occur outside Polynesia, such as *fago*, for the Ifaluk in Micronesia (Lutz 1988).

9. However, *'ofa* has not undergone the same process of appropriation by Europeans, and self-conscious reappropriation as an identity marker, as has *aloha* in Hawai'i.

10. Tonga seems to be unusual in having this distinction between *'ofa* and *faka'ofa*. In some other Polynesian languages the emphasis on pity and concern associated with *faka'ofa* is incorporated within the main term; for example, see Kirkpatrick 1983, 111–113 for *ka'oha*.

11. In Tonga to "kiss" (*'uma*) is to press the nose and mouth to the other person's cheek while sharply drawing in breath through the nose. Formerly, to *'uma* was to press nose to nose as in the Maori *hongi* (Cook in Beaglehole 1961, 269).

12. The "grandparent syndrome" observed in Hawai'i (Jordan et al. 1969, 60) also occurs to some extent in Tonga. Older parents tend to prolong the indulgence period, delaying stricter discipline and expectations of household labor for the younger children, especially when there are many older children in the family.

13. In this sense the expression of *'ofa* differs from that of *alofa* in Samoa. Mageo notes that Samoan parents do not "serve" their children, as this would be treating them as if they were of higher status (1988, 51). Children serve food to the adults

and eat last. There has been considerable change in habits of cooking and eating in Tonga, and possibly the situation was formerly more like contemporary Samoa. Cook recorded that "inferiors" did not eat with "superiors" (1777, in Beaglehole 1967, 170), and on formal occasions this is true even today.

14. An anonymous reader of the thesis on which this book is based made the important observation that these lessons in saying *ko au* teach children to focus on selfhood within the context of a dyad rather than as isolated individuals.

15. Vason described inferior chiefs sending men to higher chiefs to *fadongyeer* and stated that a higher chief could have up to five hundred men working for him at a time (Orange 1840, 139).

16. Van der Grijp provides an interesting discussion of the conflicts business-people experience between their traditional obligations and the requirements of successful capitalist enterprise (1993, 124).

17. Herda (1988, 89–90) has pointed out the difficulty of assessing just how *tu'a* perceived their duties (*fatongia*) in precontact Tonga, given the paucity of data on commoners and the conflicting nature of existing accounts.

18. Many of the questions were not primarily intended to produce quantitative data (see appendix 1).

19. Unfortunately the wording of the question—"Are there things you have to do that you don't like?"—was confusing as it did not make clear the sense of being *obliged*. Many Tongans say, when speaking English, "I have to do . . ." when they simply mean "I do . . ."

20. Some Tongan participants at the fourth Tongan History Conference, in 1990, suggested that *tau'atāina* is constructed from *tau* (we), *'atā* (free, unrestrained), and *ina* (laugh, especially in derision, an impolite term). *Ina* is also a suffix forming adjectives or intransitive verbs (Churchward 1959, 241). Gordon has pointed out that Tongan Mormons use *tau'atāina ke fili* (freedom to choose) as a direct translation of "free will" (1990, 213).

21. In contrast, independence in the sense of being capable of bathing, dressing, and so on without assistance is encouraged very early in life.

22. My discussion of gender is concerned with contemporary notions of gender among *kau tu'a*; for analyses of traditional gender roles and their transformations see Gailey 1980, 1987b; Herda 1987, 1988; James 1983, 1990; Ralston 1990a, 1990b. Much of this work forms part of the wider body of research reevaluating gender relations in the Pacific, such as Hanson 1982; Ralston 1988, 1993; and Ralston and Thomas 1987.

23. Mariner states that *nofo ma'u* referred to married women's fidelity and warriors' loyalty to their chief (Martin 1981, 318).

24. It is unclear whether the emphasis on women "staying" was present in precontact Tonga or was a result of the missionaries' insistence that women's place was in the home—or, indeed, whether the missionaries' influence served to strengthen an existing tendency.

25. Marcus points out the similarities between the *talavou*, the Tahitian *taure'are'a*, and the Samoan *taule'ale'a* (1978:257).

26. This can have serious health consequences, as Tongan women are often reluctant to seek help for breast or gynecological problems or to have pap tests or breast examinations (Niumeitolu 1993).

27. Wifely fidelity appears to have been expected in precontact Tonga (Martin 1981, 325; Waldegrave 1834, 194) and was of course strongly encouraged by the European missionaries.

28. Descriptions of the operation and convalescence can be found in Gifford 1971b, 188–189; Martin 1981, 459; and Bott n.d., 23–26. Only the Tuʻi Tonga was left unsupercised in precontact Tonga, unless the operation was performed when he was overseas.

29. Supercision and circumcision are called *kaukau* (to cleanse) and *tefe* (the vulgar term), and circumcision is known also as *kamu* (to cut around). Unsupercised or nowadays uncircumcised boys are called *kou* or *kotā*, the latter being the impolite term. Also, the prefix *taʻe* (not, un-) is added to the terms *kaukau*, *tefe*, and *kamu* to indicate an uncircumcised state.

30. Bott (n.d., 27) refers to the *katoanga o e ngata* (the celebration of the end [of childhood]) for girls of chiefly or *matāpule* families.

31. Waldegrave reported in 1834 that women were tatooed on their legs and feet "with small stars as a spotted stocking" (1834, 194).

CHAPTER 5: CHILDREN'S EVERYDAY LIVES

1. Examples of these drawings can be found later in this chapter.

2. Anthropological studies of Tongan kinship have stressed the formal kin terms and roles: see Biersack 1974, 1982; Gifford 1971b; and Kaeppler 1971a. See also Bott 1972 and James 1987, 4 for details of the use of kinship terms for relationships between chiefly titles, such as "younger brother" (*tehina*) and "older brother" (*taʻokete*) titles. Bott 1972 also shows how kinship idioms are used in formal kava ceremonies.

3. As with other kin terms there has been a narrowing of the application of sibling terms. Formerly sibling terms were "extended to at least third cousins." Today these terms often are used only for true siblings and first cousins, and "more distant cousins are referred to descriptively" (Kaeppler 1978b, 202n35). Much depends on how closely the relations interact, so that Seini referred to both her MZD, who lived with her, and her MMBDD, who was a frequent visitor, as "sisters."

4. If a paternal relative is a child's "mother" by fosterage or adoption, she will be of higher status than the child.

5. However, the "aunty" role is not as marked as in Hawaiʻi: see Linnekin 1980.

6. The most frequently described *ʻilamutu/faʻētangata* relationship in the literature on traditional Tonga is that of the Tuʻi Tonga and his eldest sister's oldest daughter, the Tamahā: see Bott 1981, 34; Gifford 1971b, 80; and Kaeppler 1971a, 183. On formal occasions such as weddings and funerals *ʻilamutu* are often chosen to be the *fahu*, that is, "the one who is ceremonially or ritually superior." The *fahu* receives the best of the food and *koloa* redistributed on such occasions. However, *fahu*

is not a kinship term synonymous with *'ilamutu*, as is assumed in some of the kinship literature. For this and other reasons there is "much confusion and misunderstanding" in this literature concerning the *fahu* (Rogers 1977, 167). For discussions of the *fahu* see Biersack 1982, 188; Bott 1981, 18; Gailey 1980, 299; Gifford 1971b, 18; James 1983, 236–237; Kaeppler 1978b, 197; Moengangongo 1988. Some Tongans today refuse to recognize *fahu* rights, and many younger Tongans only learn of the significance of the *fahu* institution through Tongan studies classes at school.

7. The role of the *'ulumotu'a*, or *'ulu 'i fāmili*, is significantly weakened today: see Aoyagi 1966, 151–154; Decktor Korn 1977, 156; Morton 1987, 55. The group of households under the leadership of the *'ulumotu'a* was formerly called the *matakali* (Morton 1972, 48–51).

8. Mothers do not use separate kin terms for sons and daughters—both are *tama*. This term can indicate a woman's or couple's children, and daughters may be *tama fafine* (female children).

9. The father's first cousins (female) are also *mehekitanga* to his children, but more distant cousins are *fa'ē* ("mothers") or just *kāinga*. The use of *kāinga* terminology has narrowed in modern Tonga so that specific *kāinga* terms often are "applied only to parents and their siblings while those more distant are simply referred to as *kāinga*" (Kaeppler 1978b, 202n35).

10. All who are *tu'a* to the deceased should *liongi*, although as Kaeppler has observed, it is common nowadays for people to *liongi* "improperly" or not at all (1978b, 197).

11. Aoyagi mentions similar *tapu* between same-sex siblings as between fathers and children; younger siblings were not to eat the elders' leftovers or wear their clothes (1966, 162). These *tapu* are rarely observed today.

12. The brother-sister relationship has special significance in many Pacific cultures (see, for example, Marshall 1983).

13. James states that the goddess Hikule'o was "the most potent deity in the Tongan pantheon" (1991b, 306).

14. It is not clear whether separate sleeping areas were a feature of commoners' dwellings in former times. Anderson stated that "men, women and children lye in the same place without seperation, unless a few who have a stiff kind of mat that stands by itself and forms a low partition" (1777, in Beaglehole 1967, 941). Cook also noted that family members "sleep on the floor wherever they please to lay down, the unmarried men and women each by themselves, or if the family is large they have small huts without to which they retire to sleep" (168). These huts may have been for the adolescent boys, and today many boys still use such huts.

15. The relationship between a woman and her husband's sister is ideally one of avoidance. The wife thus takes on the avoidance relationship that existed beteen the man and his sister during adolescence. The wife should not share her sister-in-law's clothes, comb, mats, and so on, and the women are *tapu* to one another at childbirth (Aoyagi 1966, 163; Beaglehole and Beaglehole 1941b, 73). Today, as with the *tapu* associated with the brother-sister relationship, these restrictions are weakening, but

the husband's sister may still attempt to assert her higher status by making labor demands of her sister-in-law. On the other hand, a person's relationship with his or her same-sex sibling's spouse, and the same-sex siblings of his or her spouse "are characterized by license and joking" (Bernstein 1983, 43).

16. Gailey and James have both examined the transformations of women's roles in Tonga, but come to somewhat different conclusions. Gailey (1980, 1981, 1987a, 1987b) has argued that women have generally been disadvantaged by postcontact changes. She claims that women have lost their power as sisters and that "missionary redefinitions of marital responsibilities particularly disfavored wives" (1980, 313). James (1983, 1990) has shown the situation to be more complex, noting that postcontact changes gave women "at once more and less freedom and securities as wives" (1983, 241). She also has pointed out that sisters have in fact retained a significant measure of their "chiefly" position (1990).

17. Mariner reported that young, marriageable commoner women lived with the chiefs and *matāpule*, to attend them or their wives; once married, these women moved to live with their husbands on the agricultural land, this being the period before village settlement (Martin 1981, 325). This custom presumably left girls not yet of marriageable age, and boys, to help with household chores and productive activities.

18. Some Holonga households had washing machines, but because the only water source was a yard tap, the machines had to be filled and emptied manually and could not be used to rinse the clothes. In addition, the frequent power cuts rendered the machines useless.

19. The role of adolescent girls at cooperative events such as *koka'anga* (tapa-dyeing sessions) is more clearly one of helping. While the adult women paste and dye the tapa the girls prepare and serve food and drinks, clean up, hand around fresh dye and pasting materials, and look after babies and toddlers.

20. The census shows that of the "employed population"—that is, those recognized as economically active—only 2.2 percent of women are involved in agriculture for subsistence or cash (Statistics Department 1991a, xxvii). Although the administrative report on the census readily acknowledges the problematic nature of its assessment of economic activity, the Sixth Development Plan does not, stating only that "17.8 percent of women over 15 years are reported as economically active" (Central Planning Department 1991, 66).

21. See Perminow's account of the situation of rural youth, who find it virtually impossible to use their formal education to build any social status within their local community, given their positioning within the social hierarchies (1993).

22. Haberkorn's survey was more specifically aimed at discovering employment aspirations than was mine. Many respondents to my question simply answered *"ngāue"* (work) or "look for a job" without specifying the type of employment desired.

23. The role of play in learning to learn, or "deuterolearning" as Bateson called it, has become an important field of study, particularly by Vygotskian researchers. Vygotsky also claimed that play involves the acquisition of understanding of social rules (1978).

24. Bott has indicated that chiefly children of about five and older were assigned attendants who were the children of *matāpule* or even commoners from the same *kāinga*. They became friends and were able, when alone together, to put aside their different social rank and status to talk and play freely (n.d., 21).

25. Ochs describes a similar pattern in Western Samoa (1988, 160).

26. Tonga has also had a television station since 1988; it broadcasts daily within certain hours, with programs mainly from the American networks. Using this channel is expensive: one has to buy an unscrambler and pay a monthly subscription fee. There were approximately five hundred subscribers by late 1989 (*Matangi Tonga* 1989c, 31).

CHAPTER 6: LEARNING TO BE POTO

1. Tongan practice differs from that reported by Ochs for Western Samoa (1988, 158). She states that people do not talk *to*, or *with* babies, only *about* them.

2. People of any age use the same pattern on parting, calling each other's names or calling "*Nofoā ē?*" (stay) or " '*Aluā ē?*" (go) depending on the circumstances.

3. Borofsky, in his analysis of "acquiring traditional knowledge" in Pukapuka (1987), describes observation and imitation as the most important forms of learning. However, he considers only that knowledge related to physical and other practical skills. In Tonga, appropriate value-oriented behavior is both formally and informally taught to children, and this form of learning is given more cultural emphasis than the taken-for-granted learning of physical skills. Levy's study of Tahiti also shows this stress on the importance of "advising" children (1973, 449).

4. Lindstrom also states that questioning "is severely controlled so to protect the circulation of knowledge on the island" (1990, 45).

5. Although I use the dichotomy between formal and informal here I acknowledge the problems it entails, as discussed by Strauss (1984). The dichotomy she prefers, between intentional and incidental learning, is equally problematic, because any given learning event may involve both these forms. I use "formal" here without the implication that it is restricted to Western-type schooling or is otherwise "out-of-context" learning (195); rather, it is teaching that is not spontaneous and that entails stricter observance of the status rules concerning speech.

6. Ngata's comments here and throughout were made in English.

7. Māhina defines *talatupu'a* as a mixture of imaginary and real situations and *fananga* as describing "strictly imaginary events" (1990, 37).

8. In Samoan, disobedience is *fa'alogogatā*, literally, "hard to listen" (Mageo 1988, 44).

9. There are many terms used when referring to scolding, including *le'o lahi* (shout), *tafulu* (scold, growl), *kaila* (shout, scream), *'itangi* (scold), *ngaohi'i* or *ngāhi'i* (berate, abuse).

10. Variable factors in communicative accommodation include who is speaking to the child, the setting and the activity involved, and the child's age (Schieffelin and Ochs 1986b, 174).

11. Gallimore and Howard describe the way in which Hawaiian children's overtures to adults change over time, to become less intrusive (1969b, 14), as in Tonga.

CHAPTER 7: SANCTIONED VIOLENCE

1. Aggression and violence are distinct but overlapping phenomena. Violence is "the intentional rendering of physical hurt" (Riches 1986, 4), and aggression is violence, or threatened violence, motivated by hostile or angry feelings. This distinction allows for the fact that some violent behavior is not perceived as motivated by anger.

2. After death these souls resided in Pulotu, a mythical island to the west of Tonga (Collocott 1921a; Martin 1981, 312–314). *Tu'a*, Mariner claims, had no souls, "or such only as dissolve with the body after death" (Martin 1981, 299). Mariner adds that some *tu'a* "have the vanity to think they have immortal souls" (313). Lātūkefu states that *tu'a* were believed to turn into vermin at death (1975, 12). In Collocott's description of "the spirit" (*laumālie*, used today as soul or spirit) it is not clear if this belief is attributed to *hou'eiki* and/or *tu'a*.

3. These souls and beings are often referred to today as *tēvolo*, and *'Otua* is the term for the Christian God. Beliefs in the ability of *tēvolo* to intervene in human affairs persist.

4. Not all "miseries" were regarded as punishments, as there were *"Hotooa Pow"* (*'otua pau'u*, mischievous gods) who caused "petty evils and troubles, not as a punishment, but indiscriminately, from a pure mischievous disposition" (Martin 1981, 298). These troubles included leading travelers astray; tripping, pinching, and jumping on them; and causing bad dreams (305).

5. Appparently adults were also sacrificed (Beaglehole 1967, 917, 1049, 1308; Collocott 1921a, 158; Rowe 1976, 114). Samwell stated that chiefs would pay homage to the Tu'i Tonga at the time of the *'inasi* (firstfruits ceremony) by killing a number of their dependents in his presence by blows to the head with a club (Beaglehole 1967, 1049). Ferdon has speculated that the sacrifices of children to effect a cure for illness were originally carried out using adults and were intended to propitiate the gods and transfer the health and strength of the victim (1987, 150; see Collocott 1921a, 158). Cummins claims the last human sacrifice was in 1842 (1977, 239).

6. *Nima kū* appears to have been a common practice. Clerke, in 'Eua with Cook's expedition in 1773, claimed that "at least ¾ of them have only one; and at least ¼ neither, of their little Fingers" (in Beaglehole 1961, 758; also see Cook in Beaglehole 1961, 268 and Anderson in Beaglehole 1967, 947). The practice has also been referred to in the literature as *tootoo nima* (Martin 1981, 349), *to'o nima* (Kaeppler 1971b, 209), and *kau'inima* (Lātūkefu 1974, 8).

7. Some accounts were highly emotive and exaggerated. Farmer, for example, wrote that when people wanted to propitiate the gods they gave food offerings, "and sometimes their young children too; the first joint of whose little finger they pro-

ceeded to cut off. If that had already been presented, they cut off the second joint, and then the third; or if all the joints had been sacrificed on one hand they began with the other; and then they held up the bleeding hands in the hope of softening an angry god" (1976, 128).

8. Given the many examples of beatings and killings (not only by chiefs, but also by others, such as husbands to adulterous wives), it seems odd that Ferdon commented that "there is remarkably little in the early historic literature regarding the punishment employed in the control of Tongan society" (1987, 40).

9. Gifford (1971b, 183–185) and Lātūkefu (1975, 12) give details of the kinds of punishments dispensed by the hou'eiki and their kau tangata (strong men drawn from among the chiefs' attendants). It is difficult to assess the relationship between chiefs and commoners in the period before the emergence of the Tupou dynasty. It has been in the interests of the monarchy to emphasize the cruelty and tyranny inherent in the previous polity, and the church also has a vested interest in focusing on the negative features of the "unenlightened" past. In a careful assessment of the literature, Herda has concluded that only pōpula and hopoate (slaves) and kautu'avivi (low-born commoners) were regarded as of no account and treated cruelly. She argues that ordinary tu'a were related to chiefs and therefore their lives and welfare "were an emotional matter of considerable concern" (1988, 90).

10. The law specifies that these be administered using a cat-o'-nine-tails, but in practice a cane is used. Any whipping must be ordered or approved on review by the cabinet and is administered by the chief jailer or district jailer in the presence of a magistrate (Law of Tonga 1967, Cap. 15, section 32).

11. The Statistical Abstract of 1993 provides no comparable figures.

12. Some of the Ritchies' informants claimed that physical punishment was not traditional in Maori childrearing (1989, 130), and this has also been argued by Schwimmer (1964 cited in Fergusson, Fleming, and O'Neill 1972, 149). A similar claim has been made for Hawai'i (Grimshaw 1989, 37; Pukui 1942, 377) and Samoa (Leacock 1987, 182). However, Mageo disagrees with Leacock and suggests that the physical punishment of children in Samoa "is a practice of long duration" (cited in Caton 1990, 298). Firth's account of Tikopia indicates that physical punishment was seldom used and was not harsh (1970). Clearly, any generalization about Polynesia as a whole is problematic, and the dearth of information about socialization during the precontact and early contact period, for all of the island groups, makes it impossible to disentangle the threads of tradition from more recent influences.

13. For accounts of the treatment of children in Euro-American history, see Aries 1962; Breiner 1990; de Mause 1976; Greven 1973; Hardyment 1983; Hunt 1970; Miller 1985, 1987; Miller and Swanson 1958.

14. Many examples can be given of Biblical justifications for child beating: "Thou shalt beat him with the rod, and shalt deliver his soul from hell"; "He that spareth the rod hateth his son: but he that loveth him chasteneth him betimes"; "Chasten thy son while there is hope, and let not thy soul spare for his crying"; "Foolishness is bound in the heart of a child, but the rod of correction shall drive it far from him" (Proverbs 13:24; 19:18; 22:15; 23:14).

15. For persistent crying during teething a *faito'o* (healer) may be called in to *tafa nifo*, cut the baby's gum.

16. Harkness and Super (1983) have argued that cultures divide human development into stages, the timing of which varies cross-culturally, as do the kinds of developmental issues regarded as primary to each stage. For some ethnographic examples see Hamilton 1981; Kirkpatrick 1983; Martini and Kirkpatrick 1981; Poole 1985. In Tonga the more general stages are simply *pēpē* (infant), *tamasi'i* (child), and *talavou* and *finemui* (late adolescent). The stages in learning to walk are also used to indicate development (sitting up, crawling, and so on).

17. Gifford recorded that mothers would attempt to quiet fretful babies by telling them that Faingaa and Sisi, two deities trapped beneath the sea, would come to get them (1971a, 200). Churchward states that *pīnō nō* and *palepalengākau* (bogeys, demons) and *nifoloa* (a long-toothed demon or giant) were also used as threats to frighten children into obedience (1959, 411).

18. The Ritchies' claim that in Polynesia "nobody bothered" to train children under two and that punishment is not usually used during the transition to "yard child" (1981, 189–190) clearly does not apply to the Tongan case.

19. Spillius reported that the children of *hou'eiki* are punished less frequently than others because "only the parents and the *mehikitanga* [sic] feel really free to punish children of high rank" (1958, 63).

20. The Beagleholes claimed that it was rare for men to hit children and said "the whippings and beatings are women's work" (1941b, 82). My own research did not support this claim.

21. The judge "said he was unable to conclude that the 10 strokes inflicted upon a nine year old boy for persistent misconduct is excessive. 'It might be abroad, but not in Tonga!' " (*Matangi Tonga* 1992b, 32).

22. The same sound is made to babies during episodes of playful smacking.

23. Freeman 1983 and Gerber 1975 have stated that the expected response to punishment in Western Samoa is to sit, cross-legged and submissive. Beating a seated child, usually with a belt, as in Samoa, was described by a Tongan doctor as "like a traditional punishment" in Tonga, but I did not hear any other reference to it and certainly did not witness it. In fact children who attempt to sit down are usually told to stand.

24. *'Oi* is an interjection (as in "Oh!"), *au* means "me/myself," and *ē* adds emphasis, so roughly translated *'oiauē* means "Oh my!"

25. *Tā vale* is similar to the concept of *hana'ino* (mistreat or mishandle) in Hawai'i (Korbin 1990). However, *hana'ino* covers a broader category of actions.

26. Although I made it clear to the people I knew in Tonga that I did not personally support the use of physical punishment and resisted the pressure on me to physically discipline my own son, I only directly intervened on one occasion. I did so because I felt involved: My little neighbor, Folau, was being beaten because he had untruthfully blamed his older cousin for stealing a package of my cookies. My son had told the cousin of this, and he and another cousin began to beat Folau. I called to them to stop, but they ignored me. Then, when Folau's mother appeared, I cried

out to her to stop them, that I didn't care about the cookies, and she spoke to them quietly. They stopped and laughed about the incident, but over the next hour or so I heard Folau cry four or five times as they occasionally hit, threatened, or teased him because he had both stolen and lied. There were many other occasions when I thought of intervening, but as an unrelated person, outside the status system, I was not in a position to do so. My intervention might have shamed the people involved, or caused them to react, depending on the circumstances, with anger, derision, or amusement.

27. Changing household for any reason is seldom a matter of choice for young people, especially females, as parental permission is usually required (see Cowling 1990c, 104).

28. A "child" is a person under fourteen and a "young person" is aged between fourteen and sixteen for the purposes of this law. Apart from the inexact nature of the term "unnecessary suffering," the wording of this law is also problematic in the lower age limit given for offenders. Because children under sixteen are often responsible for disciplining other children, the possibility of serious abuse exists without recourse in the law.

29. There is also underreporting of child sexual abuse, which the Ministry of Police recognizes as an increasing problem (Report of the Minister of Police for 1987, 80). Only ten cases of indecent assault of a child under twelve (Law of Tonga 1967, Cap. 15, section 115) were reported for 1985–1987. Sexual assault in general is underreported, and the police admit that those cases reported are "part of a much more extensive and worrying hidden aspect of sexual abuse" (Report of the Minister of Police for 1986, 79).

30. "Western" is used here for convenience, but each country has its own definition of "child abuse" encoded in law and enacted in the practices of social workers and other officials, as well as a range of definitions within popular culture (see Doek 1991).

31. There exists a vast body of literature on child abuse in "the West," encompassing greatly different perspectives and conclusions. A recent text that usefully summarizes this literature is Corby 1993.

32. There are important exceptions such as Raum's Chaga Childhood, which gives a detailed and thoughtful account of punishment (1967, 225–231).

33. For examples of this research see Korbin 1981a, 1990, 1991; Scheper-Hughes 1987b; and many contributions to Child Abuse and Neglect: The International Journal. Much of this work focuses on the more dramatic and/or life-threatening forms of maltreatment, but for an exception see Freeman on "the darker side of Samoan life" (1983, 278), including the harsh punishment of children.

34. Scheper-Hughes (1987a, 7) warns of the dangers of presenting pessimistic and overstated accounts of this darker side of parenting. To avoid this bias it is important to examine issues such as punishment within the broader context of childhood.

35. Ralston has stated that for precontact Tonga "there is little evidence of physical or domestic violence against women. Given their place of importance as sisters

one cannot imagine that women would have remained in abusive marital relationships" (1990a, 112). Because women have retained much of their importance as sisters, yet do frequently remain in abusive relationships, it appears that other factors are operating.

36. Rape as domestic violence is rarely discussed. Under Tongan law a man cannot be charged with the rape of his wife "under any circumstances" (*Law of Tonga* 1967, Cap. 15, section 109).

37. Levy has argued for Tahiti that physical punishment is used to encourage nonaggression and that Tahitian socialization encourages timid, gentle behavior (1978). He does not address the question of physical punishment itself as aggressive behavior. Other studies of "nonviolent" societies have also neglected this issue (e.g., Montagu 1978). On the other hand, the question of whether physical punishment in childhood necessarily leads to aggressiveness in adulthood remains unresolved in the child development and child abuse literature (e.g., Mussen et al. 1984, 175).

CHAPTER 8: THE SOCIALIZATION OF EMOTION

1. The ten "fundamental emotions" these theorists claim to exist are interest, joy, surprise, sadness, anger, disgust, contempt, fear, shame/sadness, and guilt (Izard and Buechler 1980, 168). See also the work of Ekman on universal facial expressions of emotion (Ekman 1974; Ekman, Friesen, and Ellsworth 1972).

2. Apart from biologically based arguments about the universality of emotions, there also exist existential factors to consider. Myers has argued that the existential situation of all people in a "sociomoral order" creates universality in a logical sense; he states that "the range and logical forms of emotions are universal in so far as they define or interpret the relationships of the subject (self) to the world" (1988, 591; and see Harris and Saarni 1989, 8 for a survey of similar claims about children's experiences). Many useful surveys of the various approaches to the study of emotion can be found; see, for example, Averill 1980a; Boucher 1979; Lutz and White 1986; Mesquita and Frijda 1992; Plutchik and Kellerman 1980; Scherer and Ekman 1984a, 1984b.

3. Work on the social bases of emotion has been carried out by philosophers (e.g., Solomon 1977); sociologists (e.g., Kemper 1978); cognitive theorists (e.g., Averill 1980a, 1982); developmental psychologists (e.g., Lewis and Saarni 1985a); and anthropologists, particularly ethnopsychologists (e.g., Lutz 1986, 1988).

4. Key texts in the study of the socialization of emotion include Brazelton 1983, Harkness and Kilbride 1983, Lewis and Saarni 1985a, Michalson and Lewis 1985, Plutchik and Kellerman 1983, Saarni and Harris 1989, Scherer and Ekman 1984b.

5. The pronoun system in Tongan is complex, with subjective and objective; definite and indefinite; inclusive and exclusive; and single, dual, and plural forms. Furthermore, each possessive pronoun has ordinary, emotional, and emphatic registers.

6. Parsons lists "bizarre talking, irrational anger, attacking family members, running away and hiding, crying out, swearing and hysteria (*āvea*), and greatly increased

strength" as symptoms of spirit possession and notes that in recent years the Department of Health has redefined such behavior as "psychiatric" and that this redefinition can transform an "acute but readily cured 'illness' " into a long-term psychiatric disturbance (1985, 95).

7. Another distressing life situation is dealing with the effects of modernization; Parsons has identified *lolo mai* as the associated illness (1984, 86). See also Cowling 1990a, 77; Parsons 1985, 99.

8. See White's analysis of the "disentangling discourse" used by A'ara speakers on Santa Isabel in the Solomon Islands, which "rhetorically transmutes 'anger' to 'sadness' " (1990, 63). Later in this chapter I show that in Tonga anger is also transformed into humor.

9. A leading Tongan doctor, however, ignored social causes and blamed personality disorders (Ranger 1990, 11; see Cowling 1990d). Analyses of the complex factors contributing to youth suicide in other Pacific societies can be found in Hezel 1987, 1989; Hezel, Rubinstein, and White 1985; Macpherson and Macpherson 1987; Norton 1988; Rubinstein 1987.

10. Hezel 1989 also found that the increase in suicides was accompanied by an increased rate of child abuse and neglect. Hezel's review has disturbing implications for Tonga because the rate of "modernization" in Tonga is escalating rapidly and the kingdom is now heading toward the middle of the "scale of transition."

11. Another form of speech that expresses anger is *talatuki* (cursing). Mariner gives an early account of curses (Martin 1981, 356).

12. Some research has shown that as well as re-cognition, this process involves emotional expressions (e.g., laughing) that actually alter emotional states through biological "feedback mechanisms" (Lewis and Saarni 1985b, 6). In other words, smiling and laughing can actually make one feel happier.

13. See Borofsky's 1987 account of competitive games and status rivalry on Pukapuka, where humor plays a similar role. Marcus notes that "the ups and downs of relative status resulting from sequences of rivalry are . . . also a form of entertainment and amusement for Tongans" (1978, 256).

14. Analyses of related concepts of *hakā'ika* in the Marquesas (Kirkpatrick 1983, 113–115; 1985) and *ha'amā* in Tahiti (Levy 1972; 1973, 334–340) can usefully be compared with the concept of *mā* in Tonga. Analyses of the cultural construction of shame or embarrassment can also be found in many of the contributions to the 1983 *Ethos* issue on self and emotion (Levy 1983).

15. Bernstein has described in more detail the various forms of teasing: *fakahua* (friendly bantering or joking), *fakapangopango* (good-natured mocking), *manuki* (mocking and ridicule), and *fakamatalili* (teasing to provoke anger) (1983, 61–63). Another form, which she does not discuss is *luma* (taunting and ridicule); *luma* is closely associated with *fakamatalili*: both are intended to provoke an angry reaction.

16. In rare cases mental or physical impairments may be blamed on maltreatment by parents (see Spillius 1958, 63).

17. Another important form of parody is found in the behavior of the *fakaleitī*: see James 1994a.

18. It is interesting to note that in Samoan *soso* means "agitated," "silly," "demented," and "trickster" (Mageo 1989a, 198n39).

19. Because both *tau* and *langi* are polysemic, this phrase has multiple interpretations. Churchward translates it as "the singing [*langi*] has hit the mark [*tau*]" (1959, 282), meaning it is enthusiastic. The translation "reaching the sky" was suggested by the Tongan scholar 'Okusitino Māhina (personal communication).

20. The term *mate* (die, become unconscious) is also used in this sense, as well as for extreme fear, grief, and so on.

21. This movement had the political effect of uniting the support of the people of Ha'apai and Vava'u for Tupou I and the missionaries (Cummins 1979, 182).

22. Anderson, in Tonga with Cook, claimed that *tuki* was sometimes performed "in other distressing situations" (Beaglehole 1967, 907), but I have found no other references to this practice.

23. Mariner claimed that before his time in Tonga the chief widow of the Tu'i Tonga was strangled on his death (Martin 1981, 348), and Bott states that on the death of a great chief some of his mother's brother's children would be killed (Bott with Tavi 1982, 54). Neither gives further details.

24. These studies include the Rakau Maori studies of Beaglehole and Ritchie 1958, Earle 1958, James Ritchie 1963, and Jane Ritchie 1957. Although James Ritchie later admitted that "rejection" was an inappropriate term, this early interpretation influenced later work such as Crocombe 1973. The Beagleholes have given several accounts of this transition, for Pukapuku (1941a), the "Kowhai" Maori (1946), and Tonga (1941b). In regard to Tonga they claim that "from the age of eighteen months or so onwards, the children are thrown on their own resources" (1941b, 82). The age at which this transition period is said to occur in Polynesian societies varies significantly, between eighteen months and seven to eight years of age.

25. Levy suggested that the early indulgence of Tahitian children gave them a "strong core," helping them cope with later "frustrations and corrections" (1973, 459). He also argued that the encouragement of exhibitionist, aggressive behavior in infancy gave children "latent capabilities" for these behaviors in certain contexts in later life, helping to reduce the pressure for conformity and nonaggression experienced otherwise.

26. Other responses included success and reward (16.7 percent), religion (8.6 percent), getting something they wanted (5.7 percent), someone apologizing to them (4.8 percent), asking forgiveness, and being obedient (4.3 percent each).

27. Sleep is one of the "distancing mechanisms" Levy identified in the Tahitians' handling of negative emotions (1973, 495–498).

CHAPTER 9: BECOMING TONGAN

1. The recent political events in Tonga have led to a flurry of articles: see Campbell 1992a, 1994; Hau'ofa 1994; Hills 1991a, 1991b; James 1994b; Lawson 1994. The Tongan news magazine *Matangi Tonga* is an excellent source on political developments, with numerous interviews with key figures.

2. Bott suggested that "one reason for the *kāinga* putting up with cruelty [in pre-contact Tonga] was that the chief was the embodiment of themselves; if he was great, they were great; if he was a fool, they were fools" (Bott with Tavi 1982, 71).

3. It is interesting that the winning speech was published in the strongly conservative *Tonga Chronicle*, although this was one of the only news publications at the time. Since then the independent press has flourished in Tonga, with several publications strongly supporting the pro-democracy movement.

4. Tonga's constitution was amended on March 8, 1991, to allow for the naturalization of 426 foreigners (mostly Chinese) who had purchased Tongan passports in a highly controversial revenue-raising venture. This brought the question of Tongan identity into sharp focus and helped to make the broader issues of political reform a matter of much wider public concern.

5. One difference was that half as many boys as girls answered this and other questions at the end of the questionnaire. This difference largely reflected the different approaches of males and females to the exercise, with the latter taking the questionnaire more seriously, writing longer responses, yet also completing the questionnaire in the allotted time.

6. In a survey of Tongan migrants living in Sydney, Australia, Faiva found that the majority preferred the stricter discipline of "the Tongan way" and felt that *pālangi* children "appear to have too much freedom" (1989, 41).

7. I was unable to obtain figures for earlier years, but people I spoke with, including police, insisted that gang rape was previously very rare.

8. See Perminow's 1993 account of *'apitanga* (evangelist meetings at which youth are exhorted against the dangers of alcohol). Perminow argues that alcohol is used as a metaphor for the general dangers to young people's morality through exposure to urban (Westernized) life.

9. In 1995 I began research with Tongan migrants in Melbourne, Australia, funded by a University of Melbourne Research Fellowship. This work, intended to be the beginning of a long-term study of Tongan migrants, focuses on transformations in concepts of cultural identity and tradition in the context of migration, from the perspective of child socialization.

GLOSSARY

'alu   to go

anga   nature, behavior, way of being

anga fakafefine   female nature and behavior

anga fakapālangi   the Western way

anga fakatangata   male nature and behavior

anga fakatonga   the Tongan way, Tongan tradition and culture

anga lelei   nice, good nature and behavior, well-behaved, kind

'api   household compound, land allotments

'api kolo   village allotment, used for dwellings

'āvanga   spirit-caused illness

ē   particle used to add emphasis to speech, usually spoken with a questioning tone

'eiki   chief, person of chiefly rank

fa'a   often (preposed)

fa'ē   mother (includes mother's sisters)

fa'ē tangata   "male mother" (i.e., mother's brother; also *tu'asina*)

fahu   person who is superior in a ritual context (often, but not always, the child of one's *mehekitanga*)

faingofua   easy, comfortable

fa'iteliha   to do as one pleases

faito'o   healer, to heal

faka   pertaining to, like, causing (prefix)

faka'apa'apa   respect, show deference to

faka'ehi'ehi   to avoid, avoidance

fakafotu   the children of a woman's brother

fakahela   tiring, causing tiredness

fakahoha'a   troublesome, to cause trouble

fakalakalaka   progress, development (from *laka*: march)

fakaleitī   "like a lady" (i.e., male effeminates; also *fakafāfine*)

fakalongolongo   silence, to remain quiet

fakama'uma'u   to be restrained, to keep in one's feelings

fakamolemole   please, sorry, to apologize

faka'ofa   pitiable, unfortunate

fakapikopiko   to be lazy

fakapōpula'i   to enslave, to force

fakasosiale   social night, school dance

fāmili   general term for relatives, often used now to indicate nuclear family or kin maintaining close ties (from "family")

fānau   children

fatongia   duty, obligation

fe'ofa'aki   to have *'ofa* for one another

fe'ofo'ofani   to be friendly with one another

fie   to want, to imagine oneself to be, with connotation of pretension (prefix or pre-posed)

fiefia   to be happy

fie lahi   wanting to be "big"; thinking oneself important

fie poto   to show off, think oneself clever

fie 'eiki   to act inappropriately in a chiefly manner, to be arrogant

finemui   females between about fourteen and early twenties

fono   public meeting

fonua   land, country, island, people, placenta

hou'eiki   chiefly people (plural of *'eiki*)

'ilamutu   man's sister's children

'ita   anger, to be angry

kāinga   relative, extended family

ko au   it is I, I am (response to having one's name called)

koka'anga   meeting to make and dye tapa

koloa   valuables, wealth (particularly fine mats and decorated bark cloth)

kovi   bad, wrong

kui   grandparents

lahi   big, older, senior

longo   to be quiet, silent

loto   inside, heart, mind, site of subjectivity and will

loto lelei   good, nice heart and mind, agreeable, willing

loto mamahi   hurt feelings, sad, upset, inwardly angry

mā   to be embarrassed, ashamed

māfana   warm, warmth

mālie   bravo, good

mamahi   physical and/or mental pain, to be sorry or sorrowful (can have a connotation of anger)

mana   sacred power, associated with chiefs and the gods

matāpule   minor chief or chief's attendant and spokesman

mā'uli   traditional midwives

mehekitanga   father's sister

mohe   to sleep

mo'ui   life, way of life

ngatu   decorated bark cloth (tapa)

ngāue   work, to work

nofo   to stay, to sit, way of living

'ofa   love, concern, compassion, generosity

ongo'i   to feel, to perceive, to hear

pālangi (previously *papālangi*)   Westerners, Europeans

pau'u   mischievous, naughty

pele   favorite child

pēpē   from "baby"

pēpē 'i loto   "baby inside" (i.e., fetus)

poto   clever, socially competent, capable

pule   authority

pusiaki   fosterage, adoption

si'i   little; as an emotional article can mean poor, dear, etc.

tā or *taa'i*   to hit (also *pā*)

ta'ahine   girl

talangata'a   disobedient, disobedience

talangofua   obedient, obedience (literally, easy to tell)

talavou   males between about fourteen and early twenties

tama   child

tamai   father (includes father's brothers)

tamasi'i   boy

tapu   restrictions, prohibitions

tau'atāina   freedom, independence

tauhi   helper, to help, to care for

tau ō?   shall we go?

tā vale   to hit foolishly

te u taa'i koe   I'll hit you

tēvolo   "devil," spirit, ghost

tokanga   to look after, supervise, pay attention to, notice

tokoni   to help

totonu   right, correct, proper

tu'a   commoner, back, outside

tuku e tangi   stop crying

tutu   beating bark for bark cloth

'ulungāanga   characteristic behavior or nature

'uma   "kiss" (pressing the nose to another's cheek with a sharp intake of breath)

'umu   underground oven using heated rocks

vale   foolish, ignorant, socially incompetent, crazy

BIBLIOGRAPHY

Abu-Lughod, L., and C. Lutz.

1990.   "Introduction: Emotion, discourse, and the politics of everyday life." In *Language and the politics of emotion*, ed. C. Lutz and L. Abu-Lughod, 1–23. Cambridge: Cambridge University Press.

Afeaki, E.

1983.   "Tonga: The last Pacific kingdom." In *Politics in Polynesia*, ed. R. Crocombe and A. Ali, 56–78. Fiji: Institute of Pacific Studies, University of the South Pacific.

Afeaki, S.

1975.   "Permanent migration from Tonga." In *Land and migration*, ed. S. Fonua, 62–72. Papers presented at a seminar sponsored by the Tonga Council of Churches, Nuku'alofa: Tonga Council of Churches.

Ahlburg, D.

1991.   *Remittances and their impact: A study of Tonga and Western Samoa*. Pacific policy paper, no. 7. Canberra: National Centre for Development Studies, Research School of Pacific Studies, Australian National University.

Aoyagi, M.

1966.   "Kinship organisation and behaviour in a contemporary Tongan village." *Journal of the Polynesian Society* 75, no. 2:141–176.

Aries, P.

1962.   *Centuries of childhood: A social history of family life*. New York: Vintage Books.

Averill, J.

1980a.   "A constructivist view of emotion." In *Emotion: Theory, research, and experience*, ed. R. Plutchik and H. Kellerman. Vol. 1: *Theories of emotion*, 305–340. New York: Academic Press.

1980b.   "The emotions." In *Personality: Basic aspects and current research*, ed. E. Staub, 134–199. Englewood Cliffs, N.J.: Prentice-Hall.

1982.   *Anger and aggression: An essay on emotion*. New York: Springer-Verlag.

Babadzan, A.

1988.   "Kastom and nation-building in the South Pacific." In *Ethnicities and nations: Processes of interethnic relations in Latin America, Southeast Asia, and the Pacific*, ed. R. Guidieri, F. Pellizzi, and S. Tambiah, 199–228. Austin: University of Texas Press.

Bain, K.

1967.   *The Friendly Islanders: A story of Queen Salote and her people*. London: Hodder and Staughton.

Baker, P., J. Hanna, and T. Baker, eds.
1986.   *The changing Samoans: Behavior and health in transition.* New York: Oxford University Press.

Baker, T.
1986.   "Changing socialization patterns." In *The changing Samoans: Behavior and health in transition,* ed. P. Baker, J. Hanna, and T. Baker, 146–173. New York: Oxford University Press.

Bakker, M.
1979.   *A demographic analysis of the population of Tonga, 1777–1975.* South Pacific Commission occasional paper, no. 14. Noumea: South Pacific Commission.

Barlow, K.
1985.   "Learning cultural meanings through social relationships: An ethnography of childhood in Murik society, Papua New Guinea." Ph.D. diss., University of California, San Diego.

Barnouw, V.
1963.   *Culture and personality.* Homewood, Ill.: Dorsey.

Battaglia, D.
1990.   *On the bones of the serpent: Person, memory, and mortality in Sabarl Island society.* Chicago: University of Chicago Press.

Beaglehole, E.
1938–   Tongan field journal. Microfilm in Australian National University Menzies
1939.   Library, PMB994.
1940.   "Psychic stress in a Tongan village." *Proceedings of the Sixth Pacific Science Congress of the Pacific Science Association* 4:43–52.

Beaglehole, E. , and J. Ritchie.
1958.   "The Rakau Maori studies." *Journal of the Polynesian Society* 67, no. 2:132–154.

Beaglehole, E., and P. Beaglehole.
1941a. "Personality development in Pukapukan children." In *Language, culture, and personality: Essays in memory of Edward Sapir,* ed. L. Spier, A. Hallowell, and S. Newman, 282–298. Menasha, Wisc.: Sapir Memorial Publication Fund.
1941b. *Pangai: A village in Tonga.* Wellington: Polynesian Society.
1946.   *Some modern Maoris.* Christchurch: New Zealand Council for Education Research.

Beaglehole, J. C. ed.
1961.   *The journals of Captain James Cook on his voyages of discovery.* Vol. 2. Cambridge: Cambridge University Press.
1967.   *The journals of Captain James Cook on his voyages of discovery.* Vol. 3, parts 1 and 2. Cambridge: Cambridge University Press.

Bell, R.
1977a. "Socialization findings re-examined." In R. Bell and L. Harper, *Child effects on adults,* 53–84. Hillsdale, N.J.: Lawrence Erlbaum Associates.

1977b. "History of the child's influence: Medieval to modern times." In R. Bell and L. Harper, *Child effects on adults*, 30–42. Hillsdale, N.J.: Lawrence Erlbaum Associates.

Benguigui, G.

1989. "The middle classes in Tonga." *Journal of Pacific Studies* 98, no. 4:451–463.

Bergeron, G.

n.d. "History of Tonga." Ms., 1–45. Catholic Archives, Nuku'alofa, Tonga, Box 10D.1.

Bernstein, L.

1983. "*Ko e lau pē* (it's just talk): Ambiguity and informal social control in a Tongan village." Ph.D. diss., University of California, Berkeley.

Biersack, A.

1974. "Matrilaterality in patrilineal systems: The Tongan case." Typed ms. held by the Menzies Library, Australian National University.

1982. "Tongan exchange structures—beyond descent and alliance." *Journal of the Polynesian Society* 91, no. 2:181–212.

1990a. "Under the Toa tree: The genealogy of the Tongan chiefs." In *Culture and history in Tonga*, ed. J. Siikala, 80–105. Transactions of the Finnish Anthropological Society, no. 27. Helsinki: The Finnish Anthropological Society.

1990b. "How Tonga kept its independence: Or, the origin of an unsteady state." Paper presented to departmental seminar. Department of Anthropology, Research School of Pacific Studies, Australian National University, August 29.

1990c. "Blood and garland: Duality in Tongan history." In *Tongan culture and history: Papers from the First Tongan History Conference held in Canberra 14–17 January 1987*, ed. P. Herda, J. Terrell, and N. Gunson, 46–58. Canberra: Department of Pacific and Southeast Asian History, Research School of Pacific Studies, Australian National University.

Bollard, A.

1974. "The impact of monetization on Tonga." Master's thesis, University of Auckland.

Borofsky, R.

1987. *Making history: Pukapukan and anthropological constructions of knowledge.* Cambridge: Cambridge University Press.

Bott, E.

1972. "Psychoanalysis and ceremony." In *The interpretation of ritual: Essays in honour of A. I. Richards*, ed. J. La Fontaine, 205–237. London: Tavistock.

1981. "Power and rank in the kingdom of Tonga." *Journal of the Polynesian Society* 90, no. 1:7–81.

n.d. "H.M. Queen Sālote on Tongan traditions." Bott-Spillius Papers, Manuscripts and Archives Collection, New Zealand and Pacific Collection, Auckland University Library, New Zealand, Box 11, Folder 6.

Bott, E., with the assistance of Tavi.
1982.   *Tongan society at the time of Captain Cook's visits: Discussions with Her Majesty Queen Sālote Tupou.* Wellington: Polynesian Society.

Boucher, J.
1979.   "Culture and emotion." In *Perspectives on cross-cultural psychology,* ed. A. Marsella, R. Tharp, and T. Ciborowski, 159–178. New York: Academic Press.

Brady, T., ed.
1976.   *Transactions in kinship: Adoption and fosterage in Oceania.* ASAO monograph, no. 4. Honolulu: University Press of Hawai'i.

Brazelton, T.
1983.   "Precursors for the development of emotions in early infancy." In *Emotion: Theory, research, and experience,* ed. R. Plutchik and H. Kellerman. Vol. 2: *Emotions in early development,* 35–56. New York: Academic Press.

Breiner, S.
1990.   *Slaughter of the innocents: Child abuse through the ages and today.* New York: Plenum.

Brenneis, D.
1990.   "Shared and solitary sentiments: The discourse of friendship, play, and anger in Bhatgaon." In *Language and the politics of emotion,* ed. C. Lutz and L. Abu-Lughod, 113–125. Cambridge: Cambridge University Press.

Briggs, J.
1970.   *Never in anger: Portrait of an Eskimo family.* Cambridge: Harvard University Press.

Bugental, D.
1985.   "Unresponsive children and powerless adults: Co-creators of affectively uncertain caregiving environments." In *The socialization of emotions,* ed. M. Lewis and C. Saarni, 239–261. New York: Plenum.

Butler, B., and D. Turner, eds.
1987.   *Children and anthropological research.* New York: Plenum.

Campbell, I.
1992a.   "The emergence of parliamentary politics in Tonga." *Pacific Studies* 15, no. 1:77–97.

1992b.   "A historical perspective on aid and dependency: The example of Tonga." *Pacific Studies* 15, no. 3:59–75.

1992c.   *Island kingdom: Tonga ancient and modern.* Christchurch: Canterbury University Press.

1994.   "The doctrine of accountability and the unchanging locus of power in Tonga." *Journal of Pacific History* 29, no. 1:81–94.

Carroll, V., ed.
1970.   *Adoption in eastern Oceania.* ASAO monograph, no. 1. Honolulu: University of Hawai'i Press.

Cassell, J., ed.
1987.   *Children in the field: Anthropological experiences.* Philadelphia: Temple University Press.

Caton, H., ed.

1990. *The Samoa reader: Anthropologists take stock*. Lanham, N.Y.: University Press of America.

Census of Population and Housing.

1976. Vol. 1: Administrative report and tables. Nuku'alofa, Tonga: Government Printer.

Central Planning Department.

1981. *Fourth Five-year Development Plan, 1980–1985*. Nuku'alofa, Tonga: Government Printer.

1987. *Fifth Five-year Development Plan, 1986–1990*. Nuku'alofa, Tonga: Government Printer.

1991. *Sixth Five-year Development Plan, 1991–1995*. Nuku'alofa, Tonga: Government Printer.

Churchward, C.

1959. *Tongan-English dictionary*. Tonga: Government Printer.

1985. [original 1953]. *Tongan grammar*. Tonga: Vava'u Press.

Clifford, J., and G. Marcus, eds.

1986. *Writing culture: The poetics and politics of ethnography*. Berkeley: University of California Press.

Collocott, E.

1921a. "Notes on Tongan religion." *Journal of the Polynesian Society* 30, no. 119:152–163, no. 120:227–240.

1921b. "The supernatural in Tonga." *American Anthropologist* 23, no. 4:415–444.

1923a. "Sickness, ghosts, and medicine in Tonga." *Journal of the Polynesian Society* 32, no. 127:136–142.

1923b. "Marriage in Tonga." *Journal of the Polynesian Society* 32, no. 128:221–228.

1928. *Tales and poems of Tonga*. Bernice P. Bishop Museum bulletin, no. 46. Honolulu: Bishop Museum Press.

Collocott, E., and J. Havea.

1922. *Proverbial sayings of the Tongans*. Bernice P. Bishop Museum occasional papers, no. 8, 3. Honolulu: Bishop Museum Press.

Cook-Gumperz, J., and W. Corsaro.

1986. "Introduction." In *Children's worlds and children's language*, ed. J. Cook-Gumperz, W. Corsaro, and J. Streek, 1–11. Berlin: Mouton de Gruyter.

Cook-Gumperz, J., W. Corsaro, and J. Streek, eds.

1986. *Children's worlds and children's language*. Berlin: Mouton de Gruyter.

Corby, Brian.

1993. *Child abuse: Towards a knowledge base*. Buckingham: Open University Press.

Coult, A.

1959. "Tongan authority structure: Concepts for comparative analysis." *Kroeber Anthropological Society Papers* 20:56–70.

Cowling, W.

1990a. "Eclectic elements in Tongan folk belief and healing practice." In *Tongan culture and history: Papers from the First Tongan History Conference held in*

Canberra 14–17 January 1987, ed. P. Herda, J. Terrell, and N. Gunson, 72–92. Canberra: Department of Pacific and Southeast Asian History, Research School of Pacific Studies, Australian National University.

1990b. "Motivations for contemporary Tongan migration." In *Tongan culture and history: Papers from the First Tongan History Conference held in Canberra 14–17 January 1987*, ed. P. Herda, J. Terrell, and N. Gunson, 187–205. Canberra: Department of Pacific and Southeast Asian History, Research School of Pacific Studies, Australian National University.

1990c. "On being Tongan: Responses to concepts of tradition." Ph.D. diss. Macquarie University, Sydney, Australia.

1990d. "Mental illness is not the only cause of suicides in Tonga." *Matangi Tonga* 5, no. 6:38–40.

Cummins, H.

1977. "School and society in Tonga, 1826–1854: A study of Wesleyan mission schools, with special emphasis upon curriculum content and its influence on political and social development." Master's thesis, Australian National University.

1979. "Holy war: Peter Dillon and the 1837 massacres in Tonga." *Essays from the Journal of Pacific History*, comp. B. MacDonald, 177–191. Canberra: Australian National University.

1980. "Missionary chieftain: James Egan Moulton and Tongan society, 1865–1909." Ph.D. diss., Australian National University.

————, ed.

1972. "Sources of Tongan history: A collection of documents, extracts, and contemporary opinions in Tongan political history, 1616–1900." Ms. held in Pacific Records Room, Department of Pacific and Southeast Asian History, Research School of Pacific Studies, Australian National University.

Cyclopaedia of Tonga.

1907. Sydney: McCarron and Stewart.

D'Andrade, R.

1984. "Cultural meaning systems." In *Culture theory: Essays on mind, self, and emotion*, ed. R. Shweder and R. LeVine, 88–119. Cambridge: Cambridge University Press.

Davis-Floyd, R.

1988. "Birth as an American rite of passage." In *Childbirth in America: Anthropological perspectives*, ed. K. Michaelson, 153–172. South Hadley, Mass.: Bergin and Garvey.

de Bres, J.

1974. *How Tonga aids New Zealand: A report on migration and education*. Wellington: South Pacific Action Network and Citizens Association for Racial Equality.

Decktor Korn, S.

1974. "Tongan kin groups: The noble and the common view." *Journal of the Polynesian Society* 83, no. 1:5–13.

1975. "Household composition in the Tonga Islands: A question of options and alternatives." *Journal of Anthropological Research* 31, no. 3:237–259.

1977. "To please oneself: Local organization in the Tonga Islands." Ph.D. diss. Washington University, Missouri.

1978a. "After the missionaries came: Denominational diversity in the Tonga Islands." In *Mission, church, and sect in Oceania.* ed. J. Boutilier, D. Hughes, and S. Tiffany, 395–422. ASAO monograph, no. 6. Ann Arbor: University of Michigan Press.

1978b. "Hunting the ramage: Kinship and the organization of political authority in aboriginal Tonga." *Journal of Pacific History* 13, no. 1:107–113.

de Mause, L., ed.

1976. *The history of childhood.* London: Souvenir Press.

Doek, J.

1991. "Management of child abuse and neglect at the international level: Trends and perspectives." *Child Abuse and Neglect: The International Journal* 15, no. 1:51–56.

Draguns, J.

1979. "Culture and personality." In *Perspectives on cross-cultural psychology,* ed. A. Marsella, R. Tharp, and T. Ciborowski, 179–207. New York: Academic Press.

Dubanoski, R.

1982. "Child maltreatment in European- and Hawaiian-Americans." *Child Abuse and Neglect: The International Journal* 5, no. 4:457–465.

Dubanoski, R., and K. Snyder.

1980. "Patterns of child abuse and neglect in Japanese- and Samoan-Americans." *Child Abuse and Neglect: The International Journal* 4, no. 4:217–225.

Earle, M.

1958. *Rakau children from six to thirteen years.* Wellington: Victoria University Press.

Ekman, P.

1974. "Universal facial expressions of emotion." In *Culture and personality: Contemporary readings,* ed. R. LeVine, 8–15. Chicago: Aldine.

Ekman, P., W. Friesen, and P. Ellsworth.

1972. *Emotion in the human face: Guidelines for research and an integration of findings.* New York: Pergamon.

Englberger, L.

1983. *Review of past food and nutrition surveys in Tonga.* Nuku'alofa: Central Planning Department.

Ennew, J.

1986. *The sexual exploitation of children.* Cambridge: Polity Press.

Ewing, K.

1990. "The illusion of wholeness: Culture, self, and the experience of inconsistency." *Ethos* 18, no. 3:251–278.

1991. "Can psychoanalytic theories explain the Pakistani woman? Intrapsychic autonomy and interpersonal engagement in the extended family." *Ethos* 19, no. 2:131–160.

Faiva, 'O.
1989.   *The Tongans in Manly-Warringah: A community survey*. Manly, Australia: Health Promotion Unit, Manly Hospital and Community Services.

Faletau, M.
1982.   "Changing roles for Tonga's women." *Pacific Perspective* 11, no. 2:45–55.

Farmer, S.
1976.   [original 1855]. *Tonga and the Friendly Islands*. Canberra: Kalia.

Feinberg, R.
1990.   "What's so funny about that? Fieldwork and laughter in Polynesia." In *The humbled anthropologist: Tales from the Pacific* ed. P. De Vita, 53–60. Wadsworth modern anthropology library. Belmont, Calif.: Wadsworth.

Feldman, H.
1981.   "*Kapekape*: Contexts of malediction in Tonga." *Maledicta* 5:143–150.

Ferdon, E.
1987.   *Early Tonga as the explorers saw it, 1616–1810*. Tucson: University of Arizona Press.

Fergusson, D., J. Fleming, and D. O'Neill.
1972.   *Child abuse in New Zealand*. Wellington: Government Printer.

Fiefia, N.
1981.   "Education in Tonga." Ms. held in Basilica Library, Nuku'alofa, Tonga.

Fifita, S.
1975.   "Problems of the land: People's view." In *Land and migration*, ed. S. Fonua 31–42. Papers presented at a seminar sponsored by the Tonga Council of Churches, Nuku'alofa: Tonga Council of Churches.

Finau, S.
1979.   "Marriage and family life in Tonga: Strategies to strengthen marriages and family life in Tongan villages through the Free Wesleyan Church of Tonga." Project for D.Min., School of Theology, Claremont, Calif.

Firth, R.
1970.   [original 1936]. *We, the Tikopia: A study of kinship in primitive Polynesia*. Boston: Beacon.

Fleming, S., with M. Tuku'afu.
1986.   *Women's work and development in Tonga*. University of New England Smallholder Project, occasional paper, no. 10. Armidale, Australia: University of New England.

Fogelson, R.
1982.   "Person, self, and identity: Some anthropological retrospects, circumspects, and prospects." In *Psychosocial theories of the self*, ed. B. Lee with K. Smith, 67–109. New York: Plenum.

Fonua, P.
1988.   "Tonga's eating problems." *Matangi Tonga* 3, no. 1:14–15.
1992.   "Death at Vaiola." *Matangi Tonga* 7, no. 3:10–18.

Freeman, D.

1983. *Margaret Mead and Samoa: The making and unmaking of an anthropological myth.* Canberra: Australian National University Press.

Gailey, C.

1980. "Putting down sisters and wives: Tongan women and colonization." In *Women and colonization: Anthropological perspectives*, ed. M. Etienne and E. Leacock, 294–322. New York: Praeger.

1981. "Our history is written . . . in our mats: State formation and the status of women in Tonga." Ph.D. diss., New School for Social Research, New York. Available through University Microfilms, Ann Arbor, Mich.

1987a. "State, class, and conversion in commodity production: Gender and changing values in the Tongan Islands." *Journal of the Polynesian Society* 96, no. 1:67–79.

1987b. *Kinship to kingship: Gender hierarchy and state formation in the Tongan Islands.* Austin: University of Texas Press.

1987c. "Culture wars: Resistance to state formation." In *Power relations and state formation*, ed. T. Patterson and C. Gailey, 35–56. Washington, D.C.: American Anthropological Association.

1992. "A good man is hard to find: Overseas migration and the decentered family in the Tongan Islands." *Critique of Anthropology* 12, no. 1:47–74.

Gallimore, R., J. Boggs, and C. Jordan.

1974. *Culture, behavior and education: A study of Hawaiian-Americans.* Beverley Hills, Calif.: Sage.

Gallimore, R., and A. Howard, eds.

1969a. *Studies in a Hawaiian community: Na makamaka o Nanakuli.* Pacific anthropological records, no. 1. Honolulu: Bernice P. Bishop Museum.

1969b. "Hawaiian lifestyle." In *Studies in a Hawaiian community: Na makamaka o Nanakuli*, ed. R. Gallimore and A. Howard, 10–16. Pacific anthropological records, no. 1. Honolulu: Bernice P. Bishop Museum.

Gautier, K.

1977. "What one calls discipline another calls abuse." In *Samoans in Hawaii: Selected readings*, ed. N. Young, 51–53. Honolulu: General Assistance Center for the Pacific College of Education, University of Hawai'i.

Gerber, E.

1975. "The cultural patterning of emotions in Samoa." Ph.D. diss., University of California, San Diego.

1985. "Rage and obligation: Samoan emotion in conflict." In *Person, self, and experience: Exploring Pacific ethnopsychologies*, ed. G. White and J. Kirkpatrick, 121–167. Berkeley: University of California Press.

Gergen, K.

1985. "Social constructionist inquiry: Context and implications." In *The social construction of the person*, ed. K. Gergen and K. Davis, 3–18. New York: Springer-Verlag.

Gergen, K., and K. Davis, eds.
1985. *The social construction of the person*. New York: Springer-Verlag.

Gifford, E. W.
1971a. [original 1924]. *Tongan myths and tales*. Bernice P. Bishop Museum bulletin, no. 8. Honolulu. New York: Kraus Reprint.
1971b. [original 1929]. *Tongan society*. Bernice P. Bishop Museum bulletin, no. 61. Honolulu. New York: Kraus Reprint.

Gladwin, T.
1961. "Oceania." In *Psychological anthropology: Approaches to culture and personality*, ed. F. Hsu, 135–171. Homewood, Ill.: Dorsey.

Goodnow, J., and J. Cashmore.
1982. "Culture and performance." Paper presented at the annual meeting of the Jean Piaget Society, Philadelphia. June.

Gordon, T.
1990. "Inventing the Morman Tongan family." In *Christianity in Oceania: Ethnographic perspectives*, ed. J. Barker, ASAO monograph, no. 12:197–219. Lanham, N.Y.: University Press of America.

Greven, P.
1973. *Childrearing concepts, 1628–1861: Historical sources*. Itasca, Ill.: Peacock.

Grijp, P. van der
1993. *Islanders of the south: Production, kinship, and ideology in the Polynesian kingdom of Tonga*. Leiden: Koninklijk Instituut voor Taal-, Land- en Volkenkunde Press.

Grimshaw, P.
1989. "New England missionary wives, Hawaiian women, and 'The cult of true womanhood'." In *Family and gender in the Pacific: Domestic contradictions and the colonial impact*, ed. M. Jolly and M. Macintyre, 19–44. Cambridge: Cambridge University Press.

Gunson, N.
1990. "The Tonga-Samoa connection, 1777–1845: Some observations on the nature of Tongan imperialism." *Journal of Pacific History* 25, no. 2: 176–187.

Haberkorn, G.
1981. "Education and migration in the Kingdom of Tonga." Development Studies Centre Seminar. Ms. held in University of the South Pacific library, Tonga campus. 3 September.

Halatuituia, L., S. Latu, and M. Moimoi.
1982. "Women's co-operatives in Tonga." *Pacific Perspective* 11, no. 2:13–17.

Hallowell, A.
1955. *Culture and experience*. Philadelphia: University of Pennsylvania Press.

Hamilton, A.
1981. *Nature and nurture: Aboriginal child-rearing in north-central Arnhem Land*. Canberra: Australian Institute of Aboriginal Studies.

Hammond, J.
1988. "Visualizing themselves: Tongan videography in Utah." *Visual Anthropology* 1, no. 4:379–400.

Handelman, D.
1983. "Shaping bureaucratic reality: Dialectic and disjunction in the bureaucratic synthesis of child-abuse in urban Newfoundland." *Social Analysis* 13:3–36.

Hanson, F. A.
1982. "Female pollution in Polynesia?" *Journal of the Polynesian Society* 91, no. 3:335–381.
1989. "The making of the Maori: Culture invention and its logic." *American Anthropologist* 91, no. 4:890–902.

Hardyment, C.
1983. *Dream babies: Childcare from Locke to Spock*. London: Jonathan Cape.

Harkness, S.
1992. "Human development in psychological anthropology." In *New directions in psychological anthropology*, ed. T. Schwartz, G. White, and C. Lutz, 102–122. Cambridge: Cambridge University Press.

Harkness, S., and C. Super.
1983. "The cultural construction of child development." *Ethos* 11, no. 4:221–231.

Harkness, S., and P. Kilbride.
1983. "Introduction: The socialization of affect." *Ethos* 11, no. 4:215–220.

Harre, R., ed.
1986. *The social construction of emotions*. Oxford: Basil Blackwell.

Harris, G.
1989. "Concepts of individual, self, and person in description and analysis." *American Anthropologist* 91, no. 3:599–612.

Harris, P., and C. Saarni.
1989. "Children's understanding of emotion: An introduction." In *Children's understanding of emotion*, ed. C. Saarni and P. Harris, 3–24. Cambridge: Cambridge University Press.

Hau'ofa, E.
1977. *Our crowded islands*. Suva: Institute of Pacific Studies, University of the South Pacific.
1978. "The pangs of transition: Kinship and economy in Tonga." *Australian and New Zealand Journal of Sociology* 14, no. 2:160–165.
1994. "Thy kingdom come: The democratization of aristocratic Tonga." *Contemporary Pacific* 6, no. 2:414–427.

Heelas, P.
1986. "Emotion talk across cultures." In *The social construction of emotions*, ed. R. Harre, 234–266. Oxford: Basil Blackwell.

Heelas, P., and A. Lock, eds.
1981. *Indigenous psychologies: The anthropology of the self*. London: Academic Press.

Helu, F.
1983.   "Thinking in Tongan society." In *Thinking: The expanding frontier*, ed.
        W. Maxwell, 43–56. Philadelphia: Franklin Institute Press.
1991.   "Tonga and the chosen ones." *Pacific Islands Monthly* 61, no. 2:5.

Herda, P.
1987.   "Gender, rank, and power in eighteenth-century Tonga." *Journal of Pacific
        History* 22, no. 4:195–208.
1988.   "The transformation of the traditional Tongan polity: A genealogical con-
        sideration of Tonga's past." Ph.D. diss., Australian National University.

Herda, P., J. Terrell, and N. Gunson, eds.
1990.   *Tongan culture and history: Papers from the First Tongan History Conference held
        in Canberra 14–17 January 1987*. Canberra: Department of Pacific and
        Southeast Asian History, Research School of Pacific Studies, Australian
        National University.

Hereniko, V.
1992.   "When she reigns supreme: Clowning and culture in Rotuman weddings." In
        Clowning as critical practice: Performance humor in the South Pacific, ed.
        W. Mitchell, 167–191. Pittsburgh: University of Pittsburgh Press.
1994.   "Clowning as political commentary: Polynesia, then and now." *Contempo-
        rary Pacific* 6, no. 1:1–28.

Hezel, F.
1987.   "In search of the social roots of mental pathology in Micronesia." In *Con-
        temporary issues in mental health research in the Pacific Islands*, ed. A. Robillard
        and A. Marsella, 12–31. Honolulu: Social Science Research Institute, Uni-
        versity of Hawai'i.
1989.   "Suicide and the Micronesian family." *Contemporary Pacific* 1, nos. 1 and
        2:43–74.

Hezel, F., D. Rubinstein, and G. White, eds.
1985.   *Culture, youth, and suicide in the Pacific: Papers from an East-West Center con-
        ference*. Honolulu: East-West Center.

Hills, R.
1991a. "The 1990 election in Tonga." *Contemporary Pacific* 3, no. 2:357–378.
1991b. *Tonga's constitution and the changing state*. Regime change and regime mainte-
        nance in Asia and the Pacific discussion paper, no. 4. Canberra: Department
        of Political and Social Change, Australian National University.

Hollan, D.
1992.   "Cross-cultural differences in the self." *Journal of Anthropological Research* 48,
        no. 4:283–300.

Holland, D., and J. Valsiner.
1988.   "Cognition, symbols, and Vygotsky's developmental psychology." *Ethos* 16,
        no. 3:247–272.

Holland, D., and N. Quinn, eds.
1987.   *Cultural models in language and thought*. Cambridge: Cambridge University
        Press.

Hosea, C.
1987.   "Who is to be blamed?" *Tonga Today* 1, no. 4:26.

Howard, A.
1970.   *Learning to be Rotuman*. New York: Teachers College Press.
1974.   *Ain't no big thing: Coping strategies in a Hawaiian-American community*. Honolulu: University Press of Hawai'i.
1985a. "Ethnopsychology and the prospects for a cultural psychology." In *Person, self, and experience: Exploring Pacific ethnopsychologies*, ed. G. White and J. Kirkpatrick, 401–420. Berkeley: University of California Press.
1985b. "Review of J. Kirkpatrick's *The Marquesan notion of the person*." *American Anthropologist* 87, no. 2:430–431.

Howard, A., and J. Kirkpatrick.
1989.   "Social Organization." In *Developments in Polynesian ethnology*, ed. A. Howard and R. Borofsky, 47–93. Honolulu: University of Hawai'i Press.

Howard, A., R. Heighton, C. Jordon, and R. Gallimore.
1970.   "Traditional and modern adoption patterns in Hawaii." In *Adoption in eastern Oceania*, ed. V. Carroll, 21–51. ASAO monograph, no. 1. Honolulu: University of Hawai'i Press.

Hsu, F., ed.
1961.   *Psychological anthropology: Approaches to culture and personality*. Homewood, Ill.: Dorsey.
1972.   *Psychological anthropology*. New ed. Cambridge: Schenkman.

Hunt, D.
1970.   *Parents and children in history: The psychology of family life in early modern France*. New York: Basic Books.

Huntsman, J., and A. Hooper.
1975.   "Male and female in Tokelau culture." *Journal of the Polynesian Society* 84, no. 4:415–430.

Hurrelmann, K.
1988.   *Social structure and personality development: The individual as a productive processor of reality*. Cambridge: Cambridge University Press.

Ikahihifo, T., and M. Panuve.
1983.   *Report of a preliminary study of traditional medicine and practices in relation to obstetrical and gynaecological conditions and disorders amongst two communities in Tonga*. Suva: Centre for Applied Studies in Development, University of the South Pacific.

Ito, K.
1987.   "Emotions, proper behavior (*hana pono*), and Hawaiian concepts of self, person, and individual." In *Contemporary issues in mental health research in the Pacific islands*, ed. A. Robillard and A. Marsella, 45–63. Honolulu: Social Science Research Institute, University of Hawai'i.

Izard, C.
1972.   *Patterns of emotions: A new analysis of anxiety and depression*. New York: Academic Press.

1977.   *Human emotions*. New York: Plenum.
1982.   *Measuring emotions in infants and children*. Cambridge: Cambridge University Press.
1983.   "Emotions in personality and culture." *Ethos* 11, no. 4:305–312.

Izard, C., and S. Beuchler.
1980.   "Aspects of consciousness and personality in terms of differential emotions theory." In *Emotion: Theory, research, and experience*, ed. R. Plutchik and H. Kellerman. Vol. 1: *Theories of emotion*, 165–187. New York: Academic Press.

Jahoda, G.
1982.   *Psychology and anthropology: A psychological perspective*. London: Academic Press.

Jahoda, G., and I. Lewis, eds.
1988.   *Acquiring culture: Cross-cultural studies in child development*. New York: Croom Helm.

James, K.
1983.   "Gender relations in Tonga, 1780–1984." *Journal of Polynesian Studies* 92, no. 2:233–243.
1987.   "Gender relations in Tonga: A paradigm shift." Paper presented to the first Tongan History Workshop, Australian National University. 14–18 January.
1988.   "O, lead us not into 'commoditisation': Christine Ward Gailey's changing gender values in the Tongan Islands." *Journal of the Polynesian Society* 97, no. 1:31–47.
1990.   "Gender relations in Tonga: A paradigm shift." In *Tongan culture and history: Papers from the First Tongan History Conference held in Canberra 14–17 January 1987*, ed. P. Herda, J. Terrell, and N. Gunson, 93–100. Canberra: Department of Pacific and Southeast Asian History, Research School of Pacific Studies, Australian National University.
1991a. "Migration and remittances: A Tongan village perspective." *Pacific Viewpoint* 32, no. 1:1–23.
1991b. "The female presence in heavenly places: Myth and sovereignty in Tonga." *Oceania* 61, no. 4:285–308.
1992.   "Tongan rank revisited: Religious hierarchy, social stratification, and gender in the ancient Tonga polity." *Social Analysis* 31:79–102.
1993.   "Cutting the ground from under them? Commercialization, cultivation, and conservation in Tonga." *Contemporary Pacific* 5, no. 2:215–242.
1994a. "Effeminate males and changes in the construction of gender in Tonga." *Pacific Studies* 17:39–69.
1994b. "Tonga's pro-democracy movement." *Pacific Affairs* 67, no. 2:242–263.

Jolly, M., and M. Macintyre, eds.
1989a. *Family and gender in the Pacific: Domestic contradictions and the colonial impact*. Cambridge: Cambridge University Press.

Jolly, M., and N. Thomas, eds.
1992.   "The politics of tradition in the Pacific. " *Oceania* 64, no. 4. Special issue.

Jordan, C., R. Gallimore, B. Sloggett, and E. Kubany.
1969.   "The family and the school." In *Studies in a Hawaiian community: Na maka-maka o Nanakuli*, ed. R. Gallimore and A. Howard, 55–63. Pacific anthropological records, no. 1. Honolulu: Bernice P. Bishop Museum.

Kadushin, A., and J. Martin.
1981.   *Child abuse: An interactional event*. New York: Columbia University Press.

Kaeppler, A.
1971a.   "Rank in Tonga." *Ethnology* 10, no. 2:174–193.
1971b.   "Eighteenth-century Tonga: New interpretations of Tongan society and material culture at the time of Captain Cook." *Man* 6, no. 2:204–220.
1978a.   "Exchange patterns in goods and spouses: Fiji, Tonga, and Samoa." *Mankind* 11, no. 3:246–252.
1978b.   "Me'a faka'eiki: Tongan funerals in a changing society." In *The changing Pacific: Essays in honour of H. E Maude*, ed. N. Gunson, 174–202. Melbourne: Oxford University Press.
1978c.   "Melody, drone, and decoration: Underlying structures and surface manifestations in Tongan art and society." In *Art in society: Studies in style, culture, and aesthetics*, ed. M. Greenhalgh and V. Megaw, 261–274. London: Duckworth.
1985.   "Structured movement systems in Tonga." In *Society and the dance: The social anthropology of process and performance*, ed. P. Spencer, 92–118. Cambridge: Cambridge University Press.
1993.   "Poetics and politics of Tongan laments and eulogies." *American Ethnologist* 20, no. 3:474–501.

Kaho, T.
1988.   *Songs of love*. Tonga: Vava'u Press.

Kavaliku, S.
1977.   " 'Ofa! The treasure of Tonga." *Pacific Perspective* 6, no. 2:47–67.

Keeler, W.
1983.   "Shame and stage fright in Java." *Ethos* 11, no. 3:152–165.

Keene, D.
1978.   "Houses without walls: Samoan social control." Ph.D. diss., University of Hawai'i, Honolulu.

Keesing, R.
1987.   "Models, 'folk' and 'cultural': Paradigms regained?" In *Cultural models in language and thought*, ed. D. Holland and N. Quinn, 369–393. Cambridge: Cambridge University Press.
1989.   "Creating the past: Custom and identity in the contemporary Pacific." *Contemporary Pacific* 1, nos. 1 and 2:19–42.

Keesing, R., and R. Tonkinson, eds.
1982.   "Reinventing traditional culture: The politics of kastam in island Melanesia." *Mankind* 13, no. 4. Special issue.

Kemper, T.
1978.   *A social interactional theory of emotions*. New York: Wiley.

Kinloch, P.
1985.   "Midwives and midwifery in Western Samoa." In *Healing practices in the South Pacific*, ed. C. Parsons, 199–212. Honolulu: Institute for Polynesian Studies.
Kirch, P.
1984.   *The evolution of the Polynesian kingdoms*. Cambridge: Cambridge University Press.
Kirkpatrick, J.
1983.   *The Marquesan notion of the person*. Michigan: University of Michigan Research Press.
1985.   "Some Marquesan understandings of action." In *Person, self, and experience: Exploring Pacific ethnopsychologies*, ed. J. Kirkpatrick and G. White, 80–120. Berkeley: University of California Press.
Kirkpatrick, J., and G. White.
1985.   "Exploring ethnopsychologies." In *Person, self, and experience: Exploring Pacific ethnopsychologies*, ed. G. White and J. Kirkpatrick, 3–32. Berkeley: University of California Press.
Kolo, F.
1990.   "Historiography: The myth of indigenous authenticity." In *Tongan culture and history: Papers from the First Tongan History Conference held in Canberra 14–17 January 1987*, ed. P. Herda, J. Terrell, and N. Gunson, 1–11. Canberra: Department of Pacific and Southeast Asian History, Research School of Pacific Studies, Australian National University.
Korbin, J., ed.
1981a.   *Child abuse and neglect: Cross-cultural perspectives*. Berkeley: University of California Press.
1981b.   "Introduction" and "Conclusion." In *Child abuse and neglect: Cross-cultural perspectives*, ed. J. Korbin, 1–12, 205–210. Berkeley: University of California Press.
1990.   "*Hana ʻino*: Child maltreatment in a Hawaiian-American community." *Pacific Studies* 13, no. 3:7–22.
1991.   "Cross-cultural perspectives and research directions for the twenty-first century." *Child Abuse and Neglect: The International Journal* 15, no. 1: 67–78.
Koskinen, A.
1968.   *Kite: Polynesian insights into knowledge*. Annals of the Finnish Society for Missiology and Ecumenics, no. 14. Helsinki: The Finnish Society for Missiology and Ecumenics.
Kövecses, Z.
1990.   *Emotion concepts*. New York: Springer-Verlag.
Kulick, D.
1990.   "Having head and showing knowledge: Language shift, Christianity, and notions of self in a Papua New Guinea village." Ph.D diss., Department of Social Anthropology, Stockholm University.

La Fontaine, J.

1986. "An anthropological perspective on children in social worlds." In *Children of social worlds: Development in a social context*, ed. M. Richards and P. Light, 10–30. Cambridge: Polity.

Lakoff, G., and Z. Kövecses.

1987. "The cognitive model of anger inherent in American English." In *Cultural models in language and thought*, ed. D. Holland and N. Quinn, 195–221. Cambridge: Cambridge University Press.

Lātūkefu, S.

1974. *Church and state in Tonga: The Wesleyan Methodist missionaries and political development, 1822–1875*. Canberra: Australian National University Press.

1975. *The Tongan constitution: A brief history to celebrate its centenary*. Nukuʻalofa: Tongan Traditions Committee.

1980. "The definition of authentic Oceanic cultures with particular reference to Tongan culture." *Pacific Studies* 4, no. 1:60–81.

Law of Tonga, The.

1967. Rev. ed. with amendments to 1985. Nukuʻalofa: Government Printer.

Lawry, W.

1850. *Friendly and Feejee Islands: A missionary visit to various stations in the South Seas, in the year 1847*. 2d ed. London: John Mason.

1852. *Missions in the Tonga and Feejee Islands*. New York: Lane and Scott.

Lawson, S.

1993. "The politics of tradition: Problems for political legitimacy and democracy in the South Pacific." *Pacific Studies* 16, no. 2:1–29.

1994. *Tradition versus democracy in the kingdom of Tonga*. Regime change and regime maintenance in Asia and the Pacific discussion paper, no. 13. Canberra: Department of Political and Social Change, Australian National University.

Leacock, E.

1987. "The problems of youths in contemporary Samoa." In *Quest for the real Samoa: The Mead/Freeman controversy and beyond*, ed. L. Holmes, 177–188. South Hadley, Mass.: Bergin and Garvey.

Leiderman, P., S. Tulkin, and A. Rosenfeld, eds.

1977. *Culture and infancy: Variations in the human experience*. New York: Academic Press.

LeVine, R.

1973. *Culture, behavior, and personality*. Chicago: Aldine.

1974. *Culture and personality: Contemporary readings*. Chicago: Aldine.

1980. "Anthropology and child development." In *Anthropological perspectives on child development*, ed. C. Super and S. Harkness, 71–80. New directions for child development, no. 8. San Francisco: Jossey-Bass.

Levy, R.

1969a. *Personality studies in Polynesia and Micronesia: Stability and change*. Honolulu: Social Science Research Insititute, University of Hawaiʻi.

1969b. "On getting angry in the Society Islands." In *Mental health research in Asia and the Pacific*, ed. W. Caudill and T. Lin, 358–380. Honolulu: East-West Center.

1969c. "Child management structure in Tahitian families." *Journal of the Polynesian Society* 78, no. 1:35–43.

1970.   "Tahitian adoption as a psychological message." In *Adoption in eastern Oceania*, ed. V. Carroll, 71–87. Honolulu: University of Hawai'i Press.

1972.   "Tahiti, sin, and the question of integration between personality and socio-cultural systems." *Psychoanalytic Study of Society* 5:83–108.

1973.   "Tahitians: Mind and experience in the Society Islands." Chicago: University of Chicago Press.

1978.   "Tahitian gentleness and redundant controls." In *Learning non-aggression: The experience of non-literate societies*, ed. A. Montagu, 222–235. New York: Oxford University Press.

Levy, R., ed.
1983.   "Self and emotion." *Ethos* 11, no. 3. Special issue.

Lewis, M., and L. Rosenblum, eds.
1974.   *The effect of the infant on its caregiver.* New York: Wiley.

Lewis, M., and C. Saarni, eds.
1985a. *The socialization of emotions.* New York: Plenum.

1985b. "Culture and emotions." In *The socialization of emotions*, ed. M. Lewis and C. Saarni, 1–17. New York: Plenum.

Lindstrom, L.
1990.   *Knowledge and power in a South Pacific society.* Washington, D.C.: Smithsonian Institution Press.

Linnekin, J.
1980.   "Children of the land: Exchange and status in a Hawaiian community." Ph.D. diss., University of Michigan.

1983.   "Defining tradition: Variations on the Hawaiian identity." *American Ethnologist* 10, no. 2:241–252.

1990a. *Sacred queens and women of consequence: Rank, gender, and colonialism in the Hawaiian Islands.* Ann Arbor: University of Michigan Press.

1990b. "The politics of culture in the Pacific." In *Cultural identity and ethnicity in the Pacific*, ed. J. Linnekin and L. Poyer 149–173. Honolulu: University of Hawai'i Press.

Linnekin, J., and L. Poyer, eds.
1990a. *Cultural identity and ethnicity in the Pacific.* Honolulu: University of Hawai'i Press.

1990b. "Introduction." In *Cultural identity and ethnicity in the Pacific*, ed. J. Linnekin and L. Poyer, 1–16. Honolulu: University of Hawai'i Press.

Lovett, I.
1958.   "A study of Tongan children with special attention given to the pre-adolescent age group." Dip. Ed. Auckland University.

Lua, K.
1987.   "Migration into Haveluloto, Nuku'alofa." In *In search of a home*, ed.
         L. Mason and P. Hereniko, 123–128. Suva: Institute of Pacific Studies, Uni-
         versity of the South Pacific.
Lutz, C.
1983.   "Parental goals, ethnopsychology, and the development of emotional mean-
         ing." *Ethos* 11, no. 4:246–262.
1985.   "Ethnopsychology compared to what? Explaining behavior and conscious-
         ness among the Ifaluk." In *Person, self, and experience: Exploring Pacific eth-
         nopsychologies*, ed. G. White and J. Kirkpatrick, 35–79. Berkeley: University
         of California Press.
1986.   "Emotion, thought, and estrangement: Emotion as a cultural category." *Cul-
         tural Anthropology* 1, no. 3:287–309.
1988.   *Unnatural emotions: Everday sentiments on a Micronesian atoll and their chal-
         lenge to Western theory*. Chicago: University of Chicago Press.
Lutz, C., and G. White.
1986.   "The anthropology of emotions." *Annual Review of Anthropology* 15:405–436.
MacKay, M.
n.d.   "Tonga and the Friendly Islands." Microfilm RM338, Pacific Records Room,
         Department of Pacific and Southeast Asian History, Research School of
         Pacific Studies, Australian National University.
Maclean, E., and J. Badcock.
1987.   *The 1986 National Nutritional Survey of the Kingdom of Tonga: Summary report
         prepared for the National Food and Nutrition Committee*. Nuku'alofa: Central
         Planning Department.
Macpherson, C., and L. Macpherson.
1987.   "Towards an explanation of recent trends of suicide in Western Samoa."
         Man 22, no. 2:305–330.
Mageo, J.
1988.   "*Mālosi*: A psychological exploration of Mead's and Freeman's work and of
         Samoan aggression." *Pacific Studies* 11, no. 2:25–65.
1989a.   "*Aga, amio,* and *loto*: Perspectives on the structure of the self in Samoa."
         Oceania 59, no. 3:181–199.
1989b.   " 'Ferocious is the centipede': A study of the significance of eating and
         speaking in Samoa." *Ethos* 17, no. 4:387–427.
Māhina, 'O.
1990.   "Myths and history: Some aspects of history in the Tu'i Tonga myths." In
         *Tongan culture and history: Papers from the First Tongan History Conference held
         in Canberra 14–17 January 1987*, ed. P. Herda, J. Terrell, and N. Gunson, 30–
         45. Canberra: Department of Pacific and Southeast Asian History, Research
         School of Pacific Studies, Australian National University.
1992.   "The Tongan traditional history *tala-e-fonua*: A vernacular ecology-centred
         historico-cultural concept." Ph.D. diss., Australian National University.

Marcus, G.
1974. "A hidden dimension of family development in the modern kingdom of Tonga." *Journal of Comparative Family Studies* 5, no. 1:87–102.
1975a. "The ancien regime in the modern kingdom of Tonga: Conflict and change among the nobility of a Polynesian constitutional monarchy." Ph.D. diss., Harvard University.
1975b. "Alternative social structures and the limits of hierarchy in the modern kingdom of Tonga." *Bijdragen Tot de Taal-, Land en Volkenkunde* 131:34–66.
1977. "Succession disputes and the position of the nobility in modern Tonga." *Oceania* 47, no. 3:220–241; 47, no. 4:284–299.
1978. "Status rivalry in a Polynesian steady-state society." *Ethos* 6, no. 4:242–269.
1979. "Elopement, kinship, and elite marriage in the contemporary kingdom of Tonga." *Journal de la Société des Oceanistes* 35, no. 63:83–96.
1980a. *The nobility and the chiefly tradition in the modern kingdom of Tonga.* Polynesian Society, memoir 42. Wellington: Polynesian Society.
1980b. "Role distance in conversations between Tongan nobles and their 'people'." *Journal of the Polynesian Society* 89, no. 4:435–453.
1981. "Power on the extreme periphery: The perspective of Tongan elites in the modern world system." *Pacific Viewpoint* 22, no. 1:48–64.
1988. "Parody and the parodic in Polynesian cultural history." *Cultural Anthropology* 3, no. 1:68–76.
1989. "Chieftainship." In *Developments in Polynesian ethnology*, ed. A. Howard and R. Borofsky, 175–209. Honolulu: University of Hawai'i Press.
1993. "Tonga's contemporary globalizing strategies: Trading on sovereignty amidst international migration." In *Contemporary Pacific societies: Studies in development and change*, ed. V. Lockwood, T. Harding, and B. Wallace, 21–33. Englewood Cliffs, N.J.: Prentice-Hall.
Marcus, G., and M. Fischer.
1986. *Anthropology as cultural critique: An experimental moment in the human sciences.* Chicago: University of Chicago Press.
Marshall, M., ed.
1983. *Siblingship in Oceania: Studies in the meaning of kin relations.* ASAO monograph, no. 8. Lanham, N.Y.: University Press of America.
Martin, J.
1981 [original 1817]. *Tonga Islands: William Mariner's account.* 4th ed. Vava'u: Vava'u Press.
Martini, M., and J. Kirkpatrick.
1981. "Early interactions in the Marquesas Islands." In *Culture and early interactions*, ed. T. Field, A. Sostek, P. Vietze and P. Leiderman, 189–213. New Jersey: Lawrence Erlbaum Associates.
Matangi Tonga.
1989a. "Down to the nitty-gritty on AIDS." 4, no. 2:4.
1989b. "Handicapped children need help now." 4, no. 2:37–38.

1989c. "Videos branded as villains." 4, no. 5:29–31.

1992a. "Let's talk about sex—baby." 7, 1:46.

1992b. "Boy hurt by teacher." 7, no. 5:32.

1992c. "A system that favours a few." 7, no. 1:13–14.

1992d. "Boy awarded $150 after police beating." 7, no. 2:41.

Maude, A.

1971. "Tonga: Equality overtaking privilege." In Land tenure in the Pacific, ed. R. Crocombe, 106–128. Melbourne: Oxford University Press.

1973. "Land shortage and population pressure in Tonga." In The Pacific in transition: Geographical perspectives on adaptation and change, ed. H. Brookfield, 163–185. Canberra: Australian National University Press.

Mayer, P.

1970. "Introduction." In Socialization: The approach from social anthropology, ed. P. Mayer, xiii–xxx. London: Tavistock.

McArthur, N.

1967. Island populations of the Pacific. Canberra: Australian National University Press.

McBride, A.

1982. "The American way of birth." In Anthropology of human birth, ed. M. Kay, 413–430. Philadelphia: Davis.

McMurray, C., and D. Lucas.

1990. Fertility and family planning in the South Pacific. Islands/Australia working paper, no. 90/10. Canberra: National Centre for Development Studies, Australian National University.

Mead, M.

1966 [original 1928]. Coming of age in Samoa: A study of adolescence and sex in primitive societies. Harmondsworth: Penguin.

Mead, M., and M. Wolfenstein, eds.

1955. Childhood in contemporary cultures. Chicago: University of Chicago Press.

Mesquita, B., and N. Frijda.

1992. "Cultural variations in emotions: A review." Psychological Bulletin 12, no. 3:179–204.

Michalson, L., and M. Lewis.

1985. "What do children know about emotions and when do they know it?" In The socialization of emotions, ed. M. Lewis and C. Saarni, 117–139. New York: Plenum.

Middleton, J., ed.

1970. From child to adult: Studies in the anthropology of education. New York: Natural History Press.

Miller, A.

1985. Thou shalt not be aware: Society's betrayal of the child. London: Pluto.

1987. For your own good: The roots of violence in child-rearing. London: Virago.

Miller, D., and G. Swanson.

1958. The changing American parent: A study in the Detroit area. New York: Wiley.

Miller, P., and B. Moore.
1989.   "Narrative conjunctions of caregiver and child: A comparative perspective on socialization through stories." *Ethos* 17, no. 4:428–449.

Miller, P., and L. Hoogstra.
1992.   "Language as tool in the socialization and apprehension of cultural meanings." In *New directions in psychological anthropology*, ed. T. Schwartz, G. White, and C. Lutz, 83–101. Cambridge: Cambridge University Press.

Miller, P., R. Potts, H. Fung, L. Hoogstra, and J. Mintz.
1990.   "Narrative practices and the social construction of the self." *American Ethnologist* 17, no. 2:292–311.

Minturn, L., and W. Lambert.
1964.   *Mothers of six cultures: Antecedents of child rearing.* New York: Wiley.

Moengangongo, M.
1988.   "Tonga." In *Pacific women: Roles and status of women in Pacific societies*, ed. T. Tongamoa, 58–74. Suva: Institute of Pacific Studies, University of the South Pacific.

Montagu, A., ed.
1978.   *Learning non-aggression: The experience of non-literate societies.* New York: Oxford University Press.

Morgan, C.
1985.   "Competing circuits in the Vava'u social economy." Ph.D. diss., Australian National University.

Morton, H.
1990.   "Missing persons: Children in the history of Tonga." Paper presented at the Fourth Tonga History Conference, Auckland, New Zealand, May. Ms. in author's possession.
1995.   "My 'chastity belt': Avoiding seduction in Tonga." In *Taboo: Sex, identity, and erotic subjectivity in anthropological fieldwork*, ed. D. Kulick and M. Willson, 168–185 London: Routledge.
n.d.   "Pregnancy and birth in Tonga." Ms. in author's possession.

Morton, J., and M. Macintyre, eds.
1995.   "Persons, bodies, selves, emotions." *Social Analysis* (special issue) 37.

Morton, K.
1972.   "Kinship, economics, and exchange in a Tongan village." Ph.D diss. University of Oregon.
1976.   "Tongan adoption." In *Transactions in kinship: Adoption and fosterage in Oceania*, ed. I. Brady, 64–80. ASAO monograph, no. 4. Honolulu: University Press of Hawai'i.
1987.   "The atomization of Tongan society." *Pacific Studies* 10, no. 2:47–72.

Moyle, R.
1987.   *Tongan music.* Auckland: Auckland University Press.

Mussen, P., J. Conger, J. Kagan, and A. Huston.
1984.   *Child development and personality.* 6th ed. New York: Harper and Row.

Myers, F.

1986. *Pintupi country, Pintupi self: Sentiment, place, and politics among western desert Aborigines*. Washington, D.C.: Smithsonian Institution Press.

1988. "The logic and meaning of anger among the Pintupi Aborigines." *Man* 23, no. 4:589–610.

Nayacakalou, R.

1959. "Land tenure and social organisation in Tonga." *Journal of the Polynesian Society* 68, no. 2:93–114.

Needs, A.

1988. *N.Z. aid and the development of class in Tonga*. Palmerston, N.Z.: Department of Sociology, Massey University, Palmerston North.

Neill, J.

1955. *Ten years in Tonga*. London: Hutchinson.

Niumeitolu, 'O.

1993. "Tongan health: A personal view." In *A world perspective on Pacific islander migration: Australia, New Zealand, and the U.S.A.*, ed. G. McCall and J. Connell, 71–81. Sydney: Centre for South Pacific Studies, University of New South Wales.

Norton, R.

1988. "Chiefs, adolescent suicide, and the transformation of chiefly authority in Western Samoa." *Man* 23, no. 4:759–760.

1993. "Culture and identity in the South Pacific: A comparative analysis." *Man* 28, no. 4:741–759.

Ochs, E.

1982. "Talking to children in Western Samoa." *Language in Society* 11:77–104.

1986a. "Introduction." In *Language socialization across cultures*, ed. B. Schieffelin and E. Ochs, 1–16. Cambridge: Cambridge University Press.

1986b. "From feelings to grammar: A Samoan case study." In *Language socialization across cultures*, ed. B. Schieffelin and E. Ochs, 251–272. Cambridge: Cambridge University Press.

1988. *Culture and language development: Language acquisition and language socialization in a Samoan village*. Cambridge: Cambridge University Press.

1990. "Indexicality and socialization." In *Cultural psychology: Essays on comparative human development*, ed. J. Stigler, R. Shweder, and G. Herdt, 287–308. Cambridge: Cambridge University Press.

Ochs, E., and B. Schieffelin.

1983. *Acquiring conversational competence*. London: Routledge and Kegan Paul.

1984. "Language acquisition and socialization: Three developmental stories and their implications." In *Culture theory: Essays on mind, self, and emotion*, ed. R. Shweder and R. LeVine, 276–320. Cambridge: Cambridge University Press.

Orange, J.
1840.   *Narrative of the late George Vason of Nottingham*. Derby: Henry Mozley and
         Sons.

Ortner, S.
1984.   "Theory in anthropology since the sixties." *Comparative Studies in Society and
         History* 26, no. 1:126–166.

Owens, C.
1985.   "The discourse of others: Feminists and postmodernists." In *Postmodern cul-
         ture*, ed. H. Foster, 57–82. London: Pluto.

Paongo, K.
1990.   "The nature of education in pre-European to modern Tonga." In *Tongan cul-
         ture and history: Papers from the First Tongan History Conference held in Can-
         berra 14–17 January 1987*, ed. P. Herda, J. Terrell, and N. Gunson, 134–144.
         Canberra: Department of Pacific and Southeast Asian History, Research
         School of Pacific Studies, Australian National University.

Parsons, C.
1983.   "Developments in the role of the Tongan healer." *Journal of the Polynesian
         Society* 92, no. 1:31–50.
1984.   "Idioms of distress: Kinship and sickness among the people of Tonga." *Cul-
         ture, Medicine, and Psychiatry* 8, no. 1:71–93.
1985.   "Tongan healing practices." In *Healing practices in the South Pacific*, ed.
         C. Parsons, 87–107. Laie, Hawai'i: Institute for Polynesian Studies.

Perminow, A.
1993.   *The long way home: Dilemmas of everyday life in a Tongan village*. Oslo: Scandi-
         navian University Press and the Institute for Comparative Research in
         Human Culture.

Perry, D., and K. Bussey.
1984.   *Social development*. Englewood Cliffs, N.J.: Prentice-Hall.

Plutchik, R., and H. Kellerman, eds.
1980.   *Emotion: Theory, research, and experience*. Vol. 1: *Theories of emotion*. New
         York: Academic Press.
1983.   *Emotion: Theory, research, and experience*. Vol. 2: *Emotions in early develop-
         ment*. New York: Academic Press.

Poole, F.
1985.   "Coming into social being: Cultural images of infants in Bimin-Kuskusmin
         folk psychology." In *Person, self, and experience: Exploring Pacific ethnopsychol-
         ogies*, ed. G. White and J. Kirkpatrick, 183–242. Berkeley: University of
         California Press.

Powles, G.
1990.   "The early accommodation of traditional and English law in Tonga." In
         *Tongan culture and history: Papers from the First Tongan History Conference held
         in Canberra 14–17 January 1987*, ed. P. Herda, J. Terrell, and N. Gunson,
         145–169. Canberra: Department of Pacific and Southeast Asian History,
         Research School of Pacific Studies, Australian National University.

Poyer, L.

1990. "Being Sapwuahfik: Cultural and ethnic identity in a Micronesian society." In *Cultural identity and ethnicity in the Pacific*, ed. J. Linnekin and L. Poyer, 127–147. Honolulu: University of Hawai'i Press.

Pukui, M.

1942. *Hawaiian beliefs and customs during birth, infancy, and childhood*. Bernice P. Bishop Museum occasional papers 16 no. 17. Honolulu: Bishop Museum Press.

Pulea, M.

1986. *The family, law, and population in the Pacific Islands*. Suva: Institute of Pacific Studies, University of the South Pacific.

Pulu, T., and M. Pope.

1979. *Childhood days in Tonga*. Laie, Hawai'i: Bilingual Education Services.

Ralston, C.

1988. "Polyandry, 'pollution', 'prostitution': The problems of Eurocentrism and androcentrism in Polynesian studies." In *Crossing boundaries: Feminisms and the critique of knowledge*, ed. B. Caine, E. Grosz, M. de Lepervanche, 71–80. Sydney: Allen and Unwin.

1990a. "Gender relations in Tonga at the time of contact." In *Tongan culture and history: Papers from the First Tongan History Conference held in Canberra 14–17 January 1987*, ed. P. Herda, J. Terrell, and N. Gunson, 110–17. Canberra: Department of Pacific and Southeast Asian History, Research School of Pacific Studies, Australian National University.

1990b. "Deceptive dichotomies: Private/public and nature/culture. Gender relations in Tonga in the early contact period." *Australian Feminist Studies* 12: 65–82.

1993. "Maori women and the politics of tradition: What roles and power did, do, and should Maori women exercise?" *Contemporary Pacific* 5, no. 1:23–44.

Ralston, C., and N. Thomas, eds.

1987. "Sanctity and power: Gender in Polynesian history." *Journal of Pacific History* 22, no. 3. Special issue.

Ranger, D.

1990. "Mental illness rises." *Matangi Tonga* 5, no. 5:10–11.

Raum, O.

1967 [original 1940]. *Chaga childhood: A description of indigenous education in an East African tribe*. London: Oxford University Press.

Reeson, M.

1985. *Currency lass*. Sutherland, Australia: Albatross Books.

Report of the Ministry of Education for the year 1987.

1988. Nuku'alofa: Government Printer.

Report of the Ministry of Health for the year 1986.

1987. Nuku'alofa: Government Printer.

Report of the Ministry of Health for the year 1987.

1988. Nuku'alofa: Government Printer.

Report of the Minister of Police for the year 1986.
1987.   Nuku'alofa: Government Printer.
Report of the Minister of Police for the year 1987.
1988.   Nuku'alofa: Government Printer.
Riches, D.
1986.   "The phenomenon of violence." In *The anthropology of violence*, ed. D. Riches, 1–27. Oxford: Basil Blackwell.
Ritchie, James.
1963.   *The making of a Maori: A case study of a changing community*. Wellington: A. H. and A. W. Reed.
Ritchie, Jane.
1957.   *Childhood in Rakau: The first five years of life*. Wellington: Victoria University Publications.
Ritchie, J., and J. Ritchie.
1970.   *Child-rearing patterns in New Zealand*. Wellington: A. H. and A. W. Reed.
1979.   *Growing up in Polynesia*. Sydney: George Allen and Unwin.
1981.   "Child rearing and child abuse: The Polynesian context." In *Child abuse and neglect: Cross-cultural perspectives*, ed. J. Korbin, 186–204. Berkeley: University of California Press.
1989.   "Socialization and character development." In *Developments in Polynesian ethnology*, ed. A. Howard and R. Borofsky, 95–135. Honolulu: University of Hawai'i Press.
Roberts, S.
1924.   *Tamai: The life story of Hartley Roberts of Tonga*. Sydney: Methodist Book Depot.
Rogers, G.
1977.   "The father's sister is black: A consideration of female rank and powers in Tonga." *Journal of the Polynesian Society* 86, no. 2:157–181.
Rorty, A., ed.
1980.   *Explaining emotions*. Berkeley: University of California Press.
Rosaldo, R.
1984.   "Grief and a headhunter's rage: On the cultural force of emotions." In *Text, play, and story: The construction and reconstruction of self and society*, ed. E. Bruner, 178–195. Washington, D.C.: American Ethnological Society.
Rowe, G.
1976   [original 1885]. *A pioneer: Memoir of the Reverend John Thomas, missionary to the Friendly Islands*. Canberra: Kalia.
Rubinstein, D.
1987.   "Cultural patterns and contagion: Epidemic suicide among Micronesian youth." In *Contemporary issues in mental health research in the Pacific Islands*, ed. A. Robillard and A. Marsella, 127–148. Honolulu: Social Science Research Institute, University of Hawai'i.
Rutherford, N., ed.
1977.   *Friendly Islands: A history of Tonga*. Melbourne: Oxford University Press.

Saarni, C., and P. Harris, eds.
1989. *Children's understanding of emotion*. Cambridge: Cambridge University Press.
St. Johnston, A.
1883. *Camping among the cannibals*. London: Macmillan.
Scheper-Hughes, N.
1987a. "The cultural politics of child survival." In *Child survival: Anthropological perspectives on the treatment and maltreatment of children*, ed. N. Scheper-Hughes, 1–29. Dordrecht: Reidel.
————, ed.
1987b. *Child survival: Anthropological perspectives on the treatment and maltreatment of children*. Dordrecht: Reidel.
Scheper-Hughes, N., and H. Stein.
1987. "Child abuse and the unconscious in American popular culture." In *Child survival: Anthropological perspectives on the treatment and maltreatment of children*, ed. N. Scheper-Hughes, 339–358. Dordrecht: Reidel.
Scherer, K., and P. Ekman.
1984a. "Developmental approaches." In *Approaches to emotion*, ed. K. Scherer and P. Ekman, 73–75. New Jersey: Lawrence Erlbaum Associates.
————, eds.
1984b. *Approaches to emotion*. New Jersey: Lawrence Erlbaum Associates.
Schieffelin, B.
1990. *The give and take of everyday life: Language socialization of Kaluli children*. Cambridge: Cambridge University Press.
Schieffelin, B., and E. Ochs, eds.
1986a. *Language socialization across cultures*. Cambridge: Cambridge University Press.
1986b. "Language socialization." *Annual Review of Anthropology* 15:163–246.
Schoeffel, P.
1979. "Daughters of Sina: A study of gender, status, and power in Western Samoa." Ph.D. diss., Australian National University.
Schwartz, T.
1981. "The acquisition of culture." *Ethos* 9, no. 1: 4–17.
Schwartzman, H.
1978. *Transformations: The anthropology of children's play*. New York: Plenum.
Sears, R., E. Maccoby, and H. Levin.
1957. *Patterns of child rearing*. New York: Harper and Row.
Sevele, F.
1973. "Regional inequalities in socio-economic development in Tonga: A preliminary study." Ph.D. diss., University of Canterbury, Christchurch, New Zealand.
Shineberg, D.
1978. " 'He can but die . . .': missionary medicine in pre-Christian Tonga." In *The changing Pacific: Essays in honour of H. E. Maude*, ed. N. Gunson, 285–296. Melbourne: Oxford University Press.

Shore, B.
1981.   "Sexuality and gender in Samoa: Conceptions and missed conceptions."
        In *Sexual meanings: The cultural construction of gender and sexuality*, ed.
        S. Ortner and B. Whitehead, 192–215. Cambridge: Cambridge University
        Press.
1982.   *Salaʻilua: A Samoan mystery*. New York: Columbia University Press.
1989.   "*Mana* and *tapu*." In *Developments in Polynesian ethnology*, ed. A. Howard
        and R. Borofsky, 137–173. Honolulu: University of Hawaiʻi Press.
1990.   "Human ambivalence and the structuring of moral values." *Ethos* 18, no.
        2:165–179.
Shumway, E.
1971.   *Intensive course in Tongan*. Honolulu: University of Hawaiʻi Press.
1987.   "Pornography: A time bomb in Tonga." *Tonga Today* 1, no. 6:10–16.
———, trans. and ed.
1991.   *Tongan saints: Legacy of faith*. Laie, Hawaiʻi: Institute for Polynesian Studies.
Shweder, R.
1979a. "Rethinking culture and personality theory part 1: A critical examination of
        two classical postulates." *Ethos* 7, no. 3:255–278.
1979b. "Rethinking culture and personality theory part 2: A critical examination of
        two more classical postulates." *Ethos* 7, no. 4:279–311.
1980.   "Rethinking culture and personality theory part 3: From genesis and typol-
        ogy to herneneutics and dynamics." *Ethos* 8, no. 1:60–94.
1991.   *Thinking through cultures: Expeditions in cultural psychology*. Cambridge: Har-
        vard University Press.
Shweder, R., and J. Miller.
1985.   "The social construction of the person: How is it possible?" In *The social
        construction of the person*, ed. K. Gergen and K. Davis, 41–69. New York:
        Springer-Verlag.
Sissons, J.
1993.   "The systematisation of tradition: Maori culture as a strategic resource."
        Oceania 64, no. 2:97–116.
Smith, J.
1981.   "Self and experience in Maori culture." In *Indigenous psychologies: The
        anthropology of the self*, ed. P. Heelas and A. Lock, 145–159. London:
        Academic Press.
Solomon, R.
1977.   *The passions: The myth and nature of human emotions*. New York: Anchor.
1984.   "The Jamesian theory of emotion in anthropology." In *Culture theory: Essays
        on mind, self, and emotion*, ed. R. Shweder and R. LeVine, 238–254. Cam-
        bridge: Cambridge University Press.
South Pacific Alliance for Family Health.
1991.   SPAFH Family Planning Service delivery assessment report. Nukuʻalofa:
        South Pacific Alliance for Family Health.

Spennemann, D.

1986.　"Sexual division of labour in Tonga during the Dark Ages: Some evidence from the 'Atele mounds, Tongatapu." *New Zealand Archaeological Association Newsletter* 29, no. 4:250–251.

1990.　"Changing gender roles in Tongan society: Some comments based on archaeological observations." In *Tongan culture and history: Papers from the First Tongan History Conference held in Canberra 14–17 January 1987*, ed. P. Herda, J. Terrell, and N. Gunson, 101–109. Canberra: Department of Pacific and Southeast Asian History, Research School of Pacific Studies, Australian National University.

Spillius [Bott], E.

1958.　"Report on brief study of mother-child relationships in Tonga." Typed ms. provided by the Central Planning Department, Nuku-'alofa, Tonga. [Published in 1960 by the World Health Organization, Geneva.]

Statistics Department.

1975.　*Statistical abstract*. Nuku'alofa: Government Printer.

1987.　*Population census 1986 bulletin*, no. 1. Nuku'alofa: Government Printer.

1991a.　*Population census 1986*. Nuku'alofa: Government Printer.

1991b.　*Population census 1986: Supplementary copy*. Nuku'alofa: Government Printer.

1993a.　*Statistical abstract*. Nuku'alofa: Government Printer.

1993b.　*Demographic analysis of 1986 census data: Fertility, mortality, and population projections*. Nuku'alofa: Government Printer.

Stigler, J., R. Shweder, and G. Herdt, eds.

1990.　*Cultural psychology: Essays on comparative human development*. Cambridge: Cambridge University Press.

Strathern, A.

1987.　"Review of G. White and J. Kirkpatrick, *Person, self, and experience: Exploring Pacific ethnopsychologies*." *Pacific Studies* 11, no. 1:157–162.

Strauss, C.

1984.　"Beyond 'formal' versus 'informal' education: Uses of psychological theory in anthropological research." *Ethos* 12, no. 3:195–222.

Takau, L., and L. Fungalei.

1987.　"Cyclone devastation and resettlement at Sopu, Nuku'alofa." In *In search of a home*, ed. L. Mason and P. Hereniko, 118–122. Suva: Institute of Pacific Studies, University of the South Pacific.

Taliai, 'O.

1989.　"Social differentiation of language levels in Tonga." M.A. diss., University of Auckland.

Taumoefolau, M.

1991.　"Is the father's sister really 'black'?" *Journal of the Polynesian Society* 100, no. 1:91–98.

Teilhet-Fisk, J.
1991.   "To beat or not to beat, that is the question: A study on acculturation and
         change in an art-making process and its relation to gender structures." *Pacific
         Studies* 14, no. 3:41–68.

Teu, A.
1978.   "Tongan communities in California." In *New neighbours: Islanders in adapta-
         tion*, ed. C. Macpherson, B. Shore, and R. Franco, 44–46. Santa Cruz:
         Center for South Pacific Studies, University of California.

Thomas, N.
1989.   *Out of time: History and evolution in anthropological discourse*. Cambridge:
         Cambridge University Press.
1990.   "Review of C. Gailey, *Kinship to kingship: Gender hierarchy and state formation
         in the Tongan Islands*." *Oceania* 61, no. 2:197–199.

Thomson, B.
1894.   *The diversions of a prime minister: Life in the Friendly Islands, 1887–1891*.
         Edinburgh: William Blackwood and Sons.

Thorne, B.
1987.   "Re-visioning women and social change: Where are the children?" *Gender
         and Society* 1, no. 1:85–109.

Throsby, C.
1987.   "Human resources development in the Pacific: Background and overview."
         In *Human resources development in the Pacific*, ed. C. Throsby, 3–21. Pacific
         policy papers, no. 3. Canberra: National Centre for Development Studies,
         Australian National University.

Times of Tonga.
1991.   "People's opinion: What do you think is the most important political change
         needed?" April 11:4.

Tonga Chronicle.
1986a.   "In court: Mother murders infant, receives imprisonment." December 12:2.
1986b.   "25 club feet surgically corrected." December 12:3–4.
1988.   "*Popoaki talamonu.*" August 5:10.
1989.   "Village boy hangs self." January 6:2.

Tonga Today.
1987a.   "Question of corporal punishment in schools." 1, no. 3:35.
1987b.   "Editorial: Is Tonga a free nation?" 1, no. 3:1–2.

Toren, C.
1988.   "Making the present, revealing the past: The mutability and continuity of
         tradition as a process." *Man* 23, no. 34:696–717.
1990.   *Making sense of hierarchy: Cognition as social process in Fiji*. London: Athlone.
1993.   "Making history: The significance of childhood cognition for a comparative
         anthropology of mind." *Man* 28, no. 461–478.

Tu'inukuafe, E.
1990.   "Tongans in New Zealand—a brief study." In *Tongan culture and history:
         Papers from the First Tongan History Conference held in Canberra 14–17 Janu-*

ary 1987, ed. P. Herda, J. Terrell, and N. Gunson, 206–214. Canberra: Department of Pacific and Southeast Asian History, Research School of Pacific Studies, Australian National University.

Tu'itani, S.
1986. "Video brings home unsavory intruders." *Tonga Chronicle*, December 12:8.

Tulkin, S.
1977. "Dimensions of multicultural research in infancy and early childhood." In *Culture and infancy: Variations in the human experience*, ed. P. Leiderman, S. Tulkin, and A. Rosenfeld, 567–586. New York: Academic Press.

Tupouniua, P.
1977. *A Polynesian village: The process of change in the village of Hoi, Tonga*. Suva: South Pacific Social Sciences Association.

Tyler, S.
1978. *The said and the unsaid: Mind, meaning, and culture*. New York: Academic Press.

Urbanowicz, C.
1973. "Tongan adoption before the Constitution of 1875." *Ethnohistory* 20, no. 2:109–123.
1977. "Integrating tourism with other industries in Tonga." In *The social and economic impact of tourism on Pacific communities*, ed. B. Farrell, 88–94. Santa Cruz: Center for South Pacific Studies, University of California.
1978. "Tourism in Tonga." In *Hosts and guests*, ed. V. Smith, 83–92. Oxford: Basil Blackwell.
1979. "Comments on Tongan commerce with reference to tourism and traditional life." *Pacific Viewpoint* 20, no. 2:179–184.

Uzgiris, I., ed.
1979. *Social interaction and communication during infancy*. San Francisco: Jossey-Bass.

Valentine, C.
1963. "Men of anger and men of shame: Lakalai ethnopsychology and its implications for sociopsychological theory." *Ethnology* 2, no. 4:441–477.

Valeri, V.
1989. "Death in heaven: Myths and rites of kinship in Tongan kingship." *History and Anthropology* 4:209–247.

Vygotsky, L.
1978. *Mind in society: The development of higher psychological processes*. Cambridge: Harvard University Press.

Waldegrave, W.
1834. "Extracts from a private journal kept on board HMS *Seringapatam* in the Pacific 1830. Read 24th June 1833." *Journal of the Royal Geographic Society* 3:168–196.

Wallace, A.
1970. *Culture and personality*. 2d ed. New York: Random House.

Watson-Gegeo, K., and D. Gegeo.
1986.   "The social world of Kwara'ae children: Acquisition of language and values."
        In *Children's worlds and children's language*, ed. J. Cook-Gemperz, W. Corsaro,
        and J. Streek, 109–127. Berlin: Mouton de Gruyter.

Watson-Gegeo, K., and G. White.
1990.   *Disentangling: Conflict discourse in Pacific societies*. Stanford, Calif.: Stanford
        University Press.

Weiner, M.
1971.   "Ethnomedicine in Tonga." *Economic Botany* 25:423–450.

Weisner, T., and R. Gallimore.
1977.   "My brother's keeper: Child and sibling caretaking." *Current Anthropology*
        18, no. 2:169–180.

Wentworth, W.
1980.   *Context and understanding: An inquiry into socialization theory*. New York:
        Elsevier.

Wertsch, J., ed.
1985.   *Culture, communication, and cognition: Vygotskian perspectives*. Cambridge:
        Cambridge University Press.

West, Rev. T.
1865.   *Ten years in South-Central Polynesia: Being reminiscences of a personal mission
        to the Friendly Islands and their dependencies*. London: James Nisbet.

Whitcombe, J.
1930.   *Notes on Tongan ethnology*. Bernice P. Bishop Museum occasional papers 9
        no. 9. Honolulu: Bishop Museum Press.

White, G.
1985.   "Premises and purposes in a Solomon Islands ethnopsychology." In *Person,
        self, and experience: Exploring Pacific ethnopsychologies*, ed. G. White and
        J. Kirkpatrick, 328–366. Berkeley: University of California Press.
1990.   "Moral discourse and the rhetoric of emotions." In *Language and the politics of
        emotion*, ed. C. Lutz and L. Abu-Lughod, 46–68. Cambridge: Cambridge
        University Press.
1992.   "Ethnopsychology." In *New directions in psychological anthropology*, ed.
        T. Schwartz, G. White, and C. Lutz, 21–46. Cambridge: Cambridge Univer-
        sity Press.

White, G., and J. Kirkpatrick, eds.
1985.   *Person, self, and experience: Exploring Pacific ethnopsychologies*. Berkeley: Uni-
        versity of California Press.

Whitehead, T., and L. Price.
1986.   "Summary: Sex and the fieldwork experience." In *Self, sex, and gender in
        cross-cultural fieldwork*, ed. T. Whitehead and M. Conaway, 289–304.
        Urbana: University of Illinois Press.

Whitehead, T., and M. Conaway, eds.
1986.   *Self, sex, and gender in cross-cultural fieldwork*. Urbana: University of Illinois
        Press.

Whiting, B., ed.

1963. *Six cultures: Studies of childrearing.* New York: Wiley.

Whiting, B., and C. Edwards.

1988. *Children of different worlds: The formation of social behavior.* Cambridge: Harvard University Press.

Whiting, B., and J. Whiting.

1975. *Children of six cultures: A psycho-cultural analysis.* Cambridge: Harvard University Press.

Williams, T., ed.

1975. *Psychological anthropology.* The Hague: Mouton.

Williksen-Bakker, S.

1990. "Vanua: A symbol with many ramifications in Fijian culture." *Ethnos* 55, no. 3–4:232–247.

Wood-Ellem, E.

1987. "Queen Sālote Tupou of Tonga as Tuʻi Fefine." *Journal of Pacific History* 22, no. 4:209–227.

ABOUT THE AUTHOR

Helen Morton's longstanding interest in Tonga began in 1979 with a month-long visit. A teaching position at a girls' highschool there, which led to her marriage into a Tongan family, ultimately transformed her life, both personally and professionally. She later studied anthropology at Macquarie University in Sydney and received her PhD from the Australian National University in Canberra. Morton is presently a research fellow at La Trobe University in Melbourne. Her research focuses on Tongan children and migration.

CPSIA information can be obtained at www.ICGtesting.com
Printed in the USA
BVOW04s1319130114

341511BV00004B/47/A